AUTHENTICITY IN CULTURE, SELF, AND SOCIETY

Authenticity in Culture, Self, and Society

Edited by

PHILLIP VANNINI
Royal Roads University, Canada

J. PATRICK WILLIAMS,
Nanyang Technological University, Singapore

Routledge
Taylor & Francis Group
LONDON AND NEW YORK

First published 2009 by Ashgate Publishing

2 Park Square, Milton Park, Abingdon, Oxfordshire OX14 4RN
52 Vanderbilt Avenue, New York, NY 10017

Routledge is an imprint of the Taylor & Francis Group, an informa business

First issued in paperback 2020

British Library Cataloguing in Publication Data
Authenticity in culture, self, and society
1. Authenticity (Philosophy) 2. Social sciences - Philosophy
I. Vannini, Phillip II. Williams, J. Patrick, 1970-
300.1

Library of Congress Cataloging-in-Publication Data
Vannini, Phillip.
Authenticity in culture, self, and society / by Phillip Vannini and J. Patrick Williams.
p. cm.
Includes index.
ISBN 978-0-7546-7516-7
1. Culture. 2. Cultural awareness. 3. Authenticity (Philosophy). 4. Group identity. 5. Consumption (Economics)--Psychological aspects. I. Williams, J. Patrick, 1970- II. Title.

HM621.V455 2009
306.01--dc22

2008045386

ISBN 13: 978-0-7546-7516-7 (hbk)
ISBN 13: 978-0-367-60318-2 (pbk)

Contents

List of Figures

Notes on Contributors

Sarah Burgess holds a B.A. in Creative Writing and in Sociology, a B.Sc. in Physics, and an interdisciplinary M.A. from the University of Victoria. She is currently pursuing a Ph.D. in Physics at the University of Toronto. Her poems have appeared in a number of Canadian literary magazines, including *the Malahat Review*, *Prism International*, and *Grain*. A series of poems on science will appear in *The New Quarterly* in Fall 2007.

Lynn Charman holds a M.A. degree in Professional Communication from Royal Roads University. Following an extensive career in broadcast network television as a producer, director and writer, Lynn is currently in the Public Affairs Bureau for the province of British Columbia.

Alessandro Ferrara is Professor of Political Philosophy at the University of Rome, Tor Vergata. He is author of *Reflective Authenticity: Rethinking the Project of Modernity* (Routledge, 1998), *Modernity and Authenticity: A Study of the Social and Ethical Thought of Jean Jacques Rousseau* (SUNY Press, 1993), *The Force of the Example: Explorations in the Paradigm of Judgement* (Columbia University Press, 2007), *Justice and Judgment: The Rise and the Prospect of the Judgment Model in Contemporary Political Philosophy* (SAGE, 1999), as well as several other books and many journal articles in Italian, German, and English.

Alexis T. Franzese recently completed her doctoral study in Sociology at Duke University. Her dissertation research addressed the relationship between the need for social approval and authentic behavior. Alexis now continues her studies of authenticity as she pursues her doctorate in Clinical Psychology at Duke University, in which she investigates the mental health consequences of feeling inauthentic. Her writings have appeared in *Sociology Compass* and *Demography.*

Jaber F. Gubrium is Professor and Chair of the University of Missouri-Columbia Sociology department. He previously has taught at Marquette University and the University of Florida, was a Fulbright scholar at Tampere University, Finland, in 1996, and has been a visiting professor at Tampere, at Lund University in Sweden, and at the Universities of Copenhagen and Odense in Denmark. He is author and co-editor of 28 books, including his most recent *Analyzing Narrative Reality* (Sage Publications, 2009). His areas of specialization are aging and the life course, social interaction, identity, qualitative methods, and narrative analysis.

Joshua Guilar is the Director of the School of Communication and Culture at Royal Roads University. His most recent book is titled *The Power of Authenticity* (DeVorss, 2007). In 2007, Joshua received a grant from the Canadian Council on Learning to conduct a project titled ALENENEC (Homeland): Learning from Place, Spirit and Traditional Language. The research focuses on understanding a class in which learners integrate traditional knowledge regarding place and language with their personal and career development. In addition to studying the nature of learning from place, the research seeks a better understanding of the ethics of research in Aboriginal communities.

Daphne Holden, Ph.D. is an independent researcher who is currently funded by the Mertz Gilmore Foundation to look at how the Coalition of Immokalee Workers (an immigrant workers center in Immokalee, Florida) uses human rights to make social change. Her research has focused on the reproduction of inequality and emotions and she has published in the *Journal of Contemporary Ethnography*, *Social Forces*, and *Social Problems*. Most recently, her article in *Symbolic Interaction* (2007) examines how founders of an intentional community used a discourse of authenticity to maintain power over newcomers.

James A. Holstein is Professor of Sociology at Marquette University in Milwaukee. He is author and editor of over 20 books, including *Inner Lives and Social Worlds* (Oxford University Press, 2003) and *The Self We Live By* (Oxford University Press, 2000). His interests in identity work, talk, and social interaction relate to various dimensions of authenticity as they reference inner life.

Joseph A. Kotarba is Chair and Professor of Sociology at the University of Houston. He is co-editor of *The Existential Self in Society* (University of Chicago Press, 1984) and *Postmodern Existential Sociology* (AltaMira Press, 2002), and the author of *Growing Old with Rock 'n' Roll* (Left Coast Press, 2007) as well as several articles on popular music, youth culture, existential sociology and symbolic interactionism which have appeared in journals such as *Symbolic Interaction* and the *Journal of Contemporary Ethnography*.

Gary J. Krug is Associate Professor of Communication Studies at Eastern Washington University. He is the author of *Communication, Technology, and Social Change* (Sage, 2005) as well as several articles on cultural studies issues which have appeared in such journals as the *Journal of Contemporary Ethnography*, *Studies in Symbolic Interaction*, *Cultural Studies ← → Critical Methodologies*, *Critical Public Health*, and the *Journal of Health Psychology*.

Jörn Lamla is Assistant Professor at the Justus-Liebig-University in Giessen within the department of Sociology. Author of five books and over 40 journal articles, he has recently completed a research project titled "CyberCash" which focuses on everyday practices of consumption in the virtual economy and the role of authenticity in consumption and consumerism. He has published widely in the areas of social theory, political sociology, sociology of consumption, and qualitative research methods.

Philip Lewin holds an M.A. degree in Sociology and is currently a doctoral student at the University of Georgia. His interests center around the areas of culture and work, while his particular research emphasizes how individuals challenge structures of domination through personal acts of resistance and how those acts bear upon the dignity and selfhood of those who perform them. In addition to his work on punks, he has studied high school debate subculture and everyday forms of resistance within work settings.

E. Doyle McCarthy, Professor of Sociology at Fordham University, is a social theorist working in the fields of the sociology of knowledge and culture and the interdisciplinary field of emotion studies. She was Senior Editor of the *International Journal of Politics, Culture, and Society* (1996-2000), a member of the Executive Committee of the International Society for Research on Emotions (2004-2007), and is currently serving on the editorial board of *La Critica Sociologica*. She is author of *Knowledge as Culture: The New Sociology of Knowledge* (Routledge, 1996) and co-editor with David D. Franks of *The Sociology of Emotions* (1989), the first edited collection of papers in the sociology of emotions. Her current work examines modern and late-modern emotionality.

Chaim Noy in an independent scholar whose research interests focus on semiotics, communication and performance in everyday life. He teaches at the Hebrew University of Jerusalem, and at the Sapir and David Yellin colleges, in Israel. His recent research projects include ethnographies of driving and of mobilities in Jerusalem, Israel, and oral and inscriptional performances in tourism. Noy's recent book publications include *A Narrative Community* (Wayne State University Press, 2006), which deals with tourists' storytelling performances, and a co-edited volume with Erik Cohen, titled *Israeli Backpackers* (SUNY Press, 2005). He has published articles and book chapters on reflexive and experimental methodologies (*Forum in Qualitative Sociology*, *International. Journal of Social Research Methodology*), performance (*Text & Performance Quarterly*), tourism (*Annals of Tourism Research*), gender, and socio-linguistics.

Douglas Schrock is Assistant Professor of Sociology at Florida State University. Much of his research focuses on how transsexuals' construct and experience authenticity. He has shown how transsexual support group members interactionally construct childhood and denial narratives (published in *Social Psychology Quarterly*) and how transsexuals individually tell sexual stories (published in *Archives of Sexual Behavior*) in order to authenticate their differently-gendered selves. He has also examined how transsexuals' bodily transformation shapes their experience of authenticity (published in *Gender & Society*) and how transgendered activists use the promise of authenticity to mobilize transgendered people to participate in social movement work (published in *Social Problems*). In addition, he has analyzed how community elites use authenticity to maintain power over others (published in *Symbolic Interaction*) and the interactional struggle over authentic manhood in a batterer intervention program (forthcoming in *Gender & Society*).

Michael Schwalbe earned his Ph.D. in Sociology from Washington State University in 1984 and is Professor of Sociology at North Carolina State University. He is the author of numerous journal articles and five books, including *Unlocking the Iron Cage: The Men's Movement, Gender Politics, and American Culture* (Oxford, 1996), *The Sociologically Examined Life* (McGraw-Hill, 1998/2005), *Remembering Reet and Shine: Two Black Men, One Struggle* (University Press of Mississippi, 2004), and *Rigging the Game: How Inequality is Reproduced in Everyday Life* (Oxford, 2008).

Phillip Vannini is Associate Professor in the School of Communication and Culture at Royal Roads University in Victoria, BC, Canada. His research on self and authenticity—which has appeared in *Symbolic Interaction* and *Studies in Symbolic Interaction*—has primarily pertained to the emotional experience of authenticity, its biographical and narrative dimensions, as well as its relation to values and self-meanings. Phillip has also investigated the significance of authenticity in youth subcultures and music audiences in articles published in *Theory, Symbolic Interaction*, and in a book co-authored with Joseph Kotarba titled *Understanding Society through Popular Music* (Routledge, 2009). Together with Dennis Waskul he is the editor of *Body/Embodiment* (Ashgate, 2006). He is also the editor of *Material Culture and Technology in Everyday Life: Ethnographic Approaches* (Peter Lang, 2008).

Dennis D. Waskul is an Associate Professor of Sociology at Minnesota State University, Mankato. He is author of *Self-Games and Body-Play: Personhood in Online Chat and Cybersex* (Peter Lang, 2003) co-editor of *Body/Embodiment* (Ashgate, 2006), and *net.SeXXX: Readings on Sex, Pornography, and the Internet* (Peter Lang, 2004). His published empirical works have explored a variety of topics including Internet sex, fantasy role-playing, and chronic illness.

Andrew J. Weigert is Professor of Sociology at the University of Notre Dame. His interests include prairie reconstruction and interactionist perspectives on self, morality, and hope via the intersection of pragmatism and social constructionism. Recent writings include "Self," with Vik Gecas in Handbook of Symbolic Interactionism; "Vocation" with Anthony Blasi in Vocation and Social Context; "Pragmatic thinking about self, society, and natural environment: Mead, Carson, and beyond" in *Symbolic Interaction*; and a book, *Religious and Secular Views on Endtime* (Mellen Press, 2004).

J. Patrick Williams earned his Ph.D. from the University of Tennessee after studying in the departments of Sociology and Cultural Studies, and is currently an Assistant Professor of Sociology at Nanyang Technological University in Singapore. For several years, Patrick has focused on the experiential and cultural dimensions of authenticity in youth subcultures, most notably the straightedge subculture. He has published ethnographic research on identity, subculture, and/or digital culture in several peer-reviewed journals including *Social Problems, Symbolic Interaction*, *Journal of Contemporary Ethnography*, *Deviant Behavior*, and *Sociology Compass*, as well as in two edited books: *Gaming as Culture: Essays in Social Reality, Identity and Experience in Fantasy Games*, and *Youth Subcultures: Exploring Underground America.* He is the co-editor of two books, *Gaming as Culture: Essays in Social Reality, Identity and Experience in Fantasy Games* (McFarland, 2006), and *The Players' Realm: Studies in Video Games and Gaming* (McFarland, 2007). He is currently preparing a new book on youth subculture studies for Polity Press.

Acknowledgments

Phillip and Patrick would like to acknowledge first and foremost the assistance of Neil Jordan and the Ashgate Publishing production team for their kindness, patience, and efficiency. In addition, Phillip would like to acknowledge Royal Roads University's Research Office for facilitating some of the work that went into the production of this book, as well as the School of Communication and Culture at Royal Roads University for creating the most ideal collegial atmosphere that scholarly work can ever wish for. Phillip also wishes to thank Viktor Gecas for his mentorship; without it this book would have never come to light. Patrick would like to acknowledge Arkansas State University's Office of Research and Technology Transfer and the Faculty Research Committee for granting reassignment time to devote to the book.

Chapter 1
Authenticity in Culture, Self, and Society

Phillip Vannini and J. Patrick Williams

Framing Authenticity

In their 2007 book entitled *Authenticity: What Consumers Really Want*, James Gilmore and Joseph Pine argue that contemporary industrial and information societies are being commodified and virtualized, with everyday life becoming saturated with "toxic levels of inauthenticity [that] we're forced to breathe" (43). The authors cite a variety of issues to support their claim, including the ideas that most of the emails we get are not from people we know or feel we should trust; less news comes from the first-hand accounts of journalists in the field, but is rather recycled in the blogosphere; previously unnecessary terms such as "real person" have emerged in the field of customer service to describe who we are trying to reach; friends are not "really" friends unless we confirm them on our MySpace or Facebook accounts. Their list goes on with an underlying theme rooted in technology and consumption: namely, contemporary shifts in mediated reality and experience are pushing consumer populations to yearn for authenticity.

For the sociologically mindful, questions quickly emerge from reading their claims. How can the alleged crisis of (in)authenticity be empirically studied, and in what ways are individuals and groups being affected—emotionally, psychologically, socially, spiritually? And perhaps more basically, are the processes they describe really creating "toxic levels" of inauthenticity? How does one measure that toxicity? Or asked differently, how does one distinguish the authentic from the inauthentic, the real from the fake, the genuine from the fraudulent, the true from the false? In order to decide whether such questions can even be answered, we must first ask a more basic question. What is authenticity?

Each of these questions require care in answering, for recent decades have witnessed the growth of a schism in how social scientists understand the very nature of social reality, and thus the nature of authenticity itself. Much of traditional sociology has approached the world from a realist perspective that assumes the obdurateness of reality and social facts. Gender, race, and other social phenomena are considered real in the same way a building is real: no matter how you try, you can't wish one or the other out of existence. Peter Berger and Thomas Luckmann's (1967) seminal book, *The Social Construction of Reality*, however, marked a watershed moment in which the underlying assumptions of the realist perspective were called into doubt. Through a precise and sustained critique, they questioned the foundations of the social facts paradigm. Skin color, for example, which had long been assumed to be an objective marker of a racial identity, came to be seen as infinitely variable. Moreover, it became obvious that through language, socialization, and cognition do we go about placing people into arbitrary racial (and other) categories. Over the last forty years, the social constructionist perspective has gained increasing popularity across many social science disciplines.

The realist-constructionist dichotomy relates directly to both academic and lay assumptions about authenticity. To get a sense of a realist perspective, we need look no further than the *Oxford English Dictionary* (OED). There, authenticity is first defined as being "in accordance with *fact*, as being *true in substance*." Consider recent photo advertisements by two rival vodka makers. Swedish brand Absolut pictures its vodka bottle with a halo above its neck and the description "Absolut perfection" below, while in a competing ad a bottle of Russia's Stolichnaya vodka (complete with its display of four gold medals) is presented underneath the slogan "Choose authenticity." Both advertisements promote the sense that their product is authentic vodka, unblemished and true in substance. Of course, the question of whether the Swedes or the Russians make a more authentic vodka remains unanswered. The OED also defines authenticity "as being what it professes *in origin or authorship*; as being *genuine*." Fighting against an alleged graduate school curriculum that stifles one's creativity in lieu of procedural rules, Don Jacobs' (2008) book, *The Authentic Dissertation: Alternative Ways of Knowing, Research, and Representation*, offers "a road map for students who want to make their dissertation more than a series of hoop-jumping machinations that cause them to lose the vitality and meaningfulness of their research."[1] In this second definition we get the sense that authenticity is rooted in creativity and self-expression rather than in conformity to social forces. A third definition offered by the OED characterizes the authentic as that which is "*real, actual*." Here the authentic stands against replicas, pretense, and posing—a narrative common in popular culture, as Gilmore and Pine demonstrate in chapter after chapter of their book. What each of these definitions share in common is the reification of authenticity in everyday culture and discourse. Authenticity is to be understood as an inherent quality of some object, person or process. Because is it inherent, it is neither negotiable nor achievable. Authenticity cannot be stripped away, nor can it be appropriated. In short, the object, person or process in question either *is* authentic or is *not*, period.

The ironic part of all this is that contemporary culture industries invest their lifeblood in producing the very authenticity they tell us cannot be manufactured. In his 1997 book, *Creating Country Music*, Richard Peterson dissects decades of popular music as he explores just this issue—the fabrication of authenticity by profit-seekers. Peterson keys us into the modern myth of authenticity, then deconstructs that myth by arguing that authenticity is a socially constructed phenomenon that

1 From the Routledge website: http://www.routledgeeducation.com/books/The-Authentic-Dissertation-isbn9780415442237.

shifts across time and space. Peterson's study is but one of many by sociologists in recent years that critique realist assumptions of authenticity. Yet such work has remained relatively dispersed within sociology until now. Drawing primarily from social constructionism, interpretivism, phenomenology, and symbolic interactionism, the chapters in this book tackle issues such as the experience of authenticity in the context of work and aesthetic production, the construction of authenticity in the formation of collective memory, the value of authenticity in consumer culture, material culture, and music fields, as well as the relation between authenticity and identity, and between insincerity and inauthenticity. Aware and weary of sociology's realist heritage, the authors collectively advance a balanced and pragmatic vision of the concept of authenticity from a variety of qualitative methodological perspectives.

But the question still remains—what is authenticity. Beyond our belief that authenticity is a socially constructed phenomenon, we recognize that authenticity is "ultimately an evaluative concept, however methodical and value-free many of the methods for establishing it may be" (Van Leeuwen 2001:392). Authenticity may be seen as some sort of ideal, highly valued and sought by individuals and groups as part of the process of becoming. Alternatively, authenticity is often something strategically invoked as a marker of status or method of social control. Authenticity is not so much a state of being as it is the objectification of a process of representation, that is, it refers to a set of qualities that people in a particular time and place have come to agree represent an ideal or exemplar. As culture changes—and with it, tastes, beliefs, values, and practices—so too do definitions of what constitutes the authentic. Authenticity is thus a "moving target" (Peterson 2005:1094). A sociology of authenticity must attend to the socially constructed, evaluative, and mutable character of the concept, as well as its impact on a number of social dimensions. In the remainder of this chapter and the rest of the book, we consider the relevance and significance of authenticity in terms of culture, self, and society. Part 1 focuses on definitional and conceptual issues, on the ontological and epistemological foundations of our interpretivist approach to authenticity, and on authenticity and inauthenticity as values and ideals. Part 2 examines personal authenticity, that is, the authenticity of self and the formation and maintenance of authentic self-concepts, personas, and identities. Finally, Part 3 analyzes authenticity in the context of small groups, subcultures, discourses, and contemporary culture and society at large. In what follows we briefly describe the content and relevance of each chapter and situate it into the background of the relevant literature.

The Concept, Value, and Ideal of Authenticity

Following this introduction, Alessandro Ferrara begins Chapter 2 by outlining three important denotations of authenticity. Authenticity can refer to a moral identity functioning as a source for normativity, to the impetus of the cultural movement toward self-realization typical of the twentieth century (see also Lewin and Williams this volume), and the force of example and the ideal and practice of exemplarity. Ferrara dedicates his attention especially to the latter, which he constructs by drawing a philosophical and theoretical cartography of diverse approaches to authenticity. His cartography maps out a terrain of oppositions between substantialist and intersubjective, centered and decentered, integrative and antagonistic, and spontaneity-based versus reflexivity-based approaches to authenticity. Ferrara's own inclination is toward a type of authenticity that is fully reflective, as he finds that a reflective view of authenticity best allows one to tap into the cognitive moment of the relation that the self has with itself, into the self's orientation to knowledge, and the practical moment of commitment to value-based action.

Ferrara's chapter represents an elaboration, clarification, and follow-up to his influential 1998 publication, *Reflective Authenticity*. In that seminal monograph Ferrara brought together numerous and diverse strains of philosophical, psychoanalytical, and sociological thought to bear upon the question of authenticity. Ferrara's vision—in both that book and in this chapter—is to show that the idea and value of authenticity, rather than autonomy, is the quintessential node of modern and Western philosophical thinking. In defending his arguments from critiques and misunderstandings of his earlier work, Ferrara here confirms his view that an approach to self and authenticity based on reflexivity "provide[s] us with ways of thinking of limits to the self-shaping power of the self without either locating these limits outside the self or invoking the dubious notion of an essential self to be true to."

In Chapter 3 Andrew Weigert reflects on the meaningfulness of personal authenticity. Taking an explicitly interactionist approach Weigert conceptualizes the self as an emergent project, as well as the very creative subject and object of that process. Weigert orients his theoretical attention to the temporal properties of personal authenticity, grounding it into the present from the perspectives of the past and the present and their differing motives and motivational sources. Authenticity is to be found in volitional acts unfolding in problematic situations—and more precisely in those acts which index the self's motivation to feel and act in congruence with personal values. Weigert further extends authenticity into the territory of hope, which he views as central to self-functioning, to meaning formation, and to individual and collective motivation. In doing so Weigert transcends the micro level of the social psychological dynamics of authenticity. For him authenticity connects into wider dialectics of social responsibility, ameliorative reform, and a growing cosmopolitan consciousness.

Weigert's primary reference to the authenticity literature is by way of Viktor Gecas (1986, 1991, 1994, 2000, 2001) who—following the lead of Turner (1976; Turner and Schutte 1981)—emphasized the meaningfulness of authenticity for the self-concept and its interlinking with larger cultural processes. Gecas's key contribution laid in particular in his vision of authenticity as motive and motivating resource that is as essential to the self as the better known self-esteem and self-efficacy. Gecas argued that authenticity can serve as both motive and motivation (also see Franzese this volume; Vannini and Burgess this volume) since both work equally well as operative knowledge of self by the self and as expressions of the self's sociality and agency. In his writings Gecas also linked authenticity to the culture of modernity and the struggles of both the self and social movements within that period.

Any intelligent reflection on the value of authenticity has to be carried out while keeping in mind the importance of its counterpart: inauthenticity. Inauthenticity is not only inevitable, but, according to Dennis Waskul in Chapter 4, even desirable at times. Inauthenticity, insincerity, or simply the necessity to abandon moral struggles and say "to hell with it!" are common features of everyday life, and even of a good life. To explain this important point Waskul takes the reader through a contrived autoethnographic exploration, a breaching social experiment, and a flight of fancy. As he tries to stay true to himself and others for a full day Waskul finds himself incapacitated by the continuous struggles to define what is authentic and morally honest versus what is inauthentic and socially right. And after angering students, coworkers, and family members with his authentic and sincere ways Waskul concludes that not only is inauthenticity necessary, it is often desirable.

Waskul's chapter eloquently captures the complexity of dramaturgic approaches to the ideal of authenticity. According to Goffman (1959) we wear masks and perform roles for others not because we fancy ourselves thespian-like histrionic characters, but because our expressive action is first and foremost directed at the maintenance of relationships through the saving of face. From a dramaturgic perspective, therefore, the value of authenticity does not reside in choosing a role with which we feel as little distance as possible. Rather, the value of authenticity and inauthenticity lies in being a "more or less person" rather than one's own "true self" all the time. A "more or less person" inevitably exists through concealment and information control. A more or less person is an actor that understands that social life demands secrecy and thus a certain measure of insincerity and inauthenticity. In pointing out how acting honestly is conceptually different from acting sincerely, Waskul highlights how there is virtue in inauthenticity and thus how impression management is not the epitome of inauthenticity but the very root of what it means to be a functional, socialized, integrated, and lovable member of society.

Discussions of authenticity and inauthenticity are legion within the ever-expanding field of cultural studies, and especially within the interdisciplinary subfield of subculture studies. Classic ethnographic accounts of music-based subcultures, countercultures, lifestyle enclaves, scenes, or simply peer groups (e.g. Frith 1981) have shown that concerns with authenticity lie at the roots of group membership, group collective identity and values, personal and social identity formation and maintenance, and status (e.g. Coco and Woodward 2007; Levitt and Hiestand 2004; Moore 2004; Riley and Cahill 2005; Widdicombe and Wooffitt 1990; Williams 2006; Williams and Copes 2005). But aside from the more micro-sociological concerns with authenticity as congruence to group ideology and with the personal authenticity of group members, the very existence of subcultures and the great diversity of contemporary lifestyle projects of the self bears testament to the widespread preoccupation with individual self-realization, choice, self-expression, and connectedness with like-minded and like-hearted others, typical of late modern culture and society (Ferrara 1999; Holstein and Gubrium 2000; Taylor 1991).

As Lewin and Williams argue in Chapter 5, authenticity is both a moral quest toward the value and practice of self-discovery and an effort to attain identity and stability in the ever-fluctuating and (relatively) anchor-less maelstrom of fleeting trends, panics, and doubts of postmodern society. By de-emphasizing play, irony, pastiche, style, and conspicuous display of taste in subcultures, and by emphasizing instead existential and ideological commitment to a movement's ideals, Lewin and Williams show how the value of authenticity is alive and strong in the punk subcultural scene they studied. To the subculturalists amongst whom they conducted their fieldwork, being authentic stands for being creative, for rejecting the status quo, for the values of self-reflection, self-discovery, originality, and for a concern with deep felt humanity—typical of the Romantic philosophy of the individual (Boyle 2004; Taylor 1991). The value of authenticity, in this case, is by living to "laws of [one's] own being" and choice (Trilling 1992:73).

The Experience and Practice of Personal Authenticity

The chapters contained in Part 2 of the book shift away from broad cultural values and ideals and toward the theme of personal authenticity. By personal authenticity we refer to both an individual's experience of authenticity (i.e. "self authenticity") and to the interpersonal dynamics surrounding the formation and maintenance of authentic social identities and personas. The chapters in this part of the book have two distinguishing characteristics. First, they treat authenticity phenomenologically, that is, as an affective, cognitive, narrative, and self-reflective experience. Second, rather than treating authenticity as a philosophy or normative ideal (see e.g., Golomb 1995), they view authenticity as an individual and collective practice, a project of the self (cf. Giddens 1991), subject to intrapersonal and interpersonal assessment.

In Chapter 6, Alexis Franzese offers a kind of counter-narrative to Waskul's chapter on inauthenticity, providing a substantial amount of empirical evidence to suggest that authenticity does matter. Through analysis of open-ended interview questions Franzese also finds that experiences of authenticity are highly variable across age and gender. And just as importantly, she notes, there are times and situations when people willingly set their quest for authenticity aside. In this sense Franzese's findings echo the conclusions reached by O'Connor (2006), Sloan (2007), Vannini (2006, 2007, 2008), Weigert (1988, 1991), and Wolkomir and Powers (2007) who—in various research sites and working from different perspectives—agree that emotional experiences of authenticity are nuanced, multi-faceted, complex, and highly dependent on context (cf. Turner and Billings 1991).

Franzese's chapter epitomizes the usefulness of Ralph Turner's (Turner and Schutte 1981) epistemological approach to authenticity. In a seminal contribution dating back almost three decades, Turner and Schutte (1981) argued—setting aside in exemplary fashion concerns with whatever objectively and metaphysically may constitute authenticity—that authenticity is but an affective experience: the experience of feeling congruent to one's sense of true self, or in other words of feeling true to one's ideal self (also see Erickson 1995; Gordon 1989; Harter 2005; Salmela 2005; Schwalbe 1993). For Turner (and for Franzese) it does not matter whether one *is* or *is not* authentic. What matters instead is whether one *feels* that one is being authentic or not. Turner's phenomenological twist on authenticity was ingenious, and his equally simple and elegant methodological approach to the study of authenticity—which consisted of simply asking people how they felt about their experiencing of authenticity and inauthenticity—opened the ground for systematic empirical investigations of authenticity like Franzese's and Vannini's and Burgess's.

In Chapter 7 Vannini and Burgess deal with the thorny issue of motivation. Staying true to their symbolic interactionist affiliation, the authors are careful in their declaration that authenticity motivates behavior. Such a linear relation could be seen to reduce the self and individual behavior to a mere effect of authenticity, to a simple by-product of authenticity as an external, deterministic force. But as Vannini and Burgess argue authenticity is not a causal force or a drive, but instead socialized willpower. Their argument builds upon Gecas's (1986, 1991; also see Weigert this volume) argument that authenticity ought to be seen, similarly to self-esteem and self-efficacy, as a motive and a source of motivation for the self, being as it is nothing but an individual's self-appraisal of one's values and worth as a congruent person. Drawing upon interview data with academics, Vannini and Burgess find that in the context of doing scholarly research the will to act authentically translates into the quest for peak experiences, into appreciation for the value of creativity, and into the power of authenticity as a deeply meaningful aesthetic experience.

The work-related conduct of scholars is a particularly interesting one, and several authors have focused on authenticity and on the related concept of emotional labor to investigate service work by subordinate employees with little or no autonomy (e.g. Hochschild 1983; Erickson and Wharton 1997; Erickson and Ritter 2001). In the words of Turner (1976)—who made a distinction between organization "men" (or institutional selves), and mavericks (or impulsive selves)—scholars would appear to a casual observer to be impulsive selves. But as Vannini and Burgess highlight, academic life is far from being an overly individualistic, impulse-driven quest for intellectual self-fulfillment. Professors rely heavily on the definition of their roles to achieve a sense of authenticity, and even in their quest for aesthetic fulfillment spontaneity is often surrendered in order to produce work that, while satisfactory to the self, is useful and appreciated by significant and generalized others. Thus, not unlike Fine (1996) who found that authenticity in the context of chefs' work was subject to considerable compromise and negotiation, Vannini and Burgess's study evidences the need to treat authenticity not only as an experience but also as an intersubjective accomplishment shaped by the dominant conventions of a particular social world.

Chapters 6 and 7 present an approach to personal authenticity as self-referential. In Chapter 8, Jaber Gubrium and James Holstein take a fully situational approach to the concept. For them authenticity is more ubiquitous, shared amongst a group of interacting individuals, and dependent on situationally-relevant conditions, expectations, standards, and practices—or what they call the auspices of authenticity. This is because, they suggest, authenticity claims "underpin all assertions of identity, emotion, truth, accuracy, and reliability." In subverting the traditional distinction made by Trilling (1971) between sincerity (i.e. being true to others) and authenticity (being true to oneself) Gubrium and Holstein de-individualize authenticity, bringing claims to authentic communicative action away from the ego and into the social context where individuals meet their challenges.

Gubrium and Holstein do not deny that at a different level authenticity may be experienced as a self-feeling (though that too, arguably, is subject to an internal dialogue occurring under particular auspices), but their analytical attention is of a different nature. For them authenticity is a form of interactional work: a practical, mundane matter that concerns the construction, exchange, consumption, and interpretation of public claims to genuineness, truth, and self-congruency. Authenticity work is skilful and craft-like, and it does *not* go unnoticed until it is challenged. This is an essential part of their argument as it differs from other sociologists' beliefs that "issues of authenticity most often come into play when authenticity has been put in doubt" (Peterson 2005:1083). Gubrium and Holstein argue, our analytical attention should go to those sites where authenticity is made putatively real through interpretive judgements, accounts, and thus its actual materialization—its coming into being—under situational auspices. Ontologically, from the angle of talk and interaction writ large, it is irrelevant whether at stake is the authenticity of non-reflective objects like wine (cf. Peterson 1997, 2005) or reflective objects like the self, because in both cases authenticity comes to life through interactants' work. Thus, judgements regarding personal authenticity are not the exclusive domain of the ego, but of others as well. When others attempt to determine whether ego is being authentic or not, they do so from a different perspective than ego's, but precisely with the same resources—authenticity's auspices—and through the same kind of work: authenticity work. Sincerity and authenticity, in the end, become two sides of the same coin rather than different concepts.

Very few scholars hitherto have looked at the relation between authenticity and social position (see e.g., Bradamat 2005 in relation to ethnicity, Mason-Schrock 1996 in relation to gender and sexual preference, Reay 2002 in relation to class). Chapter 9 reports and discusses the biographies of Reet and Shine, two African-

American men who grew up in America's racially segregated south. Schwalbe's compelling storytelling and analysis show how "the lives of many men in subordinated groups are characterized by similar struggles to live authentically, without masks worn to please more powerful others." Reet and Shine, explains Schwalbe, are far from careless, playful roles, or from masks chosen amongst a wide array of choices. Reet and Shine may be personas strategically performed to evoke desired responses from one's audiences and to shield the self from the stigmata of race or failure, but first and foremost they are characters scripted into existence by an ethnic and class majority that typecasts underprivileged Others into subordinate roles. Reet and Shine's quest for authenticity is thus much different from that of the privileged scholars discussed by Vannini and Burgess. For Reet and Shine the quest for authenticity in relation to their desired identity comes with an insurmountable hurdle and a heavy price. The hurdle is racial and class hegemony and the restrictions that such a strong hegemony imposes on the repertoire of identities available to minorities like them. And the price to "choosing" one of the few available identities open to them is the self-destruction afforded by a mask that is personally and socially unbearable in the long run.

Performative and critical approaches to authenticity like Schwalbe's show that in everyday life authenticity can be far from "being in control"—one of the denotations of the Greek word for authenticity, *authentheo* (see Trilling 1971:122). Managing impressions of self on the basis of available scripts—as it is clear from both Schwalbe's and Waskul's chapters—pushes the quest for authenticity well beyond the task of a Machiavellian construction of a credible (to both self and others) front. Performative approaches to authenticity show how the expression of authentic selves is no mere situational choice, but instead action that has to follow "advocated codes of conduct" (Goffman 1963:111). Individuals, according to Auslander (1999:72) "achieve and maintain their effect of authenticity by continuously citing the norms of authenticity," and those norms are clearly compelling whether the intended effect is sincerity (Miall 1989), consistency (Noy 2004), or simply achieving a "balance between the cultural expectations of an 'ideal' performance [and] the constraints of the 'real' activity" that one undertakes (Stephenson Shaffer 2004:142).

Concluding Part 2 is Joseph Kotarba's ethnographic account of the role played by music in adult socialization. In his Chapter 10, Kotarba draws upon a postmodern blend of existentialist and phenomenological sociology to discuss the findings of fieldwork conducted amongst middle-aged male and female music fans, and in particular amongst baby boomers. Kotarba views authenticity as a form of work. First and foremost authenticity is an exercise in biography work, that is, in growing and in becoming. As a symbolic interactionist Kotarba views the becoming of self not in idealist terms as some kind of struggle to become what one essentially is meant to be. Rather for Kotarba the self in and of its own is inevitably a process of becoming. Authenticity, he argues, is a characteristic of this process: a form of openness to change and to the endless mutability of self and identity in a changing world and within the context of age-related changes in social roles. In this sense music becomes the soundtrack to one's life, and both an anchor for an ever-drifting self, as well as a vessel for its life's voyages.

Kotarba's arguments are well situated in a philosophical and theoretical background that is teeming with concepts useful to the student of authenticity. Existential philosophy, phenomenology, and its various iterations within social theory and sociology are perhaps the most quintessential starting points for any approach to authenticity. But instead of starting with Sartre, Nietzsche, or Heidegger, Kotarba begins his sociological and empirical perspective on authenticity with Alfred Schutz. Consciousness is social, reflexive, intentional, purposive—Schutz teaches us—and perhaps most important of all, practical (see also Anton 2001). That practical bent translates into a very pragmatic approach to the search for authenticity, an experience to be seen as a way of adaptation to change and as a strategy of defending the self from the basic threats that change may bring about.

The Social Production, Exchange, and Consumption of Authenticity

Part 3 of the book begins with a theoretical reflection on producing and consuming authenticity. In Chapter 11 Lamla tackles the complex issue of authenticity and the possibility of authentication within the context of contemporary capitalism and consumer culture. Lamla focuses in particular on the dynamics of authenticity claims by outlining four ideal types: a cohesive one based on the co-optation of authenticity; one based on the segmentation and diversification of authenticity; one in which dynamics between culture and the economy are coupled but relatively independent; and a final one in which the economy's dependency on cultural dynamics results in a moralization of the former.

Lamla's reflection on authenticity and consumption are to be read against the background of a large body of literature that has surveyed the (im)possibility of achieving authenticity within the context of capitalist production and consumption. Dating as far back as the classic arguments of critical theorists such as Adorno and Horkheimer, much of this literature is marked by (at best) a strong skepticism toward the idea of the culture industry producing authentic products of any kind. The critical idea underlying such scepticism is simple yet elegant: authenticity is a hook employed either to sell products and services (e.g. Beverland 2005; Rose and Wood 2005), or a hegemonic discourse through which various ideologies are articulated (Bramadat 2005; Charmé 2000; Coupland 2003; Heynen 2006). Critical arguments like Lamla's, however, are undoubtedly more nuanced as they are grounded in meso-domain constructionist analysis, fully at peace with the paradoxes of authenticity claims, and thus more germane to a current of pragmatist thought that conceptualizes claims to the authenticity of products and performances as "social accomplishments" (cf. Fine 2003, 2004; Lu and Fine 1995), and the search for authenticity as a rational and emotional response to life in a world perceived to be deeply inauthentic (Erickson 1994).

In Chapter 12 Guilar and Charman discuss the ideal and practice of authenticity within Canadian Coast Salish cultures. Drawing from their applied fieldwork and from a review of decolonized literatures on aboriginal cultures in Western Canada and North America, the authors argue that indigenous notions of authenticity are connected with collective identity, integrity, and respect of ancient tradition and spirituality. As scholars of communications, Guilar and Charman are well aware that cultural traditions—especially, orally transmitted ones—are founded within creative processes of "invention" (Hanson 1989) and re-invention; processes that generate all forms of social organization. Thus for Guilar and Charman the root of authenticity in Coast Salish society is not be found in dogmatic observance to foundational myths, but rather in the constant creative elaboration of tradition through culture-forming dialogue and intercultural communication.

As Hanson (1989:890) reminds us, "'Culture' and 'tradition' are anything but stable realities handed down intact from generation to generation," and yet it is primarily from their aura of intergenerational stability and rootedness in past mythology that they gather their authenticity. To suggest that culture and tradition are "invented" should not evoke cynical feelings or a sense of paradox. Aboriginal communities such as the Canadian Coast Salish generate and reproduce cultural values and a sense of history and tradition by way of dialogue, and dialogue is not be taken as a process of distortion of some pre-existing objective realities that awaits to be told "right." Through dialogue and the passing on of values like authenticity, ideas of tradition "become objectively incorporated into that culture by the very fact of people talking about them and practicing them" (Hanson 1989:898). Guilar and Charman's dialogic, phenomenological, and pragmatist approach to authenticity as "invented" (yet real in its consequences) lore thus escapes the vicious circle of what Derrida might call a metaphysics of presence, that is, an authenticity lying in a supposed historically fixed and essential tradition.

In Chapter 13 Holden and Schrock build on their recent work on the emotional culture of small therapy groups (see Holden and Schrock 2007) to consider the dimension of self-authenticity. Their field work focuses on "Aurora Commons," a communal therapy group founded in order to allow members to live in accord with their deepest senses of self, as well as to help them develop maximum honesty and openness with themselves and others. Aurora Commons clearly epitomizes the therapeutic culture of authenticity typical of pop-psychology and pop-philosophy movements striving for self-fulfillment by way of unbridled self-expressiveness, openness in interpersonal communication, personal growth, and rejection of restricting social conventions. But Holden and Schrock show us a socially constructed reality far from a core insider's perspective where community constitutes an exercise in freeing the self from the shackles of social norms. Quite in contrast, the authors highlight how Aurora Commons's emotional culture is the product of strategic performances and expressive acts governed by rules that specify how members are to recognize something as authentic or not.

Holden and Schrock's work beautifully synthesizes the value of an interpretivist approach to authenticity, that is, to authenticity without a "true self," as Ferrara has put in Chapter 2. By showing that the precise standards and techniques (cf. Gordon 1989) through which people build a shared agreement over what is to be considered authentic, an interpretivist approach to the production, exchange, and consumption of authenticity conceptualizes authenticity relativistically by envisioning it as an outcome of social interaction, as an emergent product of intrapersonal and interpersonal communication, and as a cultural trait that is indeterminate, fluid, "invented" and shared (and also contested, resisted, and commodified) by social agents acting within concrete everyday-life situations. Rather than reinforcing existing binary understandings which juxtapose authenticity with inauthenticity, or instead of seeking an unchanging or promissory essence of what authenticity is, such interpretivist approaches to authenticity are multidimensional, performative, and often at peace with the seeming contradictions of everyday practice.

Systematic discussions on authenticity have become more common within social psychology and the sociology of culture only in the last fifteen years or so. But the topics of tourists' experiences of authenticity and inauthenticity, of travel as a quest for the authentic, and of the authenticity of cultural expressions, rituals, and artefacts produced for tourists have been a staple of research and debates in the interdisciplinary field of travel and tourism studies for quite a bit longer (for reviews see Olsen 2003; Reisinger and Steiner 2005; Wang 1999). Explorations of authenticity in this field can hardly come into their own without taking into account MacCannell's (1973) classic work on the dramaturgy of tourists' encounters with "natives." MacCannell's approach, as forming as it has been, has however undergone the criticism of those who find authenticity to be less rigid of a concept than he did at the time. For example, DeLyser (1999) has convincingly shown how authenticity is not an end result or a premise of travel, but instead a pragmatic vehicle through which visitors and tourism workers engage in narrativization, interaction, and acquaintanceship with one another and the tourist site. Similar emergent and pragmatic approaches are evident in investigations that carefully dissect the nuances of authenticity in relation to the importance of context (e.g. Cohen 2003), who stands to benefit from it (e.g. Barthel-Bouchier 2001), and the discerning abilities of the parties involved (e.g. Gable and Handler 1996; Johnson 2007).

In an equally pragmatic and ecological fashion Chaim Noy, in Chapter 14, conceptualizes authenticity as a semiotic resource (cf. Van Leeuwen 2003) that people practically employ in order to increase the value of discourses, objects, and identities. For Noy, who reports the findings of an ethnographic study at a heritage site in Israel, it is not important to discriminate between what is authentic or inauthentic, but instead to focus on what people do to authenticate what they do or who they are. The outcome of what they do with something defined as authentic is often ideological in nature, with ideology in turn being used as a resource to confer authenticity to related objects and discourses. Authenticity is thus a cyclical process rather than a static characteristic; once constructed it is used to build, or validate, its very own manifestations and performances.

In Chapter 15 McCarthy examines memorializing practices mediated by news and infotainment channels as dramatic performances of authenticity. These performances, she notes, are displays of an emotional intensity very powerful and yet remarkably fleeting and ephemeral. This, according to McCarthy, constitutes a uniquely paradoxical postmodern spectacle of real artifice, of deeply felt manipulation, and of a kind of drama whose foundations are built on an old emotional history and yet reassembled on state-of-the-art technocultural possibilities. But in the end, it is not all fake or empty. However fleeting they may be, authenticity experiences remain rhetorically powerful emotional performances.

To appreciate the complexity of McCarthy's work one has to be mindful of Bruner's (1994) important contribution to the study of authenticity. Openly critical of postmodernist approaches that write out both the pragmatic relevance and the historical rootedness of authenticity in performative practices, Bruner embraces—rather than dismisses—the contradictions evoked by "authentic reproductions" (p. 398) such as the Lincoln commemorative tourist site in New Salem, Illinois. Authentic reproductions derive their authenticity from practice, rather than ideal, and from different meanings of the expression "authentic." As oxymoronic as it may sound, authentic reproductions of myths that were perhaps never true—such as theme park-like historic sites, or the dramatic spectacles of the social imaginary that McCarthy analyzes—directly construct meaning in several ways. Gary Krug considers the darker side of this analytical insight in chapter sixteen. Focusing on the political and cultural consequences of counter-narratives surrounding 9/11, Krug embraces a postmodernist stance *vis-à-vis* the new forms of mass-mediated social control unleashed by George W. Bush's conservative administration. Caught between positions of "fact" and "fairy" (Latour 2004), citizens live out their media-rich lives with little in the way of legitimate narratives that run counter to the official story as disseminated by the White House. Asking, "are there no more unanswered questions, no credible dissenting voices? Has closure been achieved?", Krug's study of authenticity is distinctively critical. In his conceptualization, authenticity becomes both pawn and king on the chessboard: quickly sacrificed in certain moments, yet ultimately important for those determined to win the game.

Bruner (1994) and McCarthy (Chapter 15) both get at how people gather some sense of past and contemporary history, however superficial, from spectacles, how they build and celebrate a sense of communitas, how they play with "time frames and enjoy the encounters" (Bruner 1994:398), how they consume nostalgia and the pathos of authenticity, and how they situate themselves into broader notions of progress and fraternity. Krug (Chapter 16) on the other hand leaves the reader less content with the whole idea of cultural consumption. In other words, McCarthy shows how people make authenticity meaningful, while Krug suggests ways in which the powerful might empty authenticity of meaning altogether.

These final ideas are a key feature of what sets *Authenticity in Culture, Self and Society* apart from the plethora of philosophical and economic books on the market today that have "authenticity" in their titles. It is precisely an interest in studying how authenticity is made meaningful, rather than a quest for finding the meaning of authenticity, that characterizes all of the chapters found herein. Our hope is that the reader will take away a more pragmatic, interpretivist understanding of authenticity, seeing it not as something that exists as an inherent property of some social object, but as part of a process of interaction and experience in everyday life.

References

Anton, Corey. 2001. *Selfhood and Authenticity*. Albany: State University of New York Press.

Auslander, Phillip. 1999. *Liveness.* New York: Routledge.

Barthel-Bouchier, Diane. 2001. "Authenticity and Identity: Theme-Parking the Amanas." *International Sociology*, 16:221-239.

Berger, Peter L. and Thomas Luckmann. 1967. *The Social Construction of Reality: A Treatise in the Sociology of Knowledge*. London: Penguin Press.

Beverland, Michael. 2005. "Crafting Brand Authenticity: The Case of Luxury Wines." *Journal of Management Studies*, 42:1003-1029.

Boyle, David. 2004. *Authenticity: Brands, Fakes, Spin and the Lust for Real Life*. London: Harper Perennial.

Bramadat, Paul. 2005. "Toward a New Politics of Authenticity: Ethno-Cultural Representation in Theory and Practice." *Canadian Ethnic Studies*, 37:1-20.

Bruner, Edward. 1994. "Abraham Lincoln as Authentic Reproduction." *American Anthropologist*, 96:397-415.

Charmé, Stuart. 2000. "Varieties of Authenticity in Contemporary Jewish Identity." *Jewish Social Studies*, 13:133-156.

Coco, Angela and Ian Woodward. 2007. "Discourses of Authenticity within a Pagan Community: The Emergence of the 'Fluffy Bunny' Sanction." *Journal of Contemporary Ethnography*, 479-504.

Cohen, Erik. 2003. "Backpacking: Diversity and Change." *Tourism and Cultural Change*, 1:95-110.

Coupland, Nikolas. 2003. "Socio-linguistic Authenticities." *Journal of Sociolinguistics*, 7:417-431.

DeLyser, Didia. 1999. "Authenticity on the Ground: Engaging the Past in a California Ghost Town." *Annals of the Association of American Geographers*, 89:602-632.

Erickson, Rebecca. 1994. "Our Society, Our Selves: Becoming Authentic in an Inauthentic World." *Advanced Development Journal*, 6:27-39.

—— 1995. "The Importance of Authenticity for Self and Society." *Symbolic Interaction*, 18:121-144.

Erickson, Rebecca and Amy Wharton. 1997. "Inauthenticity and Depression: Assessing the Consequences of Interactive Work." *Work and Occupations*, 24:188-213.

Erickson, Rebecca and Christian Ritter. 2001. "Emotional Labor, Burnout, and Inauthenticity: Does Gender Matter?" *Social Psychology Quarterly*, 64:146-163.

Ferrara, Alessandro. 1998. *Reflective Authenticity.* London: Routledge.

Fine, Gary. 1996. *Kitchens: The Cultures of Restaurant Work.* Berkeley: University of California Press.

—— 2003. "Crafting Authenticity: The Validation of Identity in Self-Taught Art." *Theory & Society*, 32:153-180.

—— 2004. *Everyday Genius: Self-Taught Art and the Culture of Authenticity.* Chicago: University of Chicago Press.

Frith, Simon. 1981. *Sound Effects: Youth, Leisure, and the Politics of Rock 'n' Roll.* New York: Pantheon.

Gable, Eric and Richard Handler. 1996. "After Authenticity at an American Heritage Site." *American Anthropologist*, 98:568-578.

Gecas, Viktor. 1986. "The Motivational Significance of Self Concept for Socialization Theory." Pp. 131-156 in *Advances in Group Processes 3*, edited by E.J. Lawler. Greenwich, CT: JAI Press.

—— 1991. "The Self-Concept as a Basis for a Theory of Motivation." Pp. 171-187 in *The Self-Society Dynamic: Cognition, Emotion, and Action*, edited by J. Howard and P. Callero. Cambridge: Cambridge University Press.

—— 1994. "In Search of the Real Self: Problems of Authenticity in Modern Times." Pp. 139-154 in *Self, Collective Behavior and Society*, edited by Gerald M. Platt and Chad Gordon. Greenwich: JAI Press.

—— 2000. "Value Identities, Self-Motives, and Social Movements." Pp. 93-109 in *Self, Identity, and Social Movements*, edited by Sheldon Stryker, Timothy J. Owens, and Robert White. Minneapolis: University of Minnesota Press.

—— 2001. "The Self as a Social Force." Pp. 85-100 in *Extending Self-Esteem Theory and Research*, edited by Timothy J. Owens, Sheldon Stryker and Norman Goodman. New York: Cambridge University Press.

Giddens, Anthony. 1991. *Modernity and Self-Identity: Self and Society and the Late Modern Age.* Cambridge: Polity.

Gilmore, James H., and B. Joseph Pine. 2007. *Authenticity: What Consumers Really Want.* Boston: Harvard Business School Press.

Goffman, Erving. 1959. *The Presentation of Self in Everyday Life.* New York: Anchor Books.

—— 1963. *Stigma.* Englewood Cliffs, NJ: Prentice-Hall.

Golomb, Jacob. 1995. *In Search of Authenticity.* London: Routledge.

Gordon, Steven. 1989. "Institutional and Impulsive Orientations in Selectively Appropriating Emotions to Self." Pp. 115–35 in *The Sociology of Emotions: Original Essays and Research Papers*, edited by David D. Franks and E. Doyle McCarthy. Greenwich, CT: JAI Press.

Hanson, Allan. 1989. "The Making of the Maori: Cultural Invention and its Logic." *American Anthropologist*, 91:890-902.

Harter, Susan. 2005. "Authenticity." Pp. 382-394 in *Handbook of Positive Psychology*, edited by C.R. Snyder and S.J. Lopez. London: Oxford University Press.

Heynen, Hilde. 2006. "Questioning Authenticity." *National Identities*, 8:287-300.

Hochschild, Arlie. 1983. *The Managed Heart: Commercialization of Human Feeling.* Berkeley, CA: University of California Press.

Holden, Daphne and Douglas Schrock. 2007. "'Get Therapy and Work on It:' Managing Dissent in an Intentional Community." *Symbolic Interaction*, 30:179-198.

Holstein, James and Jaber Gubrium. 2000. *The Self We Live By: Narrative Identity in a Postmodern World.* New York: Oxford University Press.

Jacobs, Don T. 2008. *Authentic Dissertation: Alternative Ways of Knowing, Research, and Representation.* Thousand Oaks: Routledge.

Johnson, Andrew. 2007. "Authenticity, Tourism, and Self-Discovery in Thailand: Self-Creation and the Discerning Gaze of Trekkers and Old Hands." *SOJOURN: Journal of Social Issues in Southeast Asia*, 22:153-178.

Latour, Bruno. 2004. "Why Has Critique Run Out Of Steam? From Matters of Fact to Matters of Concern." *Critical Inquiry*, 30:225-48.

Levitt, Heidi and Katherine Hiestand. 2004. "A Quest for Authenticity: Contemporary Butch Gender." *Sex Roles*, 50:605-621.

Lu, Shun and Gary Fine. 1995. "The Presentation of Ethnic Authenticity: Chinese Food as Social Accomplishment." *The Sociological Quarterly*, 36:535-553.

MacCannell, Dean. 1973. "Staged Authenticity: Arrangements of Social Space in Tourist Settings." *American Journal of Sociology*, 79:589-603.

Mason-Schrock, Douglas. 1996. "Transsexuals' Narrative Construction of the 'True Self.'" *Social Psychology Quarterly*, 59: 166-182.

Miall, Charlene. 1989. "Authenticity and the Disclosure of the Information Preserve: The Case of Adoptive Parenthood." *Qualitative Sociology*, 12:279-302.

Moore, Ryan. 2004. "Postmodernism and Punk Subculture: Cultures of Authenticity and Deconstruction." *Communication Review*, 7:305-327.

Noy, Chaim. 2004. "Performing Identity: Touristic Narratives of Self Change." *Text & Performance Quarterly*, 24:115-138.

O'Connor, Pat. 2006. "Young People's Constructions of the Self: Late Modern Elements and Gender Differences." *Sociology*, 40:107-124.

Olsen, Kjell. 2002. "Authenticity as a Concept in Tourism Research." *Tourist Studies*, 2:159-182.

Peterson, Richard. 1997. *Creating Country Music: Fabricating Authenticity.* Chicago: University of Chicago Press.

—— 2005. "In Search of Authenticity." *Journal of Management Studies*, 42:1083-1098.

Reay, Diane. 2002. "Class, Authenticity, and the Transition to Higher Education for Mature Students." *The Sociological Review*, 50:398-418.

Reisinger, Yvette and Carol Steiner. 2005. "Reconceptualizing Object Authenticity." *Annals of Tourism Research*, 33:65-86.

Riley, Sarah and Sharon Cahill. 2005. "Managing Meaning and Belonging: Young Women's Negotiation of Authenticity in Body Art." *Journal of Youth Studies*, 8:261-279.

Rose, Randall and Stacy Wood. 2005. "Paradox and the Consumption of Authenticity through Reality Television." *Journal of Consumer Research*, 32:284-295.

Salmela, Mikko. 2005. "What is Emotional Authenticity." *Journal for the Theory of Social Behavior*, 35:209-229.

Schwalbe, Michael. 1993. "Goffman Against Postmodernism: Emotion and the Reality of the Self." *Symbolic Interaction,* 16:334-350.

Sloan, Melissa 2007. "The 'Real Self' and Inauthenticity: The Importance of Self-Concept Anchorage for Emotional Experiences in the Workplace." *Social Psychology Quarterly*, 70:305-318.

Stephenson Shaffer, Tracy. 2004. "Performing Backpacking: Constructing 'Authenticity' Every Step of the Way." *Text & Performance Quarterly*, 24:139-160.

Taylor, Charles. 1991. *The Ethics of Authenticity.* Cambridge, Massachusetts: Harvard University Press.

Trilling, Lionel. 1971. *Sincerity and Authenticity.* New York: Harcourt Brace Jovanovich.

Turner, Ralph. 1976. "The Real Self: From Institution to Impulse." *American Journal of Sociology*, 81:989-1016.

Turner, Ralph and Jerald Schutte. 1981. "The True Self Method for Studying the Self- Conception." *Symbolic Interaction*, 4:1–20.

Turner, Ralph and Victoria Billings. 1991. "The Social Contexts of Self-Feeling." Pp. 103-122 in *The Self-Society Dynamic: Cognition, Emotion, and Action*, edited by Judith Howard and Peter Callero. New York: Cambridge University Press.

Van Leeuwen, Theo. 2003. "What is Authenticity." *Discourse Studies*, 3:392-397.

Vannini, Phillip. 2006. "Dead Poets' Society: Teaching, Publish-or-Perish, and Professors' Experience of Authenticity." *Symbolic Interaction*, 29:235-258.

—— 2007. "The Changing Meanings of Authenticity: An Interpretive Biography of Professors' Experiences." *Studies in Symbolic Interaction*, 29:63-90.

—— 2008. "Symbolic Spaces in Dirty Work: Authenticity as Resistance." *Studies in Symbolic Interaction*. 30:229-254.

Wang, Ning. 1999. "Rethinking Authenticity in Tourism Experience." *Annals of Tourism Research*, 26:349-370.

Weigert, Andrew. 1988. "To Be or Not: Self and Authenticity, Identity, and Ambivalence." Pp. 263-281 in *Self, Ego, and Identity: Integrative Approaches*, edited by D. Lampsey and F. Power. New York: Springer.

—— 1991. *Mixed Emotions: Certain Steps Toward Understanding Ambivalence.* Albany: State University of New York Press.

Widdicombe, Sue and Rob Wooffitt. 1990. "'Being' Versus 'Doing' Punk: On Achieving Authenticity as a Member." *Journal of Language and Social Psychology*, 9:257-277.

Williams, J. Patrick. 2006. "Authentic Identities: Straightedge Subculture, Music, and the Internet." *Journal of Contemporary Ethnography*, 35:173-200.

Williams, J. Patrick and Heith Copes. 2005. "'How Edge Are You?' Constructing Authentic Identities and Subcultural Boundaries in a Straightedge Internet Forum." *Symbolic Interaction*, 28:67-89.

Wolkomir, Michelle and Jennifer Powers. 2007. "Helping Women and Protecting the Self: The Challenge of Emotional Labor in an Abortion Clinic." *Qualitative Sociology*, 30: 153-169.

PART 1
The Value, Concept, and Ideal of Authenticity

Chapter 2
Authenticity Without a True Self

Alessandro Ferrara

Authenticity is a protean concept in philosophy and in the social sciences, ironically always at risk of luring us into the opposite path, into a somewhat "inauthentic" use of authenticity. It has played the role of catchword for a number of traditions—existentialism, Heidegger's analytics of Being, neo-conservative cultural criticism, certain therapeutic strands of humanistic psychology and of the human potential movement—while never succeeding, at least thus far, in fully playing what could be its potential role: to replace the pivotal role that the notion of autonomy as self-determination, in the variety of its meanings, played in an earlier stage of modernity.

As a result, today authenticity has broader currency as an implicitly used concept than as a term. More people use one version or other of this concept than there are people who use the word. For behind the notions of difference, of identity, of integrity that have enjoyed widespread currency over the past couple of decades we can still detect a deeper consonance, for defining the contours of which I still find the notion of authenticity fruitful. As first approximation, we could distinguish three major ways of understanding authenticity today.

We could understand the term against the backdrop of the history of moral theory. Then authenticity becomes associated with attitude of openness and receptiveness towards inner motives in the assessment of the moral worth of action. In authors of this tradition—Rousseau, Herder, Schiller, Kierkegaard and Sartre among others—we are offered a moral psychology where center stage is held not just by the Kantian conflict of a single *duty* (*Pflicht*) and a plurality of local and fragmentary *inclinations* (*Neigungen*), but also by an organized pattern of motives, with a hierarchy of priorities, which is best understood as an *identity*. While then autonomy-based approaches to morality principles are the only source of normativity, what sets authenticity-based approaches apart is their positing *identity* as a source of normativity co-originary and equally ranking as principles.[1]

---

1 This new way of understanding moral conflict, moral value, and the worthiness of the actor also results in the rise of a new dimension of the tragic, typical of the modern moral life—a new dimension of the tragic first highlighted by Rousseau. As the case of Julie, the main character of Rousseau's *La Nouvelle Heloise* (1968) suggests, attempts to master the motivations that deflect us from the moral principle without fully grasping the pattern underlying them may result in a no less severe undermining of the individual's

We could understand authenticity against the backdrop of the (mostly neoconservative) cultural criticism of the late 1970s and 1980s. In this case authenticity becomes synonymous with the leading ideal underlying a cultural climate, which dominated the cultural elites of the first half of the twentieth century, starting with the celebrated Bloomsbury elite, and then, in the second half of the twentieth century, thanks to the impact of the "culture industry," trickled down into becoming a mass culture bent on seeking self-realization and turning millions of ordinary lives into as many works of art.

Finally, we could understand authenticity in somewhat broader terms, against the backdrop of a newly changed philosophical horizon. In this sense authenticity becomes synonymous with *exemplarity*. It becomes the property of identities: the identities of individuals, groups, nations, congregations, parties, movements, disciplines, artistic schools. In this broader sense for a symbolic identity to attain authenticity or exemplarity, and to exert the force of the example, means to bridge the gap between *is* and *ought*, reality and principle, facts and norms, and to attain, even for a transient stage, and to actually be as it should be. An identity attains authenticity when it realizes to an outstanding extent the normative core that it sets

---

identity than the one associated with infringing principles on the spur of social pressure or personal interest. Julie is not just caught in the classical tragic predicament of being subjected to two conflicting norms, nor caught in the standard moral conflict of being torn between a norm "external to her" (in her case the norm prescribing that marriage should be arranged by the family) and her own "inclination" (a mere *Neigung*, in Kant's terminology). Instead, she is caught in a *new* kind of tragic situation, in which the conflict is between a norm that Julie understands in *autonomous* terms (as her having no right to intentionally cause the unhappiness of her parents and ruin their lives) and a feeling (her love for Saint-Preux) which in her eyes is not endowed with normative force (in which case her predicament would be tragic in the classic sense) but which nonetheless is so inextricably bound up with who she is, with her identity, that suppressing it inevitably will amount to undermining the coherence of her own self. In the words that Rousseau makes another character pronounce, that feeling is so ingrained with Julie's identity that by attempting to suppress it, as she eventually does, she'd be "effacing all the exquisite sentiments received from nature" (Rousseau 1968:II, 3) and when finally she will have "no more love left, nothing worth esteem will remain" in her either (Rousseau 1968: II, 3). In fact, after leaving her lover and marrying the person chosen by her father for her, Julie becomes a conscientious mother, a faithful wife, a loyal and affectionate friend, a charitable and generous master, but somehow we the readers are made by Rousseau feel that *she* is no longer quite *there* in any of these impersonations. She is no longer authentic. When Julie dies at Clarens, her last words convey her awareness that for her to die is only "to die once more." Rousseau then implicitly suggests that sometimes moral choices may have to be made in which the right solution is to side with our feelings, as opposed to our moral principles, if the feelings in question are crucially bound up with the cohesion of our identity or, in other words, that we may have also to act *authentically* against our own autonomously posited principles. The justification of our act rests then on our considered judgment – a peculiar type of reflective judgment – concerning the constitutive relation of the feeling at issue to our identity.

as its own guiding ideal. Identities would obviously even fail to be recognizable as such if they failed to somehow relate to their guiding ideals. But most collectivities and individuals, who are not exemplary or authentic, are a pale reflection of the embraced normativity. We call authentic only the ones which are "true" to these ideas in unprecedented ways.[2]

If we focus on this third meaning of authenticity, we need to do some conceptual work before this notion can unfold its fruitfulness for making sense of our understanding of normativity after the Linguistic Turn as well as its fruitfulness for the social sciences and for the disclosure of empirical reconstructions of certain social phenomena and trends that define our age. More specifically, I will reconstruct a number of theoretical options that are open, thereby drawing a cartography of diverse understandings of authenticity, and in the second section of this paper will defend my own concept of *reflective authenticity* from the charge of presupposing an essentialist view of authenticity. This agenda responds also to the intuition that the suspicion of embedding such a view of the self and, more broadly, of subjectivity is the single most influential factor in making the term "authenticity" less popular than other competitors.

Revisiting Authenticity: A Cartography

A cartography of varieties of authenticity can revolve around four oppositions. The first opposition concerns the notion of subjectivity underlying any view of authenticity: it could be either a *substantialist* view or an *intersubjective* one. The second opposition concerns the quality of subjectivity and, within subjectivity, of the self as *centered* or *decentered.* A third opposition allows us to contrast *integrative* and *antagonistic* conceptions of subjectivity. Finally, in the fourth place we could contrast conceptions of authenticity that emphasize *immediacy* or *spontaneity* with conceptions, like the one propounded here, that emphasize *reflectiveness* and, through reflectiveness, an intrinsic connection of authenticity to judgment.[3]

We need to avoid all confusion that might mislead us into conflating the first two dimensions. Like all philosophical concepts—autonomy, freedom, justice, equality, human dignity, and so on—authenticity is always understood within a conceptual horizon whose reflections influence the way in which the basic aspects of our target notion are perceived. Thus we have conceptions of authenticity that embed or presuppose a view of the self as coming into the world as a preformed substance of sorts, which acts instrumentally in the physical world and interacts with other similar selves, and conceptions of authenticity that presuppose a view

---

2 On the relation of authenticity to these two versions of exemplarity, see Ferrara (2008:3).

3 I have discussed these various conceptions of authenticity more extensively in Ferrara (1998:53-60).

of the self as emerging from a web of significant relations of recognition. This alternative, which concerns the genealogy of the self, has no intrinsic relation or even elective affinity with another conceptual alternative, concerning the inner structure of the self and of subjectivity—namely the alternative between conceiving the self as hierarchically structured around one or a plurality of central, overarching motivations, and conceiving the self as "decentered" or as consisting of a loose collection of juxtaposed and non hierarchical motivations. In other words, we can easily identify conceptions of authenticity which are centered and yet intersubjective, like the one put forward by Charles Taylor (1992), and views of authentic subjectivity that are decentered and yet non intersubjective, like the one implicit in Nietzsche's writings.

But let us take a closer look at these varieties of understandings of authentic subjectivity. Substantialist views of subjectivity embed the assumption that every human self comes into the world equipped with an essential core, which it tries to assert *through* its interaction with others. Some aspects of this core are non-individual, species-specific, and the various theories then differ in their descriptions of these universal human capacities: rationality, a capacity for abstraction, for using symbols, an instinct of self-preservation, compassion for others, a sense of justice, an impulse toward self-transcendence, libido and aggressiveness. Other aspects are specific and individuate single individuals: particular vicissitudes of the instincts in the light also of their relative strength, certain neurological capacities of the single brain, genetic endowment, and so on. This way of understanding subjectivity, definitively mainstream over many centuries and now in full resurgence through the fascination that the neurosciences and genetic research exert on contemporary culture, has been challenged by an intersubjectivist conception which has its forerunners in Herder and Wilhelm Von Humboldt, its most articulate defender in Hegel, underwent an early– to mid–twentieth century reincarnation in Mead's symbolic interactionist account of the birth of the self (1974) and in the object-relations tradition of psychoanalytic theory, and at the end of the twentieth century has been revisited along the lines of a theory of communicative reason by Jürgen Habermas and of a theory of recognition by Axel Honneth. This is the dimension of authenticity on which I will focus more closely in the second section: I believe that the "self-substantialist" backdrop makes it more impervious to think of an authentic self in consistent and sensible terms, whereas the intersubjectivist one provides us with the conceptual means that we need in order to conceive of authenticity in non-essentialist terms.

Whether understood as a substance, as *res cogitans*, or as the product of relations of recognition, the self can be further attributed the quality of either possessing a center—i.e., an identity which a) is a hierarchical set of self-posited normative demands, b) orients lower-level motivations as well as conduct and c) functions as an evaluative compass utilized in all important choices—or consisting of a more or less loose collection of self-representations on which continuity and ranking is conferred for practical purposes and on a very precarious basis.

Authenticity acquires a different coloring according to where we side on this conceptual divide.

For some authors the very idea that our notion of an authentic life presupposes that such life course can be captured as a coherent narrative is to be rejected. To their eyes, *narratability* is rather the epitome of *inauthenticity*. For every narrative imposes an ex-post-factum order in the material narrated, an order most often of a projective nature. Among the opposers of the centered self, Foucault, following in the footprints of Nietzsche and Bataille, equates the exemplarily fulfilled self subjectivity with the one undergoing a "limit-experience"—namely, the kind of experience capable of "'tearing' the subject from itself in such a way that it is no longer the subject as such or of making it 'completely other than itself so that it may arrive at its annihilation, its dissociation'" (Foucault 1991:31).[4] From a variety of perspectives—Humean, *lebensphilosophisch*, aesthetic modernist, poststructuralist, therapeutic, postmodernist, postcolonial, "ritual-theoretic", Goffmanian—the proponents of decentered views of the self and of subjectivity are inclined to oppose all attempts to restore an internal hierarchy between what is central and what is peripheral to a life-project, a personality, an identity and therefore to sever their implicit or explicit notion of authenticity from any such assumption. Instead, authors who embrace a view of the self and of subjectivity as coalescing around a center of gravity—call it a strong version of identity—which sorts out what is crucial and what is peripheral for the self, understand authenticity as the quality of a life whose plurality of experiences, detours, and side-narratives can be meaningfully seen as variations on a unique and recognizable theme. Authentic subjectivity, thus understood, is equally opposed to destructured or unstructured self-experience and to "coercive coherence" achieved by enforcing principles external to the self and posits *reconciliation*—reconciliation of the central motifs of the self under a unique life-project which also gives voice to, as opposed to ignore or suppress, all the emotionally salient aspects of inner life. The archetype of this way of understanding authenticity is constituted by Schiller's view of the *beautiful soul* as a human identity capable of reconciling *grace* and *dignity* and thus of obeying reason with joy (Schiller 1971:107)—namely, as a kind of human subjectivity capable of integrating cognitive rationality, moral reason and feelings without sacrificing any of them. But also Rousseau is a perfect example of this way of understanding authenticity.

Thirdly, conceptions of authenticity are polarized in *antagonistic* and *integrative* ones, depending of the relation they envisage between authentic subjectivity and the social order. Some authors equate authenticity with emancipation from the constrictions of an entrenched social order, whereas others do not bind authenticity with an emancipatory thrust. Among the first, we could count many figures within Romanticism (Schlegel, Novalis), aesthetic modernism (Baudelaire, Mallarmé) *Lebensphilosophie* (again, Nietzsche), twentieth century avant-garde (Artaud,

4 For an excellent discussion of this point and, more generally, of the poststructuralist view of the relation of subjectivity to experience, see Jay (1994).

Breton) as well as within the anti-psychiatry and the psychoanalytic tradition. Instead, authors such as Rousseau, Schiller, Herder, Kierkegaard, and others embrace the view (with very different degrees of awareness and explicitness) that social expectations, roles, and institutions cannot be understood as playing a merely constraining, "disciplinary" or repressive role but also somehow constitute the symbolic material out of which authentic selves and authentic conduct can be generated.

Various combinations of these dimensions—which, it is worth reminding, can be isolated from one another only at the level of philosophical reflection, whereas then they often are jointly operative in the concrete works of single authors—are then possible. For example, the model of authentic subjectivity underlying Herder's view that "Each human being has his own measure," Schiller's "beautiful soul" or Winnicott's notion of "creative living" shares with the anti-hierarchical and decentered model of subjectivity typical of Diderot's character, Rameau's nephew, with Musil's "man without qualities," or with Rorty's "ironic liberal" a non-antagonistic, affirmative attitude towards the social world. In contrast, the Marxian notion of subjectivity no longer alienated shares with late-nineteenth century modernist avant-garde not simply an aversion to the bourgeois order, but also the idea that the affirmation of the self necessarily entails a challenge against the powers that be.

On the other hand, Romantic nationalism, Sartre's view of authentic subjectivity and Kierkegaard's notion of the individual who has "chosen himself," for all their diversity, share the idea that self-realization presupposes individuation, and individuation in turn presupposes the internal structuration of subjectivity in terms of a centre and a periphery. And, despite their different ways of relating to the world of established normativity, Rameau's nephew and Barthes's "écrivain," Baudelaire's poet as "albatross," Deleuze and Guattari's "achine désirante" Nietzsche's Zarathustra and the characters of Beckett's *Endgame*, all share a certain view of unitary and centered subjectivity as illusory.

Finally, the fourth dimension in terms of which we can distinguish conceptions of authenticity has to do with the *immediate* or *reflective* quality of the match between conduct and identity, life-course and guiding ideals. In the age of the *politics of difference,* of the *politics of recognition* and of *identity-politics*, this divide has acquired crucial salience for understanding what is meant by authenticity. All conceptions of authenticity prize the individual's ability to realize her uniqueness in the conduct of her life. According to views that emphasize *immediacy*, however, the uniqueness worth realizing, or deserving recognition, is the sum total of the features that set us apart from the rest of our fellow human beings, or that set one people apart from all the other peoples of the earth: "uniqueness" is here the result of a metaphorical subtraction—uniqueness equals the sum total of our being minus what is shared in common with others. This is what *difference* means. According to conceptions of authenticity that emphasize *reflectiveness*, instead, worth realizing is not the *factual* uniqueness of certain psychological traits but the unique way in which an individual brings together his or her "difference" with the normativity shared with other fellow human beings, the "thick" with the "thin," the universal with the particular aspects of an identity. This view of reflective authenticity, anticipated by Rousseau's moral thought, as it can be reconstructed from *Emile* and from *The New Heloise*,[5] brings together normativity and singularity without sacrificing either to the other.[6]

Non-Essentialist Authenticity, or Authenticity Without a True Self

In this section I would like to narrow my focus. After drawing a cartography of diverse notions of authenticity I would now like to show how the concept of reflective authenticity and its underlying view of a centered self offers us a more sensible view of subjectivity and better answers to the questions that any view of authenticity has to address: what does it mean for a self to relate to itself? What does it mean to be oneself? Notions of authenticity differ in the extent to which they allow us to answer these questions. The concept of "reflective authenticity" offers the advantage of connecting and keeping in balance, in ways that competitors such as "difference" have difficulty to match, the two distinct aspects of the relation that the self entertains with itself: namely, the *cognitive* moment of that relation, oriented towards knowing something about oneself, and the *practical* moment of that relation, oriented towards committing oneself to something.

Few other phrases of ordinary language draw together these two aspects of the relation of the self to itself better than "I love you." My gaze meets that of my lover, the rest of my world is left idling, the gleam in my lover's eye expands my soul, and I say "I love you." What am I doing with my words? Am I describing what is going on through my mind, am I offering an account of one of my mental states? Or am I expressing a commitment, namely my own commitment to relate to that person as to someone whom I love? What is the ground of the so-called "special authority of the first person," namely of the fact that no one better than me can tell whether I love that person or I don't? Does that authority rest on the assumption—by no means undisputable, as every psychoanalyst would be ready to confirm—that no one can *know* my internal states better than I do? Or does it rest on the assumption that no one else, other than me, can *enter commitments* that are then binding for me?

Thus the promise inherent in the idea of reflective authenticity is that it can best meet that challenge that any conception of authenticity has to face—to elucidate the nature of the relation of the self to itself—and that, in so doing, can provide us with a notion of authenticity entirely independent from assuming a true self which relates to its own life as an essence relates to its manifestations.

5 See Ferrara (1993:69-109).

6 In this sense, Adorno's critique of the jargon of "Eigentlichkeit" (Adorno 1973) does not apply to the view of authenticity defended here.

The first step in defending a normative view of authenticity is to respond to the criticism raised at different times by Paul Valery, Jean-Paul Sartre and René Girard against the very idea that authenticity could be understood as the one value to which the self and subjectivity should primarily attend. Drawing on the argument developed by Charles Larmore (2004a), but eventually parting way from some of his conclusions, I see this defense of authenticity as requiring that we take distance from a venerable tradition that considers *self-knowledge* the principal axis of the relation of the self to itself and the main dimension along which the self-construction of the self proceeds. From the "Know Thyself" of the Delphic oracle to the Hegelian ideal of complete self-transparency of the subject in the stage of Absolute Knowledge, to the Freudian early notion of making the unconscious conscious, for this tradition the optimally constituted self is a self that "knows" itself and the laws that govern its own motives much in the same way as it possesses knowledge of the external world. Against *this* tradition Sartre points to the paradox of the unavoidable non-coincidence of the self *qua* object of knowledge and the self *qua* active subject of knowledge. The views of authenticity that posit a complete overlap of these two aspects of the self—to fully know oneself—as their leading ideal are then denounced as intrinsically inconsistent. By definition, in fact, the knowing self must contain an extra element that the known self lacks. A different version of this argument could be reconstructed by drawing on Mead's point about the impossibility of knowing the "I" without thereby instantly turning it into a "Me" (Mead 1974:173-75).

Of course, conceptions of authenticity that equate the authentic with what is spontaneous, immediate, *un*reflective—*le naturel*, in Stendhal's terminology—are not vulnerable to this criticism. They open themselves up, however, to lots of other problems. For example, to mention just the most obvious one, these conceptions implictly set authentic action in opposition not just to "inauthentic" action, but to *social action* as such. For social action by definition presupposes that we take the expectations of others into account and that we see ourselves through the eyes of another. Equally invulnerable to the inconsistency charge—and not liable to the problematic assumption of a zero-sum opposition of the social and the authentic quality of action—are those conceptions of authenticity, such as the ones put forward by Ricoeur and Larmore, which anchor authentic conduct to the *practical*, as opposed to the *cognitive*, relation that we establish with our self. From this perspective, from whence the authentic quality of an action depends on our commitments and not on our beliefs, authenticity cannot consist of "becoming what one is" for two reasons. First, because such imperative would be tantamount to a sort of tyranny of the existent, conjugated in the singular. One could in fact object: "it is unfortunate enough that I've got the character that I've got, why should I go out of my way to realize that character even more completely?" Second, this way of conceiving authenticity misses on the fact that in entering its commitments the self is not hostage to its own past, but rather orients itself to the future and to becoming something which it still is not. The authenticity of the self does not consist in coincidence with something actual and present, but rather in "coinciding with its own essential non-coincidence" (Larmore 2004a:10).

What is problematic with anchoring authenticity primarily to self-*knowledge*? If I say "I believe that it's raining," no one can question the truth of my belief and in this immunity of the first person with respect to error a tradition that goes back to Descartes has seen the foundations of sound knowledge. In his critique of this tradition Larmore highlights the paradoxical implications of assuming that the self has a privileged cognitive access to its own mental states. What kind of knowledge could it be? It can neither be knowledge gained through observation, as the kind of knowledge that mediates our relating to the external world, nor inferential knowledge of a purely logical form. We are then left with the hypothesis of a kind of "auto-telepathy" that allows us to establish a direct contact with our mental states based on the fact that somehow we "own" them (Larmore 2004a:153). We are thus led to presuppose the existence of a mysterious faculty of sorts, whether in the form of Ryle's claim, defended in *The Concept of Mind*, that we are always "better informed" about ourselves than about anybody else (Ryle 1949:179), or in the form of Ascombe's suggestion that there exist cognitions which stem neither from observation nor from logical inference, or in the form of a faculty of "self-intimation" (Shoemaker), or in the form of a non-cognitive kind of knowledge (Tugendhat).

Against those skeptics who question the authority of the first person, Larmore develops an argument that strongly reaffirms such authority but avoids the difficulties of cognitive accounts of it by rethinking the constituting of the self as *positing* what we aim to be and expressing our commitment to such future be a certain kind of self through *avowals* or declarations. After all, we are normative beings—"strong evaluators" in the terminology of Charles Taylor (1989)—who posit their norms in full autonomy and then not always manage to live up to them (Larmore 2004a: 156). However, this reconceptualization of the act of constituting the self simply places us on a terrain that might be more favorable for giving an account of the special authority of the first person, but certainly does not eliminate the problem. For whatever the scope and significance of my *avowals*—whether I say "long live freedom" in front of a firing squad or I say "I love oysters" at a dinner party—the practice of interpretation must at some point come to a stop before my own authority *qua* "first-person" utterer of the sentence. The difference is that, if we follow the thesis of a priority of the *practical* over the *cognitive* relation of the self to itself, now we will no longer claim that "no one better than me knows" whether I care for freedom or for oysters. Rather, we will claim that no one else is in a better position than me to take up those commitments. Yet the problem is still before us: how can we vindicate this now non-cognitive form of authority of the first person?

In a section by the title "La clé du mystère" Larmore suggests to sever all conceptual connection between our *avowals* and the supposition that they might convey any sort of "self-knowledge." Borrowing Ricoeur's notion of "attestation" (Ricoeur 1994:21-23), Larmore understands our assertions about our beliefs or intentions as "stances" or "indications" about how we plan to act in the future. To make a statement is a bit like to promise. It amounts to promising something which only I am entitled to promise—"only I" not insofar as I'm the one who knows best about my true intentions, but insofar as I'm the only owner of my agency. Furthermore, my promise *creates*, as opposed to *describes*, my commitment to act in a certain way in the future, for example to act in a way appropriate for someone who says "I love you" to someone else. Such commitments need not concern important things: when the person who just proclaimed "I love oysters" declines to help herself to one being offered around, we are entitled to comment "how come? I thought you liked oysters."

Declaratives such as "I love oysters" share with promises the quality of not being susceptible to be "false," at least in the sense descriptions can be false. They can be un-truthful, "inauthentic" as it were, but "inauthentic" in a future-oriented sense—like a promise can remain unfulfilled. To tell the truth means to live by the announced or avowed commitment. Drawing on Ricoeur, Larmore at this juncture connects the identity of the self with this eminently *practical* dimension. The *authenticity* of identity cannot be reduced to constancy of character: rather it consists of my continuing to honor my commitments *despite* the changes in the meantime occurred in my character or circumstances: as for example when I stick to my word for the simple fact of having given it, even if I no longer endorse my originary reasons for giving it. Precisely in my honoring a commitment that originates from me—even though certain aspects of that me may have changed in the meantime—I constitute myself as *my*self, as the same self that has committed itself in such a way. No one else can make such a commitment, no one else can replace me in either fulfilling or breaking it. This *practical* irreplaceability gives us the key for making sense of the authority of the first person and of the special immunity I enjoy when I express my own beliefs—beliefs of the sort "I think it is going to rain."

Notice that this practical dimension of the relation of the self to itself, far from presupposing a mysterious privileged access to self-knowledge on the part of the subject, on the contrary is one of the conditions of the possibility of self-knowledge. The received paradigm has been subverted radically. It is not self-knowledge that constitutes the self and enables it to relate to the world but, on the contrary, it is the self's capacity to enter relations of recognition with others and make commitments that enables the self to achieve self-knowledge. In this sense, a significant intersection with Honneth's theory of recognition, and in particular with his recent reinterpretation of the concept of "reification," can be pointed out. Honneth, in fact, reconceptualizes reification as "forgetfulness of recognition," i.e. as a loss of awareness "of the degree to which knowledge and cognition owe their existence to an antecedent stance of involvement and recognition" (Honneth 2005:68). This forgetfulness comes in three forms. The first and the second have to do with our relation to others and to the external world (Honneth 2005:78). The third form of reification bears directly on our theme: it is "self-reification," inauthenticity, a relation of the person to her own self that embeds the same forgetfulness or, in other words, fails to make sense of one's own motives in the context of one's own whole person. But how is it possible to for me to have a non-recognitional relation to my own self? Interestingly, Honneth offers us a twofold elucidation of what it might mean to have a "self-reified" relation to oneself: in one version (the "detectivist" relation), the actor adopts a cognitive-instrumental attitude towards her inner world, in the other (the "constructivist" relation) the actor indulges in the omnipotent illusion that she can create herself by virtue of self-description solely.[7]

Be that as it may, and regardless of the specific vocabulary adopted, once it is made to include a moment of self-reflection (or of "self-recognition") the *authentic* quality (whenever this description meaningfully applies) of the self's adoption (and carrying out) of its commitments becomes invulnerable to the two major criticisms raised against authenticity. Because the relation between the self and itself is assumed to be *practical* and not cognitive, this notion of authenticity is not vulnerable to the paradox of the self-*qua*-subject by definition always exceeding the self-*qua*-object of knowledge. And furthermore, because in this practical relation no one can replace us, also the Girardian critique of authenticity as obscuring the ubiquitous and pervasive dimension of social mimetism loses its bite. No matter where the symbolic materials through which we think and form an identity come from, it is still us that bear the responsibility for the final endorsement.

Three Limitations of the Practical Self-constitution of the Self, or Bringing Reflection Back In

Much as Larmore should be credited for having contributed to free our understanding of authenticity from the limits and strictures of framing it in cognitive terms, there is still one more step that we need to take. We should also explore the limitations of his practical account of the "special authority of the first person" and for this purpose the notion of "reflective authenticity" that I've tried to outline could be of help.

In discussing my view of authenticity, Larmore has ascribed the emphasis on reflection and judgment that distinguishes "reflective authenticity" to my own inclination to see authenticity as a an overarching, paradigmatic value, distinctive of our philosophical age much in the same way as *autonomy*, despite the existence of a variety of versions of it, was distinctive of early and classical modernity (Larmore 2004b). However, also Larmore's conception, according to which authenticity is but one of several contemporary leading philosophical values,

7 See Honneth (2005:86). Honneth's third course, called "expressionism," according to which "neither do we merely perceive our mental states as objects, nor do we construct them by manifesting them to others" (2005:88) but rather builds her intentions on "an antecedent stance of recognition" *vis-à-vis* her inner world is close in many respects to the notion of "reflective authenticity" as articulated here.

cannot avoid focusing on the *quality* of the self-constitutive process set in motion by my commitments and this assessment of the quality of my commitments in turn brings the notions of reflection and judgment in the service of self-knowledge and of avoiding self-delusion back in. Queen's singer Freddy Mercury in *Innuendo* used to sing "You can be anything you want to be. Just turn yourself into anything you think that you could ever be." And film-director Almodovar, in *All about my Mother*, has the drag-queen Amparo pronounce a similar line, when he makes her say: "Authenticity means to come to correspond to what you dream of being." But is this a sensible conception of the self and what it means for it to attain authenticity?

Larmore has no difficulty admitting that not all the practical commitments of the self contribute to its constitution in the same way. "Long live freedom" and "I love oysters" cannot be equivalent in this respect. Nor is there a limit to the number of commitments that a self can enter. The authenticity of the relation of the self to itself is not affected by this variable: fundamental and decisive remains the self's intention, no matter how unrealistic it is, to be true to all of them. I find this a dubious and underthematized aspect of Larmore's approach to authenticity.

The actuality of the self's intention to stand by all of its commitments in the future—to keep what really are "self-promises"—cannot be separated from a moment of self-reflection. I obviously cannot promise you the moon. Thus the self—also in the context of its practical relation to itself—must at the very least make sure, in a cognitive sense, that the new commitment belongs to the number of the things possible: "I adore to bootstrap myself at mid-air" can never be an *authentic* commitment, avowal or "attestation." This is fairly obvious. Yet satisfying this requirement constitutes no sufficient condition. The self usually takes on a *plurality* of commitments: so we must also assume that these commitments be mutually consistent. A self which pursues *inconsistent* commitments cannot possibly be considered as equally well constituted as one which pursues mutually compatible commitments.

The same holds for a self which pursues commitments that are *empirically incompatible*: for example, "I adore glamorous living" and "I don't like to make money." Impossible, inconsistent and empirically incompatible commitments are, however, only the most blatant cases of defective commitments. Less obvious, but equally important, is the case of those commitments which violate neither criteria of formal consistency nor criteria of empirical feasibility, but seem to violate an implicit and indispensabile assumption, never mentioned by Larmore: the plurality of commitments that, by constituting the answer to the question "Who am I?", defines the identity of the self must convey a unique pattern and cannot just amount to the random juxtaposition of scattered elements. Imagine an individual who takes on every commitment that comes to his head: in January he pursues an academic career in the humanities, in February decides on being a free-lance photographer, in March he applies for an MBA at Harvard, in April he regrets that choice and tries to act in a theater company, in May he volunteers to join a humanitarian mission in tropical Africa, in June he discovers a religious calling and joins a monastery, leaving it in July to embark on a solo sailing across the Atlantic Ocean, but in August when half way through he launches an SOS and returns home to start up a small business in computer repairs. In September he decides that the prospect for his new business is not that rosy and turns to earning his living as a door-to-door salesperson for cosmetics. In October, tired of the experience of selling cosmetics he successfully applies for being hired in a law firm, but when rejected in November proceeds to open up an activity as tax-accountant, only to drop it in December in order to apply for a position as astronaut with a space agency.

In this case, we are confronted with a self whose commitments are not mutually inconsistent but nonetheless we feel that there is something defective: these commitments taken as a whole fail to add up to a meaningful identity. There is nothing wrong in any of the single commitments, nor do they violate any normativity external to the self. What seems wrong or somehow inadequate is their apparent inability, *when taken all together*, to add up to a "coherent" or "sensible" answer to the question who this person is.[8] In other words, it is as though these commitments would *subtract* something from the self, as opposed to *add up* to its constitution. Larmore's account would gain in clarity and persuasiveness, in my opinion, if it contained an explicit mention of the fact that the self is not at its complete disposal, as the idea of self-constitution via avowals and commitments might lead one to think.

Another limitation of the conceptions of authenticity which embed an overestimation of the self-formative powers of the self concerns constative utterances. If our assertions—for example, "I believe it will pour in ten minutes"—strictly do not describe an independent reality but have the status of a commitment, on our part, to a) consider reality as possessing certain properties (the probability of heavy rains, in this case) and b) to act accordingly, then does the self not come to be endowed with a kind of omnipotence in its ability to provide us with a description of the world which, false though it may be in terms of a correspondence theory of truth, nonetheless embeds a legitimate claim to the taken as intersubjectively binding? Should a Stalinist bureaucrat of the Soviet Union utter the assertion "As far as I'm concerned, snow is black," why could he not be taken—on the basis of a certain version of the theory of authenticity—not as a subject who states a false proposition, but as a subject who offers a true and valid, authentic attestation of his intention to have us perceive him as a proponent of the idea that snow is black? Doesn't the self presupposed by this view of authenticity enjoy the questionable prerogative of being in a position to construct an image of the world, through its

8 They only way in which these commitments could add up to meaningful identity is by assuming that they respond to a deliberately adopted project of living as many lives as possible. But that hypothesis implicitly proves the point: the nomadic self that deliberately chooses to explore as many life-courses as possible *is* indeed organizing its life-course around a central theme, which just happen to be bound up with celebrating plurality.

attestations of belief, which despite its apparent falsehood nonetheless raises a not easily dismissable claim to be intersubjectively binding?

Finally, a third limitation that needs to be overcome is the somewhat underspecified role of *normativity* in self-construction. The central point of Larmore's view of authenticity is that the self is constituted via the commitments it makes. Yet, in what sense do these commitments bind the self? If the commitments are made by the self, freely entered by it, why can't they be canceled by a subsequent avowal that abrogates or repels the former? Just as I can say "I love you," I can, at any subsequent moment, say "I don't love you anymore." We need not recall how practically futile and intrinsically inconsistent is the idea of an obligation to love. Equally, just as I can proclaim "I believe in God," the next day I can say "I no longer believe." From the point of view of this theory of authenticity, the overarching ideal of the coherence and sensibleness of the identity of the self—often favorably mentioned by Larmore—seems then unable to bind the self to any concrete commitment. It becomes unclear in what sense "I can do no other," Luther's saying that has become the epitome of authenticity, means anything different from "I *want* to do no other."[9] Larmore, as a matter of fact, is a defender of moral realism: by no means can a view of normativity as entirely at the disposal of the self be attributed to him. Thus he could perhaps reply that the self makes its commitments and avows them in the larger context of a moral normativity which it *discovers* to be binding for its choices. However, if we concede that commitments exist which objectively (in some sense of this word) cannot be entered and, at the same time, commitments which we cannot avoid, and if the nature of what makes certain commitments unadoptable or unrejectable is *external* to the self, in what sense can we still speak of *authenticity*? In what sense can my authenticity consist of discovering, on my part, that I'm obeying something that obliges me from without, *malgré moi* so to speak? The history of Western philosophy abounds with accounts of moral obligation that pivot around a normativity external to the self, located in nature, in cosmos, in the will of a monotheist God who is a source of morality, in ethos, in history. Why use the term "authenticity" in order to account for the normativity of obligations originating from outside the self and independently of its ability to satisfy them?

Once again, it seems to me that the concept of reflective authenticity best serves the function that we demand of a concept of authenticity: namely, to provide us

9 To locate in authenticity the key source of normativity, for the self as well as for aesthetic experience, constitutes a solution to the difficulties that we encounter in bringing together universalism and pluralism after the Linguistic Turn. Also Christine Korsgaard follows this path when she states that "an obligation always takes the form of a reaction against a threat of a loss of identity" and that we abide by obligations ultimately in order not to be forced to think of ourselves in terms different from the ones that we would like to adopt (Korsgaard 1996:102). This approach to the justification of normativity, however, does indeed incur difficulties if we fail to thematize the limits of what the self can authentically will.

with ways of thinking of limits to the self-shaping power of the self without either locating these limits outside the self or invoking the dubious notion of an essential self to be true to.

References

Ferrara, Alessandro. 1993. *Modernity and Authenticity. A Study of the Social and Ethical Thought of Jean Jacques Rousseau.* Albany, New York: SUNY Press.

—— 1998. *Reflective Authenticity. Rethinking the Project of Modernity.* London and New York: Routledge.

—— 2008. *The Force of the Example. Explorations in the Paradigm of Judgment.* New York: Columbia University Press.

Honneth, Axel. 2005. *Verdinglichung. Eine anerkennungstheoretische Studie.* Frankfurt am Main, Suhrkamp.

Jay, Martin. 1994. "The Limits of Limit-Experience: Bataille and Foucault." *Constellations-Oxford*, 2:155–174.

Korsgaard, Christine. 1996. *The Sources of Normativity.* Cambridge: Cambridge University Press.

Larmore, Charles. 2004a. *Les pratiques du moi.* Paris: Presses Universitaires de France.

—— 2004b. "Alessandro Ferrara's Theory of Authenticity." *Philosophy and Social Criticism*, 30:5-9.

Mead, George Herbert. 1974 [1934]. *Mind, Self and Society.* Chicago: University of Chicago Press.

Ricoeur, Paul. 1994. *Oneself as Another.* Chicago: University of Chicago Press.

Rousseau, Jean-Jacques. 1968. *La Nouvelle Heloïse. Julie, or the New Heloise 1761.* University Park: Pennsylvania State University Press.

Ryle, Gilbert. 1949. *The Concept of Mind.* New York: Harper & Row.

Taylor, Charles. 1989. *Sources of the Self: The Making of the Modern Identity.* Cambridge, MA: Harvard University Press.

—— 1992. *The Ethics of Authenticity*. Cambridge, MA: Harvard University Press.

Chapter 3
Self Authenticity as Master Motive

Andrew J. Weigert

Self is an ever-fertile concept for an interactionist approach to contemporary issues. As Herbert Blumer (1969:21 fn) stated, "In elevating the 'self' to a position of paramount importance and in recognizing that its formation and realization occur [...] in the joint activities of group life, symbolic interactionism provides [...] a provocative philosophical scheme [...] attuned to social experience." As such, the concept of self references a multi-dimensional phenomenon intrinsic to all social dynamics.

Interactionist writings refer to aspects of self as process, producer, product, and project (Weigert and Gecas 2003). This fourfold set of categories provides a conceptual framework for analyzing the self in social context as well as self as experience. It incorporates a substantive understanding of self as an ever emerging meaning from embodied presence and constructed attributions from self-reflection and others' impositions. An individual self is at once a meaning from the past and promise into a future around a processual present (Blumer 1969; Cronk 1987). Temporality is a central organizing concept for an interactionist and phenomenological understanding of self as both individual actor and social process.

I include the range of this conceptual framework within a "pragmatic social constructionist" perspective incorporating the realist orientation of George H. Mead and the interpretive emphasis of phenomenology. After brief clarifying remarks, this chapter has two parts. The first part looks at self in the present as from the past—that is, pluralistically defined and identified, akin to Mead's "me," and motivated by what Alfred Schutz calls "because motives." The second part focuses on self in the present as into a future—that is, emergently meaningful dependent on the responses of others and of self, and motivated by "in order to motives" (Mead 1934:173 ff; Schutz 1962:69 ff). Self exercises a "voluntative fiat" or decision to pursue a course of action in a problematic situation and in so doing motivates the transition from the experiences of the first part to the actions of the second part (Mead 1934:177 ff; Schutz 1962:67, 70). By the voluntative fiat, self claims, "I am the author of this action."

In this chapter, "authenticity"—a growing contemporary socio-cultural phenomenon relevant to adequate understandings of self—refers to self motivation and meaning. Following Mead, meaning is always in the future, or in his words, "meaning is in the response" which is not yet but continually emerges. A future emphasis includes the power of the past as habits, rituals, norms, and other physical or social partial determinants of motives for and meanings of our acts. I extend the notion of meaning-as-futurity to include the social psychological category of hope as a phenomenological transcendent. Finally, I make a realist turn to the contemporary context of intensifying global dynamics within an emerging pluralistic "self" and "community" in search of understanding, namely, cosmopolitanism.

Clarifying the State of the Question: What is Authenticity?

Within its family of meanings, I conceptualize authenticity within the general domains of self meaning and self motivation. The literature on authenticity covers a wide range of applications from the reality of an object to classification of an object to interpretation of a self (see Vannini and Williams, this volume). Here is a brief journey through meanings and applications of authenticity.

Anthropologist Charles Lindholm (2008:2) starts with a distinction between "origin," from history or genealogy, and "content," from identity or correspondence, as bases for "characterizing any *entity* as authentic" (italics added). Many authors share this starting point and attribute authenticity to an "entity." Thus, analysts address "entity questions" to physical objects: is this gem a "real" diamond? Is this painting a "real" Van Gogh? Within social worlds, analysts address "meaning questions" to cultural objects: who says the diamond is real? Who authenticates the painting as a Van Gogh? Cultural objects are authentic as they are defined by authoritative others: Who says this person is a spy? Who authenticates this person as human just like me? As a dialectical social process unifying object and subject, self raises a conundrum: self is not a real object, yet strives for and is defined by others as more or less authentic.

Self-as-real continually emerges from reflexive self affirmation of a past self-as-authentic. Attributions of self as real and authentic, however, refer to self as past identity and as future meaning, respectively. Within its family of meanings, then, I primarily locate authenticity "as characterizing self motivation." This attribution follows from understanding self as presently motivated to achieve meaning in future responses, behavioral and symbolic.

Sharply distinguishing self from identity, or physical and social embodiments of self, I formally locate authenticity as a motivating meaning of self. As such, authenticity shares the foundational aspects of self, that is, processual, emergent, reflexive, and empirically available directly to self experience and indirectly to others through actions or symbols. Authenticity, like self, is a contested meaning which is not "increasingly discovered" through physical sciences like objects in a world that is there, but which is "continually experienced and constructed" in the interplay among self, other, and institutions via cultural codes.

A root metaphor of authenticity-as-motivation is that which is self positing: "I am what I experience as who I am." One etymology of authenticity builds on the Greek roots, "auton" and "thetos." Roughly translated, the roots refer to individuals who "posit themselves" or "set themselves as a thesis" (Ferrara 1998:15). My Webster dictionary, however, gives "auton" and "entea" or "tools," as roots. The metaphor of tools suggests means of positing oneself as authentic. Indeed, "auton" or "self," as in automobile or "self mover," and "thetos" as thesis or "entea" as tools suggest a meta-perspective on "self authenticity" as "a means of self positing." This meta-perspective elicits Mead's model of self as simultaneously I-and-me, subject-and-object, within self reflexivity. Consider his echolalia, "the 'I' in memory [...] is a 'me,' but it is a 'me' which was the 'I' at the earlier time" (Mead 1934:174).

Self is emergently and interactionally social—a process where meanings of self-as-individual emerge. As a result, self positing is a social process contingent on validation with and from others as well as self's own experience as both the means and outcomes of social action. Reflecting on authenticity as a contemporary philosophical and moral issue, Charles Taylor references Mead regarding dialogical, social, and ethical aspects of self understanding versus an overly subjective turn to self as sole source of what is good and worthy. Mead's self involves an inherent dynamic toward a more inclusive, generalized self who extends the symbolic horizons of relevant communities (see Taylor, 1991:31 ff, for dialogical, existential, and moral "horizons" of self authenticity).

The scope and inclusivity of community arise as key issues, as in the idea of a cosmopolitan community, that is, a social universe shared meaningfully by all humans. With this realist turn, self authenticity is a call for personal freedom intrinsically interwoven with responsibility for others toward a shared future. Meaning is in future responses more profoundly than in present action. Within current contexts, self authenticity emerges as a signature motive for cultural carriers of a potential global community.

Self Authenticity as Master Motive and Pragmatic Meaning

I suggest an approach to self authenticity as an aspect of self motivation rather than an aspect of self as an object. I leave out of focus such factors as reflections or appraisals by others and the validating or coercive power of social structure and institutional location. The labels, "master motive" and "pragmatic meaning," refer respectively to experiences of present self-authenticity as warrant for a self claim to an intrinsic identity, and to actions of self authenticity as warrant for a self claim to a moral life. This dual approach reflects the experiential transparency of Alfred Schutz's interpretative rendition of self-as-motivated and the pragmatic developments of George H. Mead's projection of self-as-acting to reconstruct both self and social relations.

In series of papers, Viktor Gecas (1991, 1994, 2000, 2001) presents a conceptual framework for a theory of motivation based on self-motives. Interactionists have in the past sidestepped theories of motivation as a causal force in favor of a linguistic turn to vocabularies of motive. Causal theories of motivation seemed too deterministic, physicalistic, or individualistic (see Vannini and Burgess, this volume). Yet, understanding self motivation remains a central social psychological and cultural issue.

Gecas (1991) first posits self concept—that is, operative knowledge of self by self—as a cognitive basis for a theory of motivation within a symbolic interactionist perspective. Within self concept, he locates research on self motives, especially what he considers an excessive applied emphasis on self esteem. As but one dimension of self concept as motivational wellspring, overemphasizing esteem leads to inadequate understanding and misleading applications (Gecas 2001). He emphasizes self worth derived from personal efficacy, agency, or competence as a complementary realist self motive. Genuine self esteem arises from efficacious actions. Combining efficacy with esteem highlights the interplay of cognition, feeling, and striving as dimensions of self concept and a basis for an interactionist theory of motivation.

In another paper, Gecas (1994:139) names a struggle for authenticity as a central self-meaning in the contemporary world, arguing that "authenticity is a quintessentially modern problem." At the time of his writing, authenticity was relatively undeveloped as a self motive within interactionist writings. Yet, in global and societal contexts characterized by social pluralism, rapid change, movements of peoples, increasing cultural contacts, and struggles for self meaning, authenticity emerges as a definitive challenge (see Lindholm 2008:3-10). The oft quoted line by Polonius, "To thine own self be true," was accurate then, but a more apt nuance today is, "To thine own selves be true." Rebecca Erikson (1995), for example, interprets concern for authenticity as indicating a problematic yet powerful commitment to self values in a context of rapid social change.

Gecas links self authenticity to classical themes, especially Marx and alienation. He builds on Trilling (1971), suggests linkages with other self motives, and looks at possible antecedents and consequences of authenticity-inauthenticity within social action. Each self motive refers to major aspects of self experience: esteem to feelings and affect, efficacy to action and competence, and authenticity to meaning and culture. In general, he posits that self tends to act to preserve or enhance desirable experiences of positive self feeling, competent self efficacy, and authentic self meaning.

Self understanding can be pluralistic and still function as a motivating force, indeed, a force arising from a quest for self authenticity as an impulse moving selves to act and reflexively to assess their actions by multiple standards for appropriating who they believe themselves to be or not to be. Meaning, however, always lurks in the response, in potential futures, as we go about routines of repeating habits, following norms, and fulfilling cultural imperatives. Since alternative futures, reactionary or utopian, inform social movements, Gecas (2000) expands his conceptual framework by linking self to social movements through the construct of value identities.

Value identities function as future-oriented self motives which "transcend" self's situation (see Schutz and Luckmann 1989, for little, medium, and great transcendences within the lifeworld). Gecas states that value identities are "more transcendent than are identities based on roles or [...] group memberships." They "transcend specific situations" and are more "enduring" (Gecas 2000:94-95; cf. Erikson 1995:131). Values combine cognition and emotion. As "felt-values," they provide schemas for desirable futures and energies for present actions. He speculates that self authenticity "may be the most important basis of commitment to a group" (Gecas 2000:104). Social movements activating value identities highlight self authenticity as a "pull" motivation to participate in a quest for justice or fighting injustice through social reconstruction.

In summary, I structure Gecas's conceptual framework for an interactionist theory of motivation incorporating the self motives of authenticity, values, efficacy, and esteem as follows:

Self Authenticity → Self Values → Self Efficacy → Self Esteem
= Self as Motivational Force.

I read this schema as theorizing that self authenticity is the master motive that informs other self motives leading self to act now, here, and in this way (see Erickson 1995:134 for "self as a motivational force rooted in authenticity"). This schema (AVEE) orders self motives in future-orientation (values), present social action (efficacy), and resultant evaluation (esteem, which may have negative valences). This ordering links cultural meanings and values with desirable futures, cognition with affect and striving, and action with adjustment and social change—strong Meadian themes linking self as social actor with personal adjustment and societal reconstruction. The meanings of my actions and self motives remain in the future—self authenticity is a promise and project. In addition, Gecas suggests that self authenticity emerges at moments of self transcendence over the socio-material conditions of the situation.

Gecas's Authenticity-Values-Efficacy-Esteem model of self motivation builds on concomitant self awareness and self appropriation as basic processes. In a word, self authenticity functions as the master motive because it must inform the other motives in order for them to be self-relevant. Although self motivation functions more or less within all social locations and groupings, I discuss a social dynamic that strongly reflects the processual and future oriented dynamic of self, namely, social movements.

I suggest that self authenticity activated by value identities within social movements activates desirable futures through social hope. Social hope is a powerful form of future-as-motive that generates a sense of authenticity in self through fusion with that which is greater than individual self [for example, a sense of "vocation" as a university professor (see Vannini 2006), which evokes Max Weber's "Beruf," this-worldly vocation, in his Protestant Ethic thesis). In a social realist sense akin to Durkheim's emphasis on social entities as sources of self meanings, I illustrate the experience of authenticity in a collective, religious, or ideological self. The final section takes a realist turn to contemporary formulations of a cosmopolitan self as an emerging self motive relevant to the intertwining forces of globalization and self formation.

Social Movements and Social Hope

Hope in a desirable future is central to self functioning, meaning formation, and motivation. In theorizing human development, Erik Erikson (1964:116-119, 231) locates "hope" with the infant stage of trust/mistrust as one of the "virtues" or "inner strengths" that generate engagement and motivation. He elaborates on hope as a fundamental self strength and a universal requirement for psychological health. From a theological-cultural perspective, Peter Berger (1969:75 ff) wrote of hope as a "signal of transcendence" not given by or in the natural everyday world, but posited in a symbolic realm that "transcends" the life-world. The "world" in which humans experience hope exists in symbolic relevance systems which humans construct and then posit as real, perhaps as more real than the empirical world at hand.

Thinking of hope as a psychic state akin to a metaphor of "rainbows in the mind" complements developmental and cultural analyses. Snyder (2002), a psychologist, contrasts hope and optimism, with the latter restricted to cognitive expectations and successful attainment of goals through present actions. In a sense, optimism is intrinsic to empirical probabilities of success which self imputes to actions-as-means to an end. One undertakes this action because one believes that it will bring about the end which one desires—a version of Max Weber's means-end rationality. Hope, on the other hand, transcends optimism and the rationality of means. Snyder reports studies of "hope" as an efficacious factor empirically related to various desirable outcomes and suggests a theory of "positive expectancy" that goes beyond what self may reasonably expect here and now.

Snyder's analysis includes two psychological aspects: "energy" for performing an action in pursuit of a goal, and cognitive mapping or "pathways" for attaining that goal. His hope construct remains primarily cognitive with emotions playing an important "albeit contributory role" (2002:249). He and colleagues define hope as "a positive *motivational* state that is based on an interactively derived sense of successful (a) agency (goal-directed energy), and (b) pathways (planning to meet goals)" (2002:250, italics added). Hope, then, is a feature of triadic interaction among goals, agency, and pathways, that is, future states, motivational energy, and plans or means to attain a preferred future through present action. Temporality and feelings are intrinsic to hope dynamics relating present actions to desirable futures (see his figure in 2002:254). Furthermore, hope is stronger in selves who pursue personal goals in conjunction with collective goods. Hope is not a narcissistic ego-centered motivational scheme. It is realistically anchored in social relationships and shared goals.

Agency along pathways toward a goal provides the hopeful self with the psychological functions that Snyder posits, but social realist analysis includes the consequentialist question: functional for whom and for what? Social categorization is a key step. Those rainbows may be part of a system of emotional and cognitive dynamics that motivate tossing lightening bolts at the earth and others who dwell therein. Clearly, hope is a positive state for a person or in-group, but that positive state may motivate death and destruction for out-group others as non-selves. If hope were anchored in beliefs about a desirable other-worldly existence for the saved but not the damned, it may lead to the devaluation of excluded others in this earthly life. Believers in rainbows may symbolically de-humanize others, believe in and obey a Deity which legitimates killing of all who are not the "elect," and promise hope's glow in a symbolic realm only for the few on the far side of the earth. Meadian pragmatism of self authenticity is more inclusive.

From a philosophical pragmatist's perspective, Richard Rorty writes about social hope. He reasons that we must learn to "substitute *hope* for the sort of knowledge which philosophers have usually tried to attain" (1999:24, his italics) by means of assumptions and constructs that no longer allow us adequately to understand world circumstances, interpret global dynamics, communicate and negotiate democratically, and motivate ameliorative cooperation. Hegemonic a priori categories of thought led to current crises, thus the need for a new pragmatist theory of meaning:

> replacing Greek and Kantian dualisms between permanent structure and transitory content with the distinction between the past and the future [...] to show how the things which James and Dewey said about truth were a way of replacing the task of justifying past custom and tradition by reference to unchanging structure with the task of replacing an unsatisfactory present with a more satisfactory future, thus replacing certainty with *hope*" (1999:31-32, italics added).

Rorty elaborates this epistemological principle of pragmatically grounded truth that does not justify past tradition by reference to inherited a priori structures, but by initiatives to replace conventional thinking with free imaginings, just as Mead argued against positing aprioris in knowledge and morality.

Rorty develops his understanding of hope by urging "that we substitute for knowledge" a kind of "romantic hope (that is) willingness to substitute imagination for certainty" (1999:88) in order to free human agency from the constraints of the past. Following Dewey, and I would add Mead, Rorty (1999:120) believes that "Hope—the ability to believe that the future will be unspecifiably different from, and unspecifiably freer than, the past—is the condition of growth." He asserts that the socialization of children ought to allow them to acquire "an image of themselves as heirs to a tradition of increasing liberty and rising hope" (1999:121).

Throughout the eighteenth and nineteenth centuries, Rorty (1999:208-209) believes that "Europe and North America [witnessed] a massive shift in the locus of human hope: a shift from eternity to future time," or from other worldly to this worldly hope. Contemporaries now need a new document to complement Scriptural or Communist Manifesto narratives "to provide our children with inspiration and hope [...] without prophecy and claims to knowledge of the forces which determine history—if generous hope could sustain itself without such reassurances."

For such a document, Rorty (1999:238-239) looks to antiauthoritarian philosophers of freedom and justice, concerns which flow from possibilities of "utopian social hope." Socio-cultural hope generates a type of moral identity emerging from citizens' "sense of participation in a democratic society," a moral identity that enables them to go beyond a priori religious and ethnic identities and on to "an image of themselves as part of a great human adventure, one carried out on a global scale." And yet, history is lived in present circumstances as local fields of hopeful action. "If we fail in such identification [with our country], we fail in national hope. If we fail in national hope, we shall no longer even try to change our ways" (Rorty 1999:254). His final sentence amplifies these themes: "The utopian social hope which sprang up in nineteenth–century Europe is still the noblest imaginative creation of which we have record" (Rorty, 1999:277). This-worldly hope remains at the heart of empirically possible futures and thus at the heart of authentic self motivation.

In sum, Rorty affirms that social growth and positive change depend on humans learning to cooperate by acting on likely shared futures and not by reaffirming divisive past certainties. Inclusive social hope in place of inherited certitudes is a principle both of sustainable social change and personal freedoms. He calls for thinking to inform pragmatic action that is "hopeful, melioristic, experimental" (1999:24)—echos of three themes that resonate in George H. Mead's writings (see Cronk 1987:126 ff, for Mead's potential "universal community"). They are also themes in emerging movements toward "cosmopolitan" identities as authentic contemporary responses to increasing pluralism in both benign and malevolent sociocultural dynamics.

Social movements are historical phenomena in which hope is a powerful component. Henri Desroche, in "The Sociology of Hope" (1979:1), begins with the story of a miracle of the rope: "hope is a rope" as in the magical fakir's trick of tossing a rope into the air, having it stay there, and finally climbing up that free standing rope! The rope of hope transcends gravity, a foundational experience. In some traditions, a rope is dropped from heaven for us to climb up, just as other traditions spoke of sun rays visible through the clouds as Jacob's ladder to heaven. Desroche offers four "sociological concepts" for understanding hope: waking dream, collective ideation, exuberant expectations, and generalized utopia (1979:12 ff). These constructs recapitulate components of self authenticity discussed above: a "great transcendence," social realism, positive expectancy, and a desirable future hoped for in history though not yet realized.

To the extent that hope is realized in transcendent realms of ideology or religion, it partakes of the power that defies understanding. Desroche (1979:16, his italics) quotes Durkheim's comments on elementary forms of religion: "Religion is not only *a system of ideas*, it is above all a *system of forces* [...] when man lives a religious life, he believes he is participating in a force that dominates him, *but which at the same time supports him and raises him above himself* [...] the characteristic of religion is the dynamogenic influence that it exercises on consciousness." This forceful hope motivates millennial movements throughout history and is present in many violent situations today—challenges to cosmopolitanism.

Toward the end of his treatise, Desroche introduces Max Weber's distinction between an ethics of conviction and of responsibility, which I interpret respectively as akin to phenomenological self authenticity from the past that drives self's "because motives" and to pragmatic self authenticity toward the future that generates self's "in order to motives" (see next section). The quote is from Weber's "Politics as a Vocation," and includes his observation that "the ethic of conviction and the ethic of responsibility are not contradictory, they complement each other, and together they constitute the *authentic* man" (Desroche, 1979:176, italics added). Today's authentic citizen must cultivate both ethics.

Motivation emerges: what we believe we know and experience as emotion activates action. Pragmatically, reality arises from actions that both alter the world and redefine its meaning, whether in violent destruction or supportive even if antagonistic cooperation.

The social logic of hope requires that analysts interpret different types and consequences of hope as they would all social objects which are not inherently good or bad. In short, moral judgments demand analysts assess their meta-criteria and evaluative frameworks for cosmopolitan inclusivity.

Self Authenticity as Impulse toward Cosmopolitan Meaning

As mentioned above, a key self-defining moment is what Schutz (1962:67, 70), following William James, names the "voluntative fiat," when self says "yes" to a decision that initiates an action or assents to a narrative informing the action. The course of action is in the present but the pragmatic meanings of the action lie in the future. Thus, meaning remains uncertain, though typically predictable with differing levels of likelihood, as in cognitive and affective impulses emerging from physico-chemical-electrical workings of the organism.

Holstein and Gubrium (2000:230-231; also see Gubrium and Holstein this volume), for example, do not find a Romanticist "authentic" or "deeply hidden, genuine self" beneath conversationally narrated and locally enacted selves as we seek to live meaningfully. They deal with empirical narratives through which actors realize themselves as moral. I suggest adding the cultural dynamics of a search for authenticity to their understanding of self. The promissory and not-yet realized self as processual seeker of meaning is Meadian authenticity. It is a dialectic of past identity-as-because-motive and future self-meaning-as-in-order-to-motive. To live authentically in the present is to reconstruct past identities into more inclusive empirical and moral selves.

Gary Cook summarizes the parallel between Mead's understanding of empirical science as ever reformable attempts to understand and adjust to the world that is there, and of morality as ever more inclusive actions to meliorate the society in which we and now all of us live. He writes: a "successful scientific hypothesis reunifies a problematic situation and yields a more inclusive understanding of that situation. The successful moral hypothesis reconciles conflicting values in a morally problematic situation and yields a more inclusive self," and I would add, a more cosmopolitan society (Cook 1993:122). Mead's method of morality strives to incorporate the responses of all others affected by self's or society's actions—to act conjointly in ways that reflect each self's relationship to outcomes. Moral action is democratic and cooperative, even if conflictual, that enhances the lives of all. This dynamic is at once the desired process of social change and of self development. Mead's meliorism motivates his moral vision of an authentic self.

The dialectic of self and society is the motivational matrix of meaningful social action. Mead repeatedly addressed the moral ideal of acting in terms of a "new," "larger," "whole," "complete," "generalized" self, rather than an old, narrow, partial, or particular self (e.g., 1964:147 ff; 1934:144, 155, 317, 386). From his early to late writings he taught the reconstruction of society and self in the dialectics of social action. The charitable individual shares in a "growing consciousness that society is responsible for the ordering of its own processes and structure so that what are common goods [...] should be accessible to common enjoyment" (Mead, 1964:5; 497). He adds, "We vaguely call it 'progress.'" Accordingly, he emphasized historical processes of increasingly inclusive social dynamics—adumbrating globalization, social utopianism, and cosmopolitanism in his reasoning about "international mindedness," "social reform," and an "ideal universal society" implicated in the evolutionary dynamics of self motivation and societal change.

Following Aboulafia (2001), I believe that Mead prefigured the current discussion of cosmopolitanism as a construct reflecting the issues, conflicts, and promises of global dynamics. Cosmopolitanism evokes Mead's emphasis on the internal dynamic of self to become an ever more inclusive and socially relevant actor. From early essays on World War I and a working hypothesis in social reform to later essays on ethics of philanthropy and international mindedness, Mead tried to reconfigure global issues and international violence as well as tensions between individual interests and a common good—consistent themes. Even in wartime, Mead wrote "there is always to be discovered a common social interest in which can be found the solution of social strifes" (quoted in Shalin, 1987:270-271).

Analysts are developing cosmopolitanism as a fertile construct for generating a social moral sense in an increasingly interdependent and interactive global context. Ethicist Kwame Anthony Appiah (2006) takes the reader around the world, and argues for a dialogical cosmopolitanism that remains true to one's local identity (whoever and wherever that is) and embraces a sense of obligation toward and ability to understand others. He pragmatically states that "we can live in harmony without agreeing on underlying values (except, perhaps, the cosmopolitan value of living together)" (2006:78). Believers who covet the same valued object struggle all the more violently if they cannot find a more inclusive value to ground communication, compromise, and a shared future.

In a sociological framework, Ulrich Beck (2006) argues that cosmopolitanism both reflects the crisis of contemporary global interdependencies and suggests a reflexive response that offers hope. A system of independent sovereign nation-states is inadequate to current pluralist and contact-intense global contexts. Thus, selves are ambivalent and simultaneously aware of the need for new affective, cognitive, and interactional relationships. He lists five emerging realizations: a world society in crisis; salience of differences and resulting conflict; principles of empathy and perspective-taking; need for, but tendency to rebuild boundaries; intermingling of peoples so that "cosmopolitanism without provincialism is empty, provincialism without cosmopolitanism is blind" (2006:7). As a result, a cosmopolitan self suffers conflicting emotions from culturally induced ambivalence toward events, others, and self. Yet, there are opportunities for authentic answers to the ever-present challenge, "Who am I?" now that received answers no longer suffice (Beck 2006:70; cf. Weigert 1988). Cosmopolitans strive to redefine relationships from exclusionary either-or to inclusive both-and.

A striking enactment of authenticity in social reconstruction comes from peace makers in fields of deep conflict. Writing about peace making on the ground, John Paul Lederach highlights "authentic engagement" that must continue through dialogue among actors and their societies—a C. Wright Mills-sense of vocation at the intersection of biography and social structures (Lederach, 2005:23-24). Lederach finds authenticity emerging in close encounters, the "*social distance of direct conversation*" (2005:57, his italics). In words illuminating the leitmotif of this chapter, he writes that peace making demands authenticity which "requires accessibility, connection, and mutuality as means toward transcendence" of cycles of violence (2005:62-63). It calls for a voluntative fiat toward a peaceful future from those who were killing each other. And peace making is a much needed dynamic for possibilities of a cosmopolitan self.

Summary: Self Motivation to Self Completion

In summary, Gecas' conceptual framework for self motivation, AVEE, moves from a phenomenological to an interactional ordering. Self authenticity, as the core reflexive and meta-self motive in a context of global pluralism functions as the master motive for an interactionist theory of self motivation. Self-authenticity works in two directions as master motive. First, it informs other motives and renders them experientially as self motives: to experience values, efficacy, and esteem as authentic, self must experience them as mine (an early classical interactionist theme for self development)—and authenticity remains problematic since we live interactionally by inference. Self remains processual, emergent, and contingent. Nevertheless, we can realize this phenomenological moment as really who I am via the "voluntative fiat" within narratives that allow self to make a realist turn to moral action.

Second, in the realist turn, self authenticity motivates social action, since self is always a dialogical interacting process of I and Me and of self and other. The intrinsic dynamic of self motivation calls self to reconstruct society by actions and self realizations that are ever more inclusive: from narrow self to larger self in the progression toward more inclusive societies. Especially in his later essays on philanthropy and international mindedness, Mead pre-figures contemporary selves emerging within globalized pluralism and cultural cosmopolitanism.

As such, self authenticity experientially informs other self motives and transforms them into self-referential forces that self experiences as one's own. Such self authenticity activates past identities but does not translate them directly into moral action. Mead is socially progressive but not blind to the pitfalls of self formation and organized state violence. The tensions, duplicities, feignings, lies, suppressed emotions, and other Goffmanian dramaturgical presentations of self apply—but now self is concomitantly aware that self is contested, duplicitous, misleading, lying, or fraudulent because self as reflexive is available to self's awareness. Authenticity informs self in choosing actions and forming motives for acting in the present. Self motives emerge from our past but toward a desirable future and link self interests with a common good, which renders self an authentic moral actor.

For this chapter, then, self authenticity does not refer to a substantive entity that is judged real or fake, true or false, but rather to a reason for acting, a reason-become-force that is both from a known past and toward an uncertain future. At the end of his phenomenological analysis, Corey Anton states, "authenticity is the practice of openness by which we are called to fitting responses" (2001:160). In a footnote, he wrestles with the question, "was Hitler authentic?" From his phenomenological perspective, Anton does not think that a person can judge another's authenticity, only one's own. Nevertheless, he speculates that policies to alleviate German economic woes lean to the authentic, whereas defining categories of persons as less than human is inauthentic. He ends by repeating that we are all called to "fitting responses" (2001:166-167). From the perspective developed in this chapter, a fitting response includes social hope for an increasingly inclusive cosmopolitan community. This "realist turn" allows a summary judgment: Hitler's motivation was inauthentic.

In a global context of intensely and increasingly interactive pluralism of selves and others, I believe that authenticity, hope, and cosmopolitanism form a fruitful configuration of moral motivation for acting and being well, that is, true to self and other in ongoing mutual responsiveness. From a phenomenological and pragmatic social constructionist perspective, self authenticity refers to an experiential appropriation as mine of feelings, cognitions, and strivings based on a master motive demanded of us all in our quest to be who we believe we are and to act morally and inclusively toward others. Informing Mead's prefigured cosmopolitan vision is his pragmatically meliorisitc yet utopian oxymoron, a "universal community," that is potentially emerging within current historical dynamics while it remains an ideal that is not yet in history. Authentic selves struggle to find the motivation to answer the challenge.

References

Aboulafia, Mitchell. 2001. *The Cosmopolitan Self.* Urbana, IL: University of Illinois Press.

Anton, Corey. 2001. *Selfhood and Authenticity*. Albany, NY: SUNY Press.

Appiah, Kwame Anthony. 2006. *Cosmopolitanism: Ethics in a World of Strangers*. New York: Norton.

Beck, Ulrich. 2006. *Cosmopolitan Vision*. Malden, MA: Polity Press.

Berger, Peter. 1969. *A Rumor of Angels*. Garden City: Doubleday.

Blumer, Herbert. 1969. *Symbolic Interactionism*. Englewood Cliffs: Prentice-Hall.

Cook, Gary A. 1993. *George Herbert Mead: The Making of a Social Pragmatist*. Urbana, IL: University of Illinois Press.

Cronk, George. 1987. *The Philosophical Anthropology of George Herbert Mead*. New York: Peter Lang.

Desroche, Henri. 1979. *The Sociology of Hope*. Boston: Routledge & Kegan Paul.

Erikson, Erik H. 1964. *Insight and Responsibility*. New York: Norton.

Erikson, Rebecca J. 1995. "The Importance of Authenticity for Self and Society." *Symbolic Interaction*, 18:121-144.

Ferrara, Alessandro. 1998. *Reflective Authenticity*. New York: Routledge.

Gecas, Viktor. 1991. "The Self Concept as a Basis for a Theory of Motivation." Pp. 171-187 in *The Self-Society Dynamic*, edited by Judith A. Howard and Peter L. Callero. New York: Cambridge University Press.

—— 1994. "In Search of the Real Self: Problems of Authenticity in Modern Times." Pp. 139-154 in *Self, Collective Behavior and Society*, edited by Gerald M. Platt and Chad Gordon. Greenwich: JAI Press.

—— 2000. "Value Identities, Self-Motives, and Social Movements." Pp. 93-109 in *Self, Identity, and Social Movements*, edited by Sheldon Stryker, Timothy J. Owens, and Robert White. Minneapolis: University of Minnesota Press.

—— 2001. "The Self as a Social Force." Pp. 85-100 in *Extending Self-Esteem Theory and Research*, edited by Timothy J. Owens, Sheldon Stryker, and Norman Goodman. New York: Cambridge University Press.

Holstein, James A. and Jaber F. Gubrium. 2000. *The Self We Live By*. New York: Oxford University Press.

Lederach, John Paul. 2005. *The Moral Imagination: The Art and Soul of Building Peace*. New York: Oxford University Press.

Lindholm, Charles. 2008. *Culture and Authenticity*. Malden, MA: Blackwell.

Mead, George H. 1934. *Mind, Self, and Society*. Chicago: University of Chicago Press.

—— 1964. *Selected Writings*, edited by Andrew J. Reck. Indianapolis: Bobbs-Merrill.

Rorty, Richard. 1999. *Philosophy and Social Hope*. New York: Penguin.

Schutz, Alfred. 1962. *The Problem of Social Reality*. The Hague: Martinus Nijhoff.

Schutz, Alfred and Thomas Luckmann. 1989. *The Structures of the Life-World*, Vol. II. Evanston: Northwestern University Press.

Shalin, Dmitri N. 1987. "Socialism, Democracy and Reform: A Letter and an Article by George H. Mead." *Symbolic Interaction*, 10:267-278.

Snyder, C.R. 2002. "Hope Theory: Rainbows in the Mind." *Psychological Inquiry*, 13:249-275.

Taylor, Charles. 1991. *The Ethics of Authenticity*. Cambridge: Harvard University Press.

Trilling, Lionel. 1971. *Sincerity and Authenticity*. Cambridge: Harvard University Press.

Vannini, Phillip. 2006. "Dead Poets' Society: Teaching, Publish-or-Perish, and Professors' Experiences of Authenticity." *Symbolic Interaction*, 29:235-257.

Weigert, Andrew J. 1988. "To Be or Not: Self and Authenticity, Identity and Ambivalence." Pp. 263-281 in *Self, Ego, and Identity*, edited by Daniel K. Lapsley and F. Clark Power. New York: Springer-Verlag.

Weigert, Andrew and Viktor Gecas. 2003. "Self." Pp. 267-288 in *Handbook of Symbolic Interactionism*, edited by Larry T. Reynolds and Nancy J. Herman-Kinney (eds.) Lanham: Altamira Press.

Chapter 4

The Importance of Insincerity and Inauthenticity for Self and Society: Why Honesty is Not the Best Policy

Dennis D. Waskul

In this chapter I explore the importance—or lack thereof—of sincerity and authenticity for self and society. I begin with reflective fragments from a Garfinkelian social and personal experiment: for one entire day I sought complete sincerity and authenticity. To the best of my ability I was completely honest, refusing to lie to myself or others; I rigidly adhered to my values and portrayed myself to others as I authentically experience my own subjective definition of self. The disastrous results of my experiment oblige me to conclude with highly critical assessments of sincerity and authenticity. Indeed, dishonesty and inauthenticity are far more important—and morally virtuous—than we might think.

Monday, September 22, 2008: An Experiment in Complete Sincerity and Authenticity

8am, On a Crisp, Early Fall Morning in Minnesota:

Walking my five year-old daughter to school as she chatters and talks endlessly, I barely have to say a word—I'm barely given the chance. She's always excited to go to school and her excitement is frequently expressed in precisely this kind of cheery, chatterbox talk.

> "Daddy, do you think we'll have outdoor recess today?"
>
> "Uh-huh, I think so honey. It will warm up quickly this afternoon," I answer, as I close the door, exiting our home.
>
> "Daddy, is mommy gonna pick me up from school today?"
>
> "No, I'll pick you up today, sweetheart," I reply walking past our driveway.

> "Daddy, look! A puppy!"
>
> "Yes, honey, let's walk a little faster. You don't want to be late."
>
> A dozen steps later … : "Daddy, can I have a kitty?"
>
> A dozen seconds later; after I decided not to respond to the previous question: "Daddy, I'm hot. Can I take off my jacket?"
>
> "No, please leave your jacket on. It's too chilly for that," I advise her.

Her inane talk is always refreshing; I admire how she can engender such animated exhilaration for the things that are, to me, quite trivial and mundane—but today it worries me. I wonder about my capacity to carry-out this experiment—to live as she apparently does: can I match her capacity for authenticity and sincerity? As an adult, is it even possible? She says what she thinks, expresses what she feels, has little knowledge or regard for the rules of decorum; she has few other alternatives. I, on the other hand, have an advanced degree in emotional labor, interaction order, role playing, facework, and the moral rules of society. I ponder—acknowledging that I can't unlearn what has taken thirty-nine years of socialization to instill—if I can even bracket that socialization for a single day? My first test arrives sooner than I had hoped.

> Almost half-way to school my daughter asks, as she often does: "How many days until Christmas?"
>
> "Honey, Christmas is three months away."
>
> "Oh," she replies, "I just hope Santa Claus brings me a lot of toys!"
>
> Here we go, I have to be honest to her and to myself. Letting out a brief sigh, I tell her bluntly: "Look, there is no such thing as Santa Claus. Santa Claus is a fictional character, primarily created by Coca Cola in the 1930s based on tales of Saint Nick—who was actually, according to historical record, portrayed as a man in a green jacket who carried a stick to beat children who were bad; certainly not to reward children who were good. The story of Santa Claus, as you know it, is a lie. Your mommy and I buy your Christmas toys."

She stops dead in her tracks, eyes swelling with tears. I can almost hear her heart crack as she slowly exclaims "What?!" Astonishingly, she is able to compose herself enough to mutter "but, daddy, what about the birth of baby Jesus." Oh boy. Of course, I have to explain to her that, as most historians agree, Jesus was likely born in the spring—but the Catholic church opted to celebrate his birth in December, which was only to compete with Pagan winter solstice rituals. I conclude by explaining, best I could in five year-old logic, that Christmas isn't really the birthday of Jesus—it's just symbolic. The more I explain the more she dawns the all-too apparent look of devastation and confusion. To ease the pain, I assure her that she'll still get lots of presents at Christmas. In perfect timing too for the end of my little lecture we arrive to her school; I give her a hug and kiss, wiping away her tears (best as I can), and tell her to have a nice day with her classmates.

* * *

9am, Back Home: Sifting through My Wardrobe:

"What the hell am I gonna wear today?" I say aloud as I shuffle through my poorly organized collection of cotton and polyester-blend garments. On teaching days I generally dress the part, which often includes a shirt and tie but always requires tedious time at the ironing board. I have a large wardrobe of this kind of "professional attire," but all of it is clothing I wear nowhere else. On my own time my preferred garments are consistently the same: old worn jeans, a tee-shirt, and boots. "Ugh" I mutter aloud and think, once again, "what will I wear today?" Even more, I wonder "why am I agonizing over this?"

I do not feel that my clothing—regardless of what I wear—is, by any means, a significant reflection of my sincerity or authenticity. Is the "sincere me" something I buy at a store—something put on, taken off, and sold for pennies on the dollar at a garage sale? Is the "authentic me" mere threads that, in fact, conceal as much as they protect? The very question is absurd and superficial. Clothing is no more a true reflection of my sincerity or authenticity than to suggest that the "real me" is the nude body that is hidden and presumably alienated by the fibers I must wear. Indeed, nude embodiment is exceedingly complex, intersubjective, and contextual (see Barcan 2004). The clothed body and nude body are *cultural* binaries that are filled with *situational* nuances. After all, what "counts" as clothing? A fig leaf (I doubt that will pass in contemporary public space)? Underwear (I doubt my colleagues at the office would appreciate that as my total attire)? A swimsuit ("fully dressed" for a beach, but quite naked for my classroom)? Conversely, what "counts" as nude? A topless woman is partially nude, but those bodily zoning ordinances don't apply to me. Moreover, a "topless" woman isn't generally considered "partially naked" unless her nipples are visible—contemporary cleavage-copious fashions are a testimony to that—but I too have nipples, and anyone can see them without fear I may be charged with lewd exposure; even so, I'd be quite exposed if I were to teach my courses bareback. Clearly, "nude" and "clothed" are relative and situational—neither state of embodiment, in themselves, can be said to reveal any measure of my sincerity or authenticity as either a person or professor.

Still, I *must* wear clothing in public; that's not really a choice. The question is what kind, color, material, fashion, and cut. The decision is agonizing because clothing is unavoidably one of many "sign vehicles" (Goffman 1959): a source of information about a person's character. On any other day, I wouldn't have given it a second thought. Today, however, in my efforts to be utterly sincere and authentic, I am paralyzed by choices. I find no viable options; all apparel choices are garbs of artificial manufacture—at best, partial representations of a piece of one's total selfhood.

"T'hell with it!" I say aloud as I cut the difference in what I now acknowledge as an uncompromised polarity in my wardrobe. I grab a well-worn pair of jeans, but it takes me some time to find a pair free of rips and stains. I select a dress shirt, but it takes me some time to find one more casual in appearance (shying away from both white and flashy colors—I need something neutral; earth tones are best). No tie. Brown belt. I first pull-on a pair of cowboy boots, but when I look in the mirror I appear dressed for a honky-tonk; I quickly swap the cowboy boots for some old Doc Martin's. Voila! Eh, well, it's good enough at least. Nah, I need to be more sincere—it's simply the best I could do.

On a typical day, selecting and ironing my "professional attire" often takes me thirty to forty-five minutes. Today it took me more than an hour to select my clothes and I'm dissatisfied with the results. Unable to resolve the dilemma of sincere and authentic apparel choices, I am forced into either wardrobe paralyses or a compromise. I have to choose the latter for the simple and pragmatic necessity of getting on with things. Already my experiment is only a partial success. This is harder than I thought.

* * *

10:45am, Walking into My Departmental Office Complex:

> "Good morning Dennis," our office manager says to me, as she always does, with her genuine and gleamingly cheery smile. Karen is one of the sweetest and most virtuous people you will encounter in our office—and that is no insult to my colleagues, just a testimony to her outstanding personal qualities.
>
> "Good morning, Karen" I reply with a sulk.
>
> "Are you ok?" Karen asks, sensing something is wrong.
>
> "No, not really" I admit.

Perhaps in a lapse of judgment, perhaps out of need for support, I confide in Karen. No one else is around anyway, so I explain to her my ongoing experiment and how hard it has already been. She frowns and shakes her head when I admit to telling my daughter that Santa Claus isn't real—but, in her good graces, Karen does not sermonize any further (she doesn't need to). I do my best to explain and she listens intently—although often with a puzzled look on her face. She doesn't have much to say except a confident, if not grateful, "I'm glad *you're* doing this experiment and not me!"

* * *

11am, Office Hours:

Seated at my desk, I'm busy typing an article that is nearly ready for submission. I'm making good progress, which is somewhat surprising; as I write I encounter no vexing issues of sincerity or authenticity—I don't bother to reflect on what that might mean. An abrupt rapping at my door suddenly disrupts my flow of thoughts. I turn to see a colleague standing in the door way.

> "Dennis, are you busy right now?"
>
> "Ah, well, actually YES."
>
> "Oh, I'm sorry" she says—but her "expressions given" doesn't match her "expressions given-off" (Goffman 1959) nor does my response hinder her request: "Hey, I have a student in my office right now—one of my advisees—he's having a hard-time crafting the methods section for his qualitative study. I'm wondering if you'd be willing to meet with him, help work through his problems, and get him ready to collect data. Could you do that?"
>
> "I could," I reply, "but I don't want to. I have enough students of my own; I don't need to take on yours as well. I'm teaching Qualitative Methods next semester—your student is welcome to enroll. I am very busy, and you're asking way too much of me."
>
> "Well, excuse me!" she says in a tiff, as she turns and walks away.

* * *

Noon: My Ethnography Class:

After returning papers to students (most of those are at best a halfhearted attempt at ethnographic thick description based on observational data), I belly-up to the podium with a serious look on my face.

> "There are only three of you who have produced a paper that approximates what I was expecting. I congratulate you three—you know who you are. For the rest of you, it seems quite obvious that you haven't read the assigned text and haven't given this assignment a reasonable effort. You lack any natural talent or functional skills for writing—let alone ethnography—or some combination thereof."

Utter silence, as well as expressions of surprise, anger, and fear overtakes my classroom—the air is as thick as the blood that is about to spill. I feel my ass both tighten and harden as I continue. "I'm tired of wasting my time and efforts on students who are careless, unwilling to put forth their own time and effort, or—more often than not—both," I say with animated, but sharp motions of my hands that both point accusingly at the class and clench into angry fists that pound the podium. I then unleash the most toxic weapon in my shame arsenal: a long moment of very uncomfortable silence as my gaze and wrinkled forehead scans the room. No one says a word; eyes divert to the floor. "I have nothing to say to you today because, as is so apparent in your last papers, you're either not listening or it isn't registering, and"—I bellow in an even louder voice—"I've noticed many of you don't bother to take notes anyway!" as I eye-down several of the most obvious culprits. "You're wasting my time and yours. I'm tired of this pathetic charade" I say, as I walk out the door feeling as authentic as ever.

Two hours later, as it turns out, two students drop the class; two students are now seated outside the office of my department chair (refusing to look at me as I pass by, but all too comforted by the support of the other); two apologetic e-mails show up in my inbox from students expressing both cautious confusion but, mostly, pleas for help. I eat two antacids and two Tylenol; it is 2 pm and I'm too terrified to meet my next class. "Tell them I'm not well today," I say to my graduate assistant as I authorize him to cancel class while I pack-up my belongings for a hasty retreat home. Karen didn't have to ask where I was going, or why.

* * *

For the next several hours I do nothing but drive, listen to music, and even take a long nap. I try to fix myself a snack but can't decide what to eat. I opt for fast-food but, there too, I can't find anything to authenticate my hunger—do I want a burger, taco, burrito, a gyro, a sandwich, or … there are just too many choices and—not unlike my earlier experiences of wardrobe paralyses—short of settling for some kind of cuisine compromise, none (or all) of my culinary choices seem appropriate. I briefly amuse myself with the ironic realization that I'm trying to make an authentic choice to satisfy my hunger based on choices available on the dollar menu at a fast-food restaurant. So I just drive some more but, in a short while, I grow frustrated by my inability to decide what music I want to listen to. I return home again. For many hours I don't answer the phone, nor check my e-mail. In retrospect, this is the most insincere and inauthentic moments of my day; how ironic—I'm hiding from the burden and fears of total honesty and complete authenticity and, consequently, I later fully realize that I was neither.

* * *

6:30 pm: At Home with My Wife:

> "What do you think of this necklace" my wife asks—a thin silver chain with a dark, large stone encased in silver.
>
> "I think it's gaudy, something my grandmother might wear."

> "Tifff!" she utters in a hiss—a meaningless expression that is all *too* evocative of her irritated disdain for my comment. "Well, *I* think it's cute" she announces, more than says. "Since you don't like it, then what necklace would you suggest?" she taunts.
>
> "Well, cosmetics and body adornment are primarily designed to draw attention, as well as communicate status. If you want a status symbol then I'd suggest this one … " I select a necklace with a thin chain that rides high on her neckline; nothing fancy that would distract from the large diamond pendant. "But, if you wish to draw attention, and namely to your chest, then I'd suggest something like this … " I select a necklace that hangs low on her chest; again a thin chain but, this time, a slightly larger pendant to draw the viewers' gaze to her cleavage.
>
> "Jesus, do you have to be so cynical and perverted all the time?" she responds. "Don't you think that sometimes, God forbid, people might wear jewelry just because it's fun and playful? Why do all our discussions have to turn into some kind of sociology lecture?!"
>
> "I'm sorry honey, you asked my opinion. I'm just trying to be as sincere as possible." "Sincere?! Reeaally?" she says in a sarcastic tone as she proceeds to give *me* a lecture: "Don't you think I would have sincerely appreciated hearing you say 'yes, honey, I love that necklace'? Don't you think I would appreciate knowing that you sincerely value my choices, opinions, and appearances?" her voice raising in a partially angry but very sanctimonious tone—and not without justification. "You want sincerity?" she asks rhetorically, "Well how about this: fuck you!"—she bursts with her defiant finger brazenly raised to my face. "Is that sincere enough for you?" she mutters as I get an icy-cold shoulder.

No argument from me. Her show of sincerity is impeccable, no room for question or doubt there. But now it is apparent to me: her authentic sincerity is a long way from how I've defined these concepts for myself, and throughout this entire day. Indeed, I reflect on the growing realization that I've gotten this all wrong. In fact, the more I think about it, I haven't been sincere at all—nor have I been authentic—this entire day has been a complete failure. It is time to end this bleak experiment. I can only hope that my family, friends, colleagues, students, and acquaintances will forgive me; this entire experiment has hinged on a colossal oversight of ideas that were poorly conceived from the very beginning. I have many bridges and wounds to mend.[1]

1 Of course, the events described in this experiment are mostly fictional. The people, places, and raw materials of each scene are real—these interactions did, more-or-less, occur as described. I have, however, fictionalized what I actually said and did, as well as the outcomes, of those *false* definitions of sincerity and authenticity. I would never subject my family, friends, colleagues, and students to this kind of embarrassment and pain—I

The Practical Irrelevance of Sincerity and Authenticity

Sincerity refers to whether one's "real" thoughts and feelings adhere to those that are expressed. Authenticity is much more difficult to define. "In everyday life, we refer to something as authentic when we associate with it properties of genuineness, realness, and at times even originality" but, as Vannini (2006:236) rightly points out, authenticity is far more nebulous than assumed by these simplistic understandings. Instead, authenticity is a *reference* that *subjectively* accounts for the degree to which a person feels they are fulfilling commitments they have to self (Erickson 1995). (In)sincerity is most often associated with (dis)honesty. (In)authenticity is, however, necessarily referential—something people are only *made aware of* "through the processes of self-reflection and only when a self-referential or 'essential,' problem arises that calls one's habitual character into question" (Erickson 1995:127). Both sincerity and authenticity are shifting and nebulous *concepts* that are neither concrete nor tangible but *performances* that are patently emotional and affective. As much as people may value sincerity and authenticity they are relative definitions of the situation, emergent in shifting fields of meaning, attainable only in partial degrees, and rather irrelevant to self and society. Indeed, as Anselm Strauss (1969:87) rightly suggested, "social relationships could hardly exist without a certain amount of hypocrisy and conventional masking of thought and sentiment." Allow me to explain what I think Strauss meant.

Insincerity and the Importance of Information Control

On the surface, sincerity and honesty seem one in the same. To be sincere, one communicates to others "all of the situationally relevant knowledge, 'facts,' or findings which the actor is cognizant [of]" (Turner, Edgley, and Olmstead 1975:70). Although widely regarded as a paramount moral ideal social life is *not* characterized by such sincerity, as testified in my failed human experiment. Such sincerity is, in fact, quite rare and undesirable—a fact well understood by Simmel (1950:335, emphasis added) who wrote that "human social life *requires* a certain measure of secrecy":

> All of human intercourse rests on the fact that everybody knows somewhat more about the other than the other voluntarily reveals to him [or her]; and those things he [or she] knows are frequently matters whose knowledge the other person (were he [or she] aware of it) would find undesirable (Simmel 1961:321).

It is unfortunate that "evil has an immediate connection with secrecy" (Simmel 1950:331). For, as Goffman (1959) well understood, "secrets" and "lies" are less

---

care too much to jeopardize these relationships in such reckless ways. Besides, even if I were coldhearted enough to go through with this experiment, no IRB would approve the experiment, and justifiably so: this kind of "sincerity" and "authenticity" is unethical and dangerous.

vital than the requisites of *information control* (for both self and society)—and for reasons that are as virtuous as they are essential to self, social interaction, interaction order, and moral-order. In fact, it is quite normative for "people [to] select the information they communicate to others, withholding some and supplying some; information control is an important and necessary process in everyday life" (Turner, Edgley, and Olmstead 1975:70).

Information control refers to a restriction or distortion of "truth:" communicating something that a person would not (in his or her judgment) communicate if he or she were completely honest (Turner, Edgley, and Olmstead 1975). For example, it is honest to tell my children that Santa Claus is not real but, and here's my point, it's *not* sincere and certainly not virtuous. Seen in this light, information control—not idealized and romantic concepts such as sincerity and honesty—is a necessary bedrock of human social life.

Information control appears in two basic forms: concealment and distortion (Turner, Edgley, and Olmstead 1975). In concealment, relevant information is withheld; in distortion, the information given misrepresents what the person knows to be accurate or true. There are two major forms of concealment—half-truths and secrets. A half-truth is a partial disclosure that omits important details and is an "efficacious and effective means of controlling information or deception because they combine some truth and some falsehood" (Turner, Edgley, and Olmstead 1975)—the element of truth makes it creditable enough to reasonably pass in most circumstances. While all forms of information control entail some element of secrecy, for our purposes a secret is a form of information control where a person refuses to disclose relevant knowledge—perhaps, for example, remaining silent when she or he has something important to say. There are two major forms of distortion—exaggerations and lies. To exaggerate is to give more information, but of a kind that is not entirely true—typically to overstate in order to justify some desired outcome. Exaggerations are a risky form of information control because it "calls attention to itself and is more likely recognized by the other as a magnification of the truth" (Turner, Edgley, and Olmstead 1975:75). To lie is to knowingly not tell the truth and "maximizes the amount of information controlled" (Turner, Edgley, and Olmstead 1975:74).

These forms of information control are not only normative but exceedingly important to human social life. Although denigrated as "immoral" concealment and distortion are only sometimes used for the purposes of selfish manipulation or exploitation. Much more common uses of these "dishonest" tactics entail the protection of face (Goffman 1967)—one's own, as well as others'; to maintain or preserve social relationships; to create intimacy or necessary social distance; to avoid tension or conflict; and to exert control over situations so they may occur in an orderly fashion (see Turner, Edgley, and Olmstead 1975). Reflecting on the results of my personal experiment, my failure to conceal or distort information was far from virtuous—it caused pain, embarrassment, jeopardized relationships, and resulted in both tension and conflict. Indeed, far from morally suspect, deceptive, or hypocritical information control is often the *right* thing to do (Turner, Edgley, and Olmstead 1975).

I reject the facile assumption that sincerity means honesty. Sincerity and honesty are neither synonymous nor does one require the other. Most people would prefer to consider themselves sincere persons, but that is an appearance or impression that is put on—and one that many people are put on *by*. Sincerity regularly requires performances that necessarily entail dishonesty—*intentional* acts of distortion and concealment. In my experiment, I attempted to be sincere—but I failed miserably. Borrowing from Turner, Edgley, and Olmstead's (1975) forms of information control, sincerity as a father *requires* that I keep "secrets" from my children (i.e., about the "truth" of Santa Claus); sincerity as a spouse means I sometimes "conceal" my opinion (i.e., about what I think of my wife's necklace); sincerity as a person means I sometimes "exaggerate" by offering passing pleasantries that *I don't always mean* (i.e., encourage rather than berate my students, even when they disappoint me). Simply put, sincerity as a moral member of society means I control information—especially information that will hurt people and jeopardize relationships. Relationships are more important than truth, and relationships are what both social life and sincerity are all about (Turner, Edgley, and Olmstead 1975).

Inauthenticity and the Importance of the "More or Less Person"

Shakespeare's eloquent "to thine own self be true" begs cantankerous questions of both self and truth. Self is plural and multiple; people have as many selves as they have unique situations for interaction. As Mead (1934:142) famously argued "a multiple personality is in a certain sense normal." The problem (if there is one) is not "to thine own self be true" but to *which* self, under *what* circumstances, and related matters of motives (Mills 1940) and accounts (Scott and Lyman 1968)—namely *how*, and *why*. If those matters weren't difficult enough to negotiate, add the additional dilemma of how one accomplishes this Shakespearian "self truth:" what does that mean, and where do we even begin to unpack these complicated existential questions. It would take a legion of philosophers to address these issues and we'd probably be left with few useful answers. I suggest a different approach.

Selfhood is emergent in relationships (Mead 1934)—and that is hardly a postmodern argument (cf. Gergen 1991). Furthermore, self is neither a quality nor character of the person—it is something people *do* (primarily in acts of communication) and, most importantly, one cannot "do" self all by one's self. Instead, selves only exist in definite relationships to other selves (Mead 1934). The authenticity of self, then, is not an empirical problem at all—it is affective; how one *feels* about the self that is enacted and communicated, or the identity that one announces or is assumed to occupy. From this perspective, one might argue that authenticity is a subjective *appraisal* that concerns the (dis)continuity between an individual's perception and the imagined perceptions of others—between what

Goffman (1963) called "personal identity" and "social identity." Thus, it is in our Cooleyan (1964) [1902) *emotional reaction* to that relationship—between self assessments and the imagined assessments of others—where we find the core dynamics of (in)authenticity (Erickson 1995).

Rather than essentialize the concept of authenticity, I suggest authenticity is much more circumstantial; "being authentic in today's world does *not* necessarily mean that one is remaining true to some sort of unified or noncontradictory self" (Erickson 1995:135). Indeed, authenticity bears sharp resemblance to identity—which is both situational and coincidental. An identity is the self's situational definition of itself (Waskul 1998). An identity is established when others place an individual as a social object by assigning that person the same words of identity that she or he announces for her- of himself (Stone 1962). Thus, an individual has an identity—and can claim authenticity—wholly "in the coincidence of placements and announcements" (Stone 1962:93). Framing authenticity in this light dispels much of its cherished romantic ideals of rugged individualism, but it is far more pragmatic. Authenticity does not exist prior to experience but flows from it; authenticity does not reside in the person him- or herself but in fleeting and momentary acts of communication and interaction—by the person as well as others who act toward him or her. In short, authenticity is a situational *coincidence* of concurrent and emergent definitions of the situation and is, therefore, experienced in an eternal flux of the "more-or-less."

What is most central to both self and interaction (and moral-order) is not authenticity but, rather, the "more-or-less person." The "more-or-less person" embodies selves, claims identities, and occupies roles that *approximate* what one desires or expects of one's self *and* what others desire or expect from that person—rarely is it entirely one or the other. Granted, on occasion, there is a complete "fusion" (Mead 1934:273) between self and society—an ecstasy of authenticity—but those moments, as Mead (1934) argued, are rare. Instead, the normative experience of life in society is found in the ebb-and-flow of the more-or-less—experiences we most commonly express in moments of role-embracement and role-distancing (Goffman 1961).

The totality of self is far too complex for the full-embracement of authenticity, and not all role expectations solely involve the activities and values we engender for ourselves. Such are the complex facts of human social life. The words of identity that I claim for myself (sociologist, professor, father, spouse, colleague, and so on) do not fully express the totality of my self. Conversely, enacting all those identities require that I sometimes act and interact in ways that are hypocritical if not disingenuous (see Vannini 2006). Such is another source of failure in my personal experiment—I cannot embrace the "more" without an equal willingness to engage the "less"—and failure to do so is patently inauthentic: my subjective experiences as a professor are sometimes authentic, but sometimes my performances in class are hypocritical; my subjective experiences as a spouse are often authentic, but sometimes I have to tolerate moments where I merely play a role. In these ways, it is the "more-or-less person" who *fashions* a self in society and, conversely, it is "more-or-less people" for whom society is possible in the first place. Rigid adherence to authenticity is, in fact, disingenuous and antithetical to social- and moral-order. Goffman (1974:561) suggested, "we often use "real" simply as a contrast term. When we decide that something is unreal, the reality it isn't need not itself be very real." The same is true for the term "authentic" and, like reality, when we decide something is "inauthentic" the authenticity it isn't need not be very genuine—precisely what students of authenticity often fail to question.

Conclusion

Goffman (1959:13) argued that self and social order hinge on two related moral principles of any projected definition of the situation:

> Society is organized on the principle that any individual who possesses certain social characteristics has a moral right to expect that others will value and treat him [or her] in an appropriate way. Connected to this principle is a second, namely that an individual who implicitly or explicitly signifies that he [or she] has certain social characteristics ought in fact to be what he [or she] claims.

Adherence to these related moral principles is vital to interaction and moral-order. However, it is significant to note that (in)sincerity and (in)authenticity are, in large measure, quite irrelevant to these crucial dynamics. As Brissett and Edgley (1990:7) suggest: "it makes no difference in the last analysis whether an individual wishes to be deceitful or honest, manipulative or negotiable, selfish or altruistic, or for that matter simply wants to get on with what [she or] he's doing; the meaning of his enterprise will be established in the expressive/impressive dimensions of his behavior". It is the making, not faking of meaning (Geertz 1983) that is significant—and, indeed, there is a fine line between truth and deceptions, sincerity and dishonesty, the genuine and the fake. The emotional claptrap surrounding the paramount morality of sincerity and authenticity can, in fact, be reduced to one simple pragmatic fact: the authentic and sincere person believes they are the person they portray themselves to be, the disingenuous and deceitful person does not (Brissett and Edgley 1990)—and we all unavoidably experience sincere and authentic moments of both.

Self may be anchored in either institution or impulse (Turner 1976). In either case, self is "recognized in acts of volition," but those who anchor self in institution experience authenticity "in the pursuit of institutional goals" while those who anchor self in impulse define affective outbursts "as an indication of the real self [that] is breaking through a deceptive crust of institutional behavior" (Turner 1976:991-2). We all experience both, yet there are crucial and conflicting differences between the two and they offer *competing* aesthetics for authenticity. This, too, is illustrated in my failed human experiment; hypocrisy may mean either "failing to live up to one's standards" or adhering to standards even when they are "not what the individual wants to do and enjoys doing" (Turner 1976:993-4). Indeed, the entire plot of my failed human experiment is a parable about the impossibilities of consistently and universally negotiating a commitment between these competing ethics and aesthetics of authenticity. Instead, we pick and choose which is most appropriate, desirable, required, or convenient for the occasion—and *that shifting and variable act* may be the decisive moment of authenticity, while all else is little more than vocabulary of motive and remedial work.

References

Barcan, Ruth. 2004. *Nudity: A Cultural Anatomy.* New York: Berg.

Brissett, Dennis and Charles Edgley. 1990. *Life as Theater: A Dramaturgical Sourcebook.* New York: Aldine de Gruyter.

Cooley, Charles. 1964 [1902]. *Human Nature and the Social Order.* New York: Scribner's.

Erickson, Rebecca. 1995. "The Importance of Authenticity for Self and Society." *Symbolic Interaction,* 18:121-144.

Geertz, Clifford. "Blurred Genres: The Refiguration of Social Thought." Pp. 19-35 in *Local Knowledge: Further Essays in Interpretive Anthropology,* edited by Clifford Geertz. New York: Basic Books.

Gergen, Kenneth. 1991. *The Saturated Self: Dilemmas of Identity in Contemporary Life.* New York: Basic Books.

Goffman, Erving. 1959. *The Presentation of Self in Everyday Life.* Garden City, NY: Doubleday.

—— 1961. *Encounters: Two Studies in the Sociology of Interaction.* Indianapolis: Bobbs-Merrill.

—— 1963. *Stigma: Notes on the Management of Spoiled Identity.* Englewood Cliffs, NJ: Prentice-Hall.

—— 1967. *Interaction Ritual: Essays in Face-to-Face Behavior.* Chicago: Aldine.

—— 1974. *Frame Analysis: An Essay on the Organization of Experience.* Boston: Northeastern University Press.

Mead, George. 1934. *Mind, Self, and Society.* Chicago: University of Chicago Press.

Mills, C. Wright. 1940. "Situated Actions and the Vocabularies of Motives." *American Sociological Review,* 5:904-913.

Scott, Marvin and Stanford Lyman. 1968. "Accounts." *American Sociological Review,* 33:46-62.

Simmel, Georg. 1961. "Secrecy and Group Communication." Pp. 113-128 in *Theories of Society,* edited by Talcott Parsons. New York: Free Press.

—— 1950. *The Sociology of George Simmel,* edited by Kurt Wolff. New York: Free Press.

Stone, Gregory. 1962. "Appearance and the Self." Pp. 86-116 in *Human Behavior and Social Processes: An Interactionist Approach*, edited by Arnold Rose. Boston: Houghton Mifflin.

Strauss, Anselm. 1959. *Mirrors and Masks: The Search for Identity*. Chicago: Free Press.

Turner, Ralph. 1976. "The Real Self: From Institution to Impulse." *The American Journal of Sociology*, 81:989-1016.

Turner, Ronny, Charles Edgley, and Glen Olmstead. 1975. "Information Control in Conversations: Honesty is not Always the Best Policy." *Kansas Journal of Sociology*, 11:69-89.

Vannini, Phillip. 2006. "Dead Poets' Society: Teaching, Publish-or-Perish, and Professors' Experiences of Authenticity." *Symbolic Interaction*, 29:235-257.

Waskul, Dennis. 1998. "Camp Staffing: The Construction, Maintenance, and Dissolution of Roles and Identities at a Summer Camp." *Sociological Spectrum*, 18:25-53.

Chapter 5
The Ideology and Practice of Authenticity in Punk Subculture

Philip Lewin and J. Patrick Williams

By the middle of the eighteenth century the sensibilities of Enlightenment ideals had begun to incense some young intellectuals, writers, musicians and artists. Identifying themselves as Romantics, this young cabal prioritized the virtues of intuition, imagination and feeling over reason and method, replacing the notion *I think, therefore I am* with a philosophy more akin to *I feel, therefore I am* (Boyle 2004). In his short treatise on the ideal of authentic selfhood, Charles Taylor (1992) contends that the residue of these aesthetic standards has diffused into the contemporary social milieu, manifesting as a cultural preoccupation with self-realization predicated on the belief that human beings are imbued with moral codes that must be explored and clarified in order to actualize their intrinsic potentialities. Proposing that we live in a "culture of authenticity" (29), he argues that humans have come to construe themselves as beings with inner depths and that being in touch with oneself has taken on independent moral significance, supplanting prior efforts to attain connectedness with God. This chapter explores the links between this Romantic ideal of authenticity and the ideologies and cultural practices espoused by members of the punk subculture.

A great deal of Romantic sentiment originated with the thought of Rousseau, who contended that individuals should follow their inner voices and resist the pressures and callings of society in order to recover intimate moral contact with themselves. Rousseau also popularized the idea of "self-determining freedom," suggesting that people become free only when they make their own choices rather than allowing external influences to shape their lives. Extending this line of argument, Herder proposed that all people possess original ways of being human, and that failing to locate or actualize those unique modes of existence banishes them to conditions of inhumanness and incompleteness (cited in Taylor 1992). Implicit in this line of reasoning is a preference for *being* over *doing*. Romantics believed that treating the self as an instrument by subverting one's creative powers and freedom to external social forces confounded discovery and actualization of the inner voice, defeating one's life-purpose and undermining the attainment of moral purity.

Contemporary writers have denigrated this orientation to life as a malaise of modernity and have dismissed the quest for authenticity as indicative of a "culture of narcissism" typical of the "me-generation" (e.g. Bell 1976; Lasch 1979). These critics argue that striving for authenticity overemphasizes the value of the self relative to community and consequently narrows peoples' lives by making them poorer in meaning. Such critiques, we believe, neglect to consider two properties of authenticity as a cultural ideal, however. First, a moral compass generally guides the search for self-realization; it is not motivated by vanity or self-worship (Taylor 1992). And second, individuals celebrate authenticity in order to balance the extreme dislocation that characterizes life in the postmodern world, in which traditional concepts of self, community and space have collapsed. This collapse has led to a widespread internalization of doubt and an obsession with distinguishing the real from the fake (Allan 1998).

According to Turner (1976), changes in the nature of social integration within advanced industrial societies have caused individuals to uproot their self-conceptions from institutional frameworks and reanchor them in deeply felt impulses and emotions. Late capitalism has destabilized the institutions that once provided people with opportunities to *attain* meaningful self-concepts through fulfillment of social duties and roles. These changes increasingly motivate people to abandon socially obligatory identities and instead turn inward in order to *find* and feel their "real selves" and reality more generally. Consequently, whether in relation to food (Lu and Fine 1995), art (Fine 2003) or selfhood (Gergen 1991), a quest for authenticity has risen to the fore in advanced industrial societies, seducing individuals with the promise of the "really real" (Geertz 1973) and serving as a life-boat to keep them afloat in the uncertain seas of postmodernity.

Scholars have found that similar issues of ontological insecurity influence participants in youth subcultures, which emerge in response to common problems of satisfaction or adjustment (e.g., Becker 1963; Merton 1938). Albert Cohen (1955), for example, found that working class boys frustrated with their inability to compete in the status system of middle-class institutions rejected prevailing cultural means and goals, supplanting both with ones that they could more readily achieve. Similarly, Sarah Thornton's (1996) research on rave culture revealed that participants accrued status by garnering subcultural capital, which also reflexively marked them as "authentic" in contrast to the mainstream. However, while theoretically rich, such research has made little attempt to locate the quest for authenticity within the larger social context of late modernity. This chapter tackles that task, contending that the ideology of authenticity serves as something more than a vehicle to social status for young people. In what follows, we explore how the quest for authenticity among members of the punk subculture is deeply implicated in two processes: a morally oriented quest oriented toward self-discovery inspired by Romantic aesthetics and an effort to stabilize reality in the postmodern condition.

Youth Subcultures and the Study of Authenticity

Early subcultural research rarely questioned the socially constructed boundaries of subcultural collectivities. Rather, it assumed the objectivity of identity by uncritically assigning membership categories to individual participants based on their stylistic preferences or behaviors. This assumption is perhaps nowhere more evident than in Dick Hebdige's (1979) book, *Subculture: The Meaning of Style*. Focusing on the emergence and eventual diffusion of punk, he studied the mass cultural incorporation of subcultural style and argued that when "the original innovations which signify 'subculture' are translated into commodities and made generally available, they become 'frozen'" (1979:96). For Hebdige, punk was authentic only at its moment of innovative conception, after which a hegemonic culture industry transformed it into a commodity to sell back to future generations of consumers. He argued that this process of commodification destroyed punk's creativity and diluted the "forbidden" content that originally comprised its authenticity (i.e., punks' collective awareness of their marginalized social position). This realist perspective[1] privileges and reifies an etic discourse of subcultural authenticity, marginalizing those who are identified as outside of or peripheral to an "authentic" subcultural core (Williams 2006). Realist perspectives also obscure the processes of negotiation and construction through which subculturalists objectify authenticity by assuming that it constitutes something that participants have or do not have.

In more recent decades, scholars have advanced the study of subcultures through the application of a microsociological perspective. Resultant work has deemphasized the CCCS' concentration on class and resistance and given subcultural participants voice with respect to the meaning of authenticity. In particular, Thornton's (1996) research on rave culture is significant in its move beyond realism, conceptualizing authenticity as a social construction that possesses no inherent properties. Utilizing Bourdieu's (1984) concepts of distinction and cultural capital as well as Becker's (1963) concept of hipness, she explored how participants worked to construct a collective identity in contrast to an ostensibly homogenous mainstream while vying with one another for subcultural status. She found that her informants had constructed a status system predicated on the possession of subcultural capital, which was objectified through social relationships and ownership (e.g., having the right clothing) and embodied through knowledge (e.g., knowing the right people). Departing from Hebdige, Thornton re-theorized authenticity as something that one earns and subsequently works to maintain—something that is ephemeral, negotiated and processual. Following her lead, Muggleton (2002) claimed that an interest in expressing individuality rather than group affiliation trumps concern with achieving insider-status among those who subscribe to subcultural styles (see also Widdicombe 1993; 1998). His perspective—following in some respects from the work of Steve Redhead (1990:25), who notes that "'authentic' subcultures were produced by subculturalists, not the other way around"—has gained significant

1 For other examples, see, e.g., Fox (1987) and Willis (1993).

clout among scholars who sympathize with a postmodern view of youth cultures. In Muggleton's view, the "post-subculturalist" constructs authenticity in a way that eschews membership in pre-defined groups and rejects the influence of others, taking an *individualistic* approach to subcultural style. Herein lies the problem.

Research on subcultural authenticity has focused primarily on style and stylistic preference. Overemphasizing style fetishizes material culture and its consumption as indispensable dimensions of youth subculture. This brings us back to Hebdige's work on punk. Apart from exemplifying a realist conception of subcultural authenticity, such work also stands as the quintessential representation of an enduring interest in punk as a culture of display. Hebdige's semiological analysis reduced the significance of punk to its material qualities, describing its style as "noise" as opposed to "sound," maintaining that "subculture is concerned first and foremost with consumption. It operates exclusively in the leisure sphere ... It communicates through commodities [...]. It directs attention to itself; it gives itself to be read" (Hebdige 1979:90, 94-95, 101). Alas, subcultural style, so salient and intriguing to the sociological eye, has become the most commonly analyzed dimension of subculture studies. Scholars have framed, interpreted, and defined subcultures through the lens of style, despite claiming to have overcome their homological heritage (e.g., Bennett and Kahn-Harris 2004; Muggleton and Weinzierl 2003).

Like post-subculture scholars, we believe that a profit-driven culture industry routinely co-opts and distorts many elements of subculture, including style. Unlike them, however, we want to de-emphasize punk's material culture and focus instead on its value and belief systems, through which many young people continue to ground their authenticity claims. We explore how punks construct a concept of authenticity that relies on ideological commitment, emphasizing how they frame subcultural participation as part of a larger life project that is independent of external influence. We go on to reveal that this construction is remarkably congruent with the ideal of authenticity that prevails in the broader social milieu (Taylor 1992; Turner 1976). Thus, unlike many youth-subculture scholars, we argue that punk much more reflects than resists so-called mainstream culture.

Subcultural Authenticity, Selfhood and Ideological Commitment

Our study draws from an ethnography of the punk subculture in a large metropolitan area in the Southeastern US.[2] Informants consisted of self-identified punks that the first author personally knew or became acquainted with during the study. Their demographic and lifestyle characteristics were diverse. Participants ranged from eighteen to twenty-seven years of age and had a manifold of religious, political, and class backgrounds, although most could be characterized as lower-middle class, agnostic or atheist (yet, notably, there were a number of religious informants) and politically left-leaning. Educational attainment spanned from GEDs to

2 For a detailed overview of the punk subculture, see O'Hara (1999).

graduate degrees (the mode being a bachelor's degree), and the occupations of subjects ranged from service workers to white collar professionals. The lives of some participants revolved around active participation in punk scenes, whereas others maintained a more distant, personal commitment to the subculture's value system. There were no constants with respect to style display—some informants made extensive use of sartorial accoutrements while others could not readily be distinguished from those outside the subculture.

The first author undertook participant observation during five months in 2004 and five months in the winter of 2007-8. He also conducted twenty in-depth interviews with fourteen men and six women, which ranged from 45 to 120 minutes in length and focused on the experiences of participants before identifying as punk; how they became involved with the subculture; what values and beliefs they associated with punk; how they viewed punk style; how they distinguished insiders from outsiders; how acts of resistance were implicated in their subcultural participation; and what overall social and political views they held.

Three tenets of punk ideology emerged during data analysis—tenets that we have termed "rejection," "reflexivity" and "self-actualization." These tenets reflect a broader societal commitment to self-discovery that Taylor (1992), Boyle (2004) and Turner (1976) discuss at length. Taylor argues that contemporary society's morally oriented quest toward self-discovery manifests in a devotion to creation and construction, originality and opposition to the rules of society. Boyle paints a very similar picture of authenticity, adding that to be authentic means to be human—to be rooted in "felt" reality as opposed to the passionlessness of mass-production. Turner makes a parallel argument but from a social-psychological perspective, suggesting that people have come to recognize impulsive feelings and actions as emanating from the "real self" rather than stemming from conforming to society's institutional mandates. Punk subculture structures the development of authenticity in a very similar way to how these scholars describe it.

Rejection

We labeled the first value about which informants showed concern "rejection." While other empirical research has found that punks place a premium on resistance and largely reject the common sense world of "dominant culture," the nature of their resistance has remained poorly conceptualized (cf. Copes and Williams 2007; Williams 2009). Fox (1987), for example, cast punk resistance as a component of style, claiming that most participants within it lack "consciousness" and suggesting that their resistance was rooted in a vague "anti-establishment, anarchist sentiment" (352). Our interviewees, to the contrary, offered very thick analytical descriptions of their resistance to mainstream culture. Expressing unease toward socialization and dedication to a perceived inner nature, they claimed to reject consumption in the broadest sense of the word, with respect not just to commodities but also to knowledge and identity, eschewing essentially all learning directed toward enculturation. For example, when asked what punk meant to him, Blake, a 21 year old-college student said:

> Punk … involves heeding a questioning, skeptical, attitude, resisting social pressures and norms, rejecting undue and sometimes even just authority … Essentially [it] involves living the life that I want to live without regard for how others perceive and judge me.

For Blake, punk entailed a rejection of societal pressure in favor of a frame of reference oriented around the goal of living the life that he wants to live. He implied that tension exists between the pressures of societal integration and the pull of one's inner callings.

Elaborating a similar position, Cooper asserted that punk culture exists in contrast to an "ideology of acceptance." For him, this ideology referred to a lifelong "system" of societal indoctrination that constrains the potentialities of the self and perpetuates existing systems of power. The system that Cooper indicted was construed as the collective efforts of agents of socialization including schools, media, family, religion, government, and peers.[3] Informants contended that such institutions maintain the positions of those in power at the expense of others, compelling people to forsake their inner essences in order to achieve fractional and illusory gains via social approval. Agents of socialization do this by inhibiting people from exploring their inner ideas and maximizing their life experiences, working instead to promote a strict system of conformity that renders deviance harshly punishable. The punks that we interviewed believe that this system, having as its goal the establishment of a "dull and drab" (Tom, interview) culture that suits privileged others, undermines one's aesthetic potential for self-expression. Hardly narcissistic, they assigned moral significance to both the notions of self-expression and societal constraint, because the phenomenonological experience of self-as-impulse had transformed the institutional order into a set of norms (as opposed to values), which they felt arbitrarily constrained their ability to engage in genuine self-expression in order to recognize and enact the real self (Turner 1976). For example:

> Punk rock is an idea. Oversimplifying it as a style of clothing, a set of chords, or even as an attitude erodes the idea. The idea behind punk rock is that social change

3 While as sociologists we recognize the inevitability of socialization, we want to emphasize that informants repeatedly expressed the belief that they had personally derived their value and belief systems through a sustained process of introspection. Although self-identifying as punk, many claimed to reject even the subculture as a source of socialization, expressing resistance to any knowledge or information that originated in others rather than in themselves. An etic analysis of our data would not lend support for their claims, as it seems that informants resisted only mainstream sources of socialization while embracing the subculture as a valid locus of influence. In the spirit of our interpretive approach, however, we will continue to give an emic account of punk ideology that emphasizes a rejection of all socialization and a radical turn inward.

> comes from within. Many people view punkers as non-conformists and rebellious, but that too is an oversimplification. Punk rock seeks to break down an ideology of acceptance. [...] As human beings, we're socialized into thinking that the truth we seek lies somewhere hidden within ... pre-established paradigms. Things like "take comfort in that which is familiar, fear that which is unknown;" things you start learning as early as a child that never go away [...] Punk seeks to change individual mindsets as a precursor to the types of ideas that bring about change ... Punk itself will never change the world, but the impact of punk is that freedom of will gets sparked in the post-punk generation. And yes, absolutely that begins with the individual ... it is the unending process that is key. [Cooper, interview]

Dedicated to breaking down an "ideology of acceptance," other informants regularly emphasized the importance of resisting external socialization. They asserted that punk, as a movement, is oriented around the goal of ending socialization and of deconstructing social norms, beliefs, and values in order to more purely experience life. Thus, rather than representing class or generation-based resistance, punks' rhetoric of rejection reflects the modernist quest for authenticity, which "demands that [people] break the hold of external impositions and [make decisions] for [themselves] alone" (Taylor 1992:27). The irony of emphasizing resistance to socialization while staking claim to and participating in punk subculture supports Muggleton's (2002) contention that postmodern youth cultures can "be understood, somewhat paradoxically, as collective expressions and celebrations of individualism" (79). Like the subculturalists in his study, the punks in our study subjectively resolved this contradiction by exaggerating the extent to which mainstream culture was homogenous and punk subculture was heterogeneous. For example, according to Charlie: "the punk scene has so many different facets [...] there are so many different ideas in punk rock [...] but everybody is rejecting the same thing."

Many interviewees also described possessing an "I don't give a fuck" attitude. When probed with respect to what exactly they meant by this, informants spoke of their concern with self-realization and with undoing societal influence in order to lead meaningful lives. Our findings break with how other empirical work has framed punks' ambivalence. Past scholars (e.g. Baron 1989; Fox 1987; Gaines 1998) have construed the idea of "not giving a fuck" as a blasé attitude arising from the boredom and purposelessness of young people who have been socialized to be consumers and spectators, explaining the sentiment away as a product of the postmodern condition. When asked to clarify their own statements and behaviors, however, interviewees gave a rather different explanation. Tom, a 24 year old musician, had the following to say about this mentality:

> When you say "I don't give a fuck," it's kind of like the existential crisis is getting put on the table of like ... how am I supposed to go about life: making a living, supporting a family, having a career, getting educated, whatever that means these days. It's like having all of that thrust in your face and looking at it and saying, "I don't know what to do with this, I can't do anything with this,

> I'm not equipped emotionally." When I say that that guy doesn't give a fuck, I think that guy went out of his way and burned all of those bridges and said, "I don't give a fuck, I'm doing everything by my own rules." It means you've got to make your own way, you don't give a fuck what the rest of the world gives a fuck about … it's like you have all these people telling you that you have to care about these things … and I don't give a fuck about that. You know, I've got to do well for myself if I want to be an individual.

Informants' commentary did not exhibit a blasé attitude or a nihilistic orientation toward the world. Rather, interviewees claimed to reject received culture because they saw no value in it. As opposed to succumbing to feelings of purposelessness and meaninglessness, punks like Tom demonstrated a commitment to finding fulfillment in life on their own terms—an outlook that is patently postmodernist and that indicates a self-concept anchored in impulse rather than in institutions.

Interviewees also described a humanist imperative in punk that involved rejecting various forms of social inequity such as racism and sexism. They couched this imperative within a larger concern for anti-authoritarianism—expressing a desire to topple hierarchies and power structures that undermined their abilities to achieve self-realization—rather than within a normatively conceptualized commitment to social justice or equality. This is not to say that a belief in the dignity and worth of all human beings did not motivate informants' rejection of inequality and inequity to some extent, but our findings do suggest that punk ideology is more grounded in a rejection of the process of hegemonic socialization than in its consequences. Humanism thus served as a vehicle for achieving self-realization—for undoing societal influence and forging one's own meaning in life.

Rejection was not framed in black and white but rather on a continuum that involved situational relevance. The punks that we spoke with did not seem to take on an attitude that inherently and automatically rejected all forms of authority and establishment. While they regularly exhibited disdain for both authority and "the establishment," opposition to the idea of *mindlessly* internalizing the rules and beliefs that established institutions and authority figures promote better describes their position. Trevor and Henry, for example, acknowledged that some aspects of education were important. However, they expressed a strong disinclination toward the idea of allowing their schooling to sculpt them into particular types of people with particular beliefs. For another informant, Eve, punk involved making a commitment to freeing herself from external influence so that she could formulate her own viewpoints:

> It took me a couple years and a couple bad mistakes to realize that being punk doesn't have to mean fuck this—you know, fuck fill in the blank. It doesn't have to mean just rejecting everything outright just because it may seem conformist to someone else … It definitely means that instead of just sort of giving that knee jerk reaction of rejection toward things to really actively think about them and to create my own viewpoint.

Discussing her Christian faith and her friends' unwillingness to accept what they saw as a disjuncture between religion and "free" thought and expression, she went on to explain how she ... :

> managed to sort of incorporate that into my life and keep my belief system without ... I don't know ... without it interfering with my ability to think [critically]. Like, I don't use it to just cloud over, you know, the problems I have or that I see in the world.

Invoking her struggle to reconcile her punk identity with her Christian faith, Eve claimed that she came to realize that she did not have to wholly reject conventional institutions and systems of meaning in order to be punk. One may still value and participate within them, but, as a punk, she made a commitment to do so on her own terms, choosing to embrace Christianity because of a personal volition and because it felt right to her, not because of social pressure or because others defined it as worthwhile or secure.

While realist scholars might view such sentiments as proof of Eve's inauthenticity, doing so overlooks the social constructedness of subcultural identity. Sociologists have long recognized that "in our mass society, characterized as it is by cultural pluralism, each person internalizes several perspectives" which "arise through the internalization of norms; they constitute the structure of expectations imputed to some audience for whom one organizes his [sic] conduct" (Shibutani 1955:565). Relating this to subcultural identity, Fine and Kleinman (1979) have noted that subcultures are not homogeneous, static social systems, and that subculturalists maintain multiple group memberships that structure their everyday lives. While interviewees subscribed to punk as one identity, they did not always predicate that identity on a total rejection of all things non-punk. Rather, since punks constructed authenticity through self-realization, they attempted to achieve it by symbolically rejecting cultural objects that they individually defined as problematic.

Reflexivity

Following from their commitment to rejecting the influence of mainstream socialization, informants also exhibited a dedication to leading lifestyles that were accountable to their perceived genuine selves—a value that we call "reflexivity." Punks committed to it by enacting their subjectively realized belief systems through praxis in everyday life. Drawing a sharp distinction between being and doing, they expressed disdain for people who engaged in artificial performances in order to earn social approval. In social psychological terms, informants took the view that all behavior should follow from intrinsic rather than extrinsic self-efficacy.

Interviewees insisted that they could distinguish between people who were being themselves and those who were merely performing roles for instrumental purposes. How exactly they did so remained somewhat elusive. Although informants could not identify concrete qualities of so-called performers, they did contend that authentic individuals possessed a nonchalant, self-assured attitude. When asked how he distinguished between authentic and inauthentic punks, Dickie, for example, explained how

> you can just tell, you can tell when people just don't care from when they're trying, and I think that people who are trying to be something need to stop trying and just be whoever they are. Maybe it's a confidence thing in the way you show yourself to people. Like, I definitely don't think I'm trying to do anything with my haircut right now [a mohawk], and every single person that I talk to who sees it is just like "oh." You know, they're not like, "Oh wow! That's crazy! Absurd!" You know, they're kind of just like "yeah." You know, like, it's new for me, but then they're like "yeah, it looks right." You know, it fits me.

Dickie's commentary mirrors the mysterious qualities that professional jazz musicians attribute to one another: "the musician is conceived … as an artist who possesses a mysterious artistic gift setting him apart from all other people … The gift is something that cannot be acquired through education; the outsider, therefore, can never become a member of the group" (Becker 1963:85-86). Elsewhere in his interview, Dickie castigated individuals who adorned themselves in normative punk style while wearing his own hair in a mohawk. He emphasized, however, that he was not posing or posturing—his hairstyle, he claimed, unlike those of some others, reflected his real, internalized self (see also Widdicombe 1993). His friends and other so-called authentic punks, he claimed, could readily recognize this. Much like the jazz musicians in Becker's study, Dickie implied that outsiders could adopt aspects of punk style, but they would not become punk in so doing. Punk merely reflected the inborn attributes of Dickie's genuine self—attributes that emphasize creation and originality in lieu of consumption and conformity.

Dickie's commentary provides insight into the belief—expressed in some form by interviewees—that style should objectify self image. Punks accomplished this in two ways. The first was through positive inner-speculation, which involved utilizing a style that *reflects* one's unique way of being. The second is through negative disidentification from persons and things against which punks collectively rebel. Given their concern with reflexivity, informants expressed extreme distaste for people who employed styles in ways judged to be inconsistent with their self-concepts. To continue to use Dickie as an example, during a punk show he encountered two young women who, in his view, were deploying images in order to appear punk, while lacking an understanding of punk ideology.[4] Both had colorfully dyed hair, sported t-shirts donning the names of well-known punk

4 While beyond the scope of our analysis, it is important to note that the following encounter reflects past empirical work in relation to how gender dynamics operate within subcultures (see e.g., Leblanc 2001; Roman 1988). Women are regularly accused of superficiality and of possessing shallow concerns with style. That accusation has resulted in the marginalization of women within many different subcultural scenes. In the case at

bands and wore popular Converse shoes. An excerpt from field notes displays his bold, condemnatory reaction to them.

> The women again turn around and try to say something to Dickie. Before they finish their thoughts, he asks how old they are. Before they can answer, he inquires if they have high school the next day; they nod. "Because I think you're fucking retarded," he replies. He then proceeds to castigate them without restraint. He tells them that they need to "shut the fuck up" and move to the back of the venue because "no one gives a fuck that [they're there]," that they remind him of the girls from his high school, and that they "act like a bunch of fucking twelve year olds." As his assault draws to a close, the pink-haired woman retorts to the effect that she hopes he gets hurt in the pit. Dickie looks stunned and appalled … After this the women moved farther to the right of us, taking refuge with a friend. The three of them began to mock Dickie … the gist of the conversation involving how he thought himself to be "hardcore punk rock." Their friend stood up straight, looking at Dickie, repeatedly saying "I'm punk rock" in a mocking manner. [field notes, 10/21/04]

Dickie's behavior was precipitated by disgust for their attempts to project images of subcultural membership that he suspected did not reflect their genuine selves. The teenagers' trendy clothing, he said, symbolized the culture of high school that he fervently abhorred. In an interview a few days later, he described why he had reacted against the women in that way, as well as against some other people at the show with whom he had also apparently taken issue.

> I just decided they sucked—snap judgment. Like, I heard them talking, saw their crappy, cosmetic haircuts and wanted to kick their asses. I mean, it's the same idea set—punks aren't clean, they don't fucking style their hair the way they did. They're fucking filthy and dirty. They wanted to be something they weren't. They clearly came from [an affluent suburb] and went to some store in [a trendy alternative shopping area] to buy their clothes to look punk, spent hundreds of dollars on clothing and hair products, and they think they're punks, which is complete bullshit. You know, that's not true at all—they're just consumers, which to me is the worst classification. Yeah … they're just a product of consumer society … even when I send in the hawk, the second where it becomes anything where I have to style it, I'll just shave it off—send in the space monkey afterwards. There is no point..there's no point in having to wake up and style your hair.

Dickie wrote off the teenagers at the show as inauthentic because he thought that they "were trying to be something that they weren't." Studying concert participants

---

hand, it is possible that Dickie interpreted the genders of the young women as indicators of their inauthenticity, unjustly writing them off as a result.

who conformed to punk and goth styles, Widdicombe (1993; Widdicombe and Wooffitt 1990) found that several of her interviewees resisted the correlation between "membership and style [...] precisely because it implies conformity and the loss of individuality and is regarded as inauthentic" (1993:110). In our fieldwork, we found Dickie wearing a mohawk but labeling others as inauthentic because he suspected that they had bought—not created—their punk identities in order to look cool. This point represents pragmatic knowledge of the social psychological functions of social comparisons among subcultural participants. In *Beyond Subculture*, Muggleton (2002) found that subculturalists distinguished themselves from those with identical styles by claiming that their own styles came about gradually and organically, while others' emerged suddenly. Likewise, Dickie's claim of authenticity may be seen as "necessarily conditional upon the 'mass media' influenced inauthenticity of others" (Muggleton 2002:140). Interestingly, however, the two women's response to Dickie's attack suggested an alternate sense of reflexivity. After Dickie told them off, both women, as well as their friend, mocked him for attempting to cast himself as a "hardcore punk." In other words, they also accused Dickie of attempting to create a perception of himself that did not accord to who they thought he really was. This incident further underscores the point that subcultural authenticity possesses no specific properties.

Given the symbolic value attached to being rather than performing punk, study participants emphatically rejected the idea of "assumed identities," which took the form of commodities—unoriginal, constructed by others and therefore not reflexive. Informants instead asserted that one's sense of self should emerge organically through a process of active, personal creation. When asked how he distinguished among people in the local do-it-yourself (DIY)[5] scene, Charlie, for instance, classified inauthentic punks as

> people who just aren't initiating any new ideas, aren't trying to create. You can see it. If there's a lot of worship, if they treat these bands that are coming through like rock stars, it's like you're absolutely missing the point of this.

Punks thus forged a construction of authenticity that distinguished "real" from "fake" by virtue of the extent to which one created versus consumed. Other empirical work on punk has attributed this sentiment, which typically manifests in an acute rejection of consumerism and materialism, to a project of political resistance grounded in an anti-capitalist sentiment. Moore (2007), for example,

5 Participants in DIY scenes often emphasize an individualist, anti-consumptive ethic toward cultural production and everyday living. The former prong of this ethic manifests in the creation of fan zines, recording one's own musical albums, booking one's own tours, and so forth. With respect to the latter prong, the DIY ethic manifests in a manifold of activities ranging from growing one's own food to making one's own clothing. For a detailed account of the DIY ethic, see Moore's (2007) work on variable fields of cultural production.

argued that the DIY ethos enables a public sphere among young people to develop, in which they organize themselves to express dissenting viewpoints about social issues. While several of our interviewees expressed disfavor with capitalism and used punk to cultivate symbolic space in which to challenge dominant ideology, we found that the ideas of rejection and reflexivity are much more grounded in a commitment to authenticity as a cultural ideal than to political dissent. In discussing the value and meaning of DIY as a cultural ethos, informants tended to assert that it enabled them to create their own identities as opposed to purchasing ones that were manufactured in mass culture. They also suggested that it facilitated their abilities to live by their ideals as opposed to participating in a lifestyle that was inconsistent with their ideologies. While many also extolled DIY as a means through which to subvert consumer capitalism, doing so was secondary to self-expression.

Self-actualization

The ideal of authenticity that Taylor discusses also promotes being versus doing by encouraging people to make moral commitments to self-discovery and to create and abide by individual systems of values and beliefs. We refer to this dimension of authenticity as "self-actualization." While the punks that we interviewed tended to talk about their values and beliefs as if they derived them internally instead of from the subculture in which they participated, Taylor (1992:39) predicates self-actualization on an "openness to horizons of significance." Informants expressed repugnance for and frustration with ignorance and apathy, which they felt were bleeding through society because of an uncritical acceptance of the status quo. Most people, they felt, never questioned their eschatological purposes or the validity of the common sense world of everyday life. In contrast, punks embraced a DIY ethic of creation, originality and self-reliance.

> As Americans we're just fed so much crap, whether it be from our families, or our church, or our schools, and from the media … It's not very often, even for the youth now, that they really question why it is we live this way, why are we in the position we're in on a global scale, so I think that that's really important for people to question the methods we use around the world … things like that. And I think for a lot of kids, when they get into punk, that's when they really start questioning those things and really challenging themselves—challenging their beliefs … I mean going out of your way to read a book by Howard Zinn, or going out of your way to read Noam Chomsky or something, and maybe read an alternative history or an alternative view of religion that we're not necessarily force-fed by school or by religion or something like that. [Glenn, interview]

This DIY ethic was constructed through a subcultural frame of reference—built through interaction with various forms of subcultural media (e.g., song lyrics and zines) and through face-to-face interaction with other punks at events as well as in more mundane settings such as school. Glenn continued:

> And definitely once you get into punk that stuff starts to happen. You get around people who challenge your beliefs and who challenge you to look into things further ... And that's why high school is such a fertile ground for punks, because you're reaching an age where you have that angst, where if you're not accepted by the majority of people in the school, you know all the refugees can go and express themselves and actually learn something new.

Although informants generally acknowledged that the subculture played a large role in the cultivation of their values and beliefs, most claimed that punk ideology took no structured form. They insisted that it simply involved staking out an informed individuality and drawing one's own conclusions about the significance of life rather than adopting prefabricated viewpoints. What those conclusions are did not seem to matter, so long as people "do their own thing."

> It's kind of an oxymoron, to be punk rock and play by the rules. There aren't any rules! [...] There are some punk rockers in bands and they're Republicans—they're doing their own thing, you know? You may not agree with them ... but they're doing their own thing and they're not following a guideline—that kind of stuff. I know punk rockers that are Christians, you know, there's no rules to that sort of stuff ... You do your own thing on your own terms because of your own set of beliefs. The only motivation behind it is that you know you'll have self satisfaction from it. [Henry, interview]

From this perspective, punk ideology involved no pre-conceived set of beliefs, values or practices; it held that people should stay true to themselves and behave accordingly. This observation lends further support to contention that punks anchor their self-concepts in instincts and impulses rather than in institutional frameworks. Henry implied that the true self is revealed when a person does or thinks something solely because he or she wishes to do so. It is not, to the contrary, revealed when an individual adheres to high societal standards while resisting the pull of inner temptations (Turner 1976). When subjectively achieved, "self-actualization" brought about a sense of intrinsic self-esteem, a measure of self-worth that feels uniquely individualistic despite its social foundation (Brisset 1972).

Blake referred to his immersion in punk as "self-realization" and Cooper reported that upon discovering punk he felt empowered, finally connecting his true self to a culture that reflected it. Trevor defined a punk as someone who "holds true no matter what" and went on to discuss how that mantra had made him stronger, allowing him to discover who he was and to actualize his ideals more quickly in comparison to others who were not involved in the subculture. Rejecting dominant agents of social conditioning infused informants with a sense of liberation and empowerment. In other words, striving to understand one's genuine self and demanding accountability to it brought meaning and understanding into the lives of the punks that we studied. The goal of self-actualization ultimately manifested in the development of a self-concept that subjectively existed outside of social influence.

> Ideas of truth are really important. Punks always search for truth, but they have yet to find that truth in ... power relationships ... The truth punks seek is the truth derived from within ... a truth that creates real change. It is what we as [individuals] learn through experience ... [punk] is a utopia that can be open to all, a heaven of sorts that anyone can attain if they simply participate in the process. The process has no boundaries, it is only the everlasting quest to find truth, objective truth in the self, even if that truth contradicts the truth of another.

Here, Cooper illuminated the common punk sentiment that knowledge accrued through socialization merely perpetuates existing systems of power and privilege. Emphasizing the Romantic virtue of experience in lieu of rationality, he suggested that individuals should strive to develop self-concepts that *feel* valid and true—not ones that are socially defined as such. Punk facilitated this process by enabling participants to engage in cultural practices that reflected their inner essences. Among the punks we studied, it also encouraged a devotion to profound and extended introspection while maximizing the spectrum of experiential possibilities that accompanies subcultural participation. Returning to Turner (1976), we see how punk subculture provides participants with a forum that allows them to gratify deeply felt urges in order to subjectively experience their "real selves" while indemnifying them from institutional sanctioning.

Discussion and Conclusion

Whether as efforts to contest class positions or as adaptations to cultural strain, scholars have long associated youth subcultures with rebellion or inverted cultural value structures. Our empirical findings, however, suggest something different. Having probed informants about their ideological beliefs, we found that punks did not emphasize political resistance but rather freedom of self-expression—not as just punks, but as human beings. Recent scholarship has suggested that contemporary subcultural participation tends to be apolitical, not necessarily seeking to challenge "the system" but to pursue free expression (Bennett and Kahn-Harris 2004; Weinzierl and Muggleton 2003). Muggleton found that "punk politics [were] best understood in terms of personal self-determination" (2002:149). Likewise, the punks in our study did not frame their participation as political resistance, as doing so would imply that a calculated gesture of dissent rather than a genuine expression of the inner self predicated their subcultural identities.[6] However, unlike these scholars, who tend to characterize *all* subcultural life as rooted in consumption and play, we have grounded it in the modernist ethic of authenticity that in many ways derives from societal shifts in the locus of individual self-conceptions.

Gary Fine (2003) has written that the "desire for authenticity now occupies a central position in contemporary culture" (153). Similarly, scholars like Bell (1976), Lasch (1979), and Turner (1976) have noted that a devotion to self-discovery has become embedded in the value system of society at large. Just as punks seek to reconnect to the real by bypassing market relations and establishing an autonomous field of cultural production through DIY ethics, the greater lot of the Western world increasingly desires to experience things for itself. Boyle (2004) suggests that this is because humans live in a world in which people learn that the future of food is artificial, that the future of books, newspapers and medicine is virtual, and that they will soon deal entirely through computer screens rather than through people. While the punks that we studied insisted that most people are socially unconscious, tepid conformists, Boyle, to the contrary, argues that globalization has spawned a desire for anything but conformity and convention and suggests that somewhat of a revolution has occurred whereby consumers have launched a rejection of the fake, the virtual, the spun, and the mass produced. Like Turner, he claims that everyone longs for something that they can touch and put their fingers on, thereby implying that phenomena like punk will become more common as more people reject conceptions of progress that have held sway for more than two centuries. People will increasingly demand "real" human contact, "real" experience and "real" connection. This is a response to the cultural conditions of postmodernity, which call into question the assumed authenticity of selves and relationships. The drive to rediscover the "really real" challenges the postmodern notion that nothing is true and that all is for sale.

By linking punk to these cultural conditions, our work moves beyond an analysis of how subculturalists construct authentic identities, instead exploring how the broader cultural quest for authenticity and the shifting locus of self-conceptions orient subcultural participation. We found that what has ensued from the culture industry's appropriation of punk style is an attempt by some young punks to come together in order to share in a project of self-realization in which authenticity (as punk and as a human-being) is developed through commitment to three ideological tenets: rejection, reflexivity and self-actualization. Punks constituted authenticity in terms of the integrity of their search for and practice of an inner essence, while the subculture as a whole worked to countermand the ontological insecurity that typifies the postmodern condition. The subculture may thus be understood as one

6 We do wish to emphasize, however, that the informants in our study were certainly not apolitical. To the contrary, almost all were socially conscious, and many actively participated in various political causes and movements. The argument that we advance is more nuanced, suggesting that punks do not predicate their subcultural participation on the political—that the concern with self-realization tends to supersede all else.

expression—albeit in a heightened and distorted form—of a "dominant" cultural tendency, not so much challenging bourgeois hegemony as articulating an already-prevalent cultural ideology.

References

Allan, Kenneth. 1998. *The Meaning of Culture: Moving the Postmodern Critique Forward.* Westport: Praeger.

Baron, Stephen. 1989. "The Canadian West Coast Punk Subculture: A Field Study." *Canadian Journal of Sociology*, 14:289-316.

Becker, Howard. 1963. "The Culture of a Deviant Group: The Jazz Musician." Pp. 55-65 in *The Subcultures Reader*, edited by K. Gelder and S. Thornton. New York: Routledge.

Bell, Daniel. 1976. *The Cultural Contradictions of Capitalism*. New York: Basic Books.

Bennett, Andy and Keith Kahn-Harris. 2004. "Introduction." Pp. 1-18 in *After Subculture: Critical Studies in Contemporary Youth Culture*, edited by Andy Bennett and Keith Kahn-Harris. New York, NY: Palgrave.

Bourdieu, Pierre. 1984. *Distinction.* London: Routledge.

Boyle, David. 2004. *Authenticity: Brands, Fakes, Spin and the Lust for Real Life.* London: Harper Perennial.

Brisset, Dennis. D. 1972. "Towards a Clarification of Self-Esteem." *Psychiatry*, 35:255-263.

Clarke, John. 1976. "Style." In *Resistance through Rituals: Youth Subcultures in Postwar Britain*, edited by Stuart Hall and Tony Jefferson. New York: Holmes and Meier Publishers.

Cohen, Albert. 1955. *Delinquent Boys*. Glencoe, IL: The Free Press of Glencoe.

Copes, Heith, and J. Patrick Williams. 2007. "Techniques of Affirmation: Deviant Behavior, Moral Commitment, and Subcultural Identity." *Deviant Behavior* 28(2):247-272.

Fine, Gary Alan. 2003. "Crafting Authenticity: The Validation of Identity in Self-Taught Art. *Theory and Society*, 32:153-180.

Fine, Gary Alan and Sherryl Kleinman. 1979. "Rethinking Subculture: An Interactionist Analysis." *American Journal of Sociology*, 85:1-20.

Fox, Kathryn Joan. 1987. "Real Punks and Pretenders: The Social Organization of a Counterculture." *The Journal of Contemporary Ethnography*, 16:344-370.

Gaines, Donna. 1992. *Teenage Wasteland: Suburbia's Dead End Kids*. New York: Harper Perrenial.

Geertz, Clifford. 1973. *Interpretations of Culture: Selected Essays*. New York: Basic Books.

Gergen, Kenneth. 1991. *The Saturated Self: Dilemmas of Identity in Contemporary Life. New York*, NY: Basic Books.

Giddens, Anthony. 1991. *Modernity and Self-Identity: Self and Society in the Late Modern Age*. Stanford, CA: Stanford University Press.

Gilmore, James H., and B. Joseph Pine. 2007. *Authenticity: What Consumers Really Want*. Boston: Harvard Business School Press.

Hall, Stuart and Tony Jefferson. 1976. *Resistance through Rituals: Youth Subcultures in Post-War Britain*. London: Hutchinson.

Hebdige, Dick. 1979. *Subculture: The Meaning of Style*. London: Routledge.

Huq, Ryan. 2006. *Beyond Subculture: Pop, Youth, and Identity in a Postmodern World*. London: Routledge.

Lasch, Christopher. 1979. *The Culture of Narcissism: American Life in an Age of Diminishing Expectations*. New York: Norton.

Leblanc, Lauraine. 2001. *Pretty in Punk: Girls' Resistance in a Boys' Subculture*. New Brunswick: Rutgers University Press.

Lu, Shun and Gary Alan Fine. 1995. "The Presentation of Ethnic Authenticity: Chinese Food as Social Accomplishment." *The Sociological Quarterly*, 36:535-553.

Merton, Robert. 1938. "Social Structure and Anomie." *American Sociological Review*, 3:672-682.

Moore, Ryan. 2007. "Friends Don't Let Friends Listen to Corporate Rock: Punk as a Field of Cultural Production." *Journal of Contemporary Ethnography*, 36:438-474.

Muggleton, David. 2002. *Inside Subculture: The Postmodern Meaning of Style*. Oxford: Berg.

Muggleton, David, and Rupert Weinzierl (eds.) *The Post-Subcultures Reader*. Oxford: Berg.

O'Hara, Craig. 1999. *The Philosophy of Punk*. London: A.K. Press.

Redhead, Steve. 1990. *The End of the Century Party: Youth and Pop Towards 2000*. Manchester: Manchester University Press.

—— 1997. *From Subcultures to Clubcultures*. Oxford: Blackwell.

Roman, Leslie G. 1988. "Intimacy, Labor, and Class: Ideologies of Feminine Sexuality in the Punk Slam Dance." Pp. 143-184 in *Becoming Feminine: The Politics of Popular Culture*, edited by Leslie G. Roman and Linda K. Christian-Smith. London: Falmer Press.

Shibutani, Tamotsu. 1955. "Reference Groups as Perspectives." *American Journal of Sociology*, 60:562-569.

Taylor, Charles. 1992. *The Ethics of Authenticity*. Harvard: Harvard University Press.

Thornton, Sarah. 1996. *Club Cultures: Music, Media and Subcultural Capital*. Middletown, CT: Wesleyan.

Turner, Ralph. 1976. "The Real Self: From Institution to Impulse." *The American Journal of Sociology*, 81:981-1016.

Weinzierl, Rupert, and David Muggleton. 2003. "What is 'Post-subcultural Studies' Anyway?" Pp. 3-23 in *The Post-Subcultures Reader*, edited by David Muggleton and Rupert Weinzierl. Oxford: Berg.

Widdicombe, Sue. 1993. "Autobiography and Change: Rhetoric and Authenticity of "Gothic" Style." Pp. 94-113 in *Repertoiries and Readings of Texts in Action*, edited by Erica Burman and Ian Parker. London: Routledge.

—— 1998. "'But You Don't Class Yourself': The Interactional Management of Category Membership and Non-Membership." Pp. 52-70 in *Identities in Talk*, edited by Charles Antaki and Sue Widdicombe. London: Sage.

Widdicombe, Sue, and Robin Wooffitt. 1990. "'Being' Versus 'Doing' Punk: On Achieving Authenticity as a Member." *Journal of Language and Social Psychology*, 9:257-277.

Williams, J. Patrick. 2006. "Authentic Identities: Straightedge Subculture, Music, and the Internet." *Journal of Contemporary Ethnography*, 35:173-200.

—— 2007. "Youth-Subcultural Studies: Sociological Traditions and Core Concepts." *Sociology Compass*, 1:572-593.

—— 2009. "The Multi-dimensionality of Resistance in Subculture Studies." *Resistance Studies Magazine*, 2(1), http://rsmag.org.

Williams, J. Patrick, and Heith Copes. 2005. "'How Edge Are You?' Constructing Authentic Identities and Subcultural Boundaries in a Straightedge Internet Forum." *Symbolic Interaction*, 28:67-89.

Willis, Susan. 1993. "Hardcore: Subculture American Style." *Critical Inquiry*, 19:365-383.

Wood, Robert T. 2003. "The Straightedge Youth Sub-Culture: Observations on the Complexity of Sub-Cultural Identity." *Journal of Youth Studies*, 6:33-52.

PART 2
The Personal Experience and Practice of Authenticity

Chapter 6
Authenticity: Perspectives and Experiences

Alexis T. Franzese

As a result of the demands and expectations of modern society, there is a growing contradictory yearning among people to construct one's self in order to achieve material success and also to be existentially authentic—that is, to feel true to one's self. From self-help approaches (e.g. Ban Breathnach 1998), to pop philosophy (Covey 2004), and academic treatises (e.g. Dews and Law 1995) such discourses on authenticity abound. While the rise in attention to authenticity is not surprising considering the changing cultural context of our times (Erickson 1995), more surprising is the scarcity of clear scholarly conceptualizations of authenticity and of empirical research on it.

Authenticity has been conceptualized in many and radically different ways across disciplines. This alone, as Vannini and Williams point out in the introduction, is a significant problem. Such differing definitions, specific to discipline, may in part be accountable for the dearth of empirical research on the topic. While it is true that empirical research on authenticity is becoming more common, few if any available research studies provide readers with clear, straightforward, and as unmediated as possible access to what people feel and say about their authenticity and about authenticity as a value. The purpose of the research study reported in this chapter is, following Turner and Schutte's (1981) lead, to ask individuals about their experiences of authenticity and inauthenticity and to report on their answers. Authenticity, in what follows, is defined as an individual's subjective sense that their behavior, appearance, self, reflects their sense of core being. One's sense of core being is composed of their values, beliefs, feelings, identities, self-meanings, etc. I begin with a brief background on the self and authenticity; it is this body of knowledge that inspires my conceptualization.

Approaching the Study of Authenticity

Writings on authenticity span the humanities and social sciences. Philosophical attention to authenticity has focused on its moral underpinnings, social character, and its contextual dependence on culture (e.g., Anton 2001; Taylor 1991; Trilling 1971). Philosophers also consider authenticity as it relates to existential ideas about the self (e.g. Adorno 1973). In the early nineties, philosophers, such as Taylor (1991) began to tie the concept of authenticity to modernity. By building on the work of his precursor Trilling (1971), Taylor's influential discussion looked at authenticity's role in the development of individualistic culture. Both Taylor and Trilling discuss factors that may inhibit enactment of one's sense of true self. A more recent philosophical writing on authenticity by Anton (2001) considers the social conditions of authenticity and the habitual and relational nature of authenticity, noting that context influences, without determining, how we relate to others. Authenticity, according to Anton, is also not concerned exclusively with feeling good.

Psychological approaches to authenticity focus on how individuals meet the needs of the self, but evidence points to both the costs and gains of authentic behavior. This approach is evident in both the early psychological literature on social desirability and the need for social approval (e.g., Crowne and Marlowe 1964) and the literature within humanistic psychology (e.g., Bugental 1965). Empirical research on authenticity conducted by psychologists offers measurable conceptualizations of authenticity (e.g., Goldman and Kernis 2002) and provides important insights into its developmental roots in adolescence (see Harter, Bresnick, Bouchey, and Whitesell 1997; Harter, Marold, Whitesell, and Cobbs 1996).

Sociological approaches to authenticity focus on the reflexivity of the self and the negotiation of social interactions. A key distinction between the *I* and the *me* can be traced to William James ([1890] 1981) and later to George Herbert Mead (1934). James's distinction between the *I* and the *me* ([1890] 1981) describes the *me* as consisting of the physical, social, and spiritual aspects of the self. James's identification of the social component of the *me*, which concerns the human need for recognition and the idea that we present ourselves differently depending on the audience provides an early discussion of authenticity. James's attention to context is an early suggestion that there is a self to be monitored and filtered in human interaction, and by extension, that there is a true, or authentic self, at stake.

The distinction between the *I* and the *me* is related to authenticity because it uniquely identifies an individual's ability to both see oneself from one's perspective, and consider oneself from the perspective of as others. This distinction is crucial in research on impression management. According to Goffman (1959, 1967) there is a serious tension between an individual's desire for authenticity (though Goffman never used this word) and the need for social approval (George, 1998). This tension is a pivotal component in the study of authenticity, and has long been empirically overlooked (George 1998).

A cursory summary of authenticity's empirical research base in sociology (for a more extensive review see Vannini and Franzese 2008) shows authenticity's potential for self-enhancement and well-being (Turner and Billings 1991), the fact that authenticity is at stake in some work settings and can negatively influence wellbeing (Erickson and Wharton 1997), and that it is specifically the experience of managing agitation that is associated with feelings of inauthenticity (Erickson and Ritter 2001). More current research supports the idea that individuals value the perceived authenticity of others (Franzese 2007; Parvez 2006), and suggests linkages between emotion management and authenticity (Sloan 2007). Ethnographic insights suggest the need to consider that the self is not static and that authenticity is fluid over the life course (Vannini 2007). Furthermore authenticity can be considered a motivating force of the self (Gecas 1986; George 1998; Vannini and Burgess this volume), a potential means of self-enhancement (George 1998), and is a key component of the positive psychology movement (e.g., Peterson and Seligman 2004; Seligman 2002). It is within this broad research background that I present my research findings.

The Present Study

Data for this study come from semi-structured in-depth interviews conducted with twenty-one individuals during fall 2005. The interview protocol was designed to gain insights into how individuals think about, speak about, and otherwise conceptualize authenticity. The protocol addressed a core set of topics, yet also allowed for topics to spontaneously emerge. Interviewees were participants in a larger quantitative study of authenticity which aimed to sample younger and older adults. I experienced significant difficulty in identifying younger men who were willing to be interviewed.

The interview sample was predominantly composed of older adults, but was diverse in terms of gender, race/ethnicity, marital status, and education level, which averaged at a Bachelor's degree. Younger adult interviewees ranged in age from twenty-five to forty-four, and older adults from sixty-three to eighty-one. Qualitative analysis entailed three phases. First, I did an initial review of the transcripts. Second, I performed a detailed review of the transcripts which supplied themes that emerged from the guiding questions of this research. Third, I examined transcripts with specific attention to the various motivations for authentic behavior that emerged in the quantitative data analysis (not described here). I used the Constant Comparison Method (CCM), developed by Barney Glaser (Glaser 1978; Glaser and Strauss 1967), to analyze the data. The CCM employed in the study loosely followed the steps outlined by Boeije (2002): comparison within an interview, comparison between interviews within a group, and a comparison of interviews between groups.

The following sections describe insights into how participants conceptualize authenticity, and factors and contexts that inhibit or facilitate authenticity. This section is focused on summarizing and reporting data, almost in their raw form, as a means to give readers an unprecedented gaze and open access to people's talk about authenticity. This is my preferred strategy because it allows the reader more immediate, direct, and clearer access to important dimensions and aspects of the experience of authenticity than available anywhere else in the literature.

Conceptualizing Authenticity

The expression "be true to yourself" was familiar to all participants, but there was variation in what individuals perceived the expression to mean, with most responses clustered into two main themes. The modal theme was a sense that being true to oneself means living life with a level of honesty and integrity. The other theme was that a sense of being true to yourself means knowing who you are. For example, an older Black man felt that being true to oneself means living with honesty and integrity: As he put it: "it means being an honest person. There are a lot of people who say one thing and do something else." The idea that being true to yourself requires that you know who you are was vividly emphasized by an older White woman who stated: "first before you can be true to yourself you have to know who you are … Often we fudge who we are so much that we really don't know. But I guess don't do things just because you think somebody else is watching you and will judge you by what you're doing."

More than half of the respondents reported that the expression "be true to your self" is personally meaningful to them and they highlighted how it has been useful in their lives. An older White man said: "Well I've always lived by that. As well as the golden rule. But I expect to be truthful to myself and it has helped me in my work." Responses from both age groups were permeated with a sense that the ability to be oneself yields a feeling of freedom. For example, a younger White woman said "A lot of freedom I'd say. Freedom and independence is probably my primary mode of being my self." An older White woman echoed this sentiment: ".to do the things that I would like to do and think I should do might be two different things. So [to] do the things that I get enjoyment from and like doing." Other less frequent responses included a sense of being able to live with oneself, a sense of morality, and a sense of consistency. Yet, some participants reported that the statement is not personally meaningful, noting that they do not understand what it means, do not think about it, or do not find it relevant. Two younger Black women shared that although they find the statement compelling it is not personally meaningful because it is not part of their daily experience.

Similarly, there was no universal agreement on the value of authenticity. Just over half of the participants felt that the concept was important to others, while the remainder of the participants gave answers with exceptions and contingencies, felt that it was not important, or provided inconclusive answers. Participants who felt that authenticity is important to others emphasized its social value; ranging from the idea that people like authenticity and integrity, to a sense that being authentic makes people feel good. One respondent suggested that like-minded people associate with one another, one noted that is makes you dependable, and another respondent—a self-described optimist—conveyed a sense of wanting others to value authenticity. The frequency and tone of these responses is significant because they suggest that authenticity, being one's self, can be a socially desirable attribute. An older White man said: "I'm still defining being true to oneself as following your conscience and the values that are ingrained into you, and I think everybody wants to do that." The perspective that others do not value authenticity was evident in the remarks of two participants, one a younger white man who did not feel that others value authenticity "Because it's not a survival skill." The six individuals who said it depends on the circumstances at hand—a group composed equally of older and younger adults—conveyed that it may be important to some people but not others.

Factors that Facilitate and Inhibit Authenticity

I asked participants when they feel most true to themselves (cf. Turner and Schutte 1981). This question was designed to assess variations in authenticity related to both social time (and social transitions, e.g., marriage, retirement) and life time (age). Responses were almost evenly split between a belief that older age is most facilitative of authentic behavior, and that younger age is most facilitative, with the remainder of participants indicating a sense of being most authentic in middle age, that age does not matter, that the relationship is greatest at youngest and oldest ages, or provided no answer. What is most interesting about these competing perspectives is their relationship to respondents' ages. By and large, the older adults felt that it was as they aged that they were most free to be themselves. Yet, the younger adult participants who are approaching middle age and do not have the perspective of the older adults reported a sense of authenticity and freedom that is tied to youth and pre-adulthood. With some circularity, this reflects the sentiment of older adults who view their older years (post-adulthood) with the same sense of enchantment that the younger adults identified as a trademark of childhood.

Other features of life that participants believed facilitate the ability to be authentic included freedom from the expectations of others, wisdom and perspective, and engagement in other-focused activities. Some participants described social lifestyle choices such as spiritual/religious involvement and getting married as transition points facilitating the ability to behave in an authenticating way.

All but one respondent was able to recall times when it was difficult to be true to oneself. These recollections were often connected to social institutions, for example, interactions with family, the business world, the military, and with the church and religious institutions. An example of reference to church came from an older Black man who described a sense of conflict between the dogma of the church and his own feelings. He said:

> I consider myself a Christian, but there are philosophies, there are challenges that I see in the Bible, there are sometimes when I would be somewhat reluctant to say what it is. In fact, I enjoy my Sunday school teacher very much and so, I take a central stand. But uh, I enjoy her so much because she is the same kind of way, just she will, you know, she will simply say, you know, I'm not going to give all my stuff to somebody poor, and you know, I do feel that some of the time, I'm not following what the Lord says, you know, a true, true Christian.

Most interviewees reported that they would reveal their true selves at work even if it meant upsetting their colleagues. For some participants, the decision was one of personal integrity, or commitment to a work ethic and notion of doing the right thing and honoring the principal of the situation. For some, the decision required evaluation of the salience of the work situation. Integrity was prominent in the response of an older Black man who recounted a situation in which he was working in the political arena and took "positions contra to the prevailing consensus of my colleagues. And I know it bothered them and I didn't mind" Conscience and integrity were echoed by an older White man who explained:

> I have a conscience. And I know I'm, again, being my true self. You start with, well, am I normally my true self? I am. And sometimes that hurts I'm sure. It hurts me too.
>
> Interviewer: How does it hurt you?
>
> By having to be my true self when I know that it's going to, maybe, bother me financially or, or in my business relationships. I'm sure it probably has. There've been times when being my true self has affected some part of my business relations.

This example is notable because it clearly illustrates that revealing the true self may have costs, both theoretically and literally.

The situation at hand was important to a retired older White woman who said she would be her true self "if it was a principal that was at stake, yes. Even if it upset them." Protecting a principle and the importance if the issue at hand were mentioned by a younger White woman who said: "If it was, if it was important enough yeah. If it was something that would cause enough discomfort to somebody and it wasn't worth it, then it would make the relationship too tension-filled and I probably wouldn't do it. But if it's important enough I would." When asked how she would determine importance, she replied "Well I'd probably say if it affected my position enough.. if it was something that had to do with the integrity of my work yes." A retired older Black woman said similarly:

> Well that would depend on, that would depend on the situation. Now I wouldn't want to go around upsetting colleagues all the time. But, as when I chaired the department, sometimes there were people on my staff who were upset with me but it was because of decisions that I felt were in the best interest of the department or the students, and so I tried to explain why it was necessary.

Doing what one believes is right was also a theme in the response of an older White woman who recounted a story in which she bucked tradition on the job: "Because in that situation I feel that it's important for them to know who I, at least who I think I am." The confidence required for such decisions was also reported by an older White man who described that he had always worked for himself, with a helper, and had the view that "they could leave if they didn't want to be around me."

Some participants however named work environments as a venue in which they experience difficulty feeling authentic. This may be especially true of younger individuals who are just starting out in employment environments. Four of the five participants who reported that they would not reveal their true selves if it would upset their colleagues were younger individuals who often spoke about the desire to maintain congeniality in the workplace. A younger Black woman also invoked the importance of the matter, but ultimately valued not upsetting others. She said: "And if it means making somebody angry or sad or whatever and or being fake, I'd rather be fake." Similarly, a younger Black woman said she would not: "Just because I, I have it in my head that if I upset anybody then they can go tell or try to get me put out or something. So I don't. Not really. No, not at all actually." A younger White woman expressed similar thoughts: "There, there are times that I'm not completely my true self to not upset my colleagues since you have to compromise in a work situation since I'm in a lab so we're around each other all the time." An older White woman attributed her unwillingness to a belief in adults' abilities to monitor themselves. She said: "I'm not a good supervisor. I thought adults should just work and do their jobs. That's what I thought adults did. So, I didn't like confrontations. I never really confronted anybody.

There was substantial variability in how important participants consider authenticity at work. Among those who felt it least important, three of the four were younger adults who are arguably in less powerful positions in the workplace and may have to sacrifice their sense of true self to a greater extent. A younger White woman said,

> I suppose the main times it's difficult to be my true self would be when I'm having an argument with someone since I'm in a very male dominated lab … for a woman if you raise your voice, you, they think you're you know going nuts. And so I have to not do what I really want to do, to stay totally rational so they'll actually listen to me.

This quotation shows evidence of self-censorship. The interviewee's sense of gender role expectations had a strong role in determining her behavior and authenticity appears at stake in this individual's choice to sacrifice the desires of her core being.

Participants identified a variety of factors that made being true to oneself difficult at certain times: a desire to impress others, the way they were raised, a desire to uphold a certain image of oneself, social roles or obligations—specifically for career, spiritual/religious aspects of self, relationships. The need to impress people is similar, if not synonymous, with the need for social approval. When asked about what made it difficult to be true to oneself, a younger White woman stated, "I guess I always felt the need to impress people and be like whatever quote unquote perfect. Whatever perfect is." This sentiment of wanting to please others can prevent individuals from behaving in ways that match how they feel about themselves. One interviewee attributed her difficulty in being herself to a desire for congeniality, which she attributed to how she was raised. This younger White woman stated,

> In past relationships I tended to sort of lose my sense of self because I was concentrating on the other person so much. And then when I was younger I have pretty much, I had a strict home life where my father more than anything was the "you can't do this, you can't do that" [kind of father] and that kind of thing.

The sense that one's background pervasively affects one's ability to behave in an authentic fashion also came through in the response of an older Black woman who described the influence of her working class background on her desire for achievement, and ultimately her attainment of a doctoral degree.

Social institutions, such as the military and educational institutions, were also cited as creating situations in which individuals experienced obligations that made it difficult for them to be true to themselves. One older White man described that "Everything was structured, and you had to do what they said. You had to do a lot of things that you didn't particularly want to do." One older White woman described a sense of needing to meet the expectations of professors in college as having inhibited her true self:

> I really didn't have time to think: "what do I really feel about this?" I read what I was told to read and took examinations on that and found with a lot of professors that if you input your own ideas it didn't work too well. You had to kind of give them back what they fed you. Not all of them but a good many of them.

Just over half of the participants reported that there were things that prevented them from being true to themselves. This group was composed disproportionately of women and older adults. Participants reported that relationships and desire for congeniality inhibit their ability to be their true self. These responses pertained particularly to relationships with close kin, such as spouses and children, in which negotiation and flexibility are key. For example, a younger Black woman said:

> Marriage and being a mother keeps that from happening completely … Well I mean, yes, the person that you're married to, at least in my case my husband. I can talk to him about anything. However I feel that sometimes the things that I, I've opened up with and, and shared with him has changed his perception and his view.. And so I think you do even in your marriage you have to reserve something … yes I do feel the need to, you know, withhold who I really [am], or the some of my feelings, and the feelings are a part [of that].

Another participant, an older Black woman spoke about her relationship with her husband:

> Well there are very few times that I'm not true to myself now. But I guess one of them might be if I'm angry with my husband or something like that or may not necessarily want him to know I'm angry with him. I may just not say anything or just go somewhere else and not deal with or just not do anything about it or … I guess the only time that I cannot be my[self] … is when I feel that being my true self may cause someone else to feel bad or to, to be unhappy, to be uncomfortable. And I just think it's important to, to look out for people that you're around and that you mingle with, interact with.

Finally, an older White man also spoke about negotiations with family:

> I don't know. [laughter] I pretty well do what I want to do now. I mean, there are financial considerations, things like that that get in the way of what you want to do, and my interaction with my spouse, compromises and so forth … Comes up every day [laughter].

The large majority of participants reported that they feel more genuine or authentic with family, close friends, and other, closer relationships. These responses conveyed a desire for family and friends to know who one really is, a desire fueled by the shared history of family and friends. A number of participants specifically noted that it was important to them to convey their true self with their children. Some respondents alluded to the motivations for the desire to be more genuine in close relationships. For example, an older Black man attributed it to a need for reciprocity: "especially with my friends. People who[m] I trust, you know and depend on. And I, I, see that it's imperative to be my true self. Because I am depending on them to be honest and candid with me." An older White man conveyed a similar sentiment: "My family. They know what to expect from [me], I know what to expect from them. There are some surprises along the way." An older White woman wants to be able to be her true self to maintain peace in her marital relationship. She said:

> I'm constantly trying to argue with my husband that that's not what I meant or what I meant to say and you're misconstruing what I'm saying [laughing], so I really would like him to know who I really am rather than, rather than trying to oppose who he thinks I am, want, what I'm saying, or what I'm doing.

Participants who did not report situations or people with whom it was more important to be authentic, all older adults, reported that they are the same with everyone. For these individuals, not being selectively authentic was a mark of integrity, and for a number of these older adults, a key developmental transition.

Participants' views regarding whether there are situations or people with whom being one's true self does not matter as much splinter into two groups: those who said that it is not as important around strangers and acquaintances, and those who said they are the same with everyone. Authenticity does not matter with acquaintances and strangers as much because there is less investment in those relationships. For example, an older White man said: "Well, like, you go to meetings, stockholder meetings, things like that, you're meeting for the first time. I could [not] care less whether they like me [or] dislike me cause I can turn around and walk away from them without any problem." Some participants spoke about this as self-protective, particularly in the business context. A younger White woman said: "I guess it would probably be with a job. I wouldn't want to be my true self as much since I know that with coworkers they generally aren't your best friends … and so you want to show your confident self and all that." Again, participants who said that they are the same with everyone emphasized that this is a matter of personal integrity. For example, an older Black man said: "I try to be who I am to everybody. Not putting on. Not, not anything, just I, being honest and fair to people. And it works." An older White man said that company does not matter: "To me, to me it really doesn't. If that's a lifestyle you live, of being your true self. You don't, you don't do it through any particular individual. I do it for everybody." Similarly, an older Black man said "No, because I don't like to lie about things. I like to be straightforward and say 'hey apples are apples and oranges are oranges,' you know."

Although authenticity with family is highly valued, as said, participants also reported that relationships with family sometimes inhibit them from revealing their true thoughts and feelings. For these individuals, integrity was very important. Integrity was a key theme in the response of a younger White woman who distinguished between immediate and extended family, and credited her strong self-esteem and relationship with her family as a force allowing her to be her true self. She said:

> Well with my close, with my nuclear family, my parents, that really wouldn't come up. My parents pretty much support whatever I want to do.. For my more extended family I could see where sometimes they wouldn't approve of what I'm doing but it doesn't make a difference. It's what I want to do.. My parents brought me up to do what I want and I guess I've never done anything so destructive they'd be worried about me.. I know that I have a very high self esteem and it's really mainly from my parents that I really feel as if I can do what I want and they're going to support me no matter what I want to do.

An older White woman said she had previously revealed her true self to her family's dissent: "Because that was the honest thing to do. It wasn't necessarily easily done but didn't want to be living a lie you know." This idea of honesty was also a theme in the response of a younger White woman who said: "Because I like to be straight out in the open with them and, and it's more probably along the fact though that just by lying to be too much trouble.. Besides I have too many family members. I have six brothers and sisters [laughing] and it just gets around."

The idea that the loving nature of family creates a safe context was expressed by at least one participant. Other participants reported that they would not reveal their true self if it meant their families would be disappointed. For these individuals, the theme of congeniality and a desire to keep peace was a strong motivating force. An older White man said "that's a hard question because I'm sure there's been times when I really wanted maybe to say something that I held back because it would have hurt some feelings or. I'm sure there's times like that." A younger Black woman said:

> I don't like hurting people's feeling. Especially when you talk about your family members. I mean there's some people in your family you can do it with and life goes on but there's some people in your family that it would just linger and it would affect your overall relationship with that person and to me my measly little self and opinion I can toss that to the side to keep that from happening.

More than half of the participants reported that they would reveal their true selves even if it upset or disappointed their friends and acquaintances. Some participants expressed a belief that being authentic and honest is a mark of friendship, and that advice-giving in friendship can be a way of expressing one's true or most genuine self. Yet, doing so can be costly, as reported by a younger White woman who described how she upset a friend when she expressed what she considered her true self. Some participants reported that they would not have friendships with people with whom they could not be authentic. An example of this sentiment came from a younger White man who said that he would rather not have a friend than be inauthentic. This response denotes costs and benefits; the respondent shares that his desire for friends that accept him has potentially resulted in a more limited friend pool (cost), yet, as a benefit, he is able to avoid the discomfort that he says he experiences when he must submerge the true self.

Summary and Conclusion

Over a quarter century ago, only 3.4 per cent of adults surveyed reported that they often ask "who am I," while 82 per cent reported never asking themselves that question (Turner 1975). In contrast, the current study suggests, the large majority of interviewees reported that the question is personally meaningful. This is suggestive of a shift toward higher self-reflexivity. Whether this shift is the result of a change in culture, or whether the trend is due to a cohort effect is unclear, unascertainable, and perhaps unimportant. What is clear and important, however, is that questions of self and exploration of what it means to be true to oneself hold meaning for people: most people desire, at least under certain circumstances, to *feel true to themselves*.

Findings of this study show that the desire for authenticity and integrity can be a motivator of behavior and that choices about authenticity reflect individual value hierarchies. Interviewees also emphasize the large extent to which a desire for congeniality, concern with one's own self-gains, and need for social approval, can shape behavior. Authenticity, even if abstractly valued as a means of self-enhancement, may be submerged for self-protection. People have different motivations for behavior in different contexts. Overall, interview responses indicate that it is most important to people to be known and liked and valued for who they are in their relationships with family, and this is motivated by a need for personal integrity. This pattern is understandable: people want to believe that those to whom they are closest love them for whom they feel they are. However, when faced with the possibility that exposing who they are will disappoint them, people are more willing to deal with the consequences of sacrificing their true self than face the possibility that a loved one will reject those aspects of self that they consider authentic. People also greatly value authenticity with friends, but can temper this need for purposes of congeniality. In the workplace, people are less fiercely committed to being authentic, and are more willing to engage in impression management for strategic purposes such as keeping one's job.

Findings regarding group differences are particularly interesting. Authenticity appears more tenuous for women than men. The value many women place on relationships may sometimes lead them to sacrifice authenticity in order to maintain congenial relationships. This, however, may speak to a different phenomenon altogether: women may be incongruent with some personal values in maintaining some relationships, but if they value themselves as congenial and sociable individuals they also experience authenticity this way. In relation to age, I observed that both younger and older individuals believe that with aging comes an increased sense of authenticity. Authenticity is most easily exercised when one has more freedom, and this freedom is most accessible at the earliest and, with wisdom, latest parts of the life course. The data also suggest that cultural traditions and racial identity contribute to the values individuals carry and how those values are translated into behavior. Educational attainment is salient because it influences workplace activities and workplaces (through autonomy, space, scheduling) obviously vary in the extent to which they allow for authentic behavior. Relatedly, financial freedom provides the personal freedom to do what one wants. Overall, there was a sense that relationships free us to be more authentic, yet require that we temper ourselves in order to maintain those relationships.

In conclusion, a goal of this research was to enhance the social-scientific understanding of authenticity. This research found that most people hold a general concept of authenticity, defined as enactment of the true self. Yet, it also showed the existence of diverse experiences of authenticity across the lines of gender, age, and race. Although there is a strong sense of respect for the value of authenticity and pride in behaving authentically, individuals also recognize that there are times when authenticity would be too costly.

It is important to consider that in addition to the limitations of the sample, this research may also be limited by a social desirability bias. During interviews, it often seemed that participants wanted to be perceived as highly authentic individuals. This desire may have also contributed to their willingness to be interviewed on the topic, making the interview sample and the very process potentially skewed. The desire among many participants to be perceived as highly authentic is not just a point to consider as a data limitation, but also may be a crucial research finding. This desire may reflect well-learned cultural scripts about authenticity.

In addition, participants were very prone to reify the "true self." Participants spoke about the true self in ways that made it sound concrete, real, and objective. Studying authenticity inevitably puts a researcher into a place where she or he either believes what participants are stating, or the researcher attributes their talk to impression management. Thus, in the end, authenticity may itself be a motivation or a vocabulary of motives, or perhaps both (see Vannini and Burgess this volume). Authenticity, as a cultural script, may even at times be an empty motive. In this spirit, future studies should further differentiate between normative levels of impression management behaviors, such as the social graces of civilized society, and those situations in which the broader question of authenticity is at stake. The interviews made it clear that it is possible to engage in normative and socially expected impression management behaviors without authenticity being at stake. Unearthing the threshold where questions of impression management cross the boundary into questions of authenticity is a necessary step for progress in our understanding of this important concept.

References

Adorno, Theodor. 1973. *The Jargon of Authenticity.* Evanston: Northwestern University Press.

Anton, Corey. 2001. *Selfhood and Authenticity*. Albany: State University of New York Press.

Ban Breathnach, Sarah. 1998. *Something More: Excavating Your Authentic Self.* New York: Warner Books.

Boeije, Hennie. 2002. "A Purposeful Approach to the Constant Comparative Method in the Analysis of Qualitative Interviews." *Quality & Quantity*, 36:391-409.

Bugental, James. 1965. *The Search for Authenticity: An Existential-Analytic Approach to Psychotherapy*. New York: Holt, Rinehart, and Winston.

Covey, Stephen. 2004. *The 8th Habit: From Effectiveness to Greatness*. New York: Simon & Schuster.

Crowne, Douglas and David Marlowe. 1964. *The Approval Motive: Studies in Evaluative Dependence*. New York: John Wiley & Sons.

Dews, Barney and Carolyn Leste Law (eds). 1995. *This Fine Place So Far From Home: Voices of Academics from the Working Class*. Philadelphia: Temple University Press.

Erickson, Rebecca. 1995. "The Importance of Authenticity for Self and Society." *Symbolic Interaction*, 18:121-144.

Erickson, Rebecca and Christian Ritter. 2001. "Emotional Labor, Burnout, and Inauthenticity: Does Gender Matter?" *Social Psychology Quarterly*, 64:146-163.

Erickson, Rebecca and Amy Wharton. 1997. "Inauthenticity and Depression: Assessing the Consequences of Interactive Service Work." *Work and Occupations*, 24:188-213.

Franzese, Alexis. 2007. *To Thine Own Self Be True? An Exploration of Authenticity*. Ph.D. Dissertation, Department of Sociology, Duke University, Durham, NC.

Freud, Sigmund. [1923] 1994. *The Ego and the Id*. New York: W.W. Norton.

Gecas, Viktor. 1986. "The Motivational Significance of Self Concept for Socialization Theory." Pp. 131-156 in *Advances in Group Processes 3*, edited by E.J. Lawler. Greenwich, CT: JAI Press.

George, Linda. 1998. "Self and Identity in Later Life: Protecting and Enhancing the Self." *Journal of Aging and Identity*, 3:133-152.

Glaser Barney. 1978. *Theoretical Sensitivity: Advances in the Methodology of Grounded Theory.* Mill Valley, CA: Sociology Press.

Glaser, Barney and Asnelm Strauss. 1967. *Discovery of Grounded Theory: Strategies for Qualitative Research.* Mill Valley, CA: Sociology Press.

Goffman, Erving. 1959. *The Presentation of Self in Everyday Life.* New York: Doubleday.

—— 1967. *Interaction Ritual.* New York: Doubleday.

Goldman, Brian Middleton and Michael Kernis. 2002. "The Role of Authenticity in Healthy Psychological Functioning and Subjective Well-Being." *Annals of the American Psychotherapy Association*, 5:18-20.

Harter, Susan, Donna Marold, Nancy Whitesell, and Gabrielle Cobbs. 1996. "A Model of the Effects of Parent and Peer Support on Adolescent False Self Behavior." *Child Development*, 67:360-374.

Harter, Susan, Shelley Bresnick, Heather Bouchey, and Nancy Whitesell. 1997. "The Development of Multiple Role-Related Selves during Adolescence." *Development and Psychopathology*, 9:835-853.

James, William. [1890] 1981. *The Principles of Psychology.* Cambridge, MA.: Harvard University Press.

Mead, George Herbert. 1934. *Mind, Self, and Society from the Standpoint of a Social Behaviorist.* Chicago: University of Chicago Press.

Parvez, Fareen. 2006. "The Labor of Pleasure: How Perceptions of Emotional Labor Impact Women's Enjoyment of Pornography." *Gender & Society*, 20:605-631.

Peterson, Christopher, and Martin Seligman. 2004. *Character Strengths and Virtues: A handbook and Classification.* New York: Oxford University Press.

Seligman, Martin. 2002. *Authentic Happiness: Using the New Positive Psychology to Realize Your Potential for Lasting Fulfillment.* New York: Free Press.

Sloan, Melissa. 2007. "The 'Real Self' and Inauthenticity: The Importance of Self-Concept Anchorage for Emotional Experiences in the Workplace." *Social Psychology Quarterly*, 70:305-318.

Taylor, Charles. 1991. *The Ethics of Authenticity.* Cambridge, MA: Harvard University Press.

Trilling, Lionel. 1971. *Sincerity and Authenticity.* New York: Harcourt Brace Jovanovich.

Turner, Ralph and Victoria Billings. 1991. "The Social Contexts of Self-Feeling." Pp. 103-122 in *The Self-Society Dynamic: Cognition, Emotion, and Action*, edited by J.A. Howard and P. L. Callero. Cambridge: Cambridge University Press.

Turner, Ralph and Jerald Schutte. 1981. "The True Self Method for Studying the Self Conception." *Symbolic Interaction*, 4:1–20.

Vannini, Phillip. 2007. "The Changing Meanings of Authenticity: An Interpretive Biography of Professors' Work Experiences." *Studies in Symbolic Interaction* 29:63-90.

Vannini, Phillip and Alexis Franzese. 2008. "The Authenticity of Self: Conceptualization, Personal Experience, and Practice." *Sociology Compass*, 2:1-17.

Chapter 7
Authenticity as Motivation and Aesthetic Experience

Phillip Vannini and Sarah Burgess

> The laws of nature have a beauty to which scientists are very sensitive. Without the feelings aroused by discovering this beauty, I would not feel motivated to pursue scientific research.
>
> Patrick, Professor, Natural Sciences

People work not only to earn a living but also to give meaning to their lives. Work's meaningfulness can be consequential in different ways; people may find work meaningful for the benefits it provides society, for the sense of individual accomplishment that accompanies it, or simply as a pleasant sensuous experience, an aesthetic experience that is self-fulfilling and authenticating (see Dewey 1934 [2005]). In this paper we examine authenticity experiences of academics in the context of their research work. We focus on the motivational significance of authenticity, and the aesthetic components of researchers' experiences. The work of professors seems especially suitable for the analysis of this subject matter as, in terms of professional autonomy and self-direction, scholarly work is arguably less "labor" and more a vocation—an activity marked by independent commitment, passion-driven and serious orientation, potential for aesthetic fulfillment, and existential dedication (see Stebbins 1992).

Despite most interactionists' antipathy toward the concept of motivation, we believe that symbolic interactionism sorely needs a conceptualization of motivation that does not contradict the root images (Blumer 1969; Snow 2001) of the perspective, or the basic assumptions of philosophical pragmatism. We follow Gecas (1986, 1991, 1994) in positing motivation as emergent from social interaction, and as grounded within the self and its reflexive conceptions and feelings.

Our method consisted of a twofold process of empirical data collection. The first phase involved in-depth, semi-structured interviews with a purposive sample of forty-six faculty members, employed at a mid-sized public research university located in the western United States during the academic year 2002-2003. (For more on the research design, see Vannini 2006.) In these interviews, the first author asked faculty to tell the story of how they chose their profession. He also asked them about the values, goals, and meanings they associate with their work and their identity as professors, and how these have changed over time. The second phase originated in the summer of 2005, when the second author, in collaboration

Our thesis that authenticity is a source of motivation for the self is bound to raise concern, especially with some symbolic interactionists and other sociologists who are skeptical toward the idea of motivation. In fact, as Dewey (2002 [1921]) and Mills (1970 [1940]) have remarked, the quest for "subjective 'springs' of action" (Mills 1970 [1940]:472) is moot; humans are active by nature. "Motivation is a question of direction, not origination of action" as Stone and Farberman (1970:467) succinctly put it. We generally agree with this principle. We recognize that the very idea of motivation is seemingly incongruent with the interactionist perspective because "to speak of behavior as 'motivated' is to designate behavior that is related to some specific organic drive (such as hunger or sex), to a conditioned response, to a stimulus, or to some generalized need or disposition of the organism, and to say that behavior occurs 'because' the motivation exists" (Hewitt 2002:118). The conceptualization of motivation as a psychological substratum of irresistible powers violates the basic interactionist principle that humans are not driven by "forces, drives, urges," (Hewitt 2002:118) and other "inner states that we can't ever see" (Holstein and Gubrium 2003:246). Since interactionists believe that people are active meaning-makers whose selfhood is shaped in emergent social interaction, the very idea of motivation has been dismissed. (For exceptions, though based on our arguments dissimilar from ours, see Heimer and Matsueda 1997; Katz 1994; Scheff 1997).

Our departure point, however, lies in rejecting the very definition of motivation as a mere bundle of deterministically uncontrollable and imperceptible drives, urges, impulses, and forces internal to the organism. We reject any such view of motivation, as we find it dependent on a dualistic vision of the person, which separates body and mind, and "inner" and "outer" self. Following Stone and Farberman (1970) our approach to motivation conceptualizes motivation as a direction, rather than as the origination of action. Yet, we do believe that direction is not random or aimless, and thus we recognize the significance of understanding its origins as well. We are not arguing for a type of motivation that works as a determining cause of conduct, but instead for a type of motivation as socialized willpower that is emergent in people's transactions with their world, that is contingent on the structural, interpersonal, and personal feasibility of their preferred plans of action, and that is itself subject to interpretation and negotiation. Rather than an overwhelming force determining conduct, therefore, we view motivation as an energetic orientation and an interpretive judgment of the self, a judgment that something is meaningful, valuable, pleasurable, and thus deserving of attention, interest, and possible goal-driven manipulation.

As theorized by Gecas (1986, 1991, 1994) the feeling of motivation—with regard to authenticity—may have positive or negative valence. In simpler words, we may find ourselves motivated or unmotivated to do something because it coheres, or it fails to be congruent with, our sense of self. The experience of authenticity generally has positive valence, and is a powerful intrinsic motivator through which we give meaning and purpose to life. We associate it with other emotions, such as satisfaction, aesthetic pleasure, joy, pride, and even euphoria—though certain emotions may matter to some more than others. The counterpart of authenticity is inauthenticity, an undesirable state that people try to avoid, since it is associated with negative feelings like self-contempt, shame, guilt, and meaninglessness. Engaging in actions that are inauthenticating typically occurs for extrinsic reasons, physiological needs in conflict with core values, occupational demands, or other external pressures. Then again, at times people may find extrinsic reasons, demands, and pressures to be meaningful and congruent with their core values, and thus feel authentic in meeting such demands and pressures. Feelings of authenticity and inauthenticity are key elements of the human condition (see Gecas 1986, 1991, 1994). They are hardly ever experienced in "pure" form, as they are most often mixed with other emotions, diluted by the negative consequences of acting authentically and honestly (see Waskul, this volume) and tinted by the inevitable presence, ranging from mild to acute, of their counterpart (Vannini 2006).

The workplace is an important arena for studying authenticating and inauthenticating experiences. In general, work activity that taps or is an expression of intrinsic motivators (i.e. activities that one wants to do because they are self-validating, aesthetically pleasant, meaningful and important, or fun) contributes to feelings of authenticity, as well as to other positive experiences, such as happiness, satisfaction, pride, and well-being (for a review see Vannini and Franzese 2008). Indeed, as Dewey (2002 [1921]:123) pointed out, "it is 'natural' for activity to be agreeable." When work of this kind is performed, Dewey continues, workers "tend to find fulfillment, and finding an outlet is itself satisfactory, for it marks partial accomplishment." But under the social and historical conditions in which we live, with the current "emphasis put upon profit as an inducement," "circumstances of productive service now shear away direct satisfaction from those engaging in it" (Dewey 2002 [1921]:122). Thus, work that is primarily extrinsically motivated (e.g. for money alone) tends to be alienating, devoid of aesthetic pleasure, and may be inauthenticating if it violates one's sense of true self.

An important structural condition of work that bears on workers' motivations, satisfactions, and authenticity is the degree of autonomy and self-direction that the workplace permits. Kohn (1977; Kohn and Schooler 1983; also see Mortimer and Lorence 1995) found work autonomy and self-direction (as measured by such work conditions as degree of supervision, routinization, and job complexity) to have a substantial effect on workers' values, intellectual flexibility, and well-being. Fine (1998) too, in his study of restaurant kitchen workers, found that conditions of autonomy from managerial and budgetary demands, as well as freedom of creative expression led to chefs' and cooks' feelings of satisfaction in their aesthetic creations. We argue that relative autonomy is also relevant for professor' feelings of authenticity and inauthenticity, and we believe that our study of the work of academic researchers can help us shed light on the role that authenticity plays within an occupational context in which intrinsic motivation and relative autonomy are highly valued and, at least sometimes, institutionally protected—a relatively unique context since much of the existing body of research on authenticity focuses on work conditions that seem to value and promote inauthenticity and insincerity.

comes from being able to understand the physical universe in a mathematically precise and experimentally testable way." For others it is the "enormous passion in the pursuit of ways to understand the universe about us and the thrill of a new and unexpected insight." The pleasures of discovery in relation to authenticity were best described by a professor in psychology, whose eyes were almost moved to tears as he spoke:

> It's a wonderful feeling to come up with an idea and discover something that didn't exist before. It's the joy of … well, there are two aspects. One aspect is the joy of conceptualizing something and seeing some idea, and then seeing if it can get done. There's a good example of that: I was reading a book chapter and I saw something that struck my attention. So I went back and read it again and again and I thought: you know what, I can test that hypothesis! Nobody had done that, and I knew I could do it in a very different way. And so I think about it and I go and draw it out. And so there is really the joy of conceptualizing something and the freedom of going in and asking nature a question. This is why I love what I do, why I love this job (Stephen, Professor, Social Sciences).

There is one important aspect that Stephen finds authenticating in research: the pleasure of finding out something, of being able to play with an idea and seeing it take shape in the research process. Such discovery, such element of uniqueness, of novelty, or originality is connected to the creative power of the self and the phenomenological experience of agency present in the feeling of authenticity (Gecas 1986; Holstein and Gubrium 2000). Elements of novel creation and discovery are authenticating simply because they allow professors to ground an aspect of their sense of true self in their work identity.

The Experience of Inauthenticity

Even though professors think that they enjoy a good amount of freedom in the way they choose to do their work, they also believe that their freedom is often restricted in many ways. Such restrictions are a source of complaint partly because they infringe on intellectual and research pursuits that are more aesthetically rewarding and authenticating. One pervasive source of restrictions is pressure originated by universities' need to maximize the "efficiency" of its faculty. Scholars have, as of late, come under pressure to adapt to the new commercialized culture of academic life (see Vannini 2006). Professors often lament that traditional pressures toward publication have now been replaced by a different set of priorities, such as pressures to turn research into an undertaking that is profitable for the university. Therefore, while research is a source of pleasure, it can also be a source of frustration, stress, anger, and resentment. As Erickson (1995) explains, the self becomes aware of its authenticity when stress occurs: when values and habitual character and conduct are called into question. Professors may feel the pinch of inauthenticity while focusing their attention on subject matter that is uninteresting to them but which they pursue because it is well funded. Assistant professors are particularly prone to being pressured into "chasing the money trail":

> Before getting tenure the liberty is fairly limited. I did feel that I had to go where the money was and I went off into a field that I wasn't very interested in. And I spent eight, nine years on that, and I'm still proud of that work but I feel that wasn't really me, there was little bit of unhappiness there, but then I came back to what I love there wasn't money there, but I don't care (Beatrice, Associate Professor, Natural Sciences).

Such practices as grant-seeking can be inauthenticating for some professors because of the nature of the work required. Grant-seeking entails a focus on business matters—such as filling out paperwork, furnishing a lab, justifying expenses, making purchases, employing various personnel. Such activities require a type of attention that offers few aesthetic rewards. When professors who are mostly interested in the pleasure of scientific discovery or creation find themselves "managing," "pushing paper," and "doing business," unhappy sentiments of inauthenticity are likely to arise:

> I'm like an entrepreneur who constantly has to bring in funding, though I hate to be a businessman. Everybody who goes into physics goes into it because they really like to do what they do, but once you become an academic you have to be a business man, you have to schmooze a little bit, you have to learn the right people to contact to bring in funding and I really do hate that part of it (Robert, Professor, Natural Sciences).

The most common feeling used to describe inauthenticity is that of falseness with oneself and a sense of loss of the true self, or separation from it. Professors act inauthentically because they understand that at times compromising their passions and what they truly value is necessary. Theoretically speaking, this is an important point. Authenticity may work as a motivator, but individuals are never at the mercy of what motivates them; motivating forces are never overpowering. In other words, complex configurations of diverse commitments, overlapping roles, and multiple needs are the subject of *constant reflection and negotiation*. Dorothy expresses this well:

> There are times when you feel inauthentic when you perform. There are times when you have to play a certain piece that you just cannot connect with. But you have to play. It's like telling a story without really knowing it. It's pretty bad. You need to connect with a piece psychologically, emotionally, spiritually, and if you do not have enough time to prepare for it, you'll feel pretty bad about yourself. Still, it's part of your role. We are public employees, and we need to provide a service to the public (Dorothy, Associate Professor, Humanities).

Inauthenticity derives from the realization that one is momentarily no longer acting in congruence with one's sense of true self. Often, these experiences of inauthenticity are closely connected to emotions of shame and guilt (Gecas 1986). As an assistant professor in philosophy explained, this is the time when the self feels "the pinch" of its own judgment:

> There are a few papers that I wrote because I needed to publish. It didn't feel great. I could feel a pinch. I was certainly aware that had it gotten any worse I would have left the field (Scott, Assistant Professor, Humanities).

Despite experiencing inauthenticity in relation to what they are truly passionate about and inspired by, both Scott and Dorothy admit that acting inauthentically in order to fulfill their expectations may give rise to a different, simultaneous feeling of authenticity. "Even though I felt untrue to my passions in writing those papers"—Scott added—"there was a certain sense of being authentic in there too. I am committed to supporting my family, no matter what it takes. So while I was feeling inauthentic as a scholar I was feeling true to my parental and spousal identity." Indeed authenticity, like motivation, has multiple and contradicting forms because social existence and selfhood have multiple and often contradicting forms. Motivators, like authenticity, do not sweep people off their feet. Yet, they regularly present themselves across a variety of situations; within such situations people interpret the intensity of their motivators, the significance of their goals, the feasibility of alternative course of actions. While we are not always able to verbalize these reflexive processes, or to make the best or even the same decision across similar contexts, we are certainly reflexive, intellectually sound, and emotionally intelligent enough to exercise agency, rather than just fall into the lap of situational expectations.

Motivators like authenticity may even decrease in importance over one's lifetime, perhaps as a result of the accumulation of experiences of inauthenticity and frustrations. For some professors, authenticity seems to disappear off their radar screen entirely. Lowlands of inauthenticity, mixed with senselessness seem to mark the life of professors who become "burned out", losing their youthful idealism and the ultimate meanings of their work. Professors who feel burned out explain that their feelings of inauthenticity often come from realizing that they are no longer committed to their identities as academics. Not only are they feeling untrue to what they strongly valued, but they feel that they are progressively losing their values and their sense of true self, and not without a great deal of chagrin. For example:

> Sure I look back and I say I'm not the idealist I used to be [...] I'm an educational opportunist. I'm not out there actively shaping my career; I'm more simply taking opportunities when they come along. [...] I feel like I'm in a holding pattern. I'm waiting to retire in three years and move out of this daycare for nineteen year

> olds. [...] I've tried to help the department, focusing on the students. I don't give a darn about the university (Russ, Associate Professor, Humanities).

A burned out professor, usually an associate or even full professor, has lost interest in research and publishing, yet s/he often looks back with melancholia at the olden days. Burned out professors cease to conduct research because "it no longer means anything, it's all bullshit," "it doesn't feel good anymore, it feels awkward, ugly, like it's being forced out of you, like it has no natural harmony with the world," and because "the world doesn't need it." Inauthenticity then in this case comes from a feeling of senselessness, the feeling that one is actively engaging in activities that have negative meaning to them and no longer feel like anything or affirm the self, morally or aesthetically.

It is necessary to make a final distinction between feelings of inauthenticity and feelings of frustrated authenticity. Feelings of frustrated authenticity relate to the perceived sense of being unable to act in congruence with one's self-values, and differ from feelings of inauthenticity proper with regard to the type of emotions experienced. The experience of frustrated authenticity consists of feeling distressed, agitated, vexed, and even discouraged in one's endeavor to act in accordance with one's values. However, one does not necessarily feel false and untrue to one's self, feelings which constitute true inauthenticity. For example, in the following excerpt we can see how Martha's attempt to be kind and helpful—qualities about herself that she deeply values—was foiled by her tenure-mentor who reminded her that her occupational duty was to spend time exclusively on activities beneficial to her quest for tenure, namely publishing:

> One day I was sitting here teaching conversational French to a bunch of students who were going to West Africa, and they didn't speak any French. They asked me if I could help and I said yes. So we're here at my desk, and right then and there my tenure mentor comes in, looking for her TA. I felt like a kid caught with a hand in the cookie jar. She'd found me. I wasn't supposed to be doing anything but teaching my classes and doing research. The next day she convened a meeting of my pre-tenure committee, and they all said: "You are never to do that again! It's the students' problem, it's their own problem. You can't do that, it has nothing to do with your tenure decision." I was so angry. If I could have quit my job, right then if I could have. I was furious. So did I feel pressured? I felt tremendous pressure. I felt unbelievably pressured. I wasn't allowed to change my syllabus, in any class because it would take additional time. It was awful! (Martha, Assistant Professor, Social Sciences).

In this sense the feeling of frustrated authenticity introduces a new point of entry onto the continuum between authenticity and inauthenticity. Frustrated authenticity is a feeling that arises when is unwilling or unable to begin to fight a battle for authenticity, whereas inauthenticity arises when the battle has been explicitly lost.

—— (eds) 2003. *Inner Lives and Social Worlds: Readings in Social Psychology.* New York: Oxford University Press.

James, William. 1890. *The Principles of Psychology*, Vol. 1. New York: Holt.

Katz, Jack. 1994. "Jazz in Social Interaction: Personal Creativity, Collective Restraint, and Motivational Explanation in the Social Thought of Howard S. Becker." *Symbolic Interaction*, 17:253-280.

Kohn, Melvin. 1977. *Class and Conformity*. Second edition. Chicago: University of Chicago Press.

Kohn, Melvin and Carmi Schooler. 1983. *Work and Personality: An Inquiry into the Impact of Social Stratification*. Norwood, NJ: Ablex Publishers.

Mead, George. 1926. "The Nature of Aesthetic Experience." *International Journal of Ethics*, 36:382-392.

—— 1934. *Mind, Self, and Society*. Chicago: University of Chicago Press.

—— 1938. "The Aesthetic and the Consummatory." Pp. 454-459 in *The Philosophy of the Act*, edited by Charles Morris. Chicago: University of Chicago Press.

Mills, C. Wright. 1970 [1940]. "Situated Actions and Vocabularies of Motive." Pp. 470-480 in *Social Psychology through Symbolic Interaction*, edited by Gregory Stone and Harvey Farberman. Waltham, MA: Xerox.

Mortimer, Jeylan and Jon Lorence. 1995. "Social Psychology of Work." Pp. 497-523 in *Sociological Perspectives on Social Psychology*, edited by Karen Cook, Gary Fine, and James House. Boston: Allyn and Bacon.

Peirce, Charles Sanders. 1931. *Studies in the Philosophy of Charles Sanders Peirce*. Boston: Harvard University Press.

Root-Bernstein, Robert. 2003. "Sensual Chemistry: Aesthetics as a Motivation for Research." *HYLE: International Journal for the Philosophy of Chemistry*, 9:33-50.

Scheff, Thomas. 1997. *Emotions, the Social Bond, and Human Reality: Part/Whole Analysis*. Cambridge: Cambridge University Press.

Schwalbe, Michael. 1986. *The Psychosocial Consequences of Natural and Alienated Labor*. Albany: SUNY Press.

Scott, Marvin and Stan Lyman. 1968. "Accounts." *American Sociological Review*, 33:46-62.

Snow, David. 2001. "Extending and Broadening Blumer's Conceptualization of Symbolic Interactionism." *Symbolic Interaction*, 24:367-377.

Stebbins, Robert. 1992. *Amateurs: Professional and Serious Leisure*. Montreal: McGill-Queen's University Press.

Stone, Gregory and Harvey Farberman (eds). 1970. *Social Psychology through Symbolic Interaction*. Waltham, MA: Xerox.

Trilling, Lionel. 1972. *Sincerity and Authenticity.* Cambridge, MA: Harvard University Press.

Turner, Ralph. 1976. "The Real Self: From Institution to Impulse." *American Journal of Sociology*, 81:989-1016.

Turner, Ralph and Victoria Billings. 1991. "The Social Contexts of Self-Feelings." Pp. 103-122 in *The Self-Society Dynamic: Cognition, Emotion, and Action*, edited by Judith Howard and Peter Callero. Cambridge: Cambridge University Press.

Turner, Ralph and Chad Gordon. 1981. "The Boundaries of the Self: The Relationship of Authenticity in the Self-Conception." Pp. 39-57 in *The Self-Concept: Advances in Theory and Research*, edited by M. Lynch, A. Norem-Hebeisen, and K. Gergen. Cambridge, MA: Ballinger.

Turner, Ralph and Jerald Schutte. 1981. "The True Self Method for Studying the Self-Conception." *Symbolic Interaction*, 4:1-20.

Vannini, Phillip. 2006. "Dead Poets' Society: Teaching, Publish-or-Perish, and Professors' Experience of Authenticity." *Symbolic Interaction*, 29:235-258.

Vannini, Phillip and Alexis Franzese. 2008. "The Authenticity of Self: Conceptualization, Personal Experience, and Practice." *Sociology Compass*, 2:1-17

Vannini, Phillip and Dennis Waskul. 2006. "Symbolic Interaction as Music: The Esthetic Constitution of Meaning, Self, and Society." *Symbolic Interaction*, 29:5-18.

Williams, J. Patrick. 2006. "Authentic Identities: Straightedge Subculture, Music, and the Internet." *Journal of Contemporary Ethnography*, 35:173-200.

Chapter 8

The Everyday Work and Auspices of Authenticity

Jaber F. Gubrium and James A. Holstein

Early in the 2008 US presidential primary season, *New York Times* columnist Maureen Dowd asked whether Democratic Party candidate Hillary Clinton could cry her way to the White House (*NY Times*, January 9, 2008). Dowd's column referred to Clinton's emotional moment before news cameras following rival candidate Barack Obama's win in the Iowa caucus. The alleged "unmistakable look of tears in [Clinton's] eyes" prompted Dowd's question. The start of her column is pertinent to everyday understandings of authenticity and we quote it at length.

> When I walked into the office Monday, people were clustering around a computer to watch what they thought they would never see: Hillary Clinton with the unmistakable look of tears in her eyes. A woman gazing at the screen was grimacing, saying it was bad. Three guys watched it over and over, drawn to the "humanized" Hillary. One reporter who covers security issues cringed. "We are at war," he said. "Is this how she'll talk to Kim Jong-il?" Another reporter joked: "That crying really seemed genuine. I'll bet she spent hours thinking about it beforehand." He added dryly: "Crying doesn't usually work in campaigns. Only in relationships" (P. A21).

These comments serve as a springboard for our concern with the authenticities of everyday life. Of interest in this particular case is the question of how genuine the tears were. Were they spontaneously from the heart or planned beforehand? Equally significant, how would this ostensibly impromptu moment be perceived by the electorate? Would it be viewed positively as a sign of Clinton's true humanity, or skeptically as manipulative campaign spin? The last reporter's assertion about the context of genuineness is especially relevant, as it deals with what we will refer to as the "auspices" of authenticity. What would be made of Clinton's tears under the auspices of a political campaign, as opposed to, say, a private personal relationship?

The comments indicate that crying can signify many things—something reassuringly "humanizing," "weakness" in the face of challenge, clumsiness with respect to campaign tactics, and political manipulation. The meanings have varied moral vectors, from being a matter of character to being an indicator of international for what might pass for authenticity, the conditions of possibility for the authentic, as it were (Foucault 1977). While authenticity work is the mechanism by which objects and events are presented and come to be treated as authentic, its operation alone cannot reveal the substance of what is or is not authentic, or the ways that local contingencies mediate the appearance of authenticity.

The term "authentic" is often associated with qualities such as truthfulness, genuineness, and realistic. An authentic person or self is one who is in touch with his or her real phenomenological and emotional experience and who reveals his or her own true thoughts, feelings, and actions (see Vannini 2006). While scholarly treatments of authenticity have produced myriad conceptualizations, our preference is to hold those in abeyance and turn instead to indigenous authenticity practices. Instead of predefining authenticity, we seek to describe how ordinary senses of the concept develop in the course of its mundane consideration. We view authenticity as a feature of everyday life, as a practical matter of providing, receiving, and judging accounts of the authentic, in particular accounts dealing with personal characteristics and interpersonal relationships.

The authenticity of objects, events, and actions is frequently conveyed in familiar expressions such as "I've been there" and "Only I know my true self." These expressions reference those who have been "on the scene" or are otherwise "in the know." One's "own story" is a claim to the authentic version of a lifetime of experience (Gubrium and Holstein 2009). But close examination of ordinary talk and interaction suggests that such conclusions are complicated by competing authenticity claims, diverse sources of knowledge, and local epistemological preferences. Authenticity is something interactionally accomplished in relation to the situated relevancies at play.

In the matter of life stories, for example, it is commonplace to consider the storyteller who has direct knowledge of the experience being narrated as having privileged access to the real story. An authentic subject—one who is in touch with the truth of matters in question—is commonly considered to possess the most genuine account. But adopting these commonsense criteria as analytic constructs is problematic. It risks confounding the researcher's topic with his or her analytic resources (see Garfinkel 1967; Zimmerman and Pollner 1970). In considering everyday authenticity claims, the researcher must be careful to clearly identify those processes and criteria that members of situations themselves use to designate genuineness. Researchers should take care to focus on indigenous criteria for authenticity and not adopt them as their own standards. This, of course, requires disciplined attention to the constructed and situated elements of authenticity, those that ordinary members put into play, not *a priori*, abstract assumptions about what is or is not authentic as popularly understood.

Approaching authenticity in terms of everyday practice centers research on how allegedly genuine persons, objects, emotions, events, and so forth, are identified in everyday life. It focuses on individuals making and responding to authenticity claims and how they, together, determine the genuine, the unreliable, the truthful, or the suspect, for the situated, practical purposes at hand. Those who receive the claims—listeners and audiences—are an important consideration. What they expect to hear in particular circumstances shapes the construction of authenticity as much as the constructive skill of the claimants (see Hyvärinen 2008).

Forms of Authenticity Work

Let us first consider how various forms of authenticity work construct the genuine. In doing so, we take up the question of *how* authenticity is done in everyday life. In the next section, we will address the *what* question, which will feature the auspices of authenticity construction (see Holstein and Gubrium 2000 for further discussion of this distinction). We draw upon our own and others' narrative and ethnographic data for illustration, making no claim that our catalog of practices and auspices is comprehensive. In the course of everyday interaction, we value authenticity because we associate it with properties of genuineness, credibility, plausibility, and the like (see Vannini 2006). But all interactional claims are not presented or treated as equally authentic. Authenticity must be "worked up" by both presenters and recipients. Interactional participants engage in myriad forms of authenticity work in order to substantiate claims to credibility, integrity, and influence. While it would be impossible to provide a comprehensive catalogue, we offer several illustrations here to suggest the range of everyday practices through which a working sense of authenticity is established by speakers and listeners.

Direct Claims

Most obviously, speakers assert authenticity by directly claiming it. Consider, for example, the ubiquity and frequency of proclamations such as "truth be told," "candidly speaking," or "can I speak freely?" Each functions as a kind of authenticity preface (see Sacks 1992b), alerting and instructing the recipient that the ensuing account is to be taken as heartfelt and/or genuine, part of the work of setting up a truthful account. The implication is that with such prefaces, the accounts that follow are more authentic than those bereft of them. Of course, recipients of such talk seldom take such remarks at face value; they may be circumspect if not cynical about what they are about to hear. Indeed, for some, an announcement such as, "I'm going to be frank with you," virtually alerts them to the prospect of insincerity or deceit. While a restaurant's marketing claim that touts, say, "Authentic Tuscan Cuisine" may shape potential patron's predispositions and dining choices, the mere prefacing claim is not likely to be sufficient to establish fully the restaurant's authenticity. As in other everyday venues, establishing and sustaining the sense of authenticity is an ongoing and multifaceted task shaped by the circumstances.

Authenticity Checks

There are myriad motives for offering particular accounts or versions of experience. People have self-serving interests or stakes in matters under consideration, something of which recipients often seem all too aware (see Potter 1996). We can assume that people want to be taken seriously, as honest, sincere brokers of their thoughts and feeling, but those evaluating accounts may nevertheless be more-or-less skeptical of what they hear. Erving Goffman (1959) tells us that expressions "given"—that is, direct narrative accounts or descriptions—may easily be manipulated. Consequently, their authenticity is always open to question. Accordingly, we also look for what Goffman called expressions "given off"—actions that are less easily controlled or manipulated—to reveal actors' actual interests, motives, or selves.

Common examples of such authenticity checks include vigilantly scrutinizing speakers for "stammering" or hurried speech, "shifty eyes," "sweaty palms," or other inadvertent signs of unease about what is being conveyed. If a speaker is unable to "look you in the eye and tell you what's on his mind," as it is often said, his authenticity is commonsensically compromised. We can also find subtle, less clichéd ways in which the presentation of selves and stories is read for signs of authenticity. For example, in a family therapy agency Jaber Gubrium (1992) studied, staff members generally discounted family members' initial accounts of their relations with one another, choosing instead to read the reality of their relationships from the way family members positioned, arranged, and comported themselves during therapy sessions. In particular, staff trusted expressions given off by way of how family members seated themselves more than they trusted explicit verbal accounts of domestic relations, which staff figured could be manipulated for self-serving purposes.

Authenticity work may combine explicit claims and uncontrolled gestures, involving both those who deliver accounts and those who receive them. Most of this work falls somewhere between the overt manipulation of authenticity prefaces and the search for uncontrollable, yet tell-tale signs of inauthenticity as illustrated above. We turn now to some elaborations of those purposeful, yet not fully planned or intentional practices.

Privileged Positioning

One important form of authenticity work involves privileged positioning. For example, those researched, as well as the researchers themselves, especially ethnographers, promote the authenticity of informants' reports by touting the extent to which informants are "there," "on the scene," or "inside" the action, so to speak (see Geertz 1988). "Being there" or "on the inside" provides a figurative as well as empirical anchor for accurate description, supplying a basis for treating such accounts as authentic because their sources are privy to first-hand experience.

Establishing a privileged position on the scene also involves authenticity work. Simply stating that one is an "insider" is generally inadequate to the task. Rather, one's location in relation to the source and scene of the account in question must be independently established. Consider the variety of techniques that Jonathan Potter (1996) enumerates in the following account offered by Jimmy, who is speaking during a relationship counseling session he is attending with his wife, Connie. At issue, among other things, is Connie's allegation that Jimmy is "an extremely jealous person." She argues her point by claiming that Jimmy was unduly aggravated by Connie's innocently "having a few drinks and messin'" with a "bloke in a pub" (Potter 1996:120). Jimmy tries to refute the charge by offering his own account of the situation and actions in question.

> Um, when these people came in, it was John and Caroline. And then they had this other fella, Dave with them as well ... Um He c- he came- they all came in the pub anyway. Well, Connie sat beside Caroline. And I sat [further back]. So you was, you was split between us. They sat in- on the other side. The only words Connie spoke to me for the rest of the evening was "Get another drink. Get another drink" (Potter 1996:163, transcript slightly modified for readability).

Potter notes that this account is full of specific references—definite characters, exact locations, and instances of precise quotation (Potter 1996:163). The description is highly detailed, not general or superficial. The result is a rich account constructed from Jimmy's point of view, presented in a fashion that allows the recipient close access to Jimmy's experiences, thoughts, and feelings. Such accounts permit the recipient to take on the position of the speaker, gaining a sense of understanding from his or her perspective. As Potter suggests, the recipient of the account watches and hears with the eyes and ears of the speaker and will be inclined to accept the version presented by the speaker. The richness of the description establishes the speaker as actually embedded in the actions described, positioning him or her to offer first-hand descriptions because he or she can claim implicitly to be an eyewitness or participant in the actions (Potter 1996:164-165).

Detailing

The provision of rich and abundant detail undergirds privileged positioning, according to Potter (1996). Detailing offers vivid representation of a scene, action, group, or person that is unlikely to be seen as invented or inauthentic. It enhances the work that establishes the sense of being "up close" or "inside" situations, thus entitling the speaker to offer seemingly genuine accounts as a witness, in situ expert, or actual subject or source of the experience (see Goodwin 1984; Sacks 1992a and 1992b).

While this is apparent in the illustration from relationship counseling, it is even more striking in witness accounts of extraordinary events. Kathleen Haspel (2007), for example, describes the striking degree to which eyewitness accounts by laypersons of the horrific scenes at ground zero on September 11, 2001 were replete with copious detail. Analyzing first-hand witness telephone calls to C-SPAN's *Washington Journal*, Haspel explains that many of the calls began by first conveying at length where the callers were and what they were doing when the World Trade Center was struck. Throughout the accounts, callers continued to describe the mundane details of where they were and what they were doing at various points in their accounts. The detailing included many acknowledgements of uncertainty, disfluencies, and displays of disorientation, yet they appeared as standard features of the accounts. Haspel argues that detailing allows the audience to actually visualize what happened with clarity and specificity as they recount their experiences step-by-step.

Mundane Embeddedness

Haspel explains further that detailed accounts are especially compelling in the way they embed extraordinary events within more familiar aspects of unfolding scenes. Alongside descriptions of 9-11 carnage and disaster, for example, witnesses frequently offered mundane details that anchored their narratives to more familiar circumstances. If most of the accounts included great human tragedy, often death, callers nonetheless designed them to be accessible to ordinary recipients by tying them to local details (Haspel 2007). Callers burnished accountable scenes with references to distance, direction, and other neutral and accessible descriptions of what they saw. They provided specifics about what they themselves were doing—their role in the drama—as the events unfolded.

Robin Wooffitt (1992) suggests that those who claim to witness extraordinary events are likely to situate their reports in relation to circumstances that ordinary people are likely to consider commonplace and familiar. Naturalizing the exceptional serves to authenticate their experience and reports of it. Prolific detail along with displays of routine, local knowledge, according to Haspel, lends "narrative authenticity" to eyewitness reports. This, coupled with eyewitness expressions of doubt and emotion, heightens the accounts' authenticity as stories of "what happened to me." According to Haspel, the blend of experience and information authenticates the speaker as a true and forthcoming witness.

Importing Dialogue

Imported dialogue can lend additional genuineness to authenticity claims. As we saw in the relationship counseling extract, when Jimmy imitated Connie as saying "Get me another drink. Get me another drink," the use of imported dialogue serves to underscore the authenticity of a report. Consider the following illustration, which highlights the strategy employed by Jimmy in the preceding example. The extract is from an interview conversation with a woman who is recounting her marital troubles and experience in marriage counseling. She speaks at this point about an especially important juncture in her understanding of her marriage.

> I had a couple of conversations with God and one he actually said, "He will be back." [pause] And so I of course read that to mean he [her ex-husband] will be back and we'll have our relationship back together again ... and um [pause] and another time [pause] I was really upset, it was [date of the incident] and, and um, I went outside at work. I was just too stressed, I couldn't work, and I went outside and said, "God, what am I supposed to do?" ... And this voice, just like in the story of Noah, said, "Let go." I called my counselor right away and I said, "Oh my God! God just told me that I have to let go of [her ex-husband]!" He [the counselor] said, "What exactly did he [God] say?" I said, "He said let go." He [the counselor] said, "Well, it may be he didn't mean let go of [the ex-husband], he meant let go of trying to control the situation" (Miller and Owens 2008:16-17).

This account could easily be dismissed as exaggerated, fabricated, or even delusional, but the inclusion of imported dialogue may produce just the opposite effect. Gale Miller and Erica Owens (2008) argue that the use of what they similarly refer to as "constructed dialogue" serves to authenticate what might otherwise be questionable claims to have spoken with God. Constructed dialogue, they contend, is a rhetorical device consisting of utterances that appear to literally report the speech of one's self or others who may or may not be physically present in ongoing social interactions (Tannen 1986, 1989). Elsewhere this has been called "reported speech" (Wooffitt 1992), "replayings" (Goffman 1974), "embedded speech" (Goffman 1981), and "active voicing" (Wooffitt 1992). Such utterances are expressed as literal quotations of one's own or others' actual words that have presumably been communicated in other conversations (Bergman 1993).

According to Miller and Owens, imported dialogue enhances the genuineness of accounts by animating speakers' descriptions (Goffman 1974) and vicariously importing real time into interpretations of the circumstances (Bergman 1993). Speakers use imported dialogue to invite listeners to vicariously engage events and conversations that took place elsewhere, and to treat them as eye witness experiences, not merely reports of those experiences. In this instance, it is especially noteworthy that the speaker quotes God, her therapist, and herself in the course of the narrative. This lays claim to close, nuanced knowledge of what all parties to the situation were saying, both ordinary and cosmic conversational partners. The imported dialogue supplies intimate detail of the reported conversations, detail that only an insider or actual partner to the dialogue could have recounted. By using direct quotations, the speaker conveys the sense that the talk did, in fact, take place, and was not imagined or fabricated. In addition, God's participation is cast as no more or less extraordinary or incredible than that of the therapist. Thus a kind of naturalness—a veridical taken-for-grantedness—is invoked without justification, offering up the extraordinary as just-one-more feature of being there (Woofitt 1992).

Showing True Commitment

When authenticity is considered in relation to identity, one's "true self" may be at issue. Authenticity work can involve showing that identity claims reflect true commitments, actual feelings or conditions of the heart, not simply overtures to fashion, social pressure, or momentary preferences. Consider the following extract where a member of a youth subculture was questioned about his identity as a "rocker." "R" is the respondent and "I" the interviewer; the transcript has been simplified for readability.

> I: When and how did you get into being a rocker?
>
> R: It must have been when I was about fourteen or fifteen, some friends at school were
>
> I: mmhm
>
> R: an they-an I said oh heavy metal's rubbish, they said nah it's not an they gave me some tapes to listen to an I did enjoy it, did like it ... and that's when I s-sort of started getting into it. Before I sort of liked things like Duran Duran and Spandau Ballet. Huh hh
>
> I: mmhmm and then I [mean how-
>
> R: [but that's cos I hadn't heard heavy metal you see (Widdicombe and Wooffitt 1995:140-141).

Sue Widdicombe and Robin Wooffitt (1995) suggest that this is an instance where the respondent has been challenged to defend his identity as an authentic rocker, as opposed to, say, a mere follower of musical fad. Widdicombe and Wooffitt note that the respondent initially indicates that he said "Oh heavy metal's rubbish." In doing so, the respondent acknowledges that coming to like it was against his initial predisposition. The authenticity of his claim to be a rocker is further underscored by the use of imported dialogue, as the respondent directly quotes himself in conversation with others. He goes on to say that he hadn't liked heavy metal before because he "hadn't heard [it]." The work being done here effectively conveys that the respondent did not take on the rocker identity simply to follow his friends, but did so because of the quality of the music itself. He did genuinely enjoy it and eventually got "into it." His commitment to being a heavy metal rocker is portrayed as genuine, as the respondent demonstrates that his decision to switch has gone against prior preferences. Again, supplying detail is important in authenticating the process of change, as is the sequencing of events that essentially "inoculates" the respondent against accusations of succumbing to peer pressure (Potter 1996).

Auspices of Authenticity

Authenticity work is not conducted in a circumstantial vacuum. It takes place in particular situations and settings. To a greater or lesser degree, circumstances present distinctive standards for claiming and accepting the authentic. While forms of authenticity work such as those just described are always operating, the places where this work unfolds offer up preferred senses of the genuine. What may be taken as a genuine in one circumstance, such as the proverbial crying in one's beer in a tavern, may be viewed as unacceptable in a situation in which crying is viewed as a diversion from the heart of the matter in view. Similarly, in Gubrium's (1992) comparative ethnography of two family therapy programs, crying and other ostensibly heartfelt expressions of feeling were taken to be genuine in the program whose orientation to domestic troubles centered on open communication, but it was shunned if not disparaged in the other program, whose therapeutic mission was based on no-nonsense hierarchies of authority. Authenticity work operated in both programs, but in relation to distinctly different understandings of expressive genuineness.

A Separate Dimension

If the gathered reporters Dowd wrote about commented on Hillary Clinton's apparent tears and, in the process, communicatively worked on the tears' authenticity, we also were told that this transpired in a newsroom. The prevailing warrant for genuineness centered in this case on its newsworthiness and political meaning. While it may be clear in this instance, it is important to point out that the auspices of authenticity are not always apparent in talk and interaction. Recall that it was Dowd who told the reader that the exchanges were taking place in a newsroom (office) and that the speakers were reporters. This adds to issues of everyday authenticity in its own right, because a different corpus of empirical material has entered into the mix, namely, ethnographic knowledge of the circumstances of the exchanges. This brings the *whats* of everyday authenticity into the picture.

The auspices of authenticity work vary widely in contemporary society, the operating criteria of which range from circumstances whose standards are rooted in sentiments, thoughts, and actions, to those with preferences based on religion, science, or even magic. The apparently genuine emotional expression taken to be authentic under the auspices of one setting may turn into a ruse for what the "real thoughts and actions of the matter" are in another, the former having invoked religion, say, and the latter science. Whether or not such invocations are religiously or scientifically justified, their everyday uses provide authenticity warrants in their own right (Hammersley 2008:120-121).

The Broad Range of Auspices

Extensive fieldwork has focused on authenticity work that transpires in institutional settings and we will take up an example of this shortly (see Gubrium and Holstein 2001). But it bears emphasizing that authenticity work is socially ubiquitous and takes place across the diverse nooks and crannies of everyday life, from schools and reformatories, to kitchens, playgrounds, and street corners. This was made apparent long ago in Clifford Shaw's (1930) study of a delinquent boy he called "Stanley," whose "own story" was presented in Shaw's book *The Jack-Roller*. In the book, Stanley informs us that the genuine criminal in his social world is no small fry, so to speak. Among his fellow inmates at the reformatory where he did time and on the neighborhood street corners where he hung out, the genuine "crook" was someone who engaged in serious crime. Because Stanley was only a petty thief, his authenticity as a consequential member of this peer group was constantly in question. Under the auspices of the reformatory or the street corner, Stanley's identity lacked the mark of authenticity expected in these settings. No amount of authenticity work on Stanley's part readily moved him into the big leagues. Stanley puts it this way, virtually pointing to the standards in place at Pontiac, the reformatory in which he did time:

> So I listened with open ears to what was said in these groups of prisoners. Often I stood awe-struck as tales of adventure in crime were related, and I took it in with interest. Somehow I wanted to go out and do the same thing myself. To myself I thought I was somebody to be doing a year at Pontiac [reformatory], but in these groups of older prisoners I felt ashamed because I couldn't tell tales of daring exploits about my crimes. I hadn't done anything of consequence. I compared myself with the older crooks and saw how little and insignificant I was in a criminal line. But deep in my heart I knew that I was only a kid and couldn't be expected to have a reputation yet. I couldn't tell about my charge, for it savored of petty thievery, and everybody looked down on a petty thief in Pontiac (108-109).

Later in the book, we learn from Stanley that the auspices of the street corner deployed similar identity preferences. Stanley may have literally been a street criminal and convict, but his "street cred" was minimal in the haunts of "real" criminals.

The Substantive Control of Authenticity

Institutions of various kinds can provide the formal contours for everyday authenticity as well as the practical controls over what is taken to be authentic. If operating preferences for conduct and, by implication, for authenticity, have been identified for places such as neighborhoods and street corners (e.g., see Anderson 1999; Whyte 1943), formally organized institutions substantively underscore expectations for what is authentic. We do not mean that the institutional auspices of authenticity are more compelling than those of informal settings in asserting standards and consequences for what is or isn't viewed as authentic. Indeed, Elijah Anderson's (1999) ethnography of the "code of the street" suggests quite the opposite. Anderson shows that locally inauthentic performances in neighborhood settings can lead to violence, even death, in the circumstances. The formality of authenticity controls, however, is greater in organizations, where the authentic and the inauthentic is specified in explicit directives, texts, the job descriptions, and in formal decision-making schemes (see Young 1995; Fox 2001:176-192).

Gubrium's (1986) ethnographic research on the descriptive organization of senility brings the significance of institutional auspices into bold relief in this way. In his fieldwork in Alzheimer's disease caregiver support groups, Gubrium heard many accounts of "what it's like" to become senile and "what it's like" to care for a loved one who is losing a mind. The accounts were continually evaluated for their genuineness. Of particular interest was how the newly emergent auspices of the Alzheimer's Disease Association (ADA)—a national organization promoting research and sponsoring local chapters and self-help groups for caregivers—shaped the substantive meaning of the disease for family members, especially the meaning of heartfelt concern and authentic caregiving.

The early 1980s were a time of transition in understanding cognitive impairment in old age. There was a sea change in the offing, from the view that senility was a normal part of aging, to the medical view that cognitive impairment was a disease. Stories told early in this period had dramatically different meanings and consequences than similar stories told later on. Early on, under the auspices of the normal aging model, stories of senility were accounts of woe, inevitability, and acceptance. Later, under the emerging auspices of the medicalized view, which the ADA promoted, there was woe to be sure, but it was combined with the search for a cure and the hope for recovery. As far as the caregiver was concerned, as the overall view of senility shifted, genuine caregiving changed from something one owed to aged love ones and simply did, to something with distinct phases of adaptation. For many, passage through the stages needed to be embraced "for everyone's sake." This had a bearing on what genuine caregiving became, altering the substantive criterion for authentic accounts of experiences that more or less accorded with the emerging understanding that caregiving had particular experiential parameters.

The various support groups Gubrium observed, which included ADA as well as non-ADA sponsored groups, struck him as quite different in the application of criteria for genuine caregiving. Some groups, especially those sponsored by the ADA, preferred highly formulaic renditions of the caregiving experience that accorded with the new understanding (cf. Loseke 2001). The ADA distributed voluminous promotional literature to local chapters that described the "characteristics" of dementia and the "stages" of caregiving, which support group participants read and shared. There were other groups—more likely to be independent—in which no particular version of these matters was valued over others. In the former groups, what rang true was articulated in more or less detail according to the ADA formula. Compelling accounts of the caregving experience tended to follow a stage-like script of what one "goes through" in the process. This combined with a stage-like understanding of what happens in time to the care receiver. In contrast, in the independent groups, participants were generally satisfied to simply and often emotionally compare notes and experiences, learning from each other about themselves and about the progress of afflicted loved ones' disease experience. Narratives in these groups emerged in terms of what social psychologists call a "social comparison process," where meaning making develops with the flow of individual comparisons rather than in terms of an overarching framework (see Festinger 1954).

In the ADA groups, infractions of local understandings were quickly noted and often textually substantiated. For example, on one occasion in one of the ADA-sponsored groups, a participant offered what Gubrium initially viewed as a rather detailed and engaging account of her husband's growing forgetfulness and her associated caregiving experience. Her authenticity work was palpable. This was followed by heartfelt comments on the need to be valiantly devoted to the care of Alzheimer's disease sufferers because of the disease's relentless ravages. As an outsider, Gubrium was absorbed by how true-to-life the story sounded, in its detail and depth. He could only think, "Yes, she's been through it; she knows what it's like firsthand. One could learn a great deal from her experience." But participants' responses showed that the authentic account in such groups doesn't take this shape, as seemingly truthful, engaging, and detailed as it otherwise seemed to be. What group members wanted to hear instead were truthful and engaging stories that accorded with a preferred experiential timeline, one paralleling Elisabeth Kübler-Ross's (1969) popular stage model of the dying process. Time and again, participants were cautioned and cautioned each other that there were distinctive aspects to caregiver adaptation. Caregivers whose accounts challenged the view that the caregiver "goes through stages of this thing" were considered to be "denying" the real story, which was seen as a distinct stage of adaptation. In such groups' formulation of the authentic story, accounts of unceasing devotion—as detailed and mundanely embedded as they were—were viewed as delusional, echoing what many ADA brochures, chapter newsletters, and facilitators conveyed about the Alzheimer's experience.

The substantive control of authenticity not only was encountered in challenges to such accounts, as they were in the neighborhoods Whyte and Anderson studied, but were referenced and could be read in texts well before and long after an account transpired. A participant could, in effect, gain knowledge of preferred authenticities without the actual experience of sharing accounts. The everyday truth of the matter in ADA-sponsored support groups was that one was being infinitely more realistic about the caregiving experience if one admitted that there were limits to devotion (a stage of the caregiving experience). This meant that, in time, one needed to think about oneself, the burden of care on the family as a whole, and should seriously consider nursing home placement for the afflicted (another stage of the process). Under the auspices of these groups, such preferred accounts were locally evident in both speech and text, as one or another participant read brochures about stages monitored utterances for how well they reflected the formula story surrounding what it meant to be an authentic caregiver.

In time, Gubrium's research informed him that the everyday authenticity of accounts needed to be figured in relation to its diverse auspices. In everyday life, authenticity cannot be evaluated in terms of fixed criteria. Abstract or decontextualized standards of genuineness don't tell us much about how authenticity operates in practice, nor about the substantive controls in place. As matters of local preference, authentic accounts were not just skillfully told and appreciated or discounted, but related to the auspices of authenticity work. As a consequence, Gubrium found that there were diverse local possibilities for being authentic in the matter of caring and providing care.

In their own way, caregivers themselves shared and understood the diversity. On one occasion in the field, a caregiver made a poignant and analytically telling remark that echoed delinquent Stanley's sensitivity to the auspices of authentic criminality. The caregiver was a participant in one of the relatively informal support groups Gubrium was observing. Commenting on the support group she had attended across town and comparing it to the group she now frequented and preferred, the caregiver flagged what was genuine for her:

> I just can't bear to go there [across town] anymore. All I heard there was stage one, stage two, and take the next step. Here, the stories you hear sound more like what I'm going through. I learn more from that and it makes me feel better (Gubrium 1986, fieldnotes).

In one narrative stroke, the remark pointed to the reflexive interface of authenticity work and its auspices (see Gubrium and Holstein 2009). The caregiver recognized that auspices matter in composing and responding to accounts and chose to alter the challenges to the accountability of her own story, thereby effecting its everyday authenticity. The upshot of this as far as auspices are concerned is that the control asserted by organizational or circumstantial auspices may be substantial, but it is not irresistible.

Conclusion

To expect a final answer to the question of what is genuine or authentic is to expect the impossible in practice. Standards, generalized criteria, or codes are not fixed in everyday life, even while they are perennially invoked in talk and social interaction. As D. Lawrence Wieder (1974) demonstrated in his pioneering study of the everyday operation of the convict code in a halfway house for drug offenders, standards of accountability, including what is truthful or genuine, are resources for, not determinants of, the everyday work of authenticity. In everyday life, authenticity should not be viewed as hovering above and monitoring experience. Rather it is a rhetorical touchstone for constructing and responding to the real in relation to persons, actions, and events. In this context, assessments of authenticity center on the question of what is genuine enough in the circumstances in which it arises. This requires an aesthetics that draws inspiration from the local preferences and the work of authenticity. To say "that's really genuine" is as much a reflexive measure of situated utility as it is a judgment about authenticity in its own right. Universalized standards that operate as a research orientation eclipse the operating esthetics of everyday life.

In today's world, with its remarkably diverse auspices of authenticity, the possibilities for being genuine, authentic, or inauthentic are more extensive than ever. There are more kinds of accounts, more circumstances, and more preferences about an increasing number of matters of "realness" than ever before. The *in situ* analysis of everyday authenticity work spotlights this expansive, complex landscape. It informs us that the moral horizons of the genuine are more intricate and variegated than they ever have been. This means, of course, that authenticity is perennially "up for grabs" in our everyday lives. Moreover, as the authentic is increasingly commodified—for everyday consumption as well as commercial profit—it risks being seen as increasingly "synthetic" (Cloud 2008). This implies burgeoning possibilities for the production of the "fake-real" (Gilmore and Pine 2007), the working genuineness of a postmodern environment.

While most of us are aware of such fabrication in the world of product marketing, advertising, and increasingly everywhere, this does not necessarily warrant wholehearted cynicism vis-à-vis the authenticities of everyday life. When it comes to everyday selves and experience, the distinction between the real and the concocted is blurred as an integral part of the world we live in. The de-differentiation (Lash 1990) of reality and its representations that characterizes postmodernity is especially germane with respect to authenticity. As a product of situated interpretive practice (see Gubrium and Holstein 1997; Holstein and Gubrium 2000), the authentic is constantly at stake throughout the course of interaction. What is and is not authentic is always a locally practical matter, presenting authenticity as an everyday concern with what is circumstantially relevant and useful.

References

Anderson, Elijah. 1999. *Code of the Street: Decency, Violence and the Moral Life of the Inner City*. New York: Norton.

Bergmann, Jörg R. 1993. *Discreet Indiscretions: The Social Organization of Gossip*. Translated by J. Bednarz, John. Hawthorne, NY: Aldine de Gruyter.

Cloud, John. 2008. "Synthetic Authenticity." *Time*, March 14, Pp. 53-54.

Festinger, Leon. 1954. "A Theory of Social Comparison Processes." *Human Relations*, 7:117-140.

Foucault, Michel. 1977. *Discipline and Punish*. New York: Vintage.

Fox, Kathryn J. 2001. "Self-Change and Resistance in Prison." Pp. 176-192 in *Institutional Selves: Troubled Identities in a Postmodern World*, edited by Jaber F. Gubrium and James A. Holstein. New York: Oxford University Press.

Garfinkel, Harold. 1967. *Studies in Ethnomethodology*. Englewood Cliffs, NY: Prentice-Hall.

Geertz, Clifford. 1988. *Works and Lives: The Anthropologist as Author*. Stanford, CA: Stanford University Press.

Gilmore, James H. and B. Joseph Pine. 2007. *Authenticity: What Consumers Really Want.* Boston: Harvard Business School Press.

Goffman, Erving. 1959. *The Presentation of Self in Everyday Life*. New York: Doubleday.

Goffman, Erving. 1974. *Frame Analysis*. New York: Harper.

Goffman, Erving. 1981. *Forms of Talk*. Philadelphia: University of Pennsylvania Press.

Goodwin, Charles. 1984. "Notes on Story Structure and the Organization of Participation." Pp. 225-246 in *Structures of Social Action,* edited by J Maxwell Atkinson and John Heritage. Cambridge, UK: Cambridge University Press.

Gubrium, Jaber F. 1986. *Oldtimers and Alzheimer's*. Greenwich, CT: JAI Press.

Gubrium, Jaber F. 1992. *Out of Control: Family Therapy and Domestic Disorder*. Thousand Oaks, CA: Sage.

Gubrium, Jaber F. and James A. Holstein (eds.) 2001. *Institutional Selves: Troubled Identities in a Postmodern World.* New York: Oxford University Press.

Gubrium, Jaber F. and James A. Holstein. 2009. *Analyzing Narrative Reality*. Thousand Oaks, CA: Sage.

Hammersley, Martyn. 2008. *Questioning Qualitative Inquiry*. London: Sage.

Haspel, Kathleen C. 2007. "Order from Chaos: The Sensemaking Structure and Therapeutic Function of Mediated Eyewitness Accounts of the September 11th Attacks." *American Communication Journal*, 1:1, http://www.acjournal.org/holdings/vol9/spring/articles/sensemaking.html.

Holstein, James A. and Jaber F. Gubrium. 2000. *The Self We Live By: Narrative Identity in a Postmodern World.* New York: Oxford University Press.

Holstein, James A. and Jaber F. Gubrium. 2008. *Handbook of Constructionist Research.* New York: Guilford Publishers.

Hyvärinen, Matti. 2008. "Analyzing Narratives and Story-Telling." Pp. 447-460 in *The Sage Handbook of Social Research Methods*, edited by Pertti Alasuutari, Leonard Bickman and Julia Brannen. London: Sage.

Kübler-Ross, Elisabeth. 1969. *On Death and Dying*. New York: Macmillan.

Lash, Scott. 1990. *Sociology of Postmodernism*. London: Routledge.

Loseke, Donileen. 2001. "Lived Realities and Formula Stories of 'Battered Women'." Pp. 107-126 in *Institutional Selves: Troubled Identities in a*

Postmodern World, edited by Jaber F. Gubrium and James A. Holstein. New York: Oxford University Press.

Miller, Gale and Erica Owens. 2008. "Constructed Dialog in Troubles Talk." Unpublished manuscript. Milwaukee, WI: Marquette University.

Peterson, Richard A. 1997. *Creating Country Music: Fabricating Authenticity*. Chicago: University of Chicago Press.

Peterson, Richard A. 2005. "In Search of Authenticity." *Journal of Management Studies* 42:1083-1098.

Poch, Bruce. 2007. "The Search for Authenticity." *Newsweek* August 20/27, p. 59.

Potter, Jonathan. 1996. *Representing Reality: Discourse, Rhetoric and Social Construction*. London: Sage.

Sacks, Harvey. 1992a. *Lectures on Conversation*, Vol. I. Oxford: Blackwell.

Sacks, Harvey. 1992b. *Lectures on Conversation*, Vol. II. Oxford: Blackwell.

Shaw, Clifford R. 1930. *The Jack-Roller: A Delinquent Boy's Own Story*. Chicago: University of Chicago Press.

Tannen, Deborah. 1986. "Introducing Constructed Dialogue in Greek and American Conversational and Literary Narrative." Pp. 311-332 in *Direct and Indirect Speech*, edited by F. Coulmas. Berlin: Moutin de Gruyter.

Tannen, Deborah. 1989. *Talking Voices: Repetition, Dialogue, and Imagery in Conversational Discourse*. Cambridge: Cambridge University Press.

Trilling, Lionel. 1972. *Sincerity and Authenticity*. Cambridge, MA: Harvard University Press.

Vannini, Phillip. 2006. "Dead Poets' Society: Teaching, Publish-or-Perish, and Professors' Experiences of Authenticity." *Symbolic Interaction* 29:235–257.

Whyte, William Foote. 1943. *Street Corner Society: The Social Structure of an Italian Slum*. Chicago: University of Chicago Press.

Widdicombe, Sue and Robin Wooffitt. 1995. *The Language of Youth Subcultures*. London: Harvester Wheatsheaf.

Wieder, D. Lawrence. 1988. *Language and Social Reality*. Landham, MD: University Press of America.

Wooffitt, Robin. 1992. *Telling Tales of the Unexpected: The Organization of Factual Discourse*. London: Harvester Wheatsheaf.

Young, Allan. 1995. *The Harmony of Illusions: Inventing Post-Traumatic Stress Disorder*. Princeton, NJ: Princeton University Press.

Zimmerman, Don H. and Melvin Pollner. 1970. "The Everyday World as a Phenomenon." Pp. 80-104 in *Understanding Everyday Life*, edited by J. Douglas. Chicago: Aldine.

Chapter 9

We Wear the Mask: Subordinated Masculinity and the Persona Trap

Michael Schwalbe

I met Matthew Mason and Anthony Atwater in the fall of 1995 while interviewing men for a book on fathers and sons. At that time, Mason and Atwater lived two doors apart in a low-income public housing complex in Chapel Hill, North Carolina. I was a middle-aged white professor, born and raised in the North. They were older, working-class black men who had grown up in the segregated South. Intrigued by their lives and personalities, I wrote a dual biography about them, *Remembering Reet and Shine: Two Black Men, One Struggle* (Schwalbe 2004).

Mason was born in 1911 to a sharecropping family. The Masons worked halves for the same white family that had once owned Mason's grandfather, and from whom Mason's great-grandfather had taken the Mason name. When the sharecropping arrangement ended in the 1920s, Mason, still a boy, had moved to Chapel Hill. In 1934 he began what became a 60-year relationship with an all-white fraternity at the University of North Carolina–Chapel Hill. His job was originally called "houseboy."

Mason's duties included cleaning, serving meals, stoking the furnace, and running errands. Over time, however, Mason's charm and wit brought him into a close relationship with the fraternity boys. He became a beloved character, "Dr. Reet," whose antics and memories made him, as one older fraternity member put it, a living legend in the fraternity's history. I wondered about the complexities of his relationship to the fraternity, through the eras of segregation and civil rights, and into the present.

Atwater was born in 1933 and had lived, or so it seemed, a different kind of life. He had never held any job for long, his alcoholism making him an unreliable worker. In his 50s he had taken up smoking crack cocaine. His drinking, drug use, and abusive behavior had alienated him from his family and most of his erstwhile friends. When I met him he lived alone, surviving on a small disability payment, deriving companionship from street people (mainly young women) who used his apartment as a place to party and crash. Despite all this, Atwater could laugh at his foibles and the shambles of his life.

Atwater struck me as an intelligent man who could have, under other conditions, done or been anything he wanted. I wondered how his potential had been squandered and how his life had gone awry. In his stories, he cast himself not only as a victim of racism, but as a man who was doubly beaten down because he had tried to fight back. I also wondered about Atwater's self-proclaimed transformation from "Shine"—a flashy hoodlum and skilled lover—to his current incarnation as "Popcorn"—a mellow, though still lusty, streetwise sage.

I expected the project to take about two years. After one year, I realized that I had miscalculated, though not because I needed more time to gather biographical information. It was, rather, a matter of realizing that the story I was best situated to tell was unfolding in front of me. This was the story of how the men dealt with being poor, old, and in decline—a story that had one natural ending. And so I followed Atwater's life for about four and a half years before he died in 2000, and Mason's life for about six and half years before he died in 2002.

My earliest impression of how Mason and Atwater were different, aside from age, was that Mason had accommodated to the racism of his day, while Atwater had resisted it. Later, I came to see that both men had accommodated and resisted, and both had paid a price, in similar ways. The key to the similarity lay not just in the alcoholism both men suffered during long periods of their lives. It was, once again, right in front of me: their personas of "Shine/Popcorn" and "Dr. Reet."

I wrote *Remembering Reet and Shine* as narrative nonfiction for a general audience. The analysis in the book stays mainly between the lines. Here I want to draw out part of the analysis more sharply, focusing on the "one struggle" that Mason and Atwater shared. Their struggle, against the constraints of racism and class oppression, was to live authentically as men.

The lives of many men in subordinated groups are characterized by similar struggles to live authentically, without masks worn to please more powerful others. This in itself isn't news; in fact, one could argue that struggles for authenticity are endemic to all social hierarchies, and that Mason and Atwater are just familiar examples. Yet there is something less often seen that an examination of these men's lives can reveal: how a protective persona can become a self-destructive trap. We can also see how a dominant group provides the seductive personas that help to perpetuate inequality.

The Emergence of Shine and Dr. Reet

William Burness Atwater Jr. was born on April 3, 1933. He was, as it turned out, the only child of an unhappy marriage. His father was a brick mason—a good trade for an uneducated southern black man of his era. His mother, the oldest daughter of a prematurely widowed tobacco farmer, had married William Sr. to escape the drudgery of the farm and the burden of responsibility for raising her younger siblings. Marriage got her off the farm, but she then had to contend with William Sr.'s inclinations to drink, gamble, and carouse.

"Burness," as he was first called, was an undersized and precocious child. He earned A's in school and sometimes did homework for his slower peers. He was fascinated by bridges and dreamed of becoming an engineer. In the summers, Burness worked on his grandfather's tobacco farm, picking immature leaves and tobacco worms off the plants. On hot days he swam naked in the creek with his older cousins, feeling ashamed of his small body. He prayed to God to give him a big dick. He also decided that farming was harder work than he ever wanted to do.

When he was nine, one of his uncles nicknamed him "Shine," supposedly because of his bright brown eyes. His parents and others of his parents' generation still called him Burness, and would always do so. His peers started calling him Shine, and most would continue to do so until the end. Even though he was formally William Jr., his mother never called him that, using "Burness" to symbolically distance the boy from his father. "Shine" she didn't like, either.

In the summer of his thirteenth year, Atwater worked part time at a sawmill with his father and uncle. This was a world where men smoked and swore and talked of drinking, gambling, fighting, and chasing women. Induction into this masculine world pulled Atwater away from his mother and toward his father. It did not, however, lead him to see much value in physical labor. As with his experience on the tobacco farm, the sawmill led Atwater to think that there had to be easier ways to make a living.

He continued to do well in school, until his sixteenth year. That year Atwater's parents bought a car that was supposed to be used to take an aging grandparent to and from church. The mistake was letting Atwater drive the car to school. Lunch-time rides with friends sometimes took the whole afternoon. Atwater's grades fell and he barely finished enough days of school to advance to the next grade. He also began to develop a reputation as a troublemaker. It didn't help that puberty had answered Atwater's prayers for a robust reproductive anatomy and made him an object of curiosity to older women.

Though he still occasionally did homework for his friends, Atwater began to disinvest in school. The segregated school he attended used out-of-date books handed down from the white schools. Atwater also saw that black folks who went to school and got degrees often got no better jobs than black folks who didn't go to school. What, then, was the point of school, Atwater thought, if whitey wasn't going to let him get ahead anyway?

After high school he spent a year doing odd jobs, helping his father with construction projects, before joining the army. Atwater thought he might try college afterwards, letting Uncle Sam foot the bill. A pregnancy resulting from a one-night stand complicated things. Atwater married the young woman before deploying to Korea. Soon thereafter a friend wrote Atwater to say that his new wife was having an affair. Atwater was upset and wanted to go home to "set things right," but the army wouldn't give him leave.

By Atwater's account, he had been a spit-and-polish soldier. But when the army wouldn't let him go home and check on his wife, he began to drink heavily, act up, and disobey orders. Eventually this earned him time in the stockade and a bad conduct discharge. When he got out of the service in 1955, he planned to go home and kill his allegedly disloyal wife. He didn't, as it turned out, and ended up having another son by her.

Still, Atwater felt that his life plans were ruined. He had wanted to use the GI Bill to go to college and become an engineer. But due to the poor math education in his high school, he needed two years of remedial work just to get into college. He was daunted by this requirement and depressed by the state of his marriage. When he drank heavily, he was not a reliable worker and couldn't hold a job. He also became violent. Despite attempts to mend the relationship, his wife got a restraining order to keep him away from her and their sons.

At this point, Atwater began to cultivate an image as a hoodlum and tough, hard-drinking lover. "Shine" was no longer just a nickname; now it was the name of a character Atwater fashioned for himself. Shine was, as Atwater put it, "wide open"—pursuing pleasure in drinking and sex, with little regard for the consequences. Shine dressed stylishly and, if affronted, didn't use his fists. "I was too small to do much dukin," Atwater said. "So I carried a knife. I liked to cut 'em and see 'em bleed. In those days, I didn't play around."

Drawing on the skills he'd learned from his father, Atwater worked sporadically in construction, doing masonry and laying concrete. Several times when he and his father worked for the same company, William Sr. mistakenly received and cashed William Jr.'s paychecks, so Atwater changed his first name to Anthony. When he was fired from construction jobs, he found menial jobs to tide him over. He never settled into a career, owned a home, or remarried after his wife divorced him in 1970.

Atwater's pattern over the years was to get drunk and cause trouble locally, then move away—to New York or DC—or go hoboing for a while, before moving back to Chapel Hill and hoping that all would be forgotten or forgiven. In his worst times in the early 1970s, he was, as one old friend put it, "down to a street wino." After multiple detox attempts over the years, Atwater had managed to quit drinking. Never able to quit smoking (he'd started at six), emphysema had sapped his strength and limited his mobility. "By the time you came around," Atwater told me, "Shine was long dead."

The Atwater I met in 1995 was known on the street as "Popcorn," or just "PC." Popcorn, Atwater told me, was an old man who had gained wisdom by suffering the hardships of addiction and street life. This was wisdom he now generously shared with people in similar straits. "They appreciate what I can teach them," he said. "Once they've been to the School of the PC, ain't no one can take advantage of them." Popcorn was not, however, a saint or a monk. He smoked crack occasionally, and sometimes traded crack for sexual favors from the young women upon whom he bestowed his sage advice.

* * *

Matthew Mason was born on June 4, 1911. His father, William Arthur "Chain" Mason, worked halves, a typical sharecropping arrangement (half the net value of the crop went to the landowner, half to the tenant farmer), for Tom Mason, the heir to the white family that had, before the Civil War, owned the black Masons.

Matthew's mother, Connie Nunn, was from one of the few black landowning families in the area. Her father, Richard Nunn, at one time owned seventy-two acres of prime farm land. The land was later lost during the Depression.

After Tom Mason died and the old plantation was sold to pay debts, the black Masons moved off the land they had been tied to for over 120 years. Young Matthew spent a year working at a tobacco factory in Durham, then moved to Chapel Hill in 1924, earning money by cleaning houses and yards. Later, he got a job as a dishwasher in a restaurant. When he was able to get his sister a job at the same restaurant, the whole family moved to town. It was 1929.

In 1931 Mason married his first wife, Fannie. She was better educated than Mason—ninth grade to his second grade—and though her father had been a notorious bootlegger, other members of her family had gone to college. At one time she too aspired to attend college, but the birth of a child out of wedlock when she was seventeen leveled her aspirations. When Mason came along, she saw a handsome, jovial, hard-working, church-going man who seemed likely to be a good partner in tough economic times.

After a year of washing dishes, Mason was promoted to waiter. Among the customers he served were members of the Phi Delta Theta fraternity. Impressed by Mason's good humor and ability to remember their names, the boys asked him to work at the fraternity house. The pay was about the same—twelve dollars a week. But to Mason it seemed like a step up, with the advantage of a less hectic work pace than in the restaurant. And so, on the Monday after Mother's Day in 1934, Matthew Mason began his job as "houseboy."

In his new job Mason served meals, cleaned, ran errands, and stoked the furnace before dawn so the house would be warm when the boys woke up. Sometimes the boys found it hard to get out of bed for morning classes. When they learned that Mason could read, they began leaving notes for him. "Matthew, get me up for my 8:00 class. Use water if necessary," a note might say. This began what evolved into a playful ritual in which Mason tried to shag the boys out of bed, and the boys resisted.

In addition to his daily chores, Mason also served the boys and their dates at parties and dances. These were welcome opportunities to earn tips and tote home leftover food. Although he occasionally helped the boys procure alcohol, Mason was not known to drink on the job during his early years at the fraternity. Despite the friendly tone that characterized his relationship with the fraternity boys, it was an era in which it was wise for a black man to keep his wits about him around his white employers.

Soon after the United States entered WWII in 1941, Mason, like many men of his age, tried to enlist in the army. He and five of his buddies signed up and reported to Fort Bragg for their pre-induction physicals. Mason's flat feet and shuffling, slue-footed gait disqualified him. On the way back to Chapel Hill, Mason's buddies teased him mercilessly. Although the rejection might have saved his life, it stung no less. Mason got drunk for three days.

By 1944 veterans began returning to school and altering campus life. The old rules of decorum seemed infantilizing to young men who had been in the military and perhaps risked their lives in combat. A drinking culture flourished and parties became more raucous. When young veterans returned to the fraternity house, they were eager to hoist a few in celebration of their safe return. Matthew Mason was invited to join in. Even if he had sat out the war, when the bottle was passed he could be one of the boys.

Around this time Mason acquired a new nickname (the boys had previously called him "Sunshine"). With a few drinks and some egging-on, Mason could be made to buck dance and sing at parties. One of the fraternity boys, reminded of a floor-show comedian he had seen in New York, dubbed Mason "Reeter Skeeter." This was usually shortened to "Reet." Later, another boy, impressed by one of Mason's alcohol-fueled performances, said he deserved a promotion—to "*Doctor* Reet." The name stuck.

If Mason occasionally drank too much at parties and came home tipsy, it seemed like a small price to pay for a good employment relationship. The fraternity boys felt genuine affection for Mason, tipping him generously when he performed tasks that went beyond his usual duties. Some of the boys grew close to Mason and his family, often staying to eat dinner when they went to pay Fannie for washing and ironing their shirts. In the early 1950s the boys devised an initiation ritual for Mason and made him an honorary brother.

Years earlier, in 1935, Matthew and Fannie had bought a small house in one of Chapel Hill's black neighborhoods. Mason took pride in owning a home. He built additions and kept the house in good shape, sometimes taking out small loans to pay for materials. Around the time he was being made an honorary brother, Mason's house needed foundation repair. It was a bigger job than Mason could do himself, and so he took out a second mortgage to pay to have the work done. Unable to repay the loan, he lost the house.

Although Mason felt terrible about being reduced to renting, he was still, after all, Dr. Reet. He had by then been with the fraternity for 20 years. He knew hundreds of brothers and could call them by name when they returned to campus for ball games and special events. He knew how to make them feel welcome and at home, and they showed their appreciation by raising a glass with Dr. Reet. With his bawdy toasts, off-color jokes, drunken antics, and trove of stories, Dr. Reet had already become a historical fixture in the fraternity's culture.

The drinking, however, accelerated, going beyond parties and special events. Now Dr. Reet might be found passed out in the coal bin, or at the bottom of the stairs. Or he might not show up to work for days. Tensions grew at home. Mason's wife and children would berate him for spending so much time with the boys and for drinking so much. The boys, too, would get scolded when they brought Dr. Reet home drunk. When Fannie died suddenly of a cerebral hemorrhage in 1963, Mason was inconsolable. He drank more, every day.

About a year later, in August, 1964, Mason remarried. His second wife, Martha, helped him recover financially. A non-drinker herself, she fought to get

Mason off the bottle. In 1972, Mason was hospitalized after being found in an alcohol-induced coma. Martha had left him at the time, because of his drinking, and he knew she wouldn't come back unless he quit. "When Matthew called to tell me he'd quit," Martha recalled, "his voice sounded different. Something told me I could believe him this time. I put a note in the collection basket and asked the minister to pray for Matthew, and he never drank again after that."

Mason semi-retired from the fraternity that year, no longer doing the twice-a-day meal serving and heavy cleaning he had done for almost 40 years. He continued to rouse the boys in the morning, do light cleaning (with Martha's help), serve at special events, and help train the new pledges. Into his early 80s he visited the fraternity house once a week to eat dinner with the boys. Twice a week they brought meals to him and Martha in their apartment. Until a few years before his death at 90, the young members, some of whose fathers and grandfathers were Phi Delts, took Dr. Reet to dinner on his birthday and tapped his memories.

The Dilemmas of Subordinated Masculinity

The lives of Mason and Atwater were profoundly shaped by the meaning of manhood in American culture. R.W. Connell (1995) argues that in every culture there is a manhood ideal, or a hegemonic form of masculinity. In US culture, the qualities associated with hegemonic masculinity include rationality, emotional self-posessession, the ability to exert control over others, potency or generativity, and heterosexual prowess. A real man signifies, through word and deed, that these qualities are natural parts of who and what he is.

Precisely how males are supposed to signify these qualities depends on age, race, ethnicity, social class, and context. The manhood act of an inner-city black teenager on a basketball court differs from the manhood act of a middle-aged white executive in a corporate boardroom. Style matters. Even so, the same core quality must be signified: a capacity to control one's self and others. Males who fail to create the impression that they possess this capacity—that they possess, in other words, an essentially masculine self—risk being discredited relative to other men.

This is not, however, *only* a matter of style. What any individual man can signify depends on the symbolic and material resources available to him, and on the signs he can credibly wield. A man with institutional authority and money can make things happen—can exert control and resist being controlled—in ways that men without such authority and resources cannot. This is why men who lack the power that comes from wealth and position often rely on physical or sexual prowess to signify manhood. Deficits in one area can be compensated for in another.

The most revered manhood act, the hegemonic ideal, may be performed by few or, in theory, no actual men. Yet it remains the standard by which all men and their self-presentations are judged. Manhood acts that fall short of the ideal are, in Connell's terms, "surbordinated masculinities." Men who perform subordinated masculinities remain identifiable as men, and can thus claim membership in the privileged gender category. But they will enjoy lower status and fewer rewards than men whose gender enactment comes closer to the hegemonic ideal.

Men who are constrained to perform subordinated masculinities—working-class men, men of color, gay men—face a dilemma. Recognizable as males, they are culturally compelled to put on a manhood act that pays homage to the hegemonic ideal. Though it can be rejected in principle, to ignore the ideal, in everyday practice, is to court the risk of being discredited—that is, being seen as incompetent, unserious, or insane—for doing gender improperly. A dilemma arises because of the confict between the expectation to signify a masculine self in accord with the hegemonic ideal, and the lack of resources necessary to do so convincingly.

The hegemonic ideal also shapes men's expectations for what they are owed by the world around them, thus creating a further dilemma. Seeing themselves as creditable men, males feel *entitled* to exert control over themselves and others. But for men locked into subordinated masculinities, this expectation is frustrated. A manhood act constructed with inadequate resources rarely yields the expected control. When the causes for this failure are ideologically obscured, the results can be self-blame and anger (Sennett and Cobb 1972; MacLeod 1995). The dilemma in this case is not merely a logical one but a painful emotional one.

As working-class black men living under a legally-sanctioned racist regime, Mason and Atwater were denied the material and symbolic resources necessary to enact the hegemonic ideal. They were thus constrained to enact a subordinated masculinity. Yet the hegemonic ideal was the standard against which they were judged and against which they judged themselves. This is the bind in which they were caught.

At one time, Atwater had dreamed of becoming an engineer. He wanted to build bridges and create useful, lasting things in the world. He wanted to be a father to his sons and do, as he once put it, "man things" with them—ball playing, fishing, and so on. He had joined the army as a way to establish his societal worth as a man and thus to receive, deservingly, the reward of monetary support for attending college. Even in his worst times, when he couldn't hold a steady job, he had at least *tried* to work and support himself.

In his masculine amibitions, Atwater was ordinary. His adolescent disdain for adult authority, his minor brawls, and his drinking were not unusual. In fact, most of Atwater's rowdy behavior, at least when he was young, did not go much beyond what is typically dismissed as a matter of boys being boys. His sexual conquests would have fallen under the same cultural rubric. Had Atwater been a (white) member of the Phi Delta Theta fraternity that employed Matthew Mason, his behavior would have been seen as normal.

Atwater's ambitions began to run aground when he saw that school would not ensure his advancement. This was not an unrealistic view. When Atwater was young, the career options for black men in the South were limited. If he went to college and stayed in North Carolina, he might become a minister or a school teacher—neither of which appealed to him. He also saw that black people who got degrees and wanted middle-class jobs had to move out of the South. Nor was he deluded about the deficits created by his second-class schooling.

Even if Atwater had been able to reconcile with his wife and moderate his drinking so that it didn't interfere with work, he might still have failed as a sole breadwinner. Few jobs in the local economy would have paid Atwater a wage adequate to support a family. His wife almost certainly would have had to work, and Atwater himself probably would have needed multiple jobs. By way of comparison, even when he worked for the fraternity, Matthew Mason at times also held jobs as a cab driver and waiter. In the college town of Chapel Hill, the working-class employment picture is much the same today.

What Atwater refused to do, though his father advised him to do it, was to scratch his head and take whatever indignities a white employer dished out. Atwater told stories of losing jobs because he snapped back at insults that other black men tolerated. Some of these stories were no doubt embellished; and no doubt Atwater's drinking was often to blame for his loss of jobs. Yet the core claims of Atwater's stories were sufficiently corroborated (by the public record and by witnesses) to make them plausible. Atwater was a proud and intelligent man with ample reasons to be angry at the world. I had no problem imagining him telling off an abusive boss.

Here again Atwater's masculine ambitions can be seen as ordinary. By his own accounting near the end of his life, he wanted to be a good father and reliable provider. He wanted the manhood status that would have come from fulfilling these roles. He also felt entitled to a fair wage and respectful treatment on the job. He wanted to be, in sum, what he understood a man should be. His weaknesses helped to undermine his ambitions, but those weaknesses were played upon by a racist society that needed to see black men fail.

Mason came closer to fulfilling his dreams. As a young man, he staked his independence on working and earning money that he could spend as he chose. When his industriousness paid off to the extent of allowing him to buy a home, it was a triumph. Even during the Depression, he and his family had enough money to get by and had extra food to share with neighbors. Within the limits of his time and place and caste, Mason did fairly well economically, for a while.

Unlike Atwater, Mason got to be a *paterfamilias*. He was, for many years, a steady provider and a playful and generous father, giving no less love to the son his wife brought to the marriage. She and Mason successfully raised six children. Among them were one school body president, two class presidents, and two valedictorians. All graduated from high school, two from college, and two from business school. For many years, Mason could feel that he had done well as a family man, supporting his dependents and equipping his children to be upwardly mobile.

Yet Mason remained yoked by a racist opportunity structure. Black men of his era were limited mainly to menial service jobs or to low-skilled labor. The subordinate status of these jobs was marked not only by low pay but often by job title. When he started at the fraternity house in 1934, Mason was twenty-three, married, and had four children. The white male undergraduate to whom he reported was called the *house manager*. It would have been unthinkable for the fraternity to employ an older white man and call him, as Mason was called, houseboy.

And while the fraternity members tipped Mason when he performed extra services or charmed them at parties, the low wages he was paid made him dependent on these discretionary disbursements. Over the years, the fraternity rescued Mason from financial scrapes on a number of occasions. But, again, this was discretionary. Mason thus remained dependent on the fraternity members' good will. As his youngest daughter put it, "If they had paid Papa an adequate wage, he wouldn't have had to go to them so often to be bailed out."

This arrangement allowed the fraternity members to see themselves as generous benefactors, not stingy employers. It also subordinated Mason as a man. Had he been paid more, he might have enjoyed the feelings of self-reliance that men learn to desire. Instead, he was forced to be an ever-needy supplicant. Little changed after Mason retired. The fraternity gave him no formal pension, but they paid his (publicly-subsidized) rent and took him meals twice a week. Mason knew that to keep these benefits coming he had to continue to show gratitude, not attitude.

World War II created a further dilemma for Mason. Before the war, Mason had a manhood edge on his young employers. He was an adult, a father, and a homeowner. His employers, though they enjoyed race and class privilege, were untested boys. But Mason's physical disabilities kept him from acquiring what became, for the next generation of American men, a principal mark of manhood: military service or, better still, combat experience. Now, despite his age and proven mettle as a father and provider, Mason's implicit manhood claims were trumped by the twenty-something veterans returning to campus after the war.

Mason's manhood deficit *vis-à-vis* his employers deepened over the next decade. Instead of becoming more financially secure as he moved into middle age, Mason remained, incongruously, an underpaid houseboy who still needed several jobs to get by and still needed financial rescuing from time to time. As he fell victim to the fraternity's drinking culture, Mason's status as a mature, self-possessed man with a stable family life became tenuous. When he lost the home he had owned for nearly twenty years, he lost much of what marked him as a man in relation to the fraternity boys, and as a creditable man in his own community.

Atwater and Mason were caught in dilemmas not of their own making. They were expected to strive to enact the hegemonic manhood ideal, or be deemed unworthy of respect as men. Atwater staked himself on toughness, sexual prowess, and resistance to being controlled by others. Mason tried to be a good father and provider. But as working-class black men in the South, they were denied the resources and opportunities necessary to achieve the hegemonic ideal. Both men responded in a way that eased the emotional pain caused by their common dilemma, but which could not resolve it and which nearly destroyed them.

The Persona Trap

A persona is more than a situational presentation of self in Goffman's (1959) sense. A persona is a set of self-presentational acts that hang together, across situations, to constitute a consistently recognizable character. In Carl Jung's (1953:166-67) terms, a persona is a mask that the ego wears in public. But why construct a persona at all? Here Goffman and Jung concur: to protect the powerful feelings attached to images of the self. The persona not only elicits desired responses from others, it insulates us from potentially injurious responses.

Shine was a persona, a cultivated public character, an act. Atwater often spoke of Shine in the third person: "Man, Shine could talk any woman into dropping her drawers," "Shine didn't play; he'd as soon cut you as look at you," "Shine was wide open," "Shine has been long dead." Atwater became Shine to elicit respect in the clubs and on the street—and the act worked. As one of Atwater's old buddies said to me, "You're writing about Shine? Man, if he don't live another day, he's lived a life! Shine's done it *all*." But Atwater also became Shine because it was too painful to be Atwater: a disgraced soldier, a failed husband and father, an alcoholic, an unreliable worker, a petty crook.

Atwater's Shine act offered the further benefit of granting him a taste of authenticity. What was living "wide open" but an expression of the unruly impulses that constituted a part of Atwater's self? Men to whom mainstream paths to success are open cannot behave this way without risking the approval upon which such success depends. As Robert Jackall (1988) shows in his study of corporate managers, it is the ambitious mid-range climbers who must stifle elements of personality that might make higher-ups uncomfortable. Perhaps, then, authenticity is to be found mainly at the very top and center—among men whose power allows them not to give a damn about pleasing others—and at the bottom margins—among men who have nothing to lose.

But for black men the problem has another layer. The persona insulates not only against failure but, as Paul Laurence Dunbar's poem suggests, against white racism (cf. Staples 1982; Majors and Billson 1992). On the one hand, white society could look at Shine and say, *Here is another black man who fancies himself a dandy and just wants to drink and fight and fuck. Like many of his kind, he is of no value as a productive citizen.* On the other hand, Atwater could say, *Shine is just how I put on sometimes; he isn't all of who I am. Besides, whitey won't let me be much else anyway, so why shouldn't I be Shine and enjoy myself?* Authenticity, such as Atwater could experience it through Shine, thus came at the cost of implicitly accepting the dominant society's condemnation.

Popcorn emerged after Shine was no longer a viable act. Again, Atwater often spoke of himself in the third person. "Popcorn," Atwater said, "can talk to these young women about life, and not talk down to them. They know I know about drugs and living on the street. I can talk to them and give them the confidence they need to get through hard times. That's why they come to the School of the PC." Looking at himself as Atwater, he might have had to conclude that his life was a mess and, at best, a cautionary tale. Fashioning himself as Popcorn, he could transform the pains of a lifetime of failure into the face of a compassionate teacher.

Dr. Reet, too, was a persona. As Dr. Reet, Matthew Mason was more than a houseboy. He was an entertainer, a comrade in mischief, and a teller of cherished tales from bygone times. For all this, and for the generous spirit he brought to the performance, Dr. Reet was genuinely loved. There was, however, another thing that Dr. Reet could do, something no less important to earning the boys' affection: let racial teasing and joking roll off his back.

When a boy might say, "Reet, get your black ass in here and clean up my room," Dr. Reet could laugh and say, "My ass ain't black; it's chocolate." Dr. Reet could refer to himself as a nigger and make it seem funny. He could listen to, and sometimes tell, racist jokes, seemingly without a ruffled feather. He could laugh at his own Sambo performances when he got drunk and started cutting up at parties. He could kid about the exclusion of blacks from white fraternities by invoking an exclusive, imaginary fraternity of his own: *Zulu Zulu Zeta*. Dr. Reet was a black man, of course; but he was a black man who could be happy and grateful, without insisting that the boys support the civil rights struggles going on around them. What Dr. Reet could thus do, that Matthew Mason alone could not, was to give the fraternity boys absolution for their privilege.

Like Atwater, who was Shine and not-Shine, Mason was Reet and not-Reet. He would sometimes self-consciously signal his donning of the persona. If I asked, How are you today, Mr. Mason? he might reply, "The *Doctor* is in," by which phrase he announced a playful mood and readiness to banter. And in telling of times when the fraternity boys' teasing went too far, Mason would describe his rare objections as a matter of "having to show them who Dr. Reet is"—meaning that he had to show them that there were limits to what even Dr. Reet would tolerate.

The personas crafted by Atwater and Mason elicited desired responses and shielded against hurtful ones. Shine got respect on the street and Dr. Reet got affection from the fraternity boys. Both men could also see themselves as more complex, worthy, and dignified than many folks gave them credit for being—based on seeing only their public performances. The dominant white society might revile hoodlums like Shine, or look with bemused pity on Sambo characters like Dr. Reet. But these denigrating views were aimed at masks that black men had to wear, not at the real human beings behind the masks. Or so Atwater and Mason could tell themselves.

There were, however, unanticipated consequences. Over time, the Shine act destroyed Atwater's ability to sustain it. The hard drinking that was part of the act led him to be violent, untrustworthy, and unemployable. As his life crumbled around him, Shine was, more and more, all that Atwater possessed. And so he embraced the act more tightly, drank more, and hollowed himself out behind the mask. This eventually brought him to the nadir of his street wino days, at which point even Shine was only a memory.

Hard drinking was also a part of what defined Dr. Reet. The antics and misadventures that Dr. Reet joined in and, later, told stories about, were often alcohol induced. For the fraternity boys, these were college hijinks. For Matthew Mason in his Dr. Reet persona, the drunken escapades extended for decades. As with Atwater, the heavy drinking nearly killed him and, if not for the loyalty of older, influential fraternity members who decreed that Dr. Reet could not be fired, would have cost him his job. The drinking also caused tension at home for Mason. His wife and children wanted their sober, playful Papa back; the fraternity boys kept returning a besotted Dr. Reet. And again like Atwater, when things began to fall apart at home, Mason could embrace Dr. Reet and, at least among the fraternity boys, be a hero.

For both men, their personas became traps, masks that couldn't be removed. This happened in part because both men were bound to the audiences that affirmed their performances. Mason could not abandon Dr. Reet without quitting his job with the fraternity. Atwater could not abandon Shine without achieving the nearly impossible: upward mobility, which, Atwater may have sensed, would have carried its own authenticity costs. Both men found themselves channeled into social worlds populated by others—black and white—who were familiar with, entertained by, and willing to applaud characters like Shine and Dr. Reet.

The problem was that the Shine and Dr. Reet personas entailed behaviors that were self-destructive and self-defeating, and thus fueled more of the same feelings of anger and shame that made the personas—and the limited balm they offered—appealing. In this sense, the persona trap mirrored the trap of alcoholism: the same practice that mitigated the pain of psychic injury ensured that the sources of injury would persist. These masks not only hid wounds, but invited more wounds, ones that would never heal.

A racist culture created the public jaws of the persona trap. But as their Shine and Dr. Reet acts spoiled relationships with family and friends, Mason and Atwater also found themselves trapped by a shrinking backstage. Both men, largely because of the alcoholism into which they fell, found themselves with fewer places where they could remove their masks and find support for being more than Shine or Dr. Reet. The fewer chances each man had to take off the mask, the harder it was to believe in the fuller human being that lay behind it.

These conditions may have created a kind of authenticity confusion for Atwater and Mason. What did it mean to be a black man? It was clear that this did not mean—and would never be allowed to mean—enacting the hegemonic ideal in the way that white men could. *No, you can't earn enough to support a family. Yes, you will be a* houseboy *even though you're a grown man.* There were, however, images of manhood seemingly reserved for black men, images like Shine the Stud and Reet the Jester. *If I can't be white*, the cultural logic leads the wearer of the mask to reason, *I can be a kind of man that whitey can't be. That's what it* means *to be black.* A desire for authenticity, as a man and as a black man, can thus seal the persona trap.

Mason and Atwater needed to be Reet and Shine for the psychic protection these personas afforded. But white society needed these personas too. White society needed black men to wear self-protective masks rather than to rebel against the conditions that made those masks necessary. White society needed black men to discredit themselves by donning masks that could be taken as signs that black men were indeed inferior and thus in their proper place: beneath white men in the social hierarchy. White society needed black men to trip themselves up by believing in their own acts, by coming to mistake their masks for their full humanity.

Much has changed since Mason and Atwater first donned their personas: legal segregation is over; civic equality is the law of the land; and job options for black men have expanded. Yet the hegemonic manhood ideal still vaunts status, wealth, and power, and still wears a white face. Black men, and especially poor and working-class black men, remain locked into a subordinated masculinity, and so they often seek compensatory manhood rewards through violence, sexual conquest, and drug use. Dr. Reet may be gone. But Shine is still here, on the streets and in prison, dying every day in search of a self trapped behind the mask.

References

Connell, Robert. 1995. *Masculinities*. Berkeley, CA: University of California Press.

Goffman, Erving. 1959. *The Presentation of Self in Everyday Life*. New York: Doubleday.

MacLeod, Jay. 1995. *Ain't No Makin' It*. Boulder, CO: Westview.

Majors, Richard, and Janet Billson. 1992. *Cool Pose: The Dilemmas of Black Manhood in America*. New York: Lexington Books.

Jackall, Robert. 1988. *Moral Mazes*. New York: Oxford University Press.

Jung, Carl. 1953. *Two Essays on Analytical Psychology*. New York: Meridian.

Schwalbe, Michael. 2004. *Remembering Reet and Shine: Two Black Men, One Struggle*. Jackson, MS: University Press of Mississippi.

Sennett, Richard, and Jonathan Cobb. 1972. *The Hidden Injuries of Class*. New York: Vintage.

Staples, Robert. 1982. *Black Masculinity*. San Francisco: The Black Scholar Press.

Chapter 10

Pop Music as a Resource for Assembling an Authentic Self: A Phenomenological-Existential Perspective

Joseph A. Kotarba

Authenticity has long been a regular topic in discussions of popular music (see Frith 1984). Popular music scholars and journalists, the music industry, and fans themselves tend to treat authenticity as an objective reality: a feature of popular music that can be discovered, assessed, measured, and evaluated. Authenticity is assumed to be a normal feature of music as much as its quality, beauty, and danceability. The popular music industry itself is particularly concerned with marketing and product definition—essential components of the construction of authenticity in all styles of popular music. As Richard Peterson (1997) has argued for example, the country music industry centered in Nashville, Tennessee, became a powerful force in popular music by producing music that was marketed and appreciated as authentic country music. The industry often works with entertainment media to generate mountains of publishable copy through stories on authenticity. Much of this writing appears as critical evaluation of performers and performances in terms of authenticity. For instance David Grazian (2003) has written at length about the importance of critics in influencing public consumer opinion on whether contemporary blues music and musicians are authentic.

The purpose of this chapter is to approach authenticity from a different and less explored perspective, that is, through the perceptions of fans, and adult fans in particular. The scholarly literature on popular music and rock 'n' roll in particular has traditionally focused on music experiences among young audiences. Specifically, the focus has been on the rock 'n' roll idiom as a feature of adolescent culture and, therefore, of teenagers' everyday life experience. As Simon Frith (1981) noted in his famous sociological text, *Sound Effects*, rock 'n' roll music has been fundamental to the experience of growing up ever since the end of World War II. Similarly, sociologists have demonstrated increasing interest over the years in rock 'n' roll music as an indicator of dramatic changes occurring in the social and cultural worlds of teenagers. We can trace this interest at least as far back as David Riesman's (1950) classic examination of the emergence of the *other-directed* personality in post-World War II American society.

Vastly underexplored, however, are the experiences of older fans such as middle-aged and older pop music fans.

Older fans are significant because they comprise the first true and complete audience for rock ‘n’ roll music, the preeminent style of popular music in our society over the past fifty years (Kotarba 2002). Although many observers still assume that rock ’n’ roll is essentially a feature of youth culture, I argue that it is a key feature of adult culture and a primary source of everyday meanings for the first generation raised on it. Authenticity is an important and useful type of meaning for this population. They grew up with amplified, dance-oriented, guitar-driven music composed for and marketed specifically to young people after World War Two. These baby boomers—born between 1945 and 1964—are getting older. Many professional and lay observers have noted in recent years the way the baby boomer generation uses relationships, occupations, investments, religion, hobbies—and medicine—to accomplish one task: to forestall, master and/or enhance the aging process. In another work (Kotarba 2009), for example I described the many ways in which people who were raised on rock ’n’ roll music and its cultural baggage have continued to use the rock ’n’ roll idiom to make sense of, celebrate, and master everyday life—through adulthood and for the rest of their lives. There, and here, I define rock ’n’ roll music very broadly as a style of popular music that: (1) is created for and marketed towards young people or people who consume music according to youthful tastes and values; (2) is primarily guitar-driven and amplified; (3) has its musicological and cultural origins in African-American musical styles; (4) is usually danceable; and (5) sounds best when played or performed loudly (also see Kotarba 1994). I define rock ’n’ roll broadly in order to include all varieties of pop music that have evolved from it (e.g., heavy metal, pop, New Age, Christian pop, and even rap/hip hop).

All told, rock ’n’ roll music and its derivatives arguably comprise the preeminent form of popular music in our society. The popular music industry that markets rock ’n’ roll continues to expand dramatically if not always economically—beyond multi-billion dollar annual sales, globalization, CDs, MP3 technology, and the Internet. The original generation of rock ’n’ rollers—the baby boomers—are now parents and, in increasing numbers, grandparents. The music and musical culture they grew up with has stayed with them, becoming the soundtrack of American culture. It is this context that provides the cultural and societal background for my analysis, which utilizes two related conceptual frameworks: phenomenology and existentialism. Phenomenology directs us to examine the situations in which authenticity in its various forms and iterations becomes relevant to the popular music fan in everyday life. Existential social thought directs us to examine the effects of these situations on the experience of self.

Phenomenology and Authenticity

Phenomenological social theory, put briefly, focuses on the social contexts of consciousness (Freeman 1980:113). As Alfred Schutz (1967) argued, consciousness is made up of practical knowledge that allows the person to navigate through everyday life. Practical knowledge allows the person to understand and even predict—take for granted, if you will—most of the events encountered in everyday life. Practical knowledge—or common sense knowledge—is acquired simply and primarily through one's membership in a community. A community's common sense becomes its members' common sense.

Objects and events are meaningful, or have meaning for us, after we actively make sense of then in concrete situations. Schutz (1967:6) referred to this as *intentionality*—we intend or make sense of things because we are confronted by them and must make sense of them to control, protect, circumvent, honor, etc. them. Yet, of all the things we encounter in everyday life, which ones do we choose to try to make sense of? Schutz (1964:125) argued that this depends on the importance of the *purpose at hand*, that is, the situation in which we find ourselves. An object can be either immediately relevant, absolutely irrelevant, or somewhere in between. In terms of the topic at hand, the need to assess the authenticity of a song, artist, or performance is likely to shift over time. I may possibly question whether REO Speedwagon today—with only one original member, Kevin Cronin—is the same REO Speedwagon I listened to 20 years ago. Nevertheless, I will only engage that issue when I must, or when it has value for me to do so. For example, REO Speedwagon's authenticity is in my primary zone of relevance when I see the notice in the newspaper that they will perform in Houston next moth and I have to decide whether I want to/should/ must buy tickets and go.

Phenomenologists go one step further in their discussion of practical knowledge. Practical knowledge is couched in words, and a*uthenticity* is first and foremost a word. Words, both in our consciousness and in our interaction—or conversations—with others accomplish tasks for us. They do this through the powerful mechanism we call *reflexivity* (Garfinkel 1967). When we talk, our words not only describe something, but they also create a world in which that something can appear and is possible (Mehan and Wood 1975). On the one hand, musical authenticity is an idea or a linguistic/rationalist device that people use to accomplish social interactional goals. The social situation at hand largely determines when, how, and why an individual will involve the idea of or word "authenticity."

On the other hand, musical authenticity is a social object that is cognitive in essence, yet is dealt with like any other feature of material objects (Mead 1934). Objects, like music performances, can be more or less authentic according to the meanings and evaluations we give them. Musical styles too can be authentic or inauthentic, and the assessment of either can be readily accomplished and justified by reference to the cultural rules governing authenticity.

In summary, phenomenology tells us that, although we take-for-granted the existence of authenticity as a feature of music and the "fact" that music can be more or less authentic or even inauthentic, we only deal with authenticity as such in situations in which authenticity can help us solve some other practical problem. Authenticity is therefore the product of intentional, reflexive, practical social interactions. Existential social thought, as we will see in a moment, suggests that the most immediate and powerful practical problem is making sense of, fortifying, reconstructing, or saving our sense of self.

The Existential Self and Authenticity

In general, most writers in fields such as literature, philosophy, and the history of ideas locate authenticity as a feature of the self. Charles Taylor (1992), for example, sees authenticity as a component of Romantic thought. In our Western civilization we are drawn to the search for the perfect or pure self, whether or not it may in fact be attainable. This search is a moral task, based upon our understanding of the value of a fulfilled (read: authentic) self for the community, society, or culture. The search for an authentic self, therefore, is for the benefit of the common good. Another group of writers (e.g., Boyle 2004) see the search for the authentic self as an artifact of the contemporary postmodern world in which we live. Life in the postmodern world lacks anchors or meaning as a result of the fact that traditional concepts of self, community, and social place are no longer viable. We feel anxious in everyday life, unable to take our sense of positive self for granted. We may not know for sure that we experience a real self, but we become obsessed with the will to avoid a fake self. In summary, we search for the authentic self by associating it with, in fact clothing it in, authentic things such as authentic popular music experiences.

Existential social thought adds a bit of a twist to this argument. The encounter with authenticity, or the search for authenticity in everyday life, does not necessarily nurture an authentic self. More likely, this encounter or search feeds some other, more empirical, facet of the self. In our postmodern culture, the notion of an authentic self is simply too abstract to be viable for members. The existential concept of the becoming of self is a useful guide in seeking the sociological answers to this problem. Existential social thought views the self: "as a unique experience of being within the context of contemporary social conditions, an experience most notably marked by an incessant sense of becoming and an active participation in social change" (Kotarba 1984:223). The incessant sense of becoming is a reflection of the contemporary need for the individual to be prepared to reshape meanings of self in response to the dictates of a rapidly changing social world. The well-integrated self accepts the reality of change and welcomes new ideas, new experiences, and reformulations of old ideas and experiences that help one adapt to change (Kotarba 1987).

The idea of becoming is one of the most important ideas in existentialist thought because it places responsibility for fashioning a self on the individual. Whereas Jean-Paul Sartre (1945) argued dramatically that we are condemned to be free and to choose who we are to become, Maurice Merleau-Ponty (1962) insisted more moderately and sociologically that we must ground our becoming-of-self in the real world in order to cope effectively with it. Thus, an effective strategy for becoming begins with a foundation of personal experience and the constraints of

's perception of inauthenticity in pop music is with contemporary popular
desire to filter available musical selections through his satellite radio
functions for his sense of self. First, he no longer has to “fish” through
adio to find the music he enjoys, a menial task for an upper-middle-
ssional. Second, his ability to conquer the threat of inauthenticity marks
rson beyond the realm of “popular” in popular music. The popular is
ransformed into the exclusive, allowing him to demonstrate the level
ver his musical experiences that he has achieved in other facets of his
fessional career and his family.

al Self

sic is endemic to modern family life, and this certainly applies to baby
Vhen they first married in the 1960s and ‘70s, they comprised the first
of Americans to introduce popular music into the formal wedding
beyond having Elvis sing “Hawaiian Honeymoon at a wedding chapel
s—sometimes with great effort. The “our songs” couples insisted on
hurch, chapel or synagogue—in concert with the overall movement to
marriage ceremonies—and ranged from Led Zeppelin’s (romantic?)
to Heaven” to the Sandpipers’ (truly romantic) “Come Saturday
Kotarba 1997).
boomer newlyweds evolved into parents, popular music became a
tant feature of self, perhaps more so than for any previous generation.
s dad was cool, for example, if he had any semblance of good taste
sic. Authenticity in music per se became relevant when it impacted
re activities involving music. Take the modern family vacation. Baby
ade the notion of a family vacation to a theme park popular and indeed
ce in the burgeoning family leisure and vacation industry. Family
s typically have some attraction related to rock ’n’ roll, such as the
ock-up of a 1950s small town main street in the Fiesta Texas Theme
Antonio. The artists performing at the amphitheaters in the Six Flags
ded (in the summer of 2006) REO Speedwagon, an Eagles reunion
as, a Chicago reunion band, and the latest version of the Jefferson
arship. It is also there that I spoke with James.
s a 56 year-old insurance executive who has taken his family of five to
heme parks, ranging form Disneyland in California to Disneyworld in
sked James to unpack his understanding of musical authenticity, and
for him determining whether the rock-a-billy, family-oriented musical
e that is pervasive at theme parks is authentic or not was a complex
d undertaking. On one hand it is not authentic; the actors and dancers
rforming authentic rock-a-billy music—in terms of arrangements,
tion, and lyrics—as Elvis or Buddy Holly did. But on the other hand
is authentic insofar as it fits the category of rock-a-billy better than
vailable category of music, as intended by the producers and show

social structure, while evolving in terms of the resources presented by culture. I argue that middle-aged Americans work with a self built to some degree on the meanings provided by the rock ’n’ roll idiom, and they continue to nurture the self within the ever-present cultural context of rock ’n’ roll.

Jack Douglas (1984) notes that there are two analytically distinct aspects of becoming-of-self with which the modern actor contends. The first is the need to eliminate or control threats to the basic security of self (e.g., meaninglessness, isolation from others, shame, death). Although existential psychotherapists like Yalom (1978) argue that chronic insecurity, or neurosis, is pervasive in our society, Douglas argues sociologically that it is more common for the sense of security to vary biographically, situationally, and developmentally. In general, adults try to shape everyday life experiences in order to avoid basic threats to the self. Basic threats to the adult self in our society would include divorce, the loss of a job, the loss of children (e.g., the empty nest syndrome), illness, disability, and poverty. The second aspect of becoming-of-self involves growth of the sense of self. Growth occurs when the individual seeks new experiences as vehicles for innovative and potentially rewarding meanings for self (Kotarba 1987). It is through growth, or self-actualization as it is often referred to today, that life becomes rich, rewarding, full, and manageable.

Accordingly, adult music fans nurture their interest in and experience with rock ’n’ roll music for two reasons. On one hand, keeping up with the music and the culture that were so important to them when growing up helps them to maintain continuity with the past and, thus, to solidify the sense of self security. On the other hand, working hard to keep rock’n’roll current and relevant to their lives helps adults grow as parents, as spiritual beings, and as friends.

The concept of the existential self tells us that the experience of individuality is never complete; the answer to the question “who am I?” is always tentative. In the postmodern world, the popular media—including popular music—serve as increasingly important audiences to the self. The self is situational and mutable (Zurcher 1977). One can be various selves as the fast-paced, ever-changing, uncertain postmodern society requires. The rock ‘n’ roll idiom serves as an important source of self-stabilizing meaning for many baby boomer fans.

Existential social thought directs us to two issues to explore. First, we should expect that, in everyday life situations, authenticity is not experienced primarily as a variable. People do not ordinarily perceive music as more or less authentic. Instead, we should be open to the discovery and description of experiences in which music provides a sense of authenticity or inauthenticity to the self, as well as a resource for making sense of a particular situation. Put differently, inauthenticity could have positive uses in every day life (also see Waskul this volume).

Second, the experience of inauthenticity, when dysfunctional for the self, may be akin to the notion of alienation. In existential thought, alienation refers to the experience of estrangement or distance from the world (Fontana 1980). This largely affective as well as rationalistic separation can result in a state of meaninglessness: if I depend on the world for meaning for my life, but it is not longer available to me, then my sense of self is suddenly void. Propositionally, if I have filled my life over time with rock 'n' roll, but realize that I not longer fit with rock 'n' roll, then I have a meaning void to fill.

By making claims of authenticity or inauthenticity in musical experiences, the individual simultaneously makes claims about the self. In the remainder of this chapter, I provide several illustrations of authenticity work in everyday life among baby boomers. I define authenticity work as the interactional process by which the assessment of authenticity in cultural phenomena, such as popular music, serves as a resource or tool for recreating, defining, verifying, or developing a viable self. This viable self may or not necessarily be perceived as authentic in so many words. There are many styles or depictions of self that can be the outcome of authenticity work. The point is that authenticity work creates a relationship between music and the self that can be positive or negative on the self, and that can lead to stagnation or growth.

Rock Music and the Experience of Authenticity in Middle Age—and Beyond

Critics and fans alike have traditionally viewed popular music, especially in terms of its rock 'n' roll iterations, as a meaning resource for youth navigating through adolescence. I explore instead the relevance of popular music for self-identity through middle age and beyond. As noted above, existential social thought tells us that the process of self-development is constant throughout life. What changes are life circumstances, the biological and affective aging process, reassessment of the past, and strategic relationships with others. As these contingencies change, so does the experience of self. As Andrea Fontana (1976) notes, the activities used during adulthood to make sense of the self are likely to be the same types of activities used to make sense of getting old. The "baby boomer" generation was the first Western generation to grow up entirely in the world of rock 'n' roll music and culture, and many baby boomers experienced rock 'n' roll as a master script for life. Therefore, this highly self-integrated cultural resource, enhanced by the power of the popular media, remains central to the self-identity of many baby boomers as they approach old age.

The issue of authenticity can appear in any number of pop music experiences. The starting point for this analysis is the argument that, in our postmodern world, we experience different selves in different situations and different social worlds (Zurcher 1977). Music can impact any or all of these selves in different ways and at different times. In another work (Kotarba 2009), I suggest nine styles of self-experience relevant to popular music. I will now present case studies to illustrate the ways authenticity work fits six of these nine selves. I will examine experiences such as listening to satellite radio, downloading music-as-informal gift giving, church music listening, political music; listening parenting-through-heavy metal, and grandparenting-through-Hannah Montana. I will examine these experiences of self in terms of the following issues: (a) The segment(s)

directors. Still, it is inauthentic to the degree that its original fans—or current sophisticated fans like James—probably do not accept it as "real" rock-a-billy. Nevertheless, for James the theme park music is moderately—but acceptably—inauthentic (or perhaps sufficiently authentic, if you will). Inauthenticity—for James and others—is not necessarily a bad thing that functions to eliminate certain musical performances from consideration. And having the perceived ability to differentiate authenticity from inauthenticity can index a valued self. As James concluded: "I love it. Going to see one of those bullshit shows is great. I get to be the music expert in my family, for a change. I can poke fun at them, but the kids are OK with that. They figure dad's an old guy—he should know." This is a clear example of how the mastery of authenticity work—regardless of the outcome of this work—contributes to a valued self. Indeed, this skill may be more valuable interactionally and internally than the actual mastery of the content of music (e.g. song titles, artists' names, lyrics, styles, date of popularity, level of popularity, and so forth.).

The Believing Self

Baby boomers learned to love, play, dissent, and celebrate through the idiom of rock 'n' roll. They also experienced spirituality through their music (Seay and Neely 1986). In adulthood, the spiritual dimension of rock 'n' roll continues to impact the self as believer. The lyrics and mood created by such performers as Van Morrison (e.g. *Astral Weeks)* and U2 (e.g. *The Joshua Tree)* provide baby boomers with non-sectarian, yet religion-friendly, soundtracks. New Age Music, such as that produced by Windham Hill, functions in much the same way.

Rock 'n' roll music has also had direct influence on spirituality by helping shape organized religious ceremonies and rituals to fit the tastes of the adult member. For example, Catholic baby boomers grew up at a time when the Church, largely as a result of the Vatican II Council, encouraged parishes to make use of local musical styles and talent. Hence, witness the emergence of the rock 'n' roll mass in the 1970s.

As baby boomers age, there is a tendency amongst them to return to organized religion. Some of that movement is obviously fueled by being married, having children, responding to pressure from grandparents, and so forth. This movement coincides with attempts among many church leaders to modernize liturgies, ministries, and relationships with the faithful (Roof 1999). The Catholic Church, for example, has shifted emphasis from medieval ecclesiastic music to more popular styles of music, thus raising the questions of authenticity I am discussing. In the debate over the appropriateness of popular church music theological concerns often emerge. I will now briefly discuss the issue of authenticity relating to two recent styles of music permeating Catholic worship: praise and worship music and the Christian singer-songwriter.

Praise and worship music originated in the youth-oriented "Jesus Movement" of the 1960s and '70s (Scheer 2007). The young people involved in this Southern

California-originated movement were seeking an alternative, a timely and user-friendly way to celebrate the basic Christian beliefs with which they were raised. Over time, this festive, exciting, upbeat musical style became integrated with the larger Christian music industry, and came to be known as praise and worship music. This style has been very inter-denominational in scope, and has gained great popularity by its use of contemporary instrumentation (e.g., amplified band instruments, keyboards, and guitars) and links with the pop music industry (e.g., concern with charts, producers, recording companies, sales, and marketing). The songs continue to be an upbeat blending of lyrics derived from both the Old and New Testaments. Major stars include Amy Grant and Michael W. Smith.

Discussions over authenticity in praise and worship music tend to focus less on the status of any particular songs than on the validity of the genre itself. *Is praise and worship music really (authentic) Christian music?* In terms of the sociological ways I am framing my argument, *the answers focus specifically on the contrasting ways popular Church music may impact the spiritual (self) of the faithful.* The proponents of praise and worship music clearly feel that any style of music that brings people closer to the Lord is authentic. The detractors, however, argue that the musical style itself is consequential and cannot be accepted arbitrarily.

Take Danielle, for example. Danielle is a 57 year-old music and choir director for a Catholic Parish. She has seen the styles of music shift greatly in the Church, beginning with Latin-based psalms in the 1950s, to the first English language songs in the 1960s to rock masses in the 1970s to the open-horizon of styles resulting from the praise and worship movement. For her, the issue of authenticity has shifted over time, just as the music has evolved. Her original position on changing musical styles matched that of the opponents of popular Church music: the style of music is the true object of evaluation and control, even more than any particular song, artist or lyric in question. As an illustration, Danielle approached praise and worship music in much the same way critics (e.g., the Parents' Music Resource Center) approached heavy metal music in the 1980s (Kotarba 1994). For Danielle and other senior music directors in the Church, authentic praise and worship music is that which is not confounded by a "star system." By star system, Danielle is referring to the ego-centered careers of some Christian music performers "who put themselves above their music and the good message they should want to convey." Therefore, for Danielle and other baby boomer musicians, authenticity in Christian music is synonymous with, parallel to, and performed into being by the humility of the performer and performance.

John Michael Talbot's music is an exemplar of authentic, contemporary, Catholic/Christian music for people of faith like Danielle. Talbot is an American Roman Catholic singer-guitarist who is also the founder of a monastic community: the Brothers and Sisters of Charity (Talbot 1999). He is the largest selling Catholic musical artist with over four million albums sold. He has authored or co-authored fifteen books. John Michael tours through the US in support of his monastic community nestled in the beautiful Ozark Mountains in Arkansas. On the surface, John Michael appears much like the high profile artists about whom

Danielle is cautious. John Michael Talbot is authentic to his followers, however, because he leads a simple lifestyle and does not personally profit from his talent and dedication. In a very postmodern way, John Michael is able to integrate his Internet site, concert tours, and many followers into a pristine, humble, and monastic lifestyle that will never make the cover of People Magazine. His persona is refreshing—and authentic—to those baby boomers who are a bit overtaken by mass culture, even of an ecclesiastic sort.

In summary, Danielle's experience illustrates how adult opponents of popular Church music are leery of the negative (read: sinful) effects the overall secular and materialist architecture of popular Church music can have on the souls (read: selves) of the faithful. Danielle's ministry may be typical insofar as her choir and musical ensemble will perform praise and worship songs without even mention of the "star" Christian artist who either composed the song or made it popular. Her more recent experiences of Church music, specifically her appreciation and support for John Michael Talbot, allows for commercial considerations that are acceptable because they (ironically) enable singer-songwriters to teach messages of humility, simplicity, and traditional spiritualism to an audience increasingly hungry for them—but prefers to hear these message on CDs.

The Political Self

Rock 'n' roll music serves as a soundtrack for situations in which baby boomers perceive themselves as political actors. Rock 'n' roll can add both atmosphere and meaning to political events. For example, New York punk poet and singer Patti Smith performed a concert in Houston on March 28, 2003, right at the beginning of the war in Iraq. The concert was originally scheduled simply to support an exhibit of her art displayed at the Museum of Contemporary Arts. The audience was overwhelmingly composed of middle-aged people, dressed up in their jeans and long (hippie) skirts. Through conversations with numerous fans after the concert, it was clear that they *enjoyed* the concert. Patti Smith's poetry and songs (e.g., *People Have the Power*) gave them a relevant and identifiable venue for sharing their overwhelmingly negative *feelings* about the war.

Families also use rock 'n' roll to relay a sense of political history to their children. For example, every year on Memorial Day in Houston, various veterans' organizations sponsor a concert and rally at the Miller Outdoor Theater. Most of the veterans present fought in the Vietnam and Gulf Wars, two wars for which rock 'n' roll served as the musical soundtrack. Most of the veterans bring their children to the event. Among all the messages and information available to the kids is the type of music popular during the war. A popular band regularly invited to perform is the Guess Who, whose "American Woman" was a major anthem among soldiers. I have observed fathers explaining the song to their teenaged and preteen children, who would otherwise view it as just another of dad's old songs. The fathers explain that the song had different meanings for different men. For some, it reminded them of girlfriends back home who broke up with them during the war. For others, the title was enough to remind them of their faithful girlfriends back home. For still others, the song reminded them of the occasions when they were sitting around camp, smoking pot and listening to any American rock 'n' roll songs available as a way of bridging the many miles between them and home. In Houston, Juneteenth and Cinco de Mayo activities function much the same way for African-American and Hispanic families, respectively. In summary, rock 'n' roll music is vital to maintaining a sense of the political self because many baby boomers learned their politics—and how to be and feel political—from Country Joe McDonald (and the Fish), Jimi Hendrix, and the Grateful Dead. Whereas the music of the 1960s and '70s may have helped liberate baby boomers from the restrictive and conservative culture(s) of their parents, this music—which now is likely to be labeled as "classic rock"—can help fans sustain a politically aware and even critical political self.

Musical inauthenticity can also serve as a powerful interactional tool in establishing one's political acumen as correct and one's political self as astute. If one's political opponent appreciates bad, inappropriate—or inauthentic—music, the very persona of that opponent can the discredited, to his or her political disadvantage. A recent example of this phenomenon was the media coverage to a survey inquiring as to the 2008 US presidential candidates' musical preferences. One could almost predict the differences between Barack Obama's and John McCain's music (http://www.obama-mccain.info/compare-obama-mccain-music.php). Since McCain is a member of the baby boomer generation, there is no surprise in learning that his favorite style of music is 1950s and '60s rock 'n' roll. He is also a big fan of ABBA, and recently purchased a CD album, "The Very Best of the Beach Boys." Again, predictably, Obama's taste in music is much more eclectic, matching the tastes of the "Generation X" of which he is a member (e.g., Miles Davis, Bob Dylan, Stevie Wonder, Bach and the Fugees). Whereas Obama's conservative critics lambasted him for pandering to his youthful and therefore unsophisticated supporters, McCain's liberal critics used his choices in music as evidence that he is old and out of touch with today's styles and values. The often heated discussion among baby boomers of candidates' musical tastes and preferences should not be surprising. This is the generation of music fans that learned to attach their very basic sense of self to musical performers and styles as adolescents and young adults. I simply ask the middle-aged reader to recall those common debates—arguments?—in the dorm or in the club on "who is better, the (pop-oriented) Beatles or the (hard rocker) Rolling Stones? The beat goes on.

The Sociable Self

As one enters adulthood, the self-identity of *friend* becomes difficult to maintain. This is especially the case among men, whose hectic and fragmented everyday lifestyle does not always leave space for the kinds of friendships typical of childhood and adolescence. Sure, middle-aged and middle-class men have business associates, bosses, subordinates golf partners, and neighbors. But friendships do not always get the time and personal investment needed to thrive.

Gift-giving is a traditional method for nurturing friendships, but what kind of gift can one male friend give another? Enter popular music. Many middle-aged men, who spend (arguably too much) time in front of a computer, will burn CDs to give to friends at school, in the neighborhood, and so forth. A gift like this marks a person to self and other as (1) someone who is thoughtful; yet (2) someone who is not caught up in the trivial materialism of gift-giving; and (3) someone who knows his music. In contrast, an inauthentic self is perhaps marked by a gift designed, manufactured, marketed, and thoughtlessly purchased solely as a gift (e.g., a fake Elvis Presley poster purchased at the mall).

Authenticity emerges as a feature of the aesthetic and affective bonding occurring through sharing the CD. For example, I recently bought a CD of the Van Morrison performance at the Austin City Limits festival in September of 2006. I was fortunate to be able to attend this concert, and thus became the envy of my many friends who are Van Morrison fans. I burnt a copy of the CD and presented it to my next door neighbor. Like many urban neighbors, we really do not get a chance to chat much, he being a busy newspaper editor and me being a busy academic. The CD gave us a social object that was fun to talk about, in contrast to boring talk about work or the kids. The CD marked us as cool, with cool musical tastes that have become timeless in our lives as we elegantly grow old with Van.

The Old Self

In an earlier work (Kotarba 2002) I wrote about the importance popular music holds for parents as a feature of family interaction, parental control, and so forth. As the baby boomers I studied age, however, their sense of self shifts from parent to that of grandparent. Interestingly, these increasingly senior citizens typically maintain their interest in popular music, although not always in the songs with which they grew up. Being a good or at least competent grandparent in our culture involves doting on grandchildren. Popular music serves as a convenient mechanism for nurturing this kind of relationship. Music is a great gift at Christmas or birthdays. Tickets to concerts are a welcomed surprise for the teenagers in the family.

The example in question is the recent Hannah Montana concert tour in 2007-2008. Robert is a 61 year-old petroleum engineer in Houston. He has two children and four grandchildren, one of whom is a pretty little eleven year-old girl who lives close by. Like all her friends and many pre-teenagers around the country, Sally is a Hannah Montana fan. When tickets went on sale for the concert at the Houston Rodeo, Sally wanted to go more than anything else in life. Her parents refused to buy her tickets for, as Robert noted, "they couldn't see spending a hundred dollars or so on a kid concert, and waiting in line for hours to boot." Sally made her plea to Grandfather Bob, in terms of her opinion of what a great birthday present would be. Being the softy he is, Robert obliged, went on-line, and was very fortunate to be able to buy two tickets at retail—still at a cost of over $100. Robert, a widower himself, actually took Sally to the concert. He told me that "Sally didn't mind. She had her cell phone with her to talk to all her friends who also went to the concert, during the concert [...] it was like they all went together! She is way too young to go to something crazy like that by herself. Similarly, Robert is a life-long Rolling Stones, Led Zepplin, Cream, and Elvis fan. The inauthenticity of Hannah Montana and her music—as forms of rock and roll—do not bother Robert at all: "It's pretty crappy stuff, but you know, these are just little kids. They do not know any better, what do you expect? It's what they like and what they get on TV. If it makes my little girl smile, then it makes me smile." Therefore, music perceived to be inauthentic does not necessarily mean that the self will find it useless or dysfunctional. Accepting another's inauthentic music may allow grandparents—and other adults if you will—achieve their ideal self of understanding, caring, and willing to sacrifice one's taste for the good of another person.

Conclusion

I have presented a sample of the many different ways in which popular music experiences, especially those involving rock 'n' roll phenomena, affect the experiences of self in later adulthood. I do not intend to generalize across all members of the demographic population that we perhaps all too casually refer to as baby boomers. My goal is simply to provide examples of how pop music serves as a practical resource for making sense of self and everyday life situations. This sense of self works well when it fits the person's vision of an ideal self crafted during an exciting period in life and history. Authenticity is important to baby boomers now—though perhaps not as much as it is to rabid teenage fans—given all the other relevant preoccupations that occupy busy adult lives. Still, a feature of adulthood is learning how to nurture and take advantage of those meaning resources that have a track record of working and contributing to one's life. As we have seen, authenticity is a complex issue when its assessment is consequential to people in everyday life. People use it, as well as its antithesis, inauthenticity, to get a firm sense of who they are in the various complex situations, roles and selves in which they routinely find themselves.

References

Douglas, Jack. 1984. "Introduction." Pp. 3-17 in *The Existential Self in Society*, edited by Joseph Kotarba and Andrea Fontana. Chicago: The University of Chicago Press.

Fontana, Andrea. 1976. *The Last Frontier*. Beverly Hills, CA: Sage.

—— 1977. "The Existential Thought of Jean-Paul Sartre and Maurice Merleau-Ponty." Pp. 101-129 in *Existential Sociology*, edited by Jack Douglas. New York: Cambridge University Press.

—— 1980. "Toward a Complex Universe: Existential Sociology." Pp. 155-181 in *Introduction to the Sociologies of Everyday Life*, edited by Jack Douglas. Boston: Allyn and Bacon.

Freeman, C. 1980. "Phenomenological Sociology and Ethnomethodology." Pp. 113-154 in *Introduction to the Sociologies of Everyday Life*, edited by Jack Douglas. Boston: Allyn and Bacon.

Frith, Simon. 1984. *Sound Effects*. New York: Pantheon.

Garfinkel, Harold. 1967. *Studies in Ethnomethodology*. Englewood Cliffs, NJ: Prentice-Hall.

Grazian, David. 2005. *Blue Chicago*. IL: University of Chicago Press.

Grossberg, Lawrence. 1992. *We Gotta Get Out of this Place*. New York: Routledge.

Kotarba, Joseph. 1984. "The Existential Self in Society: A Synthesis." Pp. 222-234 in *The Existential Self in Society*, edited by Joseph Kotarba and Andrea Fontana. Chicago: The University of Chicago Press.

—— 1994. "The Postmodernization of Heavy Metal Music: The Case of Metallica." Pp. 141-163 in *Adolescents and Their Music*, edited by Jonathon Epstein. New York: Garland.

—— 1997. "Reading the Male Experience of Rock Music: Four Songs about Women." *Cultural Studies*, 2:265-277.

—— 2002. "Baby Boomer Rock 'n' Roll Fans and the Experience of Self." Pp. 103-126 in *Postmodern Existential Sociology*, edited by Joseph A. Kotarba and John Johnson. Walnut Creek, CA: Alta Mira Press.

—— 2009. *Growing Old with Rock and Roll*. Walnut Creek, CA: Left Coast Press.

Mead, George Herbert. 1934. *Mind, Self and Society*. Chicago: University of Chicago Press.

Mehan, Hugh and H. Wood. 1975. *The Realty of Ethnomethodology*. New York: Wiley.

Merleau-Ponty, Maurice. 1962. *The Phenomenology of Perception*. London: Routledge & Kegan Paul.

Peterson, Richard. 1999. *Creating Country Music: Fabricating Authenticity*. Chicago: University of Chicago Press.

Riesman, David. 1950. *The Lonely Crowd*. New Haven, CT: Yale University Press.

Roof, Wade Clark. 2001. *Spiritual Marketplace: Baby Boomers and the Remaking of American Religion*. Princeton, NJ: Princeton University Press.

Sartre, Jean Paul. 1945. *The Age of Reason*. Paris: Gallimard.

Scheer, Greg. 1997. *The Art* of *Worship*. Baker Books.

Seay, Davin and Mary Neely. 1986. *Stairway to Heaven*. New York: Ballentine Books.

Schutz, Alfred. 1964. *Collected Papers II*. The Hague: Martinus Nijhoff.

—— 1967. *The Phenomenology of the Social World*. Evanston, IL: Northwestern University Press.

Talbot, John. 1999. *The Music of Creation: Foundations of a Christian Life*. NY: Tarcher/Putnam.

Zurcher, Louis., Jr. 1978. *The Mutable Self.* Beverly Hills, CA: Sage.

PART 3
The Interactional Production, Exchange, and Consumption of Authenticity

Chapter 11

Consuming Authenticity: A Paradoxical Dynamic in Contemporary Capitalism

Jörn Lamla

Authenticity and Social Theory

Authenticity has many meanings in social theory. Post-structuralists or radical constructivists regard authenticity as a myth, a specific cultural form of wielding power over the modern subject via self-interpretation or identity formation (e.g. Nassehi 2006:Chap.3). They emphasize that the culturally coded differences between authenticity and inauthenticity reveal authenticity's contingent nature. The same behavior—be it camouflage, excess, or even insanity—labeled inauthentic in one epoch may be an expression of authenticity in another (Trilling 1972). References to some essence of a truthful stance towards the subject's inner self, one's needs, feelings, motives, and so on, are often criticized as false consciousness. Advocates of such a concept of authenticity, the critics say, fall for the ideals of the romantic ethic.

In my view, it is indeed warranted to criticize philosophers like Charles Taylor (1991) and others on grounds of their belief of being able to differentiate between authentic and inauthentic traditions of authenticity. But in Jürgen Habermas's (1984) argument for a validity claim of "subjective truthfulness," which according to him is operative in every instance of communicative action, we may also find a starting point for a non-essentialist interpretation for the philosophical vindication of authenticity. Drawing on Goffman's (1959) concept of dramaturgic action, authenticity may be understood in a pragmatist sense without specifying any final solution for the problem of self-presentation. While Habermas holds on to psychoanalytical methods in therapeutic discourse to separate a truthful core from its systemic distortions, pragmatists are prepared to accept the empirically varying solutions to the problem of authentication as long as they stand the test of time in social interaction. To get a more precise grasp on the issue, let us confront three approaches to problems of identity and self-interpretation.

The French philosopher Paul Ricœur suggests a concept of self and identity (1992) that matches this pragmatist perspective in many ways. His concept of the self differentiates between the character of the self (identity as sameness) and its accountability (identity as selfhood). The first relates to the habitus concept and comprises all dispositions that make a person recognizable. The second refers to the validity claim of subjective truthfulness as an anchor for ethical behavior in human life. The narrative constructions of the self, following Ricœur, always oscillate and have to mediate between these two dimensions. They are therefore in flux and may react to the situational requirements of social interaction. Symbolic as well as habitual requirements depend on historically changing conditions, such as changing cultural norms of being oneself, being accountable, being authentic, and changing resource distributions that have an impact on the ability to sustain routine action and ontological security in one's course of life. But if such pragmatic solutions are to stand the test of time, their narrative reflections or reconstructions have to fulfill some further general conditions. For Ricœur (1992; see also Giddens 1991), mediation via self-identity narratives has to consider a steadfast hierarchy of praxis. At the bottom, we find narratives on single practices or sets of practices like those of consumption, shopping, and so on; further up, we find more integrated narratives related to a biography, a life plan, or the course of life in spheres like work and family; at the top, these life stories have to be integrated by an ethical narrative of the good life.

Critics of this position point to the difficulties of such integration in the complex worlds of highly differentiated societies. In contrast to the model of coherent biographical and ethical self-narratives, Jean-Claude Kaufmann (2005) argues for the predominance of the instantaneous situation in the identity formation process. In his theory, the hierarchy seems to be reversed. The narration of the self is only one form of constructing an identity, encouraged by the modern myth of authenticity. While those storylines are important and powerful in modern life, they may increasingly be in contradiction to actual experience in concrete situations. Kaufmann conceptualizes a second mode of identity formation, which is driven by emotional force and memory and produces discrepancies and fragmentations of the self. This mode depends on the situational context, consists of images, not narrations, and functions as an operative tool for managing the situation. While in one context we may identify ourselves with a football star, in another situation this same image may bring shame on us because we want to be seen as a serious intellectual. But even Kaufmann does not deny the influence of an integrative principle at work in the identity process—namely the necessity to sustain one's self-esteem (2005:196). Therefore the pragmatic self-images also depend on the social conditions of being a recognizable and accountable person. But here the solutions to the problem of identity construction are characterized by much greater diversity and fluidity.

The third approach to the problem focuses on the meso-level. Anselm Strauss (1959) did not only write an essay on identity formation that combined the Chicago tradition of symbolic interactionism with the sociology of organizations, he also developed a pragmatist theory of the segmentation and intersection of "social worlds" that is very useful here (Strauss 1993). According to Strauss, social worlds are marked by core activities that are shared by the members of that world and defended in processes of authentication and legitimation—or even in negotiations with members of other social worlds (or subworlds) in "social arenas." Authenticity is therefore an important aspect of social life even in a highly differentiated and complex society. To be sure, not every situation is contextualized by a well-defined identity of collective practices such as "being a football fan" or "taking an intellectual stance." But in most cases even spontaneous images of the self are integrated in a symbolic universe of a corresponding social world. Thus the heterogeneity and immediacy of social situations and corresponding identities do not exempt us from solving problems of authenticity or authentication. While the narrations of the self vary from one situation to the next, producing discrepancy instead of identity, the social worlds we live in nevertheless include some general rules of interaction and shared principles of recognition. The diversification and democratization of the criteria for being authentic within particular social worlds may weaken the power of the romantic myth over interactions in modern society, but they do not suspend the processes of authentication completely. On the contrary, these processes not only constitute social worlds via their shared practices and fuzzy boundaries, they are sustained by ongoing and, in terms of outcome, open struggles for recognition and resources.

The question I want to address is this: How are the structural dynamics of these struggles and authentication processes configured today? To answer this question I analyze the relation between the quest for authenticity and its conditions in economic life. We will misunderstand much of this relation if we only think about it in terms of classic critical theory, as opposing spheres of life and action. These spheres are intertwined in many ways, especially in the domain of consumption. Drawing on theories concerning social and cultural change within modern capitalism, I will first distinguish a model of four ideal types concerning the structural dynamics or drift of authenticity claims in contemporary society. Insofar all of these types have some theoretical evidence, it remains an empirical question what kind(s) of social change best describe(s) the current societal dynamic and the role of authenticity claims therein. We cannot abstractly answer whether modern beliefs in identity coherence continue or new forms of syncretism and hybridity will emerge; whether conflicts will divide social worlds fundamentally or a moral grammar of recognition will integrate them within the economically contextualized manufacturing, cooptation, defense and negotiation of authenticity. My thesis is that this dynamic gets more paradoxical in contemporary capitalism. In order to explore such paradoxes, I will conclude by adumbrating two of the relevant fields of research on consumption.

Authenticity in Contemporary Capitalism: A Model of Four Ideal Types

The first ideal-typical dynamic (a) is cohesive and may be based on an incorporation of authenticity into economic life that completely absorbs its critical aspects. The second type (b) focuses on flexible markets and the reinforced segmentation of social worlds, which may result in a diversification and increased fragmentation of authenticity. Third, we may find coupled, but relatively independent dynamics in culture and economy (c). While the market accumulates capital by commodifying

Table 11.1 The structural dynamics of authenticity claims in contemporary capitalism

	Societal integration	**Societal disintegration**
Dominance of economic values	a) Spirit of modern capitalism (e.g. consumerism)	b) Fragmentation in flexible capitalism (deconstruction)
Autonomy of cultural values	d) Markets as (political) arenas (negotiation, deliberation)	c) Cultural capitalism (coupling of separated evolutions)

cultures, authenticity claims may nevertheless be strengthened by economic valorization. Finally, instead of a loosely coupled co-evolution, the market's dependency on cultural resources may also result in a moralization or politicization of the economic sphere (d) if normative claims are extended to this arena. In order to elaborate the theoretical arguments for these ideal types let me now turn attention to each.

Consumerism: A Spirit of Modern Capitalism

In the tradition of Max Weber's ([1904/05] 1968) famous work, *The Protestant Ethic and the Spirit of Capitalism*, sociologists have repeatedly discussed the different possible relationships between culture and capitalism in modernity. Weber himself conceived of anonymous social mechanisms that made capitalism more and more independent of its cultural and ethical roots in Protestantism (e.g. market-competition). Other scholars differ, arguing for elective affinities to the cultural environment that must be sustained even when religion declines, lest the reproduction of capitalism be jeopardized. But these affinities could be more or less adjustable. While for Daniel Bell (1976) the hedonistic outcomes of post-industrialist consumer capitalism must erode the ascetic constitution of capitalistic behavior, authors like Colin Campbell (1987) regard the mass-consumer's disposition to shop for identity as a necessary condition of modern capitalism. Consumers must acquire the ability to imagine and daydream in order to act and participate as well-integrated citizens of the market society. These autonomous, imaginative hedonists, experts in manipulating their own desires (Campbell 1987:Chap.5), anchor some mode of pleasure-seeking in modern life, which is continuously fueled and disappointed by the market sphere. According to Bauman (2000) or Sennett (2006), the qualities of fast adapting consumers are even more important today than the ethics of professions. But where do these consumerist dispositions come from?

The integration of authenticity myths into economic life is crucial here. Campbell traces the history of the modern consumerist spirit back to the romantic ethic, which stems from sentimentalism, "the other protestant ethic" (1987:

Chap.6). The romantic quest for individual originality through self-expression or self-realization motivates the aesthetic creativity of modern pleasure seekers in the sphere of consumption, even if they no longer recognize this disposition as a vital source of their lifestyle projects, their interest in fashion, their everyday consumption, and so on (Eberlein 2000). New questions arise. How stable is the historical integration of the romantic myth of authenticity into the market sphere, and in what direction does it transform moral claims of authenticity? For Campbell, an ironic and dialectic constellation still marks the commercial sphere, where imaginative hedonists nowadays long for an idealized good life: "[while] romantics may sometimes have assisted commercialism, commercial interests may also have unwittingly acted so as to promote romanticism" (1987:216). "Shifting involvement" and political criticism in particular may evolve out of those romantic ideals, when individual disappointment of consumers concurs and is publicly associated with crises in collective action (Hirschman 1982:73). The student movements of the late 1960s are a case in point. But the degree to which this movement holds as a model for future forms of critique or transcendence of capitalist relationships is again an empirical question. Many social scientists and public intellectuals are skeptical in this regard.

In order to understand how capitalism is able to adapt to changing cultural environments, let us take a closer look at the much-disputed book, *The New Spirit of Capitalism* (Boltanski and Chiapello 2005). Tracing the history of capitalism, the authors distinguish economic regimes, with culture and capitalism matching in different ways. Socially speaking for instance, industrial capitalism is embedded differently than earlier family-based bourgeois capitalism. While the latter relies on small but strong networks and commitments between family members, the former is characterized by authority and the norms of hierarchical integration, where the top of an organization is responsible for the well-being of the whole and its members. A third form of capitalism is centered on norms of individual effort and achievement. Here institutionalized cultural capital provided by certificates from schools and universities is essential. Drawing on an earlier study by Boltanski and Thévenot (2006) on regimes of justification, the authors' main aim is to reconstruct the new spirit of capitalism—that is, the justifications upon which contemporary capitalism relies.

Boltanski and Chiapello's main argument is that the critique capitalism faces is in fact a catalyst for its historical change. Where critique is difficult to ignore and poses a threat to justification, it must be incorporated into the spirit of capitalism itself. The *new* capitalist spirit is now largely characterized by the fact that it has incorporated the *artistic critique*, which has been articulated since the 1960s, into its justifications. The authors distinguish artistic from social critique: while the latter refers to solidarity, justice, and social redistribution, the former relies on norms of personal autonomy and authenticity. Hence, with their integration into the new capitalist spirit, authenticity and self-realization are promoted as motives for participation in economic life by the new capitalist justification regime itself. The new spirit absorbs the critique leveled against organized capitalism of mass production and mass consumption by satisfying the desire for authentic lifestyles via product diversification—including an ecological market segment for those seeking "pure nature"—and by integrating the desire for self-realization into the organizational *leitmotif* of new management structures. But what meaning does the quest for authenticity take on under these circumstances? As we will see, integration here depends in some respect on the fragmentation of the myth of authenticity, thus combining the first and second of our four ideal types.

Deconstruction: Fragmentation in Flexible Capitalism

The new modes of justification offer appropriate standards of social esteem for flexible accumulation and its corresponding distribution of status and position. With its demands for autonomous and authentic lifestyles, artistic critique has successfully delegitimized former assessment systems that depended on social roots, economic power and responsibility, hierarchical structures and faith in authority, and/or classical work ethics. These systems have been replaced by tests that concentrate on communication skills, the ability to network, and flexibility. To achieve this, the new justification system blurs the boundaries between economic and private life—individuals are encouraged to completely immerse themselves in the context of social cooperation and display enthusiasm, trust, and personal responsibility in doing so. The price for the extension of the scope of autonomy and options for self-realization, however, is that habitualized expectations of particular careers, social security, and ethical status guarantees have to be abandoned. The mobility and independence of network nomads who swing from contact to contact and project to project, socially and spatially, without insisting on a consistent self-image, is now considered to be the most valuable asset of human capital (Boltanski and Chiapello 2005:124; Sennett 2006).

To understand how contemporary capitalism was able to incorporate authenticity and autonomy into its justifications, one has to take the impact of post-structuralism into account. The deconstruction of authenticity and autonomy by philosophers such as Derrida, Deleuze and others has helped to make them compatible with flexible production regimes (see Boltanski and Chiapello 2005:453-455). Once the quest for one's own originality is delegitimized as part of an ideological discourse on the modern self-disciplined subject, only ironic versions of authenticity survive. Flexible capitalism challenges the quest for authenticity via lifelong self-formation by providing an alternative postmodern interpretation of authenticity; one which amounts to practices of self-expression, experimentation with multiple identities, and in which individuals orient their lives toward selectable and interchangeable commercial lifestyles. This type of authenticity is based on biographical discontinuity and relies on appropriate lifestyle resources in the field of consumption.

The resulting aestheticization and fragmentation of authenticity's validity in a highly segmented market sphere reduces the generalized criteria for being authentic to fragile and simple techniques for self-presentation in decentralized communication and interaction settings, "that do not necessarily have to plumb a deep ego which they would somehow disclose" (Boltanski and Chiapello 2005:462). These processes weaken integrative capacities as well, provoking new frictions and paradoxes in the cultural environment of contemporary capitalism. Boltanski and Chiapello point this out through an example of trust. Economic projects are a new form of social cooperation that greatly rely on the development of trust, which participants have to underpin with some credible appearance of sincerity, reliability, and at least some biographical continuity. But if we are aware that our interaction partners are likely to adjust their self-image in accordance with economic contingencies, this type of interaction order can only promote a culture of mistrust. Therefore capitalism seems to be dependent on cultural resources that cannot be reproduced within its own economic regime. This problem leads to the next ideal type.

Co-evolution: Cultural Capitalism

While artistic critique may be weakened through contemporary economic regimes, the normative power of authenticity is not fully forsaken as long as it remains an important resource for embedding markets. On the contrary, we may find a strengthening of its myths within culturally and economically segmented social worlds, thus fostering a dynamic cultural separation rather than fragmentation. Take for example the brand "Mecca Cola," an alternative soft drink for Arab and Muslim customers that simulates the refused American "Coca Cola" in taste, shape, appearance and appeal. As Uri Ram (2005) has shown, local (and this often implicitly refers to authentic) culture is massively used to create new markets, with a dual effect. First, those processes enhance the relevance of cultural self-expression and identification within social worlds. Second, they are structurally modeled after the Western mode of accumulation and commodification. This seems to be paradoxical as long as the articulation of authenticity implies a critical stance on capitalistic standardization and the "Coca-Colonization" of the lifeworld. Apparently, further modes of coupling cultural and capitalistic evolution have to be taken seriously.

Using culture as its major resource, contemporary economy takes the form of "cultural capitalism." By borrowing this term from Rifkin (2000), Sighard Neckel (2005) points to a new syncretism of economy and forms of life. In cultural capitalism, culture and economy not only bind or limit each other (as the term elective affinity suggests). In addition, building and improving their relation is now at the heart of the capitalistic enterprise itself. Authenticity is one of the most important values and its creation—for instance in brands (Arvidsson 2005)—is a kind of key technology in our weightless knowledge economy. On the consumption side of capitalism, such conditions of cultural value creation may limit its flexibility. Authenticity here is not only an issue of communication skills for cultivating a trustful climate in economic bargaining or interaction. It is also necessary for lending commodities use-value and cultural aura (Appadurai 1986:44-5; Benjamin 1969). The trouble here lies in the limits of the possibility of deliberately manufacturing such cultural resources. They can be exploited, but have to be presupposed because they follow their own rules of social (re-)production. Companies can only try to create a favorable environment for such production processes to occur. Making (unpaid) co-producers out of consumers and their communities in processes of value creation is one striking mode of colonizing and exploiting culture as kind of post-industrial labor force (Lamla 2007; Voß and Rieder 2005).

Even protests against the global expansion of capitalism and commercialism by anticonsumerist movements (e.g., No Logo!, Adbusters) can be utilized as a cultural resource for the creation of new markets (Frank 1997; Heath and Potter 2004). But this demystification of counterculture should not be overstrained. Here it is important to realize that cultural validity claims retain their momentum (and must do so) even in contexts where they are exploited economically. Paths of social, cultural, and economic development are not fully controlled in this model of co-evolution. Boltanski and Chiapello (2003:443-451, 463-466) argue for a possible revival of artistic critique insofar as, for instance, green consumers try to limit the commodification of authenticity and to preserve at least some kind of boundary between the market sphere on the one hand, and aspects of an intimate life in a sphere of altruism and gift exchange on the other. The empirical question is thus whether these cultural countermovements peacefully coexist with dynamic marketization or whether they also place structural strain on the economic sphere. If we assume that they have some serious impact on capitalist expansion, the question arises whether the underlying mechanisms involve some *grammar* of moral or ethical control (Honneth 1995). While we may observe a moralization of markets (Lash and Urry 1994; Stehr 2008) here, this does not necessarily imply a moral *control* of markets. Understanding the structural dynamic of contemporary capitalism inevitably requires studying the coupling of economic and cultural value creation in more detail. Here contentious negotiations, which take up the issue of authenticity, must also be taken into account.

Negotiation and Deliberation: Markets as (Political) Arenas

In the new economic sociology, markets are conceptualized as politics or a kind of political arena (see e.g., Appadurai 1986; Bourdieu 2005; Fligstein 1996). Whether or not they function like state institutions or public deliberation, it may still be rewarding to explore the similarities in their modes of "processual ordering" (Strauss 1993). To be sure, reconstructing the political quality of negotiations in market arenas empirically is a complex task (Lamla 2006, forthcoming) and it is important not to confuse the politicization of market issues with ideas of a democratically managed economy. The spread and emergence of a critical "politics of products" (Micheletti 2003) may nevertheless hold potential for modifying the capitalist order. For authors like Ulrich Beck (1997) a lot depends on the ability to politically organize the economic power of individual consumers. But how can such an organization be accomplished under conditions of a complex social order marked by highly segmented and differentiated social worlds? Are questions of authenticity helpful or an obstacle in this regard?

There are numerous approaches for answering such a question. Some appeal to the virtues of citizens and the need to strengthen political institutions and the law accordingly. Others promote a moral, fair, or sustainable style of consumption through marketing or a reliance on boycott or "buycott" campaigns. A third approach focuses on the mass media and the commercialization of the public sphere in order to influence or subvert the means of advertisement. For all of these approaches, the myths of authenticity may be relevant, but in disparate ways. Ecology, mental health, fakeness and irony, fashion and style, religion—there are many ways of claiming (or "breaking down") authenticity in the sphere of consumption, and the only political logic we may predict is one of conflicting identities and/or social worlds. But perhaps this is not the full story. If we consider the conditions of the three previously-considered ideal types together, a fourth type of structural dynamic also becomes plausible. While on both the production and commerce sides of capitalism authenticity demands social networking and requires elaborate communication skills, the problem of value creation, on the other hand, still depends on the production of narrative identity and creativity. Between these two constraints, a civilized myth of authenticity is able to develop as long as the public arenas of the market sphere meet at least minimum standards of deliberation. Enhancing those civil conditions could be the project of the future in reshaping our civil society. It would depend on civil society's capability of establishing and stabilizing communication links across segmented social worlds in order to bridge their frames and to reintegrate artistic and social critique (Young 2006).

If we look at the integrative capacities of global civil society, it becomes clear that this fourth model is as hypothetical as the others. To put it in Manuel Castells's (1997) terms, there are lots of tensions and conflicts between modes of a "legitimizing," a "resistant" and a new "project identity" in civil society, and it is hard to predict which one (if any) will win the struggle. It may also be a mistake to assume that a dynamic of deliberative integration will emerge in the market sphere on its own. But what we can observe up to this point is a revitalization of a consumer movement, the heterogeneity of which would not at all be detrimental to the renewal of civil society as long as it served to promote public debate on contemporary capitalism. To keep it in perspective, there is no other mode of organizing a global civil society except for such decentralized political communication about issues like cultural authenticity and its social as well as economic contexts, conditions, and implications. As long as the arena for such debate is not fully amorphous and maintains some standard of rationalization, this would not disadvantage global democracy and governance. One key object of study here is the evolution of the internet as a platform for a multifaceted intersection of social and economic worlds.

Consuming Authenticity: A Paradoxical Dynamic

Consumer-markets, from caring to tourism, today extend their claims to solving the whole range of cultural problems of human life and existence, keeping the myth of authenticity alive and active. But while making authenticity an object of desire to be consumed, corresponding commodities or services nonetheless depend on consumer's coproduction of value. Thus cultural capitalism leads to paradoxical constellations. Autonomous social worlds and commercial practices of shopping increase their tensions while simultaneously heightening their level of integration.

Traditionally, sociology has taken a skeptical stance towards the quest for an authentic life within a commercial consumer culture. As Simmel (1904) demonstrated, fashion cycles are a good example for such a paradoxical form of modern sociation [*Vergesellschaftung*]. Again and again they promise individual distinction, but are actually no more than incessant variations on an unchanging theme. On the other hand we can take Benjamin's (1973) window shopper, whose perception of the endless selection of products in the Paris arcades is torn between aesthetic delight and shocked sobriety. For him, the flaneur preserves some potential for the renewal of critique within the commercial sphere.

Consuming authenticity therefore signifies an empirically open, ambivalent dynamic in contemporary capitalism, one which does not guarantee stability but may also lead to a renewal of civil engagement through bridging artistic and social critique. This is possible because struggles for authenticity latently imply struggles for recognition and therefore social reciprocity. This hypothesis can be qualified by reconstructing movements towards establishing a new ethics of gift exchange against the commercial environment in order to counterbalance the commodification of authenticity.

In a final step, I want to briefly explore two exemplary research fields where we can empirically observe an advanced and dynamic conjunction of consumption with a quest for authenticity. The first field involves romantic love and intimate relationships; the second can be found in the intersection of market and community cultures on the internet. While the first example is important from the perspective of the individual experience of a crisis of authenticity, the second can be analyzed with regard to the quality of public consumer deliberation on the issue in market arenas.

Romantic Love

As Eva Illouz demonstrated in "Consuming the Romantic Utopia" (1997), the field of consumption harbors a series of practices that are paramount to the formation and cultivation of intimate relationships and love. The romantic ideal of love, undeniably important to the quest for authenticity, became symbiotically connected to consumerist symbols in the twentieth century. Lovers make use of the world of luxury goods and symbolically charged consumer settings (i.e., going to expensive restaurants, cinemas, or on vacation) to establish and preserve their intimate relationships, escaping from everyday life together to secure their extraordinary emotional ties in eroticized frenzies and indulgences. Georges Bataille (1991) has already pointed out that the longing for an intimate self-consciousness is at the essence of all excessive practices, and Illouz (1997), drawing on Victor Turner's (1969) concept of "liminality," similarly stresses that these consumer practices systematically transcend the postmodern culture of libidinous amusement and experimentation with multiple identities. Romantic experiences do not fragment the identity of lovers but rather restore the unity they yearn for via the emotionally-loaded experience of ritual. The consumption of romantic symbols and moods can therefore certainly support the intimate facets of relationships that allow partners to guarantee each other the emotional security and stability they need for the reflexive development of their self-identities. Nevertheless, it is worth considering whether the paradoxes that are rooted in the commercialization of romantic utopia can still be balanced under the conditions of contemporary capitalism.

In this context, Illouz's (1997:178-9) exposition raises skepticism. She examines the narrative structure of the accounts her interviewees give of their intimate relationships and romantic experiences and observes that *biographical* narratives on intimacy increasingly fail to include accounts of romantically charged erotic experiences and sexual adventures. Hence, it appears as if perpetual relationship work is becoming more and more disconnected from episodic erotic experiences. What was considered a unity in the romantic ideal is reduced to two unconnected realms of experience. While narratives concerning relationship work reveal the endeavor of reconstructing a continuous self-identity, the discontinuous stories about sexual adventures reflect a pattern of experience that seeks authenticity solely by transcending the mundane and which can be interpreted as attempts to escape efforts of establishing some degree of congruency between the autobiographical narrative and life practices.

To me this demonstrates that the quest for authenticity is developing into a paradoxical venture in contemporary capitalism, one whose goal can only inadequately be attained by consumerist means. As a result, intimate relationships may develop into "pure relationships" (Giddens 1992) where both partners primarily concentrate on their mutual emotional stabilization. This kind of relationship is typified by precarious trust negotiations that hold distance to idealistic as well as commercial interventions so that therapeutic tasks can be tackled without distractions, thus ensuring the continuity of identity. Pure relationships may in some cases successfully compensate for the biographical pressures imposed upon subjects by contingencies and uncertainties of flexible markets and superficial relationship networks, which, in turn, are justified by the new spirit of capitalism. But for others, the signs of authenticity, which the commercialization of romance formerly connected to love stories, can only be experienced by a steady increase in the doses of frenzied decadence and excess that transcend the boundaries of any sober relationship work. Thus the consumption of excitement, which has lost its connection to the justifications and coherence required of an autobiographical narrative, rapidly acquires all the aspects of an addiction that bitterly disappoints as it repeatedly fails to attain the promise of authenticity.

To sum up, there seems to be a kind of dialectical movement involving a reckless immersion in consumer culture, on the one hand, and a corresponding, opposite turn towards market-free communication, on the other. While the former serves to evade the burdens of constructing a coherent narrative of the self, the latter is the result of a growing distrust in, and disappointment with, the promises of the field of consumption.

Internet Markets and Communities

Concerning the early internet's social character, a "community model" can be distinguished from the "consumption model" (Barkardjieva 2005:165). The first model refers to communication rituals, a social, non-proprietary mode of production and its norms of reciprocity that help to constitute forms of personal friendship, social belonging, trust, and continuous solidarity. But we also find forms of social exclusion and disenchanted areas of the internet where private individuals primarily make strategic use of information without any significant social contact (e.g., product search and price comparison engines). Yet this distinction holds only for Web 1.0. In the rising era of Web 2.0, the intersection of these two models is getting stronger and consumer communities are now systematically utilized to compensate a loss of trust in the virtual market sphere by adding surplus use-value to the products (user-generated content). Their non-economic activities provide forms of advertising that the market increasingly depends on. In this regard, the internet looks much like a "digital bazaar" where information is mobilized and utilized in building trustful relationships—often as a strategy to gain an economic edge (Geertz 2001).

Take, for example, the combination of review websites with marketplaces (e.g., Amazon). Here, the principles of community building and authentication via narratives on subjective experiences are partially transformed into a commercial strategy. Product reviews are in most cases less important as a source of rational information for a buying decision. Their relevance for the suppliers arises from their quality as a means of socially or culturally re-embedding consumption in an otherwise anonymous or faceless marketplace. The designs of the technical architectures of such platforms are very well considered for achieving this goal (Lamla 2007). In such commercial internet environments, a culture of deliberation is hardly able to evolve. Instead of using the authentic experience of domestic users to anchor a cooperative, egalitarian, and rational mode of problem-solving in the lifeworld, the economic exploitation of mostly unpaid work by consumers is backed by ideologies of the "perfect market," by technical and legal restrictions on community members, as well as its over-directed relation to the market sphere and not least by the consumerist habits of Western culture itself. Under these conditions, a pretended adjustment to the "autonomous" and "authentic" will of the consumers is an efficient way of generating a market-friendly community.

This process challenges the idea of balancing proprietary and non-proprietary modes of life and production in digital environments (Benkler 2006). The extent to which ideas and frames for a gift-economy, proposed by open-source movements or advocates of sharing practices, could limit the commodification and exploitation of cultural authentication practices on the internet depends not only on the community's internal formation processes. It is also predetermined by the digital bazaar's structure as an arena for negotiating cultural and economic values, i.e., by decisions and path-dependencies concerning the distribution of power, economic, and informational resources between consumers and providers at the legal and technological levels. But as long as users provoke the dominance of private property over the internet, its history as an arena for reflecting, debating and working through our self-conceptions will remain open.

References

Appadurai, Arjun. 1986. "Introduction: Commodities and the politics of value." Pp. 3-63 in *The Social Life of Things. Commodities in Cultural Perspective*, edited by Arjun Appadurai. Cambridge: Cambridge University Press.

Arvidsson, Adam. 2005. "Brands. A critical perspective." *Journal of Consumer Culture*, 5:235-258.

Barkardjieva, Maria. 2005. *Internet Society. The Internet in Everyday Life.* London: Sage.

Bataille, Georges. [1967] 1991. *The Accursed Share. An Essay on General Economy. Volume I: Consumption.* New York: Zone Books.

Baumann, Zygmunt. 2000. *Liquid Modernity. Living in an Age of Uncertainty.* Cambridge: Polity Press.

Beck, Ulrich. 1997. *The Reinvention of Politics. Rethinking Modernity in the Global Social Order.* Oxford: Polity.

Bell, Daniel. 1976. *The Cultural Contradictions of Capitalism.* New York: Basic Books.

Benjamin, Walter. 1969. "The work of art in the age of mechanical reproduction." Pp. 217-251 in *Illuminations*, edited by Hannah Arendt. New York: Schocken Books.

Benjamin, Walter. 1973. *Charles Baudelaire: A Lyric Poet in the Era of High Capitalism.* London: New Left Books.

Benkler, Yochai. 2006. *The Wealth of Networks. How Social Production Transforms Markets and Freedom.* New Haven/London: Yale University Press.

Boltanski, Luc, and Chiapello, Ève. 2005. *The New Spirit of Capitalism.* London/New York: Verso.

Boltanski, Luc, and Thévenot, Laurent. 2006. *On Justification: Economies of Worth.* Princeton: Princeton University Press.

Bourdieu, Pierre. 2005. *The Social Structures of the Economy.* Cambridge: Polity.

Campbell, Colin. 1987. *The Romantic Ethic and the Spirit of Modern Consumerism.* Oxford: Blackwell.

Castells, Manuel. 1997. *The Information Age: Economy, Society, and Culture, Volume 2: The Power of Identity.* Oxford: Blackwell.

Eberlein, Undine. 2000. *Einzigartigkeit. Das romantische Individualitätskonzept der Moderne.* [Uniqueness. Modernity's Romantic Concept of Individuality.] Frankfurt/New York: Campus.

Fligstein, Neil. 1996. "Markets as politics. A political-cultural approach to market-institutions." *American Sociological Review*, 61:656-673.

Frank, Thomas C. 1997. *The Conquest of Cool: Business Culture, Counterculture, and the Rise of Hip Consumerism.* Chicago: University of Chicago Press.

Geertz, Clifford. [1978] 2001. "The Bazaar economy: Information and search in peasant marketing." Pp. 139-145 in *The Sociology of Economic Life*, edited by Mark Granovetter and Richard Swedberg. Cambridge: Westview Press.

Giddens, Anthony. 1991. *Modernity and Self-Identity. Self and Society in the Late Modern Age.* Cambridge: Polity.

—— 1992. *The Transformation of Intimacy. Sexuality, Love, and Eroticism in Modern Societies.* Cambridge: Polity.

Goffman, Erving. 1959. *The Presentation of Self in Everyday Life.* New York: Anchor.

Habermas, Jürgen. 1984. *The Theory of Communicative Action.* Vol. 1. Boston: Beacon Press.

Heath, Joseph, and Potter, Andrew. 2004. *The Rebel Sell. Why the Culture Can't Be Jammed.* Toronto: HarperCollins.

Hirschman, Albert O. 1982. *Shifting Involvements. Private Interest and Public Action.* Princeton: Princeton University Press.

Honneth, Axel. 1995. *The Struggle for Recognition: The Moral Grammar of Social Conflicts.* Cambridge: Polity Press.

Illouz, Eva. 1997. *Consuming the Romantic Utopia. Love and the Cultural Contradictions of Capitalism.* Berkeley/Los Angeles/London: University of California Press.

Kaufmann, Jean-Claude. 2005. *Die Erfindung des Ich: Eine Theorie der Identität.* [The Invention of the Self: A Theory of Identity] Konstanz: UVK.

Lamla, Jörn. 2006. Politisierter Konsum – konsumierte Politik. Kritikmuster und Engagementformen im kulturellen Kapitalismus. [Politicized consumption – consumed politics. Criticism and involvement in cultural capitalism] Pp. 9-37 in Politisierter Konsum – konsumierte Politik, [Politicized Consumption – Consumed Politics] edited by Jörn Lamla and Sighard Neckel. Wiesbaden: VS-Verlag.

—— 2007. *Building a Market-Community. Paradoxes of Culturalization and Merchandization in the Internet.* Paper prepared for the Conference: "The institutional embeddedness of markets," Max Planck Institute for the Study of Societies, Köln, 1.-3. Februar 2007 (URL: http://www.mpifg.de/maerkte-0702/papers/Lamla_Maerkte2007.pdf).

—— forthcoming. "Consumer Citizen: The constitution of consumer democracy in sociological perspective." *German Policy Studies*, Special Issue: Reshaping consumer policy in Europe?.

Lash, Scott, and Urry, John. 1994. *Economies of Signs and Space*. London: Sage.

Micheletti, Michele. 2003. *Political Virtue and Shopping. Individuals, Consumerism, and Collective Action*. New York; Houndmills et al.: Palgrave Macmillan.

Nassehi, Armin. 2006. *Der soziologische Diskurs der Moderne.* [The Sociological Discourse of Modernity.] Frankfurt am Main: Suhrkamp.

Neckel, Sighard. 2005. "Die Marktgesellschaft als kultureller Kapitalismus. Zum neuen Synkretismus von Ökonomie und Lebensform." [Market society as cultural capitalism. On the new syncretism of economy and way of life.] Pp. 198-211 in *Triumph und Elend des Neoliberalismus*. [Neoliberalism's Triumph and Misery.] edited by : Kurt Imhof and Thomas S. Eberle. Zurich: Seismo.

Ram, Uri. 2005. "Don't drink stupid, drink committed." Die Verwässerung des Engagements. ["Don't Drink Stupid, Drink Committed": The Liquidation of Commitments.] *Forschungsjournal Neue Soziale Bewegungen*, 18:53-64.

Ricœur, Paul. 1992. *Oneself as Another.* Chicago: University of Chicago Press.

Rifkin, Jeremy. 2000. *The Age of Access: The New Culture of Hypercapitalism. Where All of Life is a Paid-For Experience*. New York: Tarcher/Putnam.

Sennett, Richard. 2006. *The Culture of the New Capitalism.* Yale: Yale University Press.

Simmel, Georg. 1904. Fashion. *International Quarterly*, 10:130-155.

Stehr, Nico. 2008. *Moral Markets: How Knowledge and Affluence Change Consumers and Products.* Boulder: Paradigm Publisher.

Strauss, Anselm L. 1959. *Mirrors and Masks: The Search for Identity*. Chicago: Free Press.

—— 1993. *Continual Permutations of Action*. New York: Aldine de Gruyter.

Taylor, Charles. 1991. *The Malaise of Modernity.* Concord: Anancy Press.

Trilling, Lionel. 1972. *Sincerity and Authenticity.* Cambridge: Harvard University Press.

Turner, Victor. 1969. *The Ritual Process, Structure and Anti-Structure*. New York: Aldine.

Voß, G. Günter, and Rieder, Kerstin. 2005. *Der arbeitende Kunde. Wenn Konsumenten zu unbezahlten Mitarbeitern werden.* [The Working Customer. When Consumers Become Unpaid Employees.] Frankfurt am Main/New York: Campus.

Weber, Max. [1904/05] 1968. *The Protestant Ethic and the Spirit of Capitalism.* London: Unwin.

Young, Iris Marion. 2006. "Responsibility and global justice. A social connection model." *Social Philosophy and Policy*, 23:102-130.

Chapter 12

Saying What We Mean; Meaning What We Say: Authentic Dialogue in Aboriginal Communities

Joshua Guilar and Lynn Charman

At the front of the school is a large, totem eagle. We meet behind the eagle in the cultural center, which is part of an impressive collection of buildings and playing fields that make up the First Nation's Tribal School on the Saanich Peninsula on Southern Vancouver Island. After greetings, we set up tables and chairs in a square so we can see each other. There is no need for explanation as each person knows their role. A researcher-instructor and I are the only non-Aboriginal people in the conversation, which has about twenty participants. The occasion for our get-together is the Cultural Advisory Committee meeting of the Tribal School Board. We are gathering to discuss a collaborative research project involving the Tribal School District and my university.

The facilitator, who is also the receptionist in the administrative office, announces the agenda for the morning. We pray, and then the agenda begins with the two non-Aboriginal researchers detailing the scope of the project: a collaborative, participatory study of traditional culture. In their comments, the researchers acknowledge how academic research had historically failed to provide benefit to First Nations. Then, it is the committee members' turn. The first to speak is Peggy, an influential member. "Historically," she says, "researchers serve themselves and not First Nations." She goes on to list her concerns about ethics and to cite research that details the ethics of research with Aboriginal communities. She sets a tone that, while being diplomatic, is deeply concerned about the colonization of her culture by researchers.

Paul's speaking turn follows. Paul is a middle-aged man, a young Elder. At first he speaks in their traditional language. We make out only a few of his words, but one phrase we both clearly recognize is a reference to white people. He compliments the work done to date on the program within the Tribal School, but says he does not want to share their culture outside the community. They have been treated badly in the past, and they do not want to give away more of their culture. Others speaking after Paul amplify this point of view by explaining their feelings about current controversies in the larger community. One example is about how condo developers have been destroying a sacred site nearby. One person tells a story about how she has shared information to inform the writing of a book, which she believes was of little benefit to her.

Everyone listens.

Then the youth begin to speak. They thank us, the two researchers. One young woman cries as she shares her feelings about being back in the community. At last, some Elders begin to speak in support of the project, given certain conditions such as more egalitarian compensation between Elders and researchers. Many support the proposal because of benefits for the youth. During a break, an Elder sitting beside me tells me, "You should be careful when you speak here. We have many people in our community with much knowledge, although they may not be called Doctor."

We talk for almost two and a half hours, but time seems to fly. As the conversation draws near to a close we ask: "perhaps we need more clarity to move forward, we have written four pages of the grant proposal at this time, the next step is writing twenty-one pages. Shall we proceed with your support?" Someone tells the facilitator she could call a vote, and she does. Everyone puts up their hand to support the proposal, which will be next taken to the school board. The meeting adjourns.

* * *

The story above is an amalgam of many conversations we have had with Coast Salish people. The story portrays many of the general features of Coast Salish dialogue that we will explain throughout this chapter. Authenticity in Aboriginal cultures is an emergent quality of dialogue and relationships within the culture. Our interaction with Aboriginal cultures has been predominantly with Coast Salish Cultures in British Columbia. Certainly there are differences in dialogue and authenticity across First Nations cultures and within Coast Salish culture. Also, each person—Aboriginal or non-Aboriginal—is different, unique. The views we give here are based on our work over the past years with Coast Salish culture but also the review of literature which is pan-Indian in scope. We use the word Aboriginal in a broad sense and do not wish to undermine differences.

Authenticity in Aboriginal cultures is a topic about which Indigenous people are reluctant to talk. To say that someone is authentic is an obvious opportunity to be razzed. I have heard Aboriginals say of one another, "he is an apple, red on the outside and white on the inside." This slam flies in the face of much that we will write in this chapter. Yet, however paradoxical and complex, authentic dialogue remains as a reality for traditional Indigenous people. In this chapter, by authenticity, we refer to being true to traditional roots (Hanson 1989), which come to be known through dialogic relations in an Aboriginal community. For most Coast Salish, authenticity means being true to traditional Coast Salish spiritual realities.

Respect to the value of authenticity begins in childhood. Walter Ong (1982) explains that oral (and Aboriginal) communities tend to be conservative and traditional because of the mental energy invested in saying over and over what has arduously been learned over the ages and this inhibits intellectual experimentation. Because knowledge is hard to acquire, those who conserve it (the Elders) are highly revered. Respect for Elders, respect for the truth, and respect for all others is intrinsic to Indigenous consciousness. Oral narratives socialize children into these norms of their group's behaviours and they are taught to listen patiently to the teachings of the Elders (Battiste and Henderson 1999). They are encouraged to "Act to everybody as if they were your own relatives" (Kluckhon 1949:347). Writing downgrades and threatens the traditional role of the Elder.

In tight-knit First Nation communities each person has a right to personal identity but also has a social responsibility to the community and to other life forms within the local environment. Members are constantly taught to be sensitive to and respect the feelings of others, to be generous, self-disciplined, and to accept a certain amount of teasing with a sense of humour. Humour is highly valued as a means of maintaining harmony. Children today as in the past are subjected to very little discipline when very young, yet they were traditionally trained to endure extremes of cold, pain and isolation to build self-reliance and courage at maturity. Children learned early they could not survive without the reciprocal benefits and obligations of community (Battiste and Henderson 1999; Peterson 1990).

Aboriginal communities tend to generate authentic members beginning with dialogues with children. These dialogues rely on the perceptiveness of older community members (Elders) appreciating the uniqueness and wholeness of children. This value for the unique differences and contribution of children contrasts with Western cultures which for the most part value (at least in practice) social stratification and inequality rather than uniqueness and wholeness. For example, Western education seeks to grade people from A to F, or fit and unfit. Aboriginal culture features non-interference and non-imposition, which lead to what is perceived to be a form of authentic communication. This perceptiveness of Aboriginal Elders comes from traditional culture: ways of speaking, an emphasis on relationship, respect, non-interference and listening.

Also, through disease, theft of their land, assimilation efforts such as residential schools, prejudice and outright violence Aboriginals have suffered mightily. Through all these hardships, Aboriginal communities have survived. Due to the challenges to First Nations' freedom to practice their own life ways, engaging in authentic dialogue amongst themselves and others requires hard work. Thus, a sense of authenticity is constructed, bit by bit, in everyday life through interaction.

Of course, dialogue takes place differently in different cultures. First Nations traditional ways of communicating and Western theories of dialogue can inform each other. The purpose of this chapter is to lay out initial ideas about Aboriginal dialogue and authenticity. First the chapter provides a background against which we can consider authentic dialogue in First Nations. Next, the essay describes four features of dialogue in Coast Salish culture. Finally, the essay summarizes ideas about Coast Salish authenticity and dialogue and how these ideas may help us live together across the larger society.

Background

Dialogue and First Nations' Ways of Communicating Interpersonally

Dialogism theories explain how we are constituted socially through communication (Anderson, Baxter, and Cissna 2004; Bakhtin 1981; Mead 1934). Dialogue has come to be a major, evolving theme in areas from communication studies through sociology and anthropology to humanistic psychology (Stewart 2006). Dialogue is not synonymous with conversation. Conversation may take place through turn-taking but dialogue is an ideal involving a respectful and honest encounter amongst people. As a form of conversation, dialogue holds promise to cure many of society's ills: from dysfunctional families, to organizations suffering from a lack of knowledge about what really matters, and to international disputes where a lack of understanding leads to unnecessary violence (Putnam and Kolb 2000). Dialogue is both an old and new normative ideal—its origins can be traced back millennia in traditional societies and through so-called civilizations.

Many First Nations people continue to communicate with one another in ways that differ greatly from the accustomed face-to-face interactions employed by the dominant society in Canada, and reflect a social etiquette that is intimately tied to their unique practices of social control (Ryan 1992; also see Greenbaum 1985; Haig-Brown 1995). Those who have studied traditional communication and culture in First Nations have written about dialogic features as essential to such cultures. For example Battiste and Henderson (2000:51) describe their societies as extended communities of relations "in which dialogue and togetherness are valued and respected." Rupert Ross (1992, 1996) has written about features such as non-interference, silence, listening, collaboration, consensus, and respect as characteristic of First Nations communication and culture. Isaacs (1999) speaks of the different language structure in First Nations' communication that creates an experiential interchange.

Dialogue, as a subject area, gained importance throughout the twentieth century and continues to be a central area of study to this day. Philosophical anthropologists such as Martin Buber (1965, 2005), Mikhail Bakhtin (1981) and the philosopher Hans Georg Gadamer (1989) have contributed to knowledge concerning dialogic practice and theory. Further, educators such as Paulo Freire (1972) have contributed a pedagogical theory of dialogue. Even physicists such as David Bohm (1996, 2004) have influenced thinking and practices such as organizational learning through knowledge about dialogue.

There is far more *written* on dialogue from Western perspectives than from Aboriginal perspectives because the latter are oral traditions. However, the Western theory that views dialogue as a process of relationship building is congruent with

Aboriginal knowledge and their dialogic traditions (Yankelovitch 1999). Thus, research on Aboriginal dialogue is a potentially rich area of study (Bohm 1996; Senge 1994; Senge, Scharmer, Jaworski, and Flowers 2006). Through traditional practices such as talking circles First Nations members developed and used dialogue as a means of governing themselves in their daily lives, for educating their people and for diplomacy. Traditional First Nations societies tend to be extended communities of relations "in which dialogue and togetherness are valued and respected" (Battiste and Henderson, 2000:51). The most important lesson an Aboriginal child learns is the value of relationships as she comes to know all the people around her and looks to them for guidance.

Those who have studied traditional communication and culture in First Nations have written about dialogic features as meaningful within such cultures. For example, Rupert Ross (1992, 1996) has written about features of traditional dialogue such as non-interference, silence, listening, collaboration, consensus, and respect as characteristic of First Nations communication and culture. The traditions of dialogue vary with First Nations' cultures but can be traced back through the tribal practices of Indigenous peoples throughout the world. Some estimate that tribal practices of dialogue go back as far back as 10,000 years (Alexander 2005). First Nations traditionally foster the necessary discipline for dialogue within their traditions from the moment a child is born, and this discipline is instilled through daily practice (Battiste and Henderson 2000; Mead 1934).

First Nations' perspectives on dialogue are found also in the works of the Four Worlds Development Project (Sacred Tree 1988) and Dan Moonhawk Alford (1994). Additional perspectives related to First Nations and dialogue come from anthropologists (e.g., Basso 1972; Kluckhorn 1949). First Nations communication and culture have much to teach about dialogue. In the words of one First Nations member,

> In our community we go to a meeting [of chief and council] and we say what we want to say. Whether you're disgruntled or whether you're happy … you have every right to go to the meetings. You know you are going to have an option to be able to get up and say what you have to say. But when we went to the meeting at the school board … [and gave our presentation] I thought we were going to sit down and have a discussion with these people … and it was "thank you very much, next!" We didn't even get to talk. And that was when I realized what we have here [in our community]. I thought is that how non-Native people treat their own people … I was utterly shocked (Broad, Boyer and Chataway 2006:54).

There are, of course, differences and similarities between theories of dialogue in Western and in First Nations cultures. These differences will create shared theories of dialogue that are intercultural. First Nations' traditional ways of communication have features such as non-interference which illuminate and extend Western ideas of dialogue—Bohm's (1996) idea of suspension, for example. The reverse is also true. Western notions of dialogue extend practices of traditional First Nations communication. For example, Ross (1996) explained how Western practices of open communication have been helpful in psychological interventions within Aboriginal communities. We may find that differences across many cultures can extend our shared understanding of dialogue.

Dialogue and Authenticity

Authenticity, as a member of a First Nations community, is emergent from dialogue, from relationships. Aboriginal thinking is not contrary to metaphysical realities (the Elders' seeing the spiritual being of the child, for example). Aboriginal thinking is also phenomenological in nature in that each person has to work out their own way for themselves. Authenticity in Aboriginal thinking is both emergent, e.g., from culture, dialogue, and relationship; metaphysical, e.g., through each person's relationship with spirit; and phenomenological—a uniqueness born of personal experience. Authenticity in Aboriginal culture is not exclusive but includes all modes of knowing—dialogical, metaphysical, phenomenological, and empirical. Authenticity is aided by Elders who value the uniqueness of the child, and with whom they do not interfere but reinforce through perception and appreciation.

Children become members of a society through the process of socialization. While the structure of this process is the same, certain values of ways of behaving are emphasized in one culture, and different behaviours are emphasized in others. For example, Western children are socialized to individualistic values, and Aboriginal children are socialized toward a more collectivist orientation. So, why do First Nations members tend to behave authentically when so many others tend toward downplaying this value, or at least to find it difficult to enact? An answer to this question comes out of the symbolic interaction theory of George Herbert Mead (1934). The idea is that people develop a sense of self by perceiving how significant others perceive them. Aboriginal children are perceived by healthy Elders as coming into this world complete, a gift and whole. The beauty of difference is valued in Aboriginal culture (Williams 2008), and authenticity plays a key role in this.

The growth of Aboriginal children begins with an early, protected, universal-identity. The young child does not feel barriers between self and the universe. Rather, the child is connected and given space by significant others such as Elders. At five or six, the child becomes more engaged in the everyday world. Again the Elders help. At five or six years of age, the Elders encourage the children out into the world to learn. Interference in the development of the child is not the norm, non-interference is. With adolescence, Aboriginal youths assume responsibility helped by the gifts with which they came into the world (Williams 2008).

Characteristics of Authentic Dialogue in Coast Salish Nations

The four features summarized here are not mutually exclusive. For example, traditional ways of speaking emphasize relationship, listening, non-interference, and respect. We give these features their own subsections to aid our understanding.

Traditional Ways of Speaking

> Language is the means through which much of Aboriginal culture is preserved. However, Aboriginal languages are currently gravely threatened by extinction. Traditional ways of speaking do not set up dichotomies of right and wrong that undermine relationship. Traditional ways of thinking do not impose a judgment valid for all people and all time. Traditional relationships respect the unique perspective of each person (Ross 1992).

Aboriginal wisdom such as is evident in Coast Salish culture is an ancient form of knowledge, which evolved separately from Western thought and is derived from a traditional and close experience with nature. This knowledge has been passed down through generations via oral traditions and taught by people who had acquired a high degree of wisdom over a lifetime of learning (Ghostkeeper 1999).

Many Aboriginal community members are currently involved in learning their traditional languages due to knowledge that Aboriginal thinking relies, at least in part, in understanding how to think in traditional language (McCarty, Romero and Zepeda 2006). However, traditional ways of speaking can influence the use of any language. Aboriginal communities are now involved in carrying on their traditions in mainstream languages such as English as well as mastering their traditional, Aboriginal languages. Obviously, speaking traditionally in adopted languages as well as mastering traditional languages is tied to authenticity. For Aboriginals, being authentic requires connecting to one's own culture, particularly through using traditional ways of speaking.

Aboriginal language is a system of sounds, which expresses the consciousness of a society and embodies the way people in that society think. By learning and speaking the language of the community, individuals absorb what Bohm (1996) referred to as participatory thought. Or as Treuer states: "Our Native language embodies a value system about how we ought to live and relate to each other … It gives a name to relations among kin, to roles and responsibilities among family members, ties with the broader clan group" (2001:87). Although Aboriginal thought can be conveyed in English, traditional Indigenous languages make thinking Aboriginal easier, which is true in all cultures.

Aboriginal languages do not include either/or dichotomies but embrace a reality in which everything is in a constant flux of creative transformation and renewal. Aboriginal languages are rich in words that represent the energy and spiritual forces that animate the temporary shapes and forms we perceive with our senses (Henderson 2000). Words in stories are not strictly a metaphor but a way of describing a reality in which at the level of life, animation and spirit, everything *is* the same, everything comes from the same energies and manifests the same patterns. Not only do Aboriginal languages have different words for things, they express a different understanding of what is important about things (Alford 1994; Ross 1996). Communicating in traditional ways requires attention and work. As one Coast Salish leader said to us, you have to wear the teachings.

Dan Moonhawk Alford (1994) has written on what distinguishes First Nations languages. He wrote that in Aboriginal languages, God is not a noun but "a verb, a process, a relationship, with no form and no gender but animate (an attitude), experienced in both manifest/-ing realms, and named in a non-arbitrary manner" (p. 4).

When Rupert Ross (1996) examined the differences in languages he noticed how comparatively harsh the English language is, how it responds to the world by encouraging judgmental and argumentative attitudes among those who speak it. In his book on Aboriginal justice, Ross (1996) describes a series of dialogues initiated by the late David Bohm entitled "Dialogues between Western and Aboriginal Scientists." Ross attended one such dialogue, hosted by Leroy Little Bear in Lethbridge, Alberta, where a group of distinguished Aboriginal scholars conversed over three days with a group of distinguished physicists. In a conversation regarding the move from Particle Theory towards Wave Theory, participants also discussed the differences between Aboriginal languages and English. The scientists and the scholars found similarities between Aboriginal and Scientific thought. For example, what many physicists refer to as Chaos Theory, some First Nations refer to as Trickster. Aboriginal languages more easily expressed these concepts than English. Though Ross confesses that the conversation was somewhat over his head, the Aboriginal people and the physicists communicated with each other easily. Ross wrote this was his introduction to the sophistication of Aboriginal languages.

As important as language is, and we appreciate the many efforts to revitalize traditional Indigenous languages, socialization may occur in any language. Although stronger cultural practices occur with traditional language, interestingly enough, important cultural elements pertaining to authenticity remain even in adopted languages. Many Aboriginals now speak English, and still teach their children their traditional (i.e., authentic) values and practices.

Respect and the Ethics of Non-Interference

Rupert Ross (1992), who spent over thirty years as a provincial Crown prosecutor, and regularly visited Northern Ontario Native communities, uncovered several ethical aspects of First Nations dialogue that have been the source of misunderstanding with other cultures. Over this period Ross developed deep personal relationships and the trust of the communities in which he worked. One of the most important principles of many Aboriginal cultures is a largely unspoken ethic of non-interference. Ross's information came from Clare Brant, a Mohawk and a practicing psychiatrist, who had studied the depths of both traditional and present-day Indigenous societies.

As Brant says, an "Indian will never interfere in any way with the rights, privileges and activities of another person ... it is forbidden, rude" (Ross 1992:12). As Brant further states, "we are loath to confront people. We are very loath to give advice to anyone if the person is not specifically asking for advice" (Ross 1992:13). By appreciating and respecting difference, many Aboriginal cultures promote the authenticity of difference.

To show how strongly this ethic is embedded in the culture Ross explained that if a group of First Nations people were riding in a car owned by the driver, no member of the group would give the driver instructions even if the car was about to hit a deer or rock slide. To do this would be interfering with the freedom of the individual. Giving advice is considered confrontational and does not support another strong ethic within First Nations society, which is harmony. The non-interference and harmony principles can partly explain how the Canadian legal system is largely dysfunctional for Aboriginals. The Canadian legal system is intentionally confrontational and First Nations people are reluctant to criticize another by testifying in court. To testify against someone in a court of law is considered an immoral act by many First Nations people.

A factor that possibly contributes to the high rate of Aboriginal incarcerations is the ethic of sincerity, a synonym of authenticity. In Aboriginal justice systems it is important to acknowledge one's misdeeds and make restitution to maintain harmony within the group. In traditional times, failing to tell the truth often led to banishment from the community. Native justice does not recognize the legal right to silence to avoid self-incrimination (Ross 1992).

How First Nations define "truth" was partly revealed from transcripts of hearings that considered an injunction to stop the first James Bay hydroelectric power development project in northern Quebec. Prior to giving his testimony, a Cree Elder was asked to swear to tell the truth. He asked the translator to explain the term "truth." When the translator explained that the truth was something that holds for all people and is valid regardless of whom is speaking, he replied: "I can't promise to tell you the truth; I can only tell you what I know" (Castellano 2000:25).

Respect for Elders, respect for truth and respect for all others are intrinsic to Aboriginal consciousness (Ghostkeeper 2004). Through oral narratives children are socialized into the norms of their group's behaviours. They are taught to be especially respectful and how to listen patiently to the teachings of the Elders (Battiste and Henderson 1999). They are taught to "act to everybody as if they were your own relatives" (Kluckhon 1949:347). The stories told by the Elders to educate the young are non-prescriptive and respect the social norm of non-interference in social relationships (Castellano 2000).

In tight knit First Nations communities each person has a right to an individualistic, personal identity but also has a social responsibility to the community and to other life forms within the local environment (Battiste and

Henderson 1999). Each person is taught to be sensitive to and respect the feelings of others, to be generous, self-disciplined and to accept a certain amount of razzing with a sense of humour. Humour is highly valued as a means of maintaining harmony. Children are rarely punished for rude behaviour. Children are rewarded for their uniqueness. As part of a collective each person has rights and advantages as well as obligations and responsibilities to the whole community (Battiste and Henderson 1999).

Silence and Listening

William Isaacs pointed out that in today's world our problems do not stem from a lack of words but rather from an "inflationary glut of words" (Isaacs 1999:46). The more words we incorporate in this modern—in a communicative sense—age, the less meaningfulness we derive from them. However, in the oral tradition of First Nations, words are powerful and must be used carefully (Alexander 2005). A commonly held belief among many First Nations is that the world emerges from the spoken word to become reality, which is a central point in interactionism, constructivism, and phenomenology (Guignon 2004).

The tradition of silence and relatively infrequent use of repetition of sentences and ideas is a unique feature of First Nations dialogue noted by Deborah Tannen (1989) in her comparative studies of various oral cultures that generally feature a high degree of repetitive exchange.

Normative ideals on dialogue require that we listen respectfully to others by suspending our opinions so that we can cultivate our own voice and draw from the intelligence that is at the center of our being. Isaacs (1999:47) refers to this as the "intelligence of the heart" and the way by which we regain the deeply shared meaning behind our words to perceive what really matters to each of us. What really matters to the heart fits with First Nations' traditions of silence, listening and respect: an essential ingredient for the empathy necessary to become the "I in the other's story for a moment, feeling, sensing, and thinking from their perspective. True empathy is always interactive and may lead to the creation of a third shared culture" (LeBaron 2004:19).

Silence does not always imply absence, sometimes it is simply the unheard or un-hearable, that which cannot be seen or experienced except in silence. This, according to Peter Cole (2000) is partly because of the nature of First Nations' languages, which allows a perception of only parts of the world. Language is "about," it is a shared space in which the language of the individual and the language of the society can enter into dialogue not only in terms of reflection but refraction and diffusion (Bakhtin 1981; Mead 1934).

Silence is often a reflection of the ethic of non-interference in which First Nations refrain from offering opinions. When Rupert Ross (1992) asked direct questions in northern Cree communities he often met with limited responses and silence. He eventually learned to speak in terms of the various options available in forming a decision as if he were thinking out loud. In response, people began to speak in an unhurried manner punctuated by long silences as they too thought out loud, weighing the variables of a given situation. They would recite and subtly emphasize facts through repetition, which had led them to their own conclusion. Ross discovered that it was important not to interrupt the conversation but to listen carefully. He observed this same dynamic at play in band meetings where everyone took turns making speeches that recited facts but gave no opinions. There was little or none of the competition that characterizes meetings in the Western tradition. Instead, the speeches appeared to go in circles often repeating facts. In the end no particular recommendation or conclusion was stated, and yet there was agreement among the group as to which facts were most significant, pointing towards the most reasonable conclusion. It was unnecessary to state the conclusion because everyone left the meeting knowing what it was. The behaviours of preferring facts to conclusions and harmony to confrontation may seem indirect. However, these behaviours demonstrate respect for existing differences within the community.

Other observed aspects of the use of silence reflect the seriousness with which First Nations people treat relationships because of their ethics of social responsibility and social obligations. Some Aboriginal people who encounter each other in public places, and who are strangers to each other, often remain silent neither acknowledging the other person nor asserting themselves. Formal introductions by others are considered "presumptuous and unnecessary" (Basso 1972:308). Entering into a social relationship is a matter that calls for caution and verbal reticence because in First Nations cultures, people cannot relate to others as "mere acquaintances" (Wieder and Pratt 1990:52). Entering into conversation implies mutual acknowledgment and the "obligation to engage in further interaction whenever the conversants' paths cross … these obligations may be quite cumbersome, for they supersede other obligations" (Weider and Pratt 1990:53). Again, we can see how Aboriginal behaviours of silence result from respect for relationship.

Parents may engage in long periods of silence at reunions following a prolonged absence such as a child attending boarding school or some other outside experience, which might have altered the child's attitudes. Until their child becomes familiar again parents often refrain from speaking (Basso 1972). Silence is strongly advised in situations where one is the recipient of an angry verbal attack. An enraged person is considered to be temporarily "crazy" and the most appropriate response is to avoid attracting attention to oneself and escalating the attack. In some First Nations cultures it is considered courteous to refrain from conversation with people who are experiencing intense emotions such as grief. Silence is also appropriate during curing or healing ceremonies that involve singing (Ibid. 1972).

In sum, whereas silence in Aboriginal culture promotes harmony, those outside the culture often see silence as indirectness. In contrast, silence can be a sincere expression of sincerity. When many Aboriginals feel the silence and protect self and others from harm, they act from a deep place of understanding.

Primacy of Relationships

A review of available literature reveals that although Indigenous cultures and languages are as diverse as the North American landscape, they share a worldview informed by the common belief that "their environment is shaped and created by living forces … Aboriginal worldviews are empirical relationships with local ecosystems, and Aboriginal languages are an expression of these relationships" (Battiste 2000:259). Peter Senge (1994; Senge, Scharmer, Jaworski and Flowers 2006) advocates the type of systems thinking that is a central part of Aboriginal life. First Nations members view the world as a series of interrelationships rather than cause and effect chains (Cajete 1999). Aboriginal people are in tune with the cycles and circular nature of time and life whereas the dominant Western perspective perpetuates a fragmented, snapshot view of life (Cajete 1999; Henderson 2000; Ghostkeeper 2004). In other words, Aboriginal peoples understand what scientists have only recently come to envision, that everything in our world is composed of energy or spirit in a continuous state of transformation or flux and therefore all time, space and events are interconnected (Ross 1996).

Many Indigenous peoples experience no separation between the physical world and the spirit world. Indigenous peoples impart to their children through ritual, storytelling and dialogue how everything comes from the Great Spirit or Creator and is one. Everything, including inanimate objects, has a soul and is to be respected (Ghostkeeper 2005). Many Aboriginal people understand that the land was a gift from the Creator; that they are of the land and guardians of their lands (Ghostkeeper 2005). The Aboriginal world view is spiritual, and traditional teachings are significant as Indigenous communities integrate their everyday life with their spiritual commitments.

For communities to subsist through direct efforts as hunters, fishers, farmers and gatherers, First Nations people had to be scientists. Indigenous knowledge is considered scientific due to its empirical nature based on systematic experimentation and observation (Cajete 1999). This knowledge differs from Western science by virtue of being highly localized and social. Native science is based on the web of relationships that exist between humans, plants, animals, natural forces, spirit and local landforms. Often the scientific judgment of Aboriginal people contradicts that of Western academic tradition and has proven to have greater validity. The inferences Aboriginal people derive from their science are not based on iterative, quantitative analysis in a controlled setting, but on a convergence of various different perspectives accumulated over generations (Cajete 1999). Because Indigenous knowledge is limited to a small region, and is rooted in personal experience, it makes no claim to universality (Battiste and Henderson 1999; Castellano 2000). By making no claim to universality, room is made for being responsible for one's own knowledge, which is a condition for sincere communication.

Trust is necessary in the accumulation of an oral literature that is based on personal experiences, which are conveyed through stories that employ mythical language. Though suspicious of second hand claims, First Nations people rarely challenge another's observations, instead they put the information in context with what they know about the past perceptiveness and integrity of the speaker. Because of the personal nature of knowledge, disparate and even contradictory perceptions are accepted as valid because they are unique to the person. Elders in a talking circle or council meeting will not argue as to whose perception is the truth, but subject the accumulated stories to collective study and consensus building. In other words, collective wisdom is arrived at through the slow, dialogic process of "putting our minds together" (Castellano 2000:26).

The extended family is the basis of Indigenous knowledge. In First Nations communities, families are much more than father, mother and siblings. Families extend to godparents, grandparents, aunts, uncles, cousins and generally the whole community. Each child receives the protection of his or her community as the community contributes to the formation of the child's identity (Battiste and Henderson 1999). From the moment of birth, First Nations children are immersed in dialogue, togetherness, and are taught the value of relationships (Battiste and Henderson 1999).

According to Angela Wilson (1996), her grandmother's stories were much more than a simple method of education. They were part of an intimate process that deeply ingrained a sense of kinship responsibility, a responsibility that conveys culture, identity and an essential sense of belonging. Through listening to stories that she could trace back through seven generations of her grandmothers she came to know what it means to be a Dakota woman. In this case, being an authentic Dakota woman took birth, time and hard work. Whereas a Western tradition of narrative socialization exists (Guignon 2004), this tradition is predominantly postmodern whereas Wilson's account above represents participatory or premodern socialization.

Conclusion

All over the globe, Aboriginal people have been denied an equal speaking ground in communicating with Westerners because the latter insist on enforcing their own codes of meaning and behaviours. An example of this is the context of treaty talks, where we have yet to create a true dialogue between negotiating partners (Turner 2004). To make progress it is vital that all parties come to a better understanding of the principles of dialogue and that non-Aboriginal people learn how to recognize and overcome deeply entrenched colonial bias shaped by history, faith, education, and consumerism in order to listen to First Nations people.

The primary reason to enter into authentic dialogue is to create mutual understanding and awareness through a respectful, interactive sharing among equals. First Nations can teach much about dialogical principles of communication. Work remains to apply these principles in efforts toward Aboriginal economic development, treaty negotiations and education, which hold potential benefits for Aboriginal communities. Empirical work is needed to determine the nature of such conversations and to understand Aboriginal complaints about the current monological processes.

This article has laid a foundation for the understanding of authentic dialogue in many Aboriginal cultures. These features are illustrated in the story about the meeting at the beginning of this article. At this meeting, all participants felt that they were in profound relationship with each other and felt they could say whatever they wished without the interference of others. People listened carefully and nobody interrupted. Participants were not primarily trying to impress or impose, they were orienting toward understanding and respecting each other. Note also that harmony was achieved and that it was the prompting of a non-Aboriginal that each member voted to support the outcome of the meeting. Finally, those with fluency spoke their own traditional language with effect.

Dialogue occurs differently in different cultures. Members of different cultures have much to teach members of other cultures about their authentic ways of speaking, dialogue, respect, listening and relationship. With a respectful attitude and through authentic dialogue in ethical collaboration with First Nations partners, we can extend existing theories and practices of dialogue toward learning how to live better together.

References

Alexander, Paul. 2005. *Coalescing the Field of Dialogue*. Union Institute and University, Ohio, USA. Unpublished Doctoral Dissertation.

Alford, D. 1994. "God is Not a Noun in Native America: Worldview Through Experiment." http://www.enformy.com/dma-berb.htm. Retrieved August 16, 2006.

Anderson, R., L. Baxter and K. Cissna. 2004. *Dialogue: Theorizing Difference in Communication Studies*. Thousand Oaks, CA: Sage.

Bakhtin, Mikhail. 1981. *The Dialogical Imagination: Four Essays by M.M. Bakhtin*. Translation by M. Holquist. Austin, TX: University of Texas Press.

—— 1986. *Speech Genres and Other Late Essays*. Translation by V. McGee. Austin, TX: University of Texas Press.

Basso, Keith. 1972. "To Give Up on Words: Silence in Apache Culture" in *Language and Social Context*, edited by P.P. Giglioli. New York: Penguin.

Battiste, Marie. 2000. "Maintaining Aboriginal Identity, Language, and Culture in Modern Society." Pp. 192-208 in *Reclaiming Indigenous Voice and Vision*, edited by Marie Battiste. Vancouver, Canada: UBC Press.

Battiste, Marie and J. Henderson. 2000. *Protecting Indigenous Knowledge and Heritage: A Global Challenge*. Saskatoon, SK: Purich Publishing Ltd.

Bohm, David. 1994. *Thought as a System*. New York: Routledge.

—— 1996. *On Dialogue*. New York: Routledge

—— 2004. *Wholeness and the Implicate Order*. New York: Routledge.

Broad, G., S. Boyer and C. Chataway. 2006. "We Are Still the Aniishnaabe Nation: Embracing Culture and Identity in Batchewana First Nation." *Canadian Journal of Communication*, 31:35-58.

Buber, Martin. 1965. *The Knowledge of Man: A Philosophy of the Interhuman.* New York: Harper & Row.

—— 2000. *I and Thou.* Toronto: Scribner.

—— 2006. "Elements of the Interhuman." Pp. 679-696 in *Bridges not Walls*, edited by John Stewart. Ninth edition. New York: McGraw Hill.

Cajete, Greg. 1999. *Native Science: Natural Laws of Interdependence.* Santa Fe, NM: Clear Light Publishers.

Castellano, Marelene Brant. 2000. "Updating Aboriginal Traditions of Knowledge." Pp. 21-35 in *Indigenous Knowledges in Global Contexts: Multiple Reading of Our Worlds*, edited by G. Dei, B. Hall, D. Goldin-Rosenberg. Toronto: University of Toronto Press.

Four Worlds Development Project. 1988. *The Sacred Tree.* University of Lethbridge: Four Worlds Development Project.

Freire, Paulo. 2000. *Pedagogy of the Oppressed.* Translated by M. Ramos. New York: The Continuum International Publishing Group.

Gadamer, H. 1989. *Truth and Method.* Second edition. Translated by J. Weinsheimer and D.G. Marshal. New York: Crossroad.

Ghostkeeper, E. 2004. "Weche Teachings: Aboriginal Wisdom and Dispute Resolution." Pp. 124-138 in *Intercultural Dispute Resolution in Aboriginal Contexts*, edited by C. Bell, and D. Kahane. Vancouver: UBC Press.

Guignon, C. 2004. *On Being Authentic.* New York: Routledge.

Haig-Brown, C. 1995. "Taking Control: Contradiction and First Nations Adult Education." Pp. 263-269 in *First Nations Education in Canada: The Circle Unfolds*, edited by M. Battiste and J. Barman. Vancouver: UBC Press.

Hanson, A. 1989. "The Making of the Maori: Culture Invention and Its Logic." *American Anthropologist*, 91: 890-902.

Henderson, J. 2000. "Ayukpachi: Empowering Aboriginal Thought." Pp. 248-278 in *Reclaiming Indigenous Voices and Vision.* Vancouver: UBC Press.

Indigenous Voice and Vision, edited by M. Battiste. Vancouver: UBC Press.

Isaacs, William. 1999. *Dialogue and the Art of Thinking Together.* New York: Currency.

Johansen, B. 2004. "Back from the (Nearly) Dead: Reviving Indigenous Languages across North America" *American Indian Quarterly*, 28: 566-582.

Kluckhorn, Clyde. 1949. "The Philosophy of the Navajo Indians." Pp. 356-384 in *Ideological Differences and World Order*, edited by F. Northrop. New Haven, CT: Yale University Press.

Lafontaine, A. 2001. *Honouring Our Heart's Call: Giving Rise to Our Voice.* Royal Roads University, Canada. Unpublished Thesis

LeBaron, M. 2004. "Learning New Dances: Finding Effective Ways to Address Intercultural Disputes." Pp. 11-27 in *Intercultural Dispute Resolution in Aboriginal Contexts*, edited by C. Bell and D. Kahane. Vancouver: UBC Press.

McCarty, T., M. Romeroand and O. Zepeda. 2006. *Reclaiming the Gift: Indigenous Youth Counter-Narratives on Native Language Loss and Revitalization.* Omaha: University of Nebraska Press.

Mead, G. 1934. *Mind, Self, and Society*, edited by Charles W. Morris. Chicago: University of Chicago Press.

Ong, W. 1982. *Orality & Literacy: The Technologizing of the Word.* Florence, KY: Routledge.

Peterson. L. 1990. *The Story of the Sechelt Nation.* Madeira Park, BC: Harbour Publishing.

Putnam, L. and D. Kolb. 2000. "Rethinking Negotiation: Feminist Views of Communication and Exchange." Pp. 76-104 in *Rethinking Organizational and Managerial Communication from Feminist Perspectives*, edited by P. Buzzanell. Thousand Oaks, CA: Sage.

Ross, Rupert. 1992. *Dancing with a Ghost.* Toronto: Penguin Books.

—— 1996. *Returning to the Teachings: Exploring Aboriginal Justice.* Toronto: Penguin Books.

Ryan, J. 1992. "Formal Schooling and Deculturation: Nursing Practice and the Erosion of Native Communication Styles." *The Alberta Journal of Education Research*, 38:91-103.

Senge, Peter. 1994. *The Fifth Discipline: The Art & Science of the Learning Organization.* New York: Currency Doubleday.

Senge, P., O. Scharmer, J. Jaworski and B. Flowers. 2006. *Presence.* San Francisco: Barrett-Koehler.

Stewart, John. 2004. "Relationships among Philosophers of Dialogue." Pp. 21-38 in *Dialogue: Theorizing Difference in Communication Studies*, edited by R. Anderson, L. Baxter and K. Cissna. Thousand Oaks, CA: Sage Publications.

Stewart, John (ed.) 2006. *Bridges not Walls.* Ninth edition. Boston, MA: McGraw Hill.

Tannen, D. 1989. *Talking Voices: Repetition, Dialogue, and Imagery in Conversational Discourse.* Cambridge: Cambridge University Press.

Treuer, A. 2006. "Ge-onji-aabadak Anishinaabe-inwewinan." (Navajo). *American Indian Quarterly*, 30:87-90.

Turner, D. 2004. "Perceiving the World Differently." Pp. 57-60 in *Intercultural Dispute Resolution in Aboriginal Contexts*, edited by C. Bell and D. Kahane. Vancouver: UBC Press.

Weider, E. and S. Praat. 1990. "Being a Recognizable Indian among Indians." Pp. 45-64 in *Cultural Communication and Intercultural Contac*, edited by D. Carbaugh. Hillsdale, NJ: Lawrence Erlbaum.

Williams, L. 2008. "Holistic Learning." Presentation at the Second Annual National Aboriginal Learning Conference. Vancouver: February 28.

Wilson, A. 1996. "Grandmother to Granddaughter: Generations of Oral History." *American Indian Quarterly*, 20:7.

Yankelovich, D. 1999. *The Magic of Dialogue.* New York: Simon & Schuster.

Chapter 13
Performing Authentic Selfhood in an Intentional Community

Daphne Holden and Douglas Schrock

In the mid-1990s, a group of therapists founded Aurora Commons (a pseudonym), a planned residential community forty miles from two midsized southeastern cities, in order to "live in accord with our deepest selves," "trust others with our deepest vulnerabilities," and "understand each other" (mission statement). They believed that in a competitive and hierarchical society, most people are unwilling to endure the pain of deeply felt emotions and are embarrassed to express them. As an antidote to this corrosive culture, the community's first goal—listed in their mission statement—is to live "authentically," which to them meant expressing emotions that are normally stifled in the interest of social conformity. For them, only an authentic self can find personal growth and be in healthy relationships. The more authentic you are the more you will grow, and the more you grow, the more authentic you will be able to be.

Based on two years of fieldwork, participant observation at over sixty community events, and multiple interviews with every community member, this chapter examines how members of Aurora Commons performed their own particular ideal of authentic selfhood. Rather than focusing on the *experience* of personal authenticity, we examine the different ways members individually and collectively *signified* their authenticity. Doing so enables us to reveal unspoken rules about how members should enact and respond to performances of authenticity. We also show how the community's founders, through guiding, ritual creation, and therapeutic proficiency had more power over the creation of authentic selfhood.

True Selves in Cultural Context

Following Turner (1976), we conceptualize authenticity as a subjective sense that people have when they feel they are acting in accordance with their "true selves." How do people know when they are experiencing their true selves? Turner (1976) pointed out two primary cultural orientations to the "true self." For those with an institutional orientation, true self resides in feelings and actions experienced as volitional and congruent with social values, such as morality and altruism. In contrast, those with impulsive orientations locate true self in feelings and action that seem impulsive, "when inhibitions are lowered or abandoned" (1976:208). Hewitt

(1994:163) points out that because these orientations to self might change over time, or even in different contexts, it is more accurate "to think of 'institutional' and 'impulsive' as culturally available modes of speaking about the self rather than as more deeply embedded modes of experiencing the self." It is within specific emotional cultures (cf. Gordon 1989) that people learn these ways of speaking about their selves such that their authenticity is apparent to others, and also learn to interpret what an authentic performance means and what kind of claim an authentic voice makes on others. As Gordon (1989:128) points out, even when feelings are experienced as impulsive and spontaneous, there are "standards and techniques" that are "socially learned and negotiated" within specific emotional cultures. Although Turner points to broad cultural discourses about true selves, we know little about how they are produced and policed within intentional communities.

Members of Aurora Commons were steeped in a type of discourse that emphasized an impulsive orientation called "liberation psychotherapy." The ideas of liberation psychotherapy are unified by two assumptions shared by a number of widespread and popular therapeutic theories: every person has an essential and good "real self" that should be the "only guide to what you 'need' to do" (Irvine 1999:31); and "conventional culture and society make individuals sick by thwarting the development of the 'real self' in the interests of social conformity" (Rice 1996:29). Although this discourse positions itself against a particular perception of conventional culture (as stifling and conformist), Turner (1976) shows how this impulsive assumption is itself becoming increasingly conventional. In this view, liberating one's "real self" involves escaping the demands of institutional life and social relationships through "processing," lowering social inhibitions and fully expressing and experiencing once-restrained emotions with others, and then connecting these emotions to childhood experiences to find their source and experience personal growth and healing.

As young adults in the 1970s, founders of Aurora Commons learned about liberation psychotherapy in alternative organizations, graduate school, and various therapeutic groups. All of the founders (eight total, four women and four men) were white and all except Robert were therapists, had been in therapy, or had worked in other human service professions. Marny, Sam, Chris, and Sara were involved in a variation of liberation psychotherapy called "primal therapy." For primal therapists, it is necessary to re-experience the pain repressed from your past to release the "true self." According to the Primal Center (2006), group work and retreats are important so that participants can "trigger each others' feelings," experience feelings in a safe environment, and see how others work through emotional pain. Liberating one's self requires unrestrained expression of emotions, especially anger and grief, and "kicking, screaming, [and] pounding on the walls for hours are essential" (Janov 1991:330). While primal therapy's techniques may seem extreme, the assumption that unrestrained expression of emotions is healthy is consistent with an impulsive orientation (Turner 1976).

In the late 1980s, founders Marny and Chris attended a retreat on community building hosted by "The Foundation for Community Encouragement" and led by

M. Scott Peck, whose 1987 best-selling book, *The Different Drum: Community-Making and Peace*, adopted two key assumptions of liberation psychotherapy. First, conventional culture makes people sick by repressing the true self in the interests of conformity. And second, the true self, uncontaminated by culture, is childlike, peaceful, and good. Peck also argued that people can and should build non-repressive communities that enable members to communicate "authentically" without worrying about "being nice" or others' judgment. People can experience their true selves only in a "true community," a group of people who do not demand pretense—unlike others in mainstream culture. In these weekend retreats participants could practice being in a true community by processing their feelings together and reaching a transcendent state free of others' judgment. After processing their feelings with twenty or so others, Marny and Chris started the "Friday Night Group" to make the experience part of their everyday lives with a group of friends. In Aurora Commons, members processed painful childhood memories together, sometimes screaming and crying.

After four years of the Friday Night Group, participants decided they wanted to extend the experience by buying land together and living out their ideals as a land-based community. They bought seventy-five acres of undeveloped land located about forty miles from two midsized southeastern cities and began moving or building homes there. At the time of the research (spring 1996-winter 1998), there were seven homes on the land with a goal of having fifteen total households eventually.

Nine newcomers found the community through local word of mouth or through having a friend there. Many reported being drawn to the community because they felt isolated and alienated from themselves and others. They liked Aurora Commons' emphasis on sharing resources and living where they could be truly themselves with the support of a close community of like-minded others. Newcomers did not have founders' background in primal therapy or Peck's community-building workshops. All the newcomers were white and had college degrees, but only one was a therapist. After newcomers attended regular weekly business meetings and at least one retreat—daylong or weekend groups where they processed personal and community problems—founders decided whether to invite them to join the community.

Performing an Authentic Self

I (Daphne) approached the community after reading a newspaper article about them. I was curious about how they practiced egalitarianism and consensus and was also intrigued by their stated emphasis on being authentic. They believed that their practices should be studied because they thought that their community was a kind of social experiment that others could learn from. We agreed that I could attend all community events and take notes, and participate to whatever extent I chose. I did not participate in the decision-making process during the business meetings or the emotionally intense psychotherapeutic processing during the retreats. I was never comfortable with some members' intense displays of emotions, such as screaming and crying, and thus my non-participation in processing was more about personal preference than an attempt at researcher objectivity. However, I did self-disclose during one-on-one conversations with members and shared personal issues and contributed to discussions during retreat check-ins and business meetings. I was a much more active participant during workdays (which involved pond restoration, road repair, and house painting) and the informal potluck dinners.

One of the first things that seemed important was how newcomers told me that they (like me) were uncomfortable with some of the founders' intense emotionality, especially their displays of anger. I also noticed that although they did not like it, they were unable to successfully challenge these practices in a community that prided itself on being egalitarian. My co-author and I initially examined how founders used a discourse of liberation psychotherapy and reproduced power inequities despite their commitment to equality (Holden and Schrock 2007). We pointed out how founders used self disclosures in a way that elicited deference from others when those disclosures were interpreted as authentic. We subsequently decided to step back and ask: how did Aurora Commons' members interactionally construct authenticity? We looked through the data for instances where someone emotionally disclosed, asking whether and how it had something to do with authenticity. We looked for common themes in how they expressed emotions and also looked at how others responded interactionally and in interviews to assess how successful they were in gaining others' attributions of authenticity. Four themes emerged in the data. We found that community members constructed authenticity by (1) demonstrating spontaneity; (2) displaying courage; (3) signifying intensity; and (4) constructing epiphanies.

Demonstrating Spontaneity

For many, being authentic means expressing what they feel spontaneously. As Gordon (1989:124) points out, for impulse-anchored selves, "real self often appears in types of emotions that are thought to be unsocialized or natural [...]. This often elicits an intense awareness of being 'fully alive'." Demonstrating spontaneity in the community commonly consisted of (1) individuals' emotional accounts that claimed that one's feelings arose "naturally" from the body and (2) disclosing in a way that appeared free from others' influence. The founders often pressured newcomers to self-disclose painful feelings, such as anger, grief, and sadness, but nevertheless preserved the idea that the forthcoming disclosures were spontaneous and unconstrained by others.

When expressing emotions, community members often linked them to their bodies, giving the impression that they were merely reporting what they felt at an intuitive level rather than thinking about others. Their emotional accounts usually situated the feeling in a particular place in the body (e.g., the stomach) and described a particular sensation (e.g., a "tightening" or "queasiness"). For example, in a business meeting founder Chris said he was upset about the lack of planning for the upcoming therapeutic retreat: "I could feel anxiety moving up from my stomach to my throat. I felt hot flashes." The implication of this and other similar claims was that their emotions arose naturally through the body and were thus authentic and unmediated by the mind or others.

Community members also followed unspoken feeling rules (Hochschild 1979) proscribing the expression of emotions felt in response to real or imagined judgments of others such as shame or embarrassment. Members never talked about feeling embarrassed, ashamed, or guilty about anything. Such emotions, as Shott (1979) has argued, are tied to social control and thus are not seen to arise "spontaneously." In this context, revealing shame would not get a member credit for doing something brave and transformative, but rather indicate that s/he was concerned about others' judgments. Instead, members often expressed sadness, grief, and anger, emotions accepted as spontaneous and authentic.

Some founders primed other members to interpret emotional disclosures as emergent rather than as responses to situations. For example, founders often cautioned retreat participants to "speak only when moved to speak" or to "speak from the heart." A few of the founders often brought scripted therapeutic tools to retreats that they learned from self-help books and groups. They used these to prime participants to interpret each others' disclosures as free from external constraint and thus authentic. Founder Michael, for example, began one retreat by asking participants to say how they felt when they introduced themselves, as in "I am Michael and I feel … " so that "we are sure we are speaking deep within ourselves."

Aurora Commons' members also reinforced the idea of emotional spontaneity by creating rituals that reflected Peck's (1987) idealized form of communication: members should take turns speaking their own personal authentic truths, instead of responding to each others' disclosures, which he calls "crosstalk." The practice of not commenting on others' authentic disclosers was most striking when I (Daphne) first observed a member break down and sob. I was surprised that no one expressed sympathy verbally or otherwise (such as nodding, hand holding, or hugging), breaking our culture's sympathy norms (Clark 1987). By avoiding responding with overt sympathy, members protected the discloser from being defined as someone who might be asking for sympathy rather than spontaneously expressing authentic feelings. Furthermore, refraining from displays of sympathy helped members define expressing emotional pain as normal and a sign of growth rather than as something that was pitiable.

During retreats and "check-ins" at business meetings, members often went around the room with uninterrupted monologues about their feelings. Even if one expressed anger toward another present member, others rarely responded. At retreats, members often passed around a "talking stick." This ritual had an explicit rule that no one was to interrupt the stick-holder as s/he discussed her or his feelings. Commenting on someone else's emotional expression could have the potential to shame the discloser and thus create an emotional culture in which people were inhibited from freely expressing themselves. The community's interaction rule forbidding crosstalk thus collectively enabled members to demonstrate emotional spontaneity.

While self-disclosing was supposed to be voluntary to qualify as authentic, some founders often subtly pressured newcomers to participate. During one retreat in which everyone but me had picked up the talking stick, Rose gestured toward me and said, "Daphne? Do you want this?" I felt embarrassed about my non-participation but felt unprepared to muster something on the spot and shook my head in dissent. I then realized that although members were cautioned to speak only when they were "moved to speak" that in fact there was situational pressure to do so. Many founders also encouraged me to self-disclose by emphasizing I would learn and grow through sharing. For example, Rose told me early on that fieldwork in the community:

> … will change the way you go about and do everything for the rest of your life. And you're a participant in this. Even if you just stand around and observe. If you want to share, you can share too […]. I would be willing to bet that if you stick around long enough you will share just like everybody else. How about them bananas, honey?!

Through such talk, some founders implicitly pressured me to self-disclose and to then interpret self-disclosure as a step toward authentic selfhood and personal growth rather than as meeting a situational demand.

Newcomers who avoided sharing were also pressured, sometimes in a more overt fashion. At one retreat, newcomer Jessica held the talking stick and said to the group, "As far as sharing personal stuff, I don't really feel like I know people well enough to do it." Founder Rose interjected irritably, "How are we supposed to know you if you don't?" No one called Rose on breaking the explicit rule forbidding interrupting stick-holders, which in effect defined the implicit rule to self-disclose as more important. It also taught newcomers that if they did not "spontaneously" self-disclose, they would be held accountable for it.

Some of the founders used the fact that not everyone participated as testimony to the authenticity of their process, despite the fact that it happened so infrequently. While a few founders pressured others (usually covertly) to self-disclose they also, in a contradictory manner, reassured newcomers and myself that processing was voluntary and that not everyone participated. Occasional noncompliance and founders' reassurances functioned to further legitimize collective claims that self-disclosure was voluntary, spontaneous, and thus authentic.

Displaying Courage

Lyng (1990) and Holyfield (1997) both point out that many people voluntarily engage in risky behaviors in order to generate intense emotions which are experienced as extraordinary and authentic. While expressing unpleasant or potentially discrediting emotions to others is not life threatening, community members constructed this action as risky because it meant showing potentially discrediting vulnerabilities to others. Members who presented themselves as being able to express emotions authentically despite their fears elicited others' attributions of authenticity.

Similar to adventure guides (Holyfield 1997), some founders primed newcomers to interpret sharing as risky work. Before I went to my first retreat, Neil and Marny counseled me about what to expect. Neil said, "I know it will be scary for you. But don't worry because we will be there for you. Maybe I'm projecting, because I know it's scary for me." Another member suggested that I bring "an old stuffed animal" to make me feel comfortable. During a break at the first retreat I attended, during which I was silent, Michael told me: "You are one courageous woman!" They were guiding me to interpret my experience as frightening and also bolstering their view of themselves as people brave enough and emotionally advanced enough to do this difficult work.

During retreats and regular meetings, community members often explicitly defined forthcoming self-disclosures as scary. They prefaced what they said with variations of, "I'm scared to say this, but … " For example, during a retreat, Marny prefaced her subsequent expression of anger at other members with the following: "I realize that I am holding back because I don't want people to get mad at me. Instead of just speaking my truth, I blame others. So what I decided to do was just to speak my truth." We see here how Marny primed others to interpret her disclosure as brave in light of her fear of others' judgment. In other words, she was telling them that she was being authentic despite an inclination to behave otherwise.

Underscoring the value community members placed on working through fear, during a retreat Kurt (Rose's adult son) said that he was scared of showing others that he was scared. He said he was "scared to talk" but thought that he should. He explained that "It is my fear that is really the issue. I've got this scared little boy inside of me." He could get points for overcoming his fear of talking about it and for making progress toward dealing with his fear of being an adult. One participant told me after the retreat how moved she was by Kurt's sharing. Kurt thus successfully elicited an attribution of authenticity by presenting himself as emotionally courageous.

Community members also conveyed the idea that self-disclosure was scary in their responses to sharers. At the end of retreats or meetings, members often congratulated disclosers in an "appreciation circle" for being "courageous" for revealing vulnerabilities and working through fear. Sometimes a member even congratulated him or herself. In the appreciation circle at the end of one retreat, Marny said, crying, "I have to appreciate myself for having the courage to say what I needed to say." By defining such self-closures as scary, community members boosted the alleged authenticity of their performances. They aligned their performances with the larger discourse that holds breaking social norms and revealing one's vulnerabilities as authenticity (Turner 1976). The discourse was a shared resource that community members used to define these performances as authentic.

Courageous performances, especially those concerned with overcoming fear, were often ritualized to heighten the perceived sacredness of authenticity. For example, rather than saying "Let's set aside this time to chat and find out how everyone is doing and be careful not to interrupt each other," participants used the "talking stick" and heightened the atmosphere of drama by making the event into a ritual. The ritual involved sitting in a circle around the stick, which was ceremoniously picked up and returned. There was always a long pause between speakers during which people stared at the floor or into space, seemingly to go deep into themselves. Participating made me feel like being on a stage, heightening my self consciousness. This ritualized self-disclosure felt scarier and more sacred than self-disclosure in everyday life. The ritual thus created the conditions under which people would be likely to interpret each others' disclosures as courageous.

By doing what seemed risky—expressing fear, vulnerability, grief, weakness, anger, or rage—community members publicly affirmed that in this community, people were emotionally liberated, or authentic enough to let everyone see their pain. They were simultaneously signifying their own liberation and the vitality of the community as a place safe enough to truly "be yourself."

Signifying Intensity

By labeling their emotional displays "intense" rather than "destructive" or "dysfunctional" (two descriptions I got from ex-members), the founders could bask in the knowledge that they were feeling deeply. Unlike self-help groups that invoke a "norm of silence" to avoid conflict (Wuthnow 1994), in this community members interpreted intense displays of anger, grief, or sadness positively. The founders often alluded to Peck's book and his idea of "pseudocommunity" to justify their intensity, especially intense anger. As Peck (1987:88-89) wrote:

> In pseudocommunity a group attempts to purchase community cheaply by pretense [...] It is an unconscious, gentle process whereby people who want to be loving attempt to be so by telling little white lies, by withholding some of the truth about themselves and their feelings in order to avoid conflict [...]. In pseudocommunity it is as if every individual member is operating according to the same book of etiquette. The rules of this book are: Don't do or say anything that might offend someone else; if someone does or says something that offends, annoys, or irritates you, act as if nothing has happened and pretend you are not bothered in the least; and if some form of disagreement should show signs of appearing, change the subject as quickly and smoothly as possible—rules that any good hostess knows. It is easy to see how these rules make for a smoothly functioning group. But they also crush individuality, intimacy, and honesty, and the longer it lasts the duller it gets.

By framing politeness and niceness as "pseudocommunity," Peck's work gave the founders a way to think of their intense expressions of anger and sadness as signifying individual authenticity and community health.

Founders were proud of their intensity. At the beginning of my fieldwork, a founder told me that she need not look for other communities, because Aurora Commons was "the most intense group around" to which a newcomer added, "It is truly amazing what we go through together." For most founders, being able to rage and cry in the context of the community signified that people were able to "know each other deeply" and "see your junk and still love you," as Marny put it. Although being authentic did not require screaming or crying, members valued those who were intense, because they displayed what community members collectively prided themselves on—being able to show each other their vulnerabilities.

Quite often during business meetings and retreats, founders Marny, Sam, and Chris—and to a lesser extent Rose and Gwen—would cry and/or scream out, seemingly out of control. For example, at one retreat, founder Chris encouraged participants to get in touch with their bodies and emotions by doing "baby breathing," a primal therapy technique in which one lies prone and breaths from the gut. During this exercise, founder Sam began to wail: "I'm so fucking angry! I can't take it anymore! I'm so fucking sick of always being so goddamned nice that I can't fucking *stand it*!" After several people placed their hands on him in support, he cried and yelled about his mother molesting him as a baby and said he would "never, never let anyone do that to me again!" Sam also raged about "always trying to please, always smiling."

Consistent with an impulsive-orientation to self (Gordon 1989; Turner 1976), Hoagland (1988:185) points out that in our culture "we tend to believe that to really feel or express something, to be authentic, we must be out of control [...]. The idea is that true desire or true anger is a matter of how intensely we feel, that such feeling only happens when we've shut off reason, and that such a state involves losing control of ourselves." Sam's public screaming and crying signified being "out of control," which signified authenticity more so than a more restrained presentation would do. At the end of the retreat in the appreciation circle others congratulated Sam for getting "so deep." Sam's intense emotionalism displayed to all that the community was a place where people could be deeply authentic.

Some newcomers complained about founders' intense displays of anger and founders were aware that their reputation was driving away potential new members. When talking about dropouts in an interview, founder Sam said, "I've heard any number of people say it was too intense," and "I think that people were scared of Rose and Marny's anger, and maybe me." At the last retreat I attended, the "separation retreat"—called by Chris and Gwen in order to allow the community to process Marny and Michael's separation—Chris described the community in which he wanted to live, implying that having to stifle intensity compromised this vision.

> Chris said that they'd start with the talking stick, and he'd like to remind people to speak only when "moved to speak." He quickly took the stick. He said that he didn't want to come this morning because he knew it would be more of that "processing shit." He said that sometimes he would get so mad at Marny because she's always the one who says "so and so is not dealing with their shit" and it makes him mad but later when he really thinks about it, he realizes that she's usually right. And now he doesn't know if he's supposed to "let everything out" or if he should be "gentle and respectful." [...] He wants the community to be "a place where everyone can be crazy and it be all right." He said that sometimes he goes on his deck and "screams and cries" and he doesn't know why, but after he does it he feels better. He said he wanted to be able to express "pain, fear, anger, and sadness" and wants others to "be there" when he needs them. At some point in all this, he started crying really hard—almost like a child would cry. [...] This was short and he seemed much better afterwards (fieldnote excerpt).

Chris indicated that he did not want to do that "processing shit" because it was painful, but he knew, like Marny said, that it was ultimately necessary. His posits "letting everything out" as being the only alternative to "being gentle," reproducing the idea that one could not gently or calmly express an authentic emotion. By crying intensely, and then recovering, he also demonstrated how cathartic it was to let everything out.

Constructing Epiphanies

Sometimes when founders expressed negative emotions, such as anger, pain, sorrow, or fear, they had epiphanies about the emotion's "real" or "root" cause, situated in childhood. In an epiphany something previously hidden about one's character is revealed (Denzin 1989). For Aurora Commons members, what was revealed was insight into their true selves.[1] Members' assumptions, reflecting their training in Primal Therapy, were that traumas from childhood left scars that could be healed only through re-experiencing the trauma and expressing the resulting emotions to others. Once the toxic emotions were experienced and expressed, members believed they could move on to healthier adult relationships. Consistent with the larger discourse of liberation psychotherapy, the emotions expressed during an epiphany were viewed as authentic because they reflected a self situated in childhood and therefore uncorrupted by a repressive culture. Sometimes members had epiphanies when founders guided them with therapeutic scripts at retreats, while at other times members came to their own epiphanies through an emotional monologue. Epiphanies simultaneously demonstrated authenticity and the desired outcome of an authentic self—personal growth.

---

1 Whereas Denzin views epiphanies as something that reveals an individual's perspective and social and historical location, we focus on how members of Aurora Commons collectively construct and perform them.

To generate an epiphany, participants linked an emotion either to their childhood or to a current issue that they had across different relationships (such as often feeling afraid of intimacy with friends and partners). While community members interpreted the expressed emotion as spontaneous and thus authentic, they did not expect that having an epiphany should always be spontaneous. In fact, for them epiphanies required hard work that most in our culture were unwilling to do because it might be emotionally painful to dredge up old emotions and memories. The founders who did this work were valued by therapeutic others as especially fearless.

During retreats, founders often guided participants to have epiphanies. For example, at one retreat Rose brought up her anger at Stacy. She complained that Stacy had distanced herself from Rose and had not told her why. After a few minutes of complaining she screamed at Stacy, "What did I do that was so terrible to you?! You have treated me abominably!" After a few more minutes of angry exchanges, Marny interjected that Chris could help them with the "tools" he learned from a recently attended workshop. Rose and Stacy agreed and Chris first asked Stacy to "take a few minutes to complain, using your whole body." Chris was guiding Stacy to be intense about her emotional expression, as Marny did when she and Steve modeled the exercise earlier. Stacy complained about how she was sick of others trying to run her life. Then Chris instructed her to reflect on the question, "What is it about my past or programming that makes this situation inevitable?" Stacy talked about how as a youngest child she felt that her family was always trying to control her. Chris's next question was, "What have you learned from this situation that you wouldn't have been able to learn otherwise?" Stacy said that she learned that "the world won't collapse if I put my foot down and say no [...] that I can take responsibility for myself." Chris congratulated Stacy for working through it, and then Stacy said she would like to take a break.

Rose and a few others went inside and I could hear the sound of her sobbing and moaning from where I was sitting on the deck. After ten minutes, she reappeared on the deck, ready to work with Chris. She said later: "And when I went to pieces and sobbed with Robert, the depth of my grief was just huge. And it wasn't just losing Stacy. That's sort of not it. It's unleashing the emotions of ancient grief. Whatever the grief was it goes back to the first time I was ever abandoned." Both Rose and Stacy's performances signified that they were progressing in their therapeutic self understanding and allowed others to bask in the feeling that the community was a special place where people could authentically express themselves.

That the community was credited with enabling such epiphanies and personal growth came up frequently in interviews with all members. Even those who did not participate in retreats thought that it was testimony to the community's safety that others could share their feelings.

> Any time you see people go through some kind of transformation on the spot—it's always significant. Like what Sam went through and his release and how the group supported him to get through that. He could have not gone through

> that without help. And he felt comfortable enough with a few people there that he was able to get released. And I've seen that happen numerous times, where somebody is really stuck and the group helps them get unstuck [Robert].

Robert referred to Sam as getting "released" and "unstuck," meaning that Sam was able to finally free himself from this childhood baggage because the community allowed him to express his emotions authentically. We can see that despite his reluctance to engage in therapeutic work himself, Robert nevertheless believed that Sam's epiphany about his current suffering (because his mother molested him when he was a baby) was a credit to the community. It was especially significant in this case because although he credited the community for Sam's "release," no one intervened or helped Sam in his monologue in any way. Though he did it alone, the witnesses to it were able to feel good about being partially responsible.

There was thus a double level of feeling evoked during the retreats and at many business meetings. First of all, the participants, such as Stacy and Rose, felt emotional epiphanies by linking their present circumstances to their pasts. Then secondly, all who witnessed such epiphanies felt moved by what seemed to be the exposed raw emotions of others and the progress others were making in working through their issues. They then interpreted this as a sign of community success. In both cases, the excitement, sorrow, and ultimately the joy of epiphanies were experienced as emerging from an authentic self.

A Flubbed Performance

It is instructive to consider a case when someone expressed feelings in an idiosyncratic way in order to evaluate the importance of the local rules the structured the development of authentic selfhood. What happens when someone does not fully understand others' expectations about what expressing oneself authentically should look like? Neil was a newcomer who consistently challenged the core group about finances and rarely used therapeutic discourse. Others told me later that there had been tension between Neil and Marny for months.

At a retreat, Neil tried but failed to gain credibility with other members with his unconventional self presentation. When he had the floor, he stepped into the center of the circle and went into a very dramatic monologue: "I would like you all to know that I am an angry person. I am angry, I am nurturing, I am passionate, I am needy, and I am loving. I am fully human and I experience myself fully. Now I am going to show you all a side of myself that I never showed anyone before." He then crouched down into a ball, tightening his muscles so that his arms were shaking, as were his clenched fists. He then emitted a long, low-pitched, crescendo howl. He then, with dry eyes, continued his monologue about going to down to a creek earlier in the day and realizing he was tense, and said "I pissed in my pants!," as he looked around the room. "And then I had to laugh at myself. I'm a full grown man pissing in my pants!" He then ceremoniously presented Rose with a rock from the creek, explaining it symbolized his gift to the community, and kissed her on the lips. He told a story that lasted about fifteen minutes about how he loved his girlfriend, newcomer Julie and how the community presented a challenge to their relationship. He finished and took his place back in the circle.

Breaking the rule again crosstalk, Sam and Chris both started to talk. Sam said, laughing, "Well, I've got a lot to say about that." Then Michael suggested that everyone think deeply before speaking and there was silence for a few minutes. Then Chris said, "I'm annoyed. Maybe what I need to do is an exercise with Marny." Marny replied, "Okay, Chris, just complain for a while." He explained that he was frustrated when Neal was speaking, saying, "I don't want to hear about him collecting a rock in the creek." He then brought up some practical issues with regard to dealing with house sites, and others joined him. Marny then said she needed to "speak her truth" and metaphorically accused Neil of harming the community, to which Neil expressed disagreement. During the "appreciation circle" (holding hands in a circle) at the end of the retreat, Neil was the only person for whom no one expressed appreciation. Neil himself pointed this out to me in a later interview.

Why wasn't Neil's performance deemed authentic? While he displayed a strongly felt emotion in an unconventional and thus potentially embarrassing way, he did not connect his anguish to a childhood issue. It was also difficult for other members to interpret his actions as coming from a "deep place" because he smoothly transformed into and out of an animal-like howler without tears or other indicators of intense emotionality. As founder Nancy put it later, echoing others, his performance "felt to me to be kind of shallow. He went into it so easily, he came out of it so easily [...] it felt like it was very planned." Neal dropped out of the community shortly after this retreat. Weeks later during a follow-up interview, he said he was still traumatized by how the community members treated him.

We can see here how other members were policing and reinforcing the boundaries of acceptability for displays of authentic emotionality when they publicly challenged his performance. Everyone there learned that if they expressed their emotions in a unique fashion, no one would defer, despite the community's stated goals of creating a safe space for emotional freedom. If they wanted to be credited as authentic, members needed to follow the rules.

Conclusion

Over the past forty years, social movement organizations (Lichterman 1996; Schrock, Holden, and Reid 2004; Taylor 1995); utopian communities (Kanter 1972); support groups (Irvine 2000; Wolkomir 2001; Wuthnow 1994), and popular culture (Kaminer 1993) have adopted a strain of liberation psychotherapy that emphasizes being authentic. It seems likely that people are increasingly judged on whether their self presentations are authentic. As this chapter shows, the standards by which people are judged as performing authentic selfhood are (re)produced at the level of interaction. If codified, the rules for performing authentic selfhood at Aurora Commons include demonstrating spontaneity, displaying courage, expressing emotions intensely, and having epiphanies. As members learned these rules, they also learned to think that authentic expressions of emotion lead to personal growth.

The founders had the most control over what counted as authentic. Because they were therapeutic experts, newcomers looked to founders as models of authenticity. Many newcomers tried to emulate founders' expressions of intensity, fear, epiphanies, and spontaneity. Founders not only modeled authenticity, they created the opportunities and used therapeutic resources (scripts and rituals) to guide others to conform to their rules of authentic expression. Those newcomers who did not emulate the founders' performances or did not follow the performance rules closely enough faced an audience less or unwilling to affirm their selves as authentic and sacred. Founders were thus the unacknowledged gatekeepers of authenticity.

In searching for their true selves and desiring to express themselves authentically, members of Aurora Commons were not unusual. In an age of job instability, high divorce rates, mobility, and rapid technological change, it becomes increasingly difficult to know who we are and our place in the world. A therapeutic culture offers a promise of liberation through finding a "true self" that transcends the vagaries of social life. However, we have seen that this promise is a false one because authenticity is constructed out of symbolic interaction, local hegemonic discourses, and situational rules. It is important to further unpack how power operates in specific contexts in order to understand how others shape the expression—and perhaps the experience—of authenticity.

References

Clark, Candace. 1987. "Sympathy Biography and Sympathy Margin." *The American Journal of Sociology*, 93:290-321.

Denzin, Norman. 1989. *Interpretive Interactionism*. Newbury Park: Sage.

Gordon, Steven L. 1989. "Institutional and Impulsive Orientations in Selectively Appropriating Emotions to the Self." Pp. 115-135 in *The Sociology of Emotions: Original Essays and Research Papers*, edited by David Franks and E. Doyle McCarthy. Greenwich: JAI.

Hoagland, Sarah. 1988. *Lesbian Ethics: Toward New Value*. Palo Alto: Institute of Lesbian Studies.

Hewitt, John P. 1994. "Self, Role, and Discourse." Pp. 155-173 in *Self, Collective Action, and Society: Essays Honoring the Contributions of Ralph H. Turner*, edited by Gerald M. Platt and Chad Gordon. New Haven: JAI Press.

Hochschild, Arlie Russell. 1979. "Emotion Work, Feeling Rules, and Social Structure." *The American Journal of Sociology*, 85:551-575.

Holden, Daphne and Doug Schrock. 2007. "'Get therapy and work on it': Managing Dissent in an Intentional Community." *Symbolic Interaction*, 30:175-198.

Holyfield, Lori. 1997. "Generating Excitement: Experienced Emotion in Commercial Leisure." Pp. 257-281 in *Social Perspectives on Emotion*, edited by Rebecca J. Erickson and Beverley Cuthbertson-Johnson. Greenwich: Jai Press Inc.

Irvine, Leslie. 1999. *CoDependent Forevermore: The Invention of Self in a Twelve Step Group*. Chicago: The University of Chicago Press.

—— 2000. "'Even Better Than the Real Thing': Narratives of the Self in Codependency." *Qualitative Sociology*, 23:9-28.

Janov, Arthur. 1991. *The New Primal Scream*. Wilmington: Enterprise Publishing, Inc.

Kaminer, Wendy. 1993. *I'm Dysfunctional, You're Dysfunctional: The Recovery Movement and Other Self-Help Fashions*. New York: Vintage Books.

Kanter, Rosabeth Moss. 1972. *Commitment and Community: Communes and Utopias in Sociological Perspective*. Cambridge: Harvard University Press.

Lichterman, Paul. 1996. *The Search for Political Community: American Activists Reinventing Commitment*. Cambridge: Cambridge University Press.

Lyng, Stephen. 1990. "Edgework: A Social Psychological Analysis of Voluntary Risk Taking." *The American Journal of Sociology*, 95:851-886.

Peck, M. Scott. 1987. *The Different Drum: Community-Making and Peace*. New York: Simon and Schuster.

Primal Center. 2006. "What Is Proper Primal Therapy as Defined by Dr. Janov?" Retrieved February 1, 2006, from http://www.primaltherapy.com/SEO/primal_therapy_proper.shtml.

Rice, John Steadman. 1996. *A Disease of One's Own: Psychotherapy, Addiction, and the Emergence of Co-Dependency*. New Brunswick: Transaction Publishers.

Schrock, Douglas, Daphne Holden, and Lori Reid. 2004. "Creating Emotional Resonance: Interpersonal Emotion Work and Motivational Framing in a Transgender Community." *Social Problems*, 51:61-81.

Shott, Susan. 1979. "Emotion and Social Life: A Symbolic Interactionist Analysis." *The American Journal of Sociology*, 84:1317-1334.

Taylor, Verta. 1995. "Watching for Vibes: Bringing Emotions into the Study of Feminist Organizations." Pp. 223-233 in *Feminist Organizations: Harvest of the New Women's Movement*, edited by Myra Marx Ferree and Patricia Yancey Martin. Philadelphia: Temple University Press.

Turner, Ralph H. 1976. "The Real Self: From Institution to Impulse." *American Journal of Sociology*, 81:989-1016.

Wolkomir, Michelle. 2001. "Wrestling with the Angels of Meaning: The Revisionist Ideological Work of Gay and Ex-Gay Christian Men." *Symbolic Interaction*, 24:407-424.

Wuthnow, Robert. 1994. *Sharing the Journey: Support Groups and America's New Quest for Community*. New York: The Free Press.

Chapter 14
Embodying Ideologies in Tourism: A Commemorative Visitor Book in Israel as a Site of Authenticity

Chaim Noy

Introduction: Tourism and Authenticities

Authenticity is a central meta-narrative in tourism, accounting for the unique appeal of this interdisciplinary field of study and remarkable growth during the last century. The key role authenticity plays in tourism is not surprising if we consider its very nature. Tourism is essentially an industry that transports people from one place—their home, to another—the destination. This corporeal travel holds a promise: to transcend mediation processes, or short-circuit representational imagery, through *actual* arrival at the desired scene. Unlike the media industry (in which authenticity also plays a constitutive role, see Peters 2001; Van Leeuwen 2001), travel is not marketed as an endeavor that entails mediated images. Rather, tourism is modernity's promise of a corporeal encounter with the Thing itself, with the genuine attraction, be it a site, place, artifact, or combinations thereof. Hence, to those who can afford it, tourism offers one of the dearest commodities available under Western-modern epistemology, namely immediate and unmediated access to (read: consumption) of the Real.[1]

In this chapter, I offer an empirical exploration of the formative role(s) authenticity plays in tourism. I pursue this aim by attending to a case study in the form of a national-military heritage site located in West Jerusalem, Israel. Through attending closely to representations in and of the site, and to artifacts exhibited in it—notably the site's commemorative visitor book, I offer a conceptual discussion of the institutional and ideological roles authenticity or authenticities play in tourism. The exploration works its way from the site as a whole to the unique exhibit/device of the visitor book, which supplies a stage for visitors' performances (Macdonald 2005; Noy 2008). In the conclusions, I thus argue that within the ecology of authenticity evinced in the commemorative site, the visitor book serves as an authenticated/authenticating surface.

---

1 I allude to Lacan's (1977) famous distinction between the orders of the Symbolic and the Real, whereby the latter relates to what lies outside language (symbolization), and is therefore ultimately unchanging and "always in its place."

At this point I would have very much liked to propose a straightforward definition of the concept of authenticity, yet "authenticity is a struggle" (as Bruner [1994:403] points out), and the literature, briefly reviewed below, suggests an array of definitions, indicating that the notion of authenticity is indeed in crisis (Van Leeuwen 2001). Hence following the literature review, I will propose a scheme that suits best the particular site I studied, which addresses authenticity through a triple perceptive, combining the notions of semiotics, performance and ideology. But first, off to the site.

The Ammunition Hill National Memorial Site (AHNMS), where I chose to conduct this research, is a heritage site located in West Jerusalem, Israel. Heritage sites and attractions supply particularly rich case studies for exploring authenticity, and the semiotic processes that mediate, frame and construct it. This is because heritage, by definition, concerns events that transpired in the past, and are inaccessible in any immediate way to tourists' bodily senses (Kirshenblatt-Gimblett 1998; Laurier 1998; on embodiment in tourism in general and in heritage sites in particular see Chhabra, Healy, and Sills 2003; Edensor 1998). As such, a special effort must be made to communicate and mediate them, in order to frame these historic sites, events, artifacts and people as both accessible and real.

Moreover, heritage plays an important role in the contemporary, heated scenes of identity politics, which seek to construct an authentic, historic narrative, on which collective identities and political claims can be validly asserted in the present (Anderson 1983; Zerubavel 1995). In their capacity of producing compelling narratives, heritage sites typically evoke the collective's "true" cultural history, and are sites at which identities are fervently and often explicitly represented and negotiated (Breathnach 2006; Bruner 1994; Chhabra, Healy, and Sills 2003; Wang 2007, and various publications in the *Journal of Heritage Tourism*).

Dean MacCannell and Beyond: Tourisms' Authenticities

An academic discussion of authenticity in tourism leads inevitably to the trailblazing works of Dean MacCannell (1973; 1999 [1976]). MacCannell argued that, since modernity is largely characterized by alienation and superficiality, tourism supplies the much sought-after experience of authenticity in our epoch. In this sense, tourism is essentially a modern industry, supplying meaning to life and a general social structure, as did religion in pre-industrial societies (MacCannell 1973). Tourist attractions are the present-day equivalents of sacred sites and sites of worship in traditional societies. As MacCannell (1973:589-590) states: "[T]ourism absorbs some of the social functions of religion in the modern world. [...] The concern of moderns for the shallowness of their lives and inauthenticity of their experiences parallels concerns for the sacred in primitive society."

While the relationship between authenticity and modernity is central to MacCannell's view, this aspect of his work has been less influential in tourism studies than his approach to authenticity and its central role in the structure of tourist attractions. MacCannell's analysis of tourist attractions and their framing, staging and division into front and back regions—all of which contribute to the construction of authenticity—builds on works published a decade earlier. Namely, Berger and Luckmann (1967), Goffman (1956) and Garfinkel (1967) supply the main impetus, which helped MacCannell drive the tourism studies wagon forward, from structural approaches into the early beginnings of post-structural explorations. MacCannell's analysis was less concerned with the authenticity of Things and their (re)production (cf. Benjamin 1968), than with the authenticity of being or of experience. "The touristic consciousness is motivated by its desire for authentic experience," he typically argued (MacCannell 1999:101). MacCannell pointed to a direct link between the state and status of being a tourist, on the one hand, and a particular type of sense or "consciousness" (the tourist's), on the other.

MacCannell's percepts have been widely elaborated, expanded upon, and also criticized (Bruner 1994). His contribution, to cite Dann (1996:8), was "as pervasive as it was radical." Cohen (1974, 1979, 1988, 1989), for instance, employed MacCannell's proposals and suggested a typology of tourists, which relies partly on the roles and intensities exhibited by the quest for authenticity within travel motivations. Cohen's early works, together with the works of Bruner (1991) and Pearce and Moscardo (1986), made MacCannell's ideas more accessible and appealing to a wider audience of researchers and laid the foundation for the surge of research on authenticity in tourism from the 1990s to the present.

Wang's (1999; 2000) contributions crucially advanced the exploration of authenticity by rejecting MacCannell's implicit assumption that there is such a thing as "objective authenticity" (or authenticity of objects), which can be correlated with the experience of authenticity. Wang (2000:71) observed that tourism is an "industry of authenticity," wherein "existential authenticity becomes a commodity." Through his use of the term "existential authenticity," Wang stressed the psychological aspects of the tourist experience, and the desires, memories and feelings that accompany this state. The tourist experience is felt and lived (Wang 2000:56). Wang's perspective weakens the link between touristic objects and the experience of authenticity in tourism, or between the objective "authenticity of knowledge" and the subjective "authenticity of feeling" (2000:48). Together with notions such as Selwyn's (1996:21-25) "hot authenticity," which is how tourists seek their own authentic selves, authenticity studies in tourism moved toward a more subjected perspective, intricately related to actual practice.

These works effectively paved the way for explorations of the role(s) of authenticity in the construction of identities—both individual and collective—in and through tourism (Noy and Cohen 2005; Taylor 2001). A case in point is my research of Israeli backpackers' narratives (Noy 2004, 2007), where I showed how authenticity is used as a semiotic resource. More than simply as a commodity (cf. Wang 2000), which I think authenticity surely is, I view authenticity as a resource that helps objects and people become worthy, a worth that can be measured symbolically and materially.

Tourists' explicit evocations of authenticity during their storytelling, served to validate and enhance their narrative performances (Noy 2004, 2007). In these performances, the Israeli backpackers I interviewed transposed authenticity, as it were, from the spaces and sights they consumed at the destinations themselves, to the performance of their travel story at home, after returning from their trips. As a result, the occasion of the interview itself became charged with the social semiotics of tourism: the backpackers told of consuming authentic places, and their performances served to authenticate who they are, and to bestow the aura of authenticity on their selves. "Importing" authenticity into their performances made their claims regarding identity and cultural capital all the more persuasive and effective (Noy 2007). More fundamentally, importing authenticity is what performatively established them *as backpackers* in the course of the interview interaction.

Other scholars have pointed out that not all tourists seek authenticity. Some present-day tourists are postmodern, at least in the sense that they are either indifferent to the markers of authenticity, or actually seek and celebrate inauthentic attractions (Ritzer and Liska 1997). This discussion is a bit tricky, because a sense of authenticity can emerge regardless of whether an attraction is viewed as "objectively authentic." Thus "genuine fakes" (Brown 1996) and other socially constructed attractions can also produce a sense of authenticity, which is why postmodern tourists may yet enjoy postmodern authenticity.

Discussions of authenticity and its vicissitudes occupy considerable volumes in the sociocultural explorations of tourism, amounting to a sub-disciplinary field of research. Yet studies of authenticity and its paradigm in related disciplines barely influenced this subfield; and except for MacCannell's work, these studies of authenticity in tourism have scarcely affected research. Thus this chapter also tries to help promote interdisciplinary examinations of authenticity.

The chapter suggests an empirically based study that views authenticity as simultaneously a semiotic resource, a performance, and an ideology in tourism. This is not to say that authenticity is not a commodity, but because it serves an ideological function, it also often serves as a valuable resource, generating genuine performances and moving experiences (Noy 2004; Stephenson 2004). The first of the three aspects in this scheme concerns authenticity's basic quality, which is the signification of originality. If a letter written by a soldier during the war is exhibited in the museum, then it can be said that it is presented as an authentic or original document (in accord with Bruner's [1994] and Van Leeuwen's [2001] first criterion of authenticity).

The second aspect concerns processes of mediation and representation of authenticity, whereby exhibits such as letters written by soldiers who died and the visitor book, are viewed as (authentic) objects and (authenticating) media simultaneously. Now the focus moves from the artifact's originality, to how, where and by whom (and to who) it is presented. Now the questions concern the authority to construct meaning and establish authenticity, and the appropriate (cultural) means by which this is accomplished. At this point I acknowledge two qualities: that authenticity is always constructed (and that there are norms regarding replication, restoration, and other manipulations, can nonetheless be judged as legitimate, see Van Leeuwen 2001); and that presentations of authenticity *validate* performances. By the term performance I refer to acts that instantiate social identities and agencies. In this sense, authenticity is a semiotic resource that partakes in these acts and serves to authorize them.

Finally, I use the term "ideology" in this chapter loosely, generally in line with Althusser's view that ideology bears experiential and epistemological hues, relating to the "'lived' relation between men and the world" (Althusser 1990:233). I find Althusser's perspective particularly appropriate because it contains two elements that also characterize authenticity in tourism. The first is that ideology relates not only to actual experience, but also to "imaginary" or "lived" experience (ibid.). This quality is particularly relevant because much of tourism concerns processes of mediation and imagination. The second element concerns the reproduction of cultural tenets, social structures, symbols and power relations, which Althusser (1971) included in his definition of ideology, and which is one function of modern tourism according to MacCannell. Thirdly, my adaptation of the concept of ideology into tourism studies is also influenced by earlier contributions, notably Adler's (1989) notion of "travel ideology," in which tourism-related phenomena are discussed in ideological terms.

Ammunition Hill: Site and Song

The AHNMS is a complex commemorating war in West Jerusalem. Inaugurated in 1975, it honors the Israeli soldiers who died in the battle on Ammunition Hill during the 1967 Six-Day War, and celebrates the victory of the Israeli Army over the Jordanian Legion, the so called "liberation" of East Jerusalem and the "unification" of the city. The complex comprises two main spaces: an outdoor site that includes commemorative monuments and the original trenches in which the fighting took place, as well as an indoor museum.

The museum presents exhibits and information about the battle on Ammunition Hill and the overall campaign for Jerusalem. Most of the features are commemorative devices, such as the Golden Wall of Commemoration, engraved with the names of the 182 soldiers who fell in the battle for Jerusalem and a short film about the Ammunition Hill Battle. In addition, many maps and pictures are employed to illustrate the battles for Jerusalem, and a variety of discursive artifacts, such as the soldiers' letters and personal journals, serve to enhance the display's authenticity and to personalize the soldiers.

The majority of my research at the AHNMS was conducted during four weeks in the summer and autumn of 2006. It is based on an examination of the visitor book itself, as well as on observations of and conversations with visitors. The majority of the visitors I observed and interviewed were either Jewish Israelis or Ultra-Orthodox Jewish tourists, mostly from North America. Both these populations strongly identify with Israel's Zionist ideology, and are supportive of the nationalistic and military ideologies promoted by the museum. I also interviewed the management, with the aim of determining the museum's ideological agenda.

Before examining the visitor book and its functions, I wish to address two aspects of concern to authenticity, and to suggest an ideological context in which a particular type of culturally constructed authenticity emerges. These constructions of authenticity supply the context within which the visitor book resides and operates as a meaning-making device.

The first point concerns the physical location of the AHNMS—on the actual site of the historic battleground. The museum's (now former) director stressed this point in our first meeting. The management's desire to capture and preserve past events explicitly and authentically was expressed by the director who, while giving me a tour, repeatedly described the site's uniqueness in the following terms: "You've got a place here where there's *something* you can actually *feel* with your own [two] feet. [You can] move through the trenches. [You can] touch the bunkers. [You can] hear the stories. And people cling to that. This guy fell *here*, that occurred *here*."[2]

With these words, the museum director addressed the significance of the site's singular location. Their use, with their repeated appeal to bodily senses and indications of proximity and immediacy ("here"), qualify his comments as an example of the discourse of authenticity. The director's description of the site's location, in response to my question regarding its power to attract visitors, suggests that he is pointing out not (only) a condition—authenticity (defined as marking originality)—but also a resource: the site's uniqueness lies in its authenticity. Indeed, because the site is not very impressive, and has not been renovated since its construction, its location is perhaps its most crucial resource in terms of attractiveness.

Since authenticity serves as a resource in the symbolic economy of tourism, it is manipulated and at least partly construed, and is only partially accurate and represents a type of "front stage reality." Consider, for instance, the fact that the historic battleground actually extends beyond the premises presently occupied by the AHNMS. A large UNRWA complex is situated to the southwest, and a couple of pre-1967 Palestinian houses still stand to the east. Thus, while part of the historic battlefield is located inside the national commemoration site, some of the historic spaces documented in the museum are inaccessible to visitors. They lie outside the premises of the AHNMS. Paradoxically, these spaces—the ex-territorial UN complex (which, to be accurate, is The West Bank Office for Palestinian Refugees in the Middle East) and the Palestinian houses—represent the type of multinational occupation of spaces in Jerusalem/Al-Quds which is precisely what the ideology of the AHNMS seeks to veil.

The director also lamented the architect's decision, during the site's construction in the early 1970s, to demolish and remove a few of the original structures and

2 Interview with C. Nir'el (August 2, 2006).

fortifications in order to make space for the museum. In this way, the AHNMS itself participated in replacing original relics with a new structure that resembles them. The director's lament can be understood in light of the shift toward authenticity in the management of tourist heritage sites and attractions during the last two decades, and the contemporary wish seemingly to preserve as much as possible from the original historic scenes (cf. DeLyser 1999).

My second point concerns something quite more abstract than the site's actual grounds and buildings. I have in mind a well-known song about the battle on Ammunition Hill. Simply entitled "Ammunition Hill," the song was written and composed by two prominent figures in the Israeli music scene (Yoram Tehar-Lev and Yair Rosenblum, respectively). It describes the battle from the perspective of the soldiers who fought there.[3] For this reason, the entire song is voiced in the first person plural, and is performed solely by men. The melodic verses are interspersed with narrative sections during which only an accordion accompanies the male singer's voice. The narratives describe specific scenes of fighting in a low and macho tone. All these characteristics combine to grant the song an aura of authenticity. It sounds as though the soldiers themselves are performing the song.

In a recent television interview, the song's writer revealed that some of the lyrics are in fact "authentic" quotes taken from an issue of the army journal *Bamahane* published shortly after the war.[4] This magazine included interviews with soldiers who received the Israeli army's medal of honor for their part in the battle. Several of the song's most memorable lines, such as that in which one of the soldiers nonchalantly says, "I don't know why I received a medal of honor, I just wanted to return safely home," actually appeared first in *Bamahane*.

In the television program Tehar-Lev and a few of the soldiers are pictured strolling on the grounds of the site. One of the soldiers notes that there are "a few technical inaccuracies" in the song, and continues (with a short chuckle), "They really didn't have 120mm mortars, you know." Nonetheless, the soldier readily agrees with the lyricist that "if it's good for the rhyme, and if that's the price for the success of such a popular song, which is a melodic memorial for the battle, then that's ok." Here again, authenticity, like other ideological social constructions, adheres only partly to the historic reality from which it derives its unique value.

The song "Ammunition Hill," well-known in Israel, functions in MacCannell's terms as an "off-site marker" (MacCannell 1999:110-111). Markers in tourism supply information about the sites they mark. Some are on-site markers, indicating *in situ* that this is the attraction, while off-site markers do so from a distance. Like many off-site markers, the song's framing function is also accomplished as

3 The song was performed by the Israeli Army's Central Command Band, 1972. It is accessible at the AHNMS's website: www.givathatachmosht.org.il/songs.php. The original animated clip is available through on the Internet at YouTube (last accessed March 25, 2008): http://www.youtube.com/watch?v=5GnTDHvWhxA.

4 "The Most Beautiful Moments of the Army Bands in Forty Years of Television Broadcasting," broadcasted on Channel 1 (Israeli National TV), February 8, 2008.

an icon. It does more than merely advertise the site as a worthy attraction (in referential terms). Through its first person voices, and the machismo narration, the song also *demonstrates* the ideology of authenticity that dominates the site. It tells not only where to go (destination), but also how and in what to believe once there (authenticity, militarism, and nationalism).

Note that the discussion of authenticity here and in all other instances relating to the AHNMS bears a gender-specific undertone. Authenticity here is intimately associated with images of hegemonic masculinity and heroic manhood, specifically with war and fighting (cf. images of masculinity in Viking Heritage sites, in Knox and Hannam 2007). However, since authenticity is meant to be perceived as an "objective quality"—the object's quality, its gender politics are veiled. While this characteristic is salient at the AHNMS, MacCannell's general discussion of authenticity has been criticized by feminists in tourism research for being gender-blind, and for its role in the maintenance of patriarchal structures (Aitchison 2001).

Approaching the Visitor Book: Discursive Authenticity

Upon entering the partly sunken structure of the museum, which is designed to resemble an underground bunker, the visitor encounters a plethora of discursive artifacts. These are mainly comprised of handwritten documents and representations thereof, spanning a variety of genres: personal letters and war journals, poems, autographs and more. Most of the exhibits were written by soldiers who fought and fell in the battle, and contribute to the ideological context of authenticity within which I will evaluate the function of the visitor book. These artifacts and exhibits are not merely instances of inscribed discourse, but entail specific instances of handwriting, which illustrate the relationship between authenticity, on the one hand, and handwriting, as an embodied mode of communication, on the other. The significance of this relationship cannot be overestimated in a heritage site dedicated to commemoration. For this reason, I wish to discuss two particular instances.

The first illustration concerns an Israeli flag exhibited in a glass frame (see Figure 14.1). This is the original flag hung by paratroopers above the Western Wall on June 7, 1967. A short text, inscribed at the time by the paratroopers, appears on its upper right corner:

> The Flag of Israel
> Hung above the Western Wall
> at the Temple Mount in Jerusalem
> By soldiers of Pl. A. of Regiment 71 of the 55th Paratrooper Division
> Today, Wednesday, June 7, at 10:15
> The "Jerusalem Liberators" Paratroop Division

Figure 14.1 Authentic 1967 flag
Source: Photo by the author.

The inscription celebrates the triumphant moment when Israeli soldiers reached the Western Wall. It does so with a (reflexive) awareness of the occasion's historic dimension. Specifically, by referring to the paratrooper division explicitly and by signing as they did, this inscription celebrates the paratroopers' division and ties the esteemed device to the renowned "liberation" of Jerusalem.

In her discussion of graffiti, Susan Stewart (1991:207, following Derrida), addressed two conceptions of spontaneous, embodied writing, according to which inscriptions can be viewed as either corrupting or cherished, "[r]adically taken as both crime and art." This is true of the preceding manifestation and of many other occurrences of handwriting at Ammunition Hill. The handwritten mode is either against the law or above it. In the former case it is a matter of vandalism (writing on national symbols is illegal in Israel), and, in the latter, as evinced in the inscription on the national flag, it is an instance to be venerated, belonging in a museum. Handwriting traces or indexes the body of those who wrote it at the moment of inscription. It is perceived as a highly authentic mode of representation not only because the flag is the original item (original items can be manipulated), but because the handwriting on the flag authenticates the flag itself, by positioning

Figure 14.2 Temporary memorial post
Source: Photo by the author.

ARMY OF ISRAEL

ZAHAL

BURIED HERE ARE
17 ~~BRAVE~~ JORDANIAN
SOLDIERS. JUNE 7 1967

Figure 14.2a Memorial inscription (detail)

it in the heart of celebrated events.[5] As Van Leeuwen (2001) stresses, authenticity is very much tied with modality, or more accurately, with the social semiotics of modality. Handwriting on the surface of the national flag dramatically brings together binaries: a collective symbol with a personal inscription.

The second illustration I wish to discuss is a photograph which is not actually situated in the museum, but rather in the Ammunition Hill offices (Figure 14.2). It hangs in the main conference room, where VIPs, donors, and other exclusive visitors are received. The director referred to it specifically during my first visit (it has since been posted on the museum's new website).

The center of the frame is filled by a handwritten, English text inscribed on cardboard, fastened to the butt of a rifle, which is stuck into the ground upside down (Figures 14.2, 14.2a). The post marks the location of the collective grave of 17 Jordanian soldiers killed in the battle. A copy of the picture (dated July 1994), was ceremoniously presented to a Jordanian Army delegation which visited the Ammunition Hill compound after the signing of the peace accord between Jordan and Israel.

Like the writing inscribed on the flag (above), here too a handwritten text is superimposed on a historic artifact and gives it meaning and value. The handwritten text evinces proximity to the "bare" ("pre-verbal") historic event, and thus acquires the precious quality of authentic representation. The physical and functional proximity of rifle to writing additionally embodies the ideology that the activities of fighting and writing are enmeshed. The unused rifle functions concretely, but also symbolically, as a necessary precondition for a cultured existence, embodied

5 In a recent television interview, one of the paratroopers who inscribed on the flag recollected the historic events. His story was incongruent with the text that appears on the flag. It might be that the decades have dimmed the paratrooper's memory of the occasion, or that there were more than one original flag. The point is that authentic artifacts are a problematical category of things.

in the appearance of the inscription. This exact notion was conveyed to me in conversation with the chairman of the Museum's Friends Society. During our first meeting, after I mentioned that I teach at a nearby campus, the chairman replied pedagogically, "You should know that the victory in this site opened and secured the way to the university campus at Mt. Scopus (where I teach)." He added, more explicitly, "If not for the army and the sacrifices made here, you (*pl.*) couldn't have studied and taught there." This notion is common in nationalist (Republican) ideologies and pervasive in Israeli highly militarized political and public discourse, whereby intellectualism is viewed as secondary to and reliant upon military might. It grounds the point I made earlier concerning how heritage sites negotiate identities. In this instance, however, at stake is not the Israeli-Arab conflict, but less overt identities and ideologies within the Israel public (Kimmerling 1993).

Note that the word "brave" was crossed out of the inscription. This act illustrates how different views may compete over interpretations of conflicted events, even immediately after these events occur. More importantly, the deletion *testifies to* the authenticity of the sign. If we consider authenticity's relation to modality, now the sign impresses as doubly authentic—both *hand*-written, *and hand*-erased.

These markers of authenticity are of a type highly characteristic to the AHNMS. They offer a glimpse into the profusion of handwritten documents, which direct us to look not so much at the issues (content) as at the where, how and on what (modality). This mode of communication suggests both authenticity and authentication. Writing, unlike talking, is a durable mode of communication, and thus ideally serves the purposes of authentication. We look at what was written back then, and we "hear" the events anew. In this context, writing is an ideal tool for engendering an awe of the authentic in the visitors (Stewart 1993).

This point is even truer in the case of *commemorative representation.* Since the museum is part of a commemorative complex, its institutional charter is precisely to mobilize authenticity, in the form of handwritten documents, in order to intensify national commitment and re-inscribe collective memory. In terms of commemorative hermeneutics, these documents can be construed as discursive monuments; they are corporeal and of texture (Macdonald 2006).

In tourism, handwritten products fall into the larger valued category of authenticity in tourism, namely "handmade artifacts" (Cohen 1988). According to Cohen, tourists accept objects as authentic, even if they are commercialized and presented in institutional settings, as long as they have been handmade by members of a particular group—in this case paratroopers—or, more generally, people who acted in the epoch being commemorated (Cohen 1988:378). Authenticity, however, can also be constructed through culturally specific means. In Sabra (native Israeli) culture, the romantic relations between handwriting and body are unique, and create a much admired informality, familiarity and intimacy, which mass-printed documents cannot achieve. Handwriting in itself conveys an ideology which ascribes to handwriting—perceived as a non-commodified/commodifiable mode of expression—a uniquely esteemed, authentic, and personalized evocation (Katriel 1986; Noy 2007:131).

Inscribing Acts of Authenticity

Bearing all this in mind, let us approach the visitor book as visitors do. Let us observe that the book is framed in two significant ways which grant it unique status as an authenticating device. First, atypically, this visitor book is not located near the site's exit. Instead, it is located deep inside the commemorative museum. While visitor books are usually placed where visitors can write their impressions after they complete their visit, this visitor book is located in one of the museum's innermost halls. It is placed near the venerating last hall, where the Golden Wall of Commemoration is located and the eternal flame flickers. Thus positioned, this visitor book is not meant to capture reflective comments or encapsulate the visitors' "gesture of closure" (Katriel 1997:71). Rather, it is part of the museum's commemorative arsenal of devices, meant to induce emotional involvement and provide an opportunity to partake in the rite of commemoration.

Second, the visitor book is actually the main attraction in the hall in which it is positioned, its centrality augmented by the structure of which it is a part. This structure is a large and impressive formation consisting of two cylindrical columns of black steel, each about one meter in diameter. The shorter column, about one meter tall, functions as a kind of table on which the book rests. Beside it is another pillar about four meters tall. And the entire composition rests on a base that is slightly elevated from the floor, so that those wishing to read (or write) in the book must step up and enter a specially designated zone. In its overall design, the structure resembles a monument or a memorial, lending the book a solemn and dignified character and designating it as a unique exhibit - perhaps even as a monument in itself.

We thus approach the pages of the visitor book and its inscribed entries (see Figure 14.3, below) with this thick framing of authenticity. The book offers surfaces for writing that are effectively part of the museum's commemorative space. They are an *extension of the physical space of the museum*. In this respect, the space provided in the visitor book is unique because whatever is registered in/on it instantly becomes part of the exhibit. In other words, these are *authentic(ating) surfaces*: Anything and everything that is documented or inscribed on them by visitors is transformed into an authentic exhibit, and thus becomes a permanent element of the museum's interior.

Figure 14.3 illustrates a typical book opening, showing a rather lively, crowded and colorful production. Openings in this book typically contain anywhere between ten and twenty entries, which include short and long texts as well as aesthetic decorations: from orthographic and para-linguistic devices (exclamation marks, aestheticized autographs), through underlying and encircling lines, to graphic symbols and drawings.

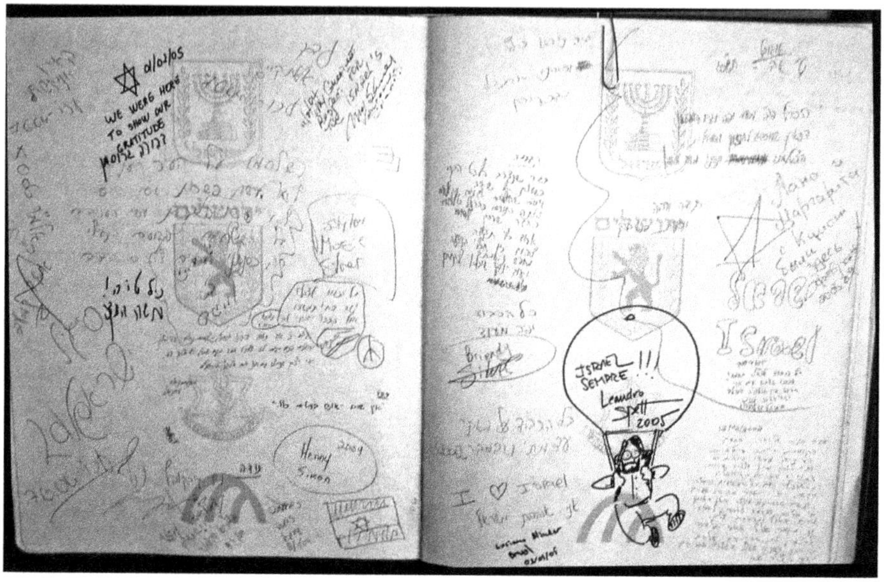

Figure 14.3 Visitor book opening: Authentic(ating) spaces
Source: Photo by the author.

Structurally speaking, the book's openings resemble the images presented above. Such is the case with the opening depicted above. Its similarities lie in the handwritten mode of inscription and the combination of verbal inscriptions with the unique symbolic (material) surfaces, on which they are inscribed. As shown in Figure 14.3, every page in the visitor book displays a vertical line made of four printed symbols. These are the symbols of the State of Israel, the City of Jerusalem, the Israel Defense Forces and the logo of the Ammunition Hill Museum. They correspond with the flags hanging nearby, and with the profusion of national and military symbols exhibited throughout the halls. These symbols serve to mark the book as a device that provides additional surfaces that are available for consumption at the AHNMS. They suggest that the pages of the book are themselves symbolic. Writing upon them is therefore already confined by and in dialogue with the semiotics and aesthetics of nationalist-militaristic commemoration.

The book's animated openings (Figure 14.3) evoke spontaneous inscriptions, created *in situ* by the visitors. These inscriptions represent and record a bottom-up form of "authentic" production. Here, again, the collective quality of the record (i.e. the various inscriptions occupying a shared space) together with its handwritten mode, endows this book with a particular type of authenticity, one that is cherished in Sabra society. As I indicated in my study of handwritten documents in Israeli backpackers' communities, "these handwritten compilations constitute the travelers' alternative to commercialized forms of tourist publications. The travelers' books are often mentioned in comparison to commercial touristic publications; in such comparisons, the former are of a unique genre, valued for their 'authenticity' and for their up-to-date nature" (Noy 2007:131). Such spontaneous expressions are highly sought after in Israeli culture, because they index a culturally esteemed notion of authenticity.

I now wish to examine two inscriptions more closely. I will precede this inquiry with a seemingly surprising finding: neither the word "authentic" nor any similar term appears anywhere in the book's more than 1,000 entries. The following inquiry seeks to address this finding, and to show how authenticity is produced without any explicit recognition of its presence. I submit the following two illustrations in their original layout. The first example is here translated from the Hebrew:

> Example 1:
>
> 30.11.05
> We were very impressed by the way
> the place is presented.
> We were very favorably influenced
> by the place.
> We extend our condolences
> to the bereaved families
> and thank all those who sacrificed their lives
> for the State of Israel.
> Meitar, Ella and Yahel

This inscription is typical of entries written by local visitors (Israeli sightseers in Jerusalem). It is in Hebrew, mainly addresses the AHNMS and expresses respect and gratitude both to the commemorative efforts of the AHNMS and to those who gave their lives during the 1967 War. As is the norm in visitor book entries, the inscription also includes the date and the names of its inscribers. While they could merely write their names, the date of their visit and where they are from, most visitors choose to create more elaborate entries. Through these detailed inscriptions, such as Example 1, the authors are made present, or are "presenced," in the site. Through the act of inscribing on these uniquely framed surfaces, the inscribers are transformed from passive visitors to active producers: they are agents participating in the national narrative of commemoration as told at the site.

The structure of this example is also typical of local visitors' entries. The first few sentences (first four lines) address the site's management, and note the positive experience it bestows. In the next section (last four lines), Meitar, Ella, and Yahel take part in the commemorative narrative and perform what they think is appropriate at this ritualistic site. Put a bit differently, after the writers thank the site, they show what they have learned and absorbed during the visit, which is to partake in the rite of commemoration by extending condolences to the deceased soldiers' families.

This reading of the entry explains why there are no indications of authenticity here or in similar entries. There is simply *no need* for such indications. Inscribing in the visitor book, in terms of both its physical location and the voice of its authors, guarantees that what is written is authentic(ated). The visitors need not mention where they are writing, or the site they are writing about. This information is considered trivial in the context of this commemorative visitor book, which is physically stationary and symbolically framed as part of the "authentic" grounds of the AHNMS.

I now turn to a second entry, which again employs no explicit markers or signifiers of authenticity, yet authenticity is nevertheless performed, albeit differently than in the first example. The writer of this entry comes from a different population of visitors: Orthodox and Ultra-Orthodox Jewish tourists from North America. Unlike the first example, this entry is written mostly in English (words originally in Hebrew are italicized and translated in square brackets).

Example 2:

Basad [abbreviation for: With God's Help]
To all the soldiers
who willingly gave
their lives for us, I
want to express all
my gratitude & emotions.
Without you, we wouldn't
be standing here today.
Thank you so much, on my
behalf & on all of the *Medinat Yisrael* [The State of Israel]
behalf for everything you
have done for us.
Sincerely,
Omry
July 3, 2006

This inscription is typical of entries written by more observant Jewish tourists. Most of it is in English, with a few special words written in Hebrew, i.e. the Holy Language (these are what sociolinguists call "code switches"). Beyond the matter of language, the difference between the entries is evident at first glance. While the first example basically addresses the site and its management, this entry directly and explicitly addresses the fallen soldiers. If the entry by Meitar, Ella, and Yahel had the AHNMS at its center, Omry's entry has the historic sacrifice at its center. It is almost as though Omry does not see the site, but rather sees *through* it.

There are of course similarities between the entries as well. In both cases, the visitors demonstrate their understanding of the narrative as told by the site, and they do so through participation—by writing in the visitor book. As is typical at commemoration sites, the visitors tell, or retell, the narrative that ties past to present via a causal link. This link suggests a justification of past events and sacrifices (present and future ones as well) by what the past has granted the present day condition ("we wouldn't be standing here today").

Yet this and similar English entries, which address the fallen soldiers directly, establish a sense of authenticity through the unique structure of their address. Directly invoking the dead positions the visitor in the same realm as those being addressed. The verse, "To all the soldiers who willingly gave their lives for us" suggests a communicative continuity between those making the address and those being addressed. This homology blurs the ontic divide between signifier and signified, and serves to place the author—in this case Omry—within the spotlight of authenticity. There is more at stake here than becoming an exhibit via inscription in the visitor book. Here the visitors talk *through* the site, and connect with the historical events and people commemorated by the site, all of which are viewed as objectively authentic.

In other words, the framing of the site and the visitor book grants museum visitors the possibility of performing authentically. Thus, different entries are able to perform authentically without explicitly indexing authenticity. From this platform, visitors are invited and enabled to communicate directly with the nation, the grieving families and the soldiers, living or dead. When this option is actualized, authentic communication results. In terms proposed by Van Leeuwen (2001, following Goffman's distinctions), at stake is the authenticity of the "encoder/transmitter." "[R]ecording and distribution technologies," Van Leeuwen notes, "become involved in the production of meaning themselves" (395). Hence there is no need for those writing in the book to indicate that the experience is "real/authentic/original" (society sanctions people who say trivial things, Sacks [1992]). The very act of inscribing (modality), the surfaces on which inscribing is performed (encoder/transmitter), and the structure of their expressions establish the writers-visitors as authentic participants.

Conclusion

> There is no serious or functional role in the production awaiting the tourist in the places they visit. Tourists are not made personally responsible for anything that happens in the establishment they visit … (MacCannell 1999:102).

In this chapter I illustrated various constructions and performances of authenticity in tourism, and specifically heritage tourism, through a case study of the AHNMS. I took my time throughout the chapter in arriving, as do tourists, at the actual device of the visitor book, which was, in a way, this chapter's (authentic) destination. I have done so because, as MacCannell has showed, no one arrives at the destination from nowhere, as a *tabula rasa*. Instead, numerous off-site markers—from advertisements and personal recollections, to representations in art, literature and cinema—permeate our modern lives, ignite our desires and inform our expectations regarding destinations.

The visitor book is positioned *within* an ecology of authenticity and at the same time it is *part of* that ecology. This ecology shares norms of modality, which concern the accepted ways of constructing and farming of authenticity, and the way it partakes in meaning-bestowing performances. This means that the semiotics of authenticity emerge due to the ways the book is framed, and because the book itself is an authenticity-framing, or authenticating, device. The pages and openings of the book are created as surfaces for tourist performances, which are uniquely endowed with (uniquely endowing) the quality of authenticity. This occurs as these performances cross the divide from the mundane (everyday) to the symbolic (tourism), and as their producers shift from being passive visitors into active agents. This transcendence, a trespassing into the land of the past and the symbolic (and the dead), charges these visitors' inscribed performances with the aura of authenticity.

MacCannell's quote demonstrates the astuteness of his observations on tourism, a quality that has made his work so appealing. Yet in the present case, the matter seems precisely the reverse. Tourists' performances in the visitor book assume their authentic quality precisely because they amount to *material productions*, whereby tourists become personally responsible for what they do. In fact, it is what they do that is what "happens in the establishment they visit"! The construction of authenticity is such that tourists' productions are made to assume the state of "objective authenticity." This is why the authenticity effect occurs implicitly, and any explicit references to authenticity on the pages of the book are absent. The tourists need not index authenticity themselves; instead, they are offered the opportunity to perform it.

Under these circumstances, the best way to conceptualize authenticity is in terms of the ideological role played out by modality. This view allows us to group together different representations and functions of authenticity, and to see how they all serve institutionally to create and sustain a "lived experience" which is both real and imagined (Althusser 1990:233). At the AHNMS, this "modality ideology" works in alliance with other ideologies. Remove authenticity from the triangle of authenticity, nationalism and militarism, and the effect of the AHNMS collapses. At this site, the ideology of authenticity's modality is in charge of epistemological issues (Althusser 1990:233), which is to say that it is responsible for letting visitors *know* or *feel* the two other grand ideologies. It is through the "lived experience" of and partaking performatively in authenticity, that militarism and nationalism are persuasively *created and embodied*. As we saw, this is accomplished cleverly, by producing a physical and aesthetic experience among the visitors, as they become ideological agents on the pages of the visitor book.

Acknowledgment

I am deeply indebted to Erik Cohen, Zohar, Phillip Vannini and an anonymous contributor to this volume, for their many constructive suggestions and learned comments.

References

Adler, Judith. 1989. "Travel as Performed Art." *American Journal of Sociology*, 94:1366-1391.

Aitchison, Cara. 2001. "Theorizing Other Discourses of Tourism, Gender and Culture: Can the Subaltern Speak (in Tourism)?" *Tourist Studies*, 1:133-147.

Althusser, Louis. 1971. *Lenin and Philosophy, and Other Essays*. Translated by B. Brewster. London: New Left Books.

—— 1990. *For Marx*. Translated by B. Brewster. London: Verso.

Anderson, Benedict. 1983. *Imagined Communities: Reflections on the Origin and Spread of Nationalism*. London: Verso.

Benjamin, Walter. 1968. *Illuminations*. New York: Harcourt.

Berger, Peter L. and Thomas Luckmann. 1967. *The Social Construction of Reality: A Treatise in the Sociology of Knowledge*. London: Penguin Press.

Breathnach, Teresa. 2006. "Looking for the Real Me: Locating the Self in Heritage Tourism." *Journal of Heritage Tourism*, 1:100-120.

Brown, Donna. 1996. "Genuine Fakes." Pp. 33-47 in *The Tourist Image: Myths and Myth Making in Tourism*, edited by T. Selwyn. Chichester: John Wiley.

Bruner, Edward. 1991. "The Transformation of Self in Tourism." *Annals of Tourism Research*, 18:238-250.

—— 1994. "Abraham Lincoln as Authentic Reproduction: A Critique of Postmodernism."*American Anthropologist*, 96:397-415.

Chhabra, Deepak, Robert Healy, and Erin Sills. 2003. "Staged Authenticity and Heritage Tourism." *Annals of Tourism Research*, 30:702-719.

Cohen, Erik. 1974. "Who is a Tourist?: A Conceptual Clarification." *Sociological Review*, 22:527-555.

—— 1979. "A Phenomenology of Tourist Experiences." *Sociology*, 13:179-201.

—— 1988. "Authenticity and Commoditization in Tourism." *Annals of Tourism Research*, 15:371-386.

—— 1989. "'Primitive and Remote': Hill Tribe Trekking in Thailand." *Annals of Tourism Research*, 16:30-61.

Dann, Graham. 1996. *The Language of Tourism: A Sociolinguistic Perspective*. Wallingford, UK: CAB International.

DeLyser, D. 1999. "Authenticity on the Ground: Engaging the Past in a California Ghost Town." *Annals of the Association of American Geographers*, 89:602-632.

Edensor, Tim. 1998. *Tourists at the Taj: Performance and Meaning at a Symbolic Site*. London: Routledge.

Garfinkel, Harold. 1967. *Studies in Ethnomethodology*. Englewood Cliffs, NJ: Prentice-Hall.

Goffman, Erving. 1956. *The Presentation of Self in Everyday Life*. Edinburgh: University of Edinburgh, Social Sciences Research Centre.

Katriel, Tamar. 1986. *Talking Straight: Dugri Speech in Israeli Sabra Culture*. Cambridge: Cambridge University Press.

—— 1997. *Performing the Past: A Study of Israeli Settlement Museums*. Mahwah, NJ: Lawrence Erlbaum Associates.

Kimmerling, Baruch. 1993. "Patterns of Militarism in Israel." *European Journal of Sociology*, 34:196-223.

Kirshenblatt-Gimblett, Barbara. 1998. *Destination Cultures: Tourism, Museums, and Heritage*. Berkeley: University of California Press.

Knox, Dan and Kevin Hannam. 2007. "Embodying Everyday Masculinities in Heritage Tourism(S)." Pp. 263-272 in *Tourism and Gender: Embodiment, Sensuality and Experience*, edited by A. Pritchard, N. Morgan, I. Ateljevic and C. Harris. Wallingford, UK: CABI.

Lacan, Jacques. 1977. *The Four Fundamental Concepts of Psycho-Analysis*. Translated by A. Sheridan. London: Hogarth Press.

Laurier, Eric. 1998. "Replication and Restoration: Ways of Making Maritime Heritage." *Journal of Material Culture* 3:21-59.

MacCannell, Dean. 1973. "Staged Authenticity: Arrangements of Social Space in Tourist Settings." *American Journal of Sociology*, 79:589-603.

—— 1999. *The Tourist: A New Theory of the Leisure Class*. Berkeley: University of California Press.

Macdonald, Sharon. 2005. "Accessing Audiences: Visiting Visitor Books." *Museum and Society*, 3:119-136.

—— 2006. "Words in Stone? Agency and Identity in a Nazi Landscape." *Journal of Material Culture*, 11:105-126.

Noy, Chaim. 2004. "Performing Identity: Touristic Narratives of Self-Change." *Text and Performance Quarterly*, 24:115-138.

—— 2007. *A Narrative Community: Voices of Israeli Backpackers*. Detroit: Wayne State University Press.

—— 2008. "Mediation Materialized: The Semiotics of a Visitor Book at an Israel Commemoration Site." *Critical Studies in Media Communication*, 25:175-195.

Noy, Chaim and Erik Cohen. 2005. *Israeli Backpackers and Their Society: A View from Afar*. Albany: State University of New York Press.

Pearce, Phillip L. and Gianna M. Moscardo. 1986. "The Concept of Authenticity in Tourist Experience." *Journal of Sociology*, 22:121-132.

Peters, John Durham. 2001. "Witnessing." *Media, Culture & Society*, 23:707-723.

Ritzer, George and Allan Liska. 1997. "'McDisneyization' and 'Post-Tourism': Complementary Perspectives on Contemporary Tourism." Pp. 96-112 in *Touring Cultures: Transformations of Travel and Theory*, edited by C. Rojek and J. Urry. London: Routledge.

Sacks, Harvey. 1992. *Lectures on Conversation*. Oxford, UK: Blackwell.

Selwyn, Tom. 1996. *The Tourist Image: Myths and Myth Making in Tourism*. Chichester: John Wiley.

Stephenson, T.S. 2004. "Performing Backpacking: Constructing 'Authenticity' Every Step of the Way." *Text and Performance Quarterly*, 24:139-169.

Stewart, Susan. 1991. *Crimes of Writing: Problems in the Containment of Representation*. New York: Oxford University Press.

—— 1993. *On Longing: Narratives of the Miniature, the Gigantic, the Souvenir, the Collection*. Durham: Duke University Press.

Taylor, John P. 2001. "Authenticity and Sincerity in Tourism." *Annals of Tourism Research*, 28:7-26.

Van Leeuwen, Theo. 2001. "What Is Authenticity?" *Discourse Studies*, 3:392-397.

Wang, Ning. 1999. "Rethinking Authenticity in Tourism Experience." *Annals of Tourism Research*, 26:349-370.

—— 2000. *Tourism and Modernity: Sociological Analysis*. Amsterdam: Pergamon.

Wang, Y. 2007. "Exploring Market Influences on Curator Perceptions of Authenticity." *Annals of Tourism Research*, 34:789-804.

Zerubavel, Yael. 1995. *Recovered Roots: Collective Memory and the Making of Israeli National Tradition*. Chicago: University of Chicago Press.

Chapter 15

Emotional Performances as Dramas of Authenticity

E. Doyle McCarthy

> The self has a history and a social history and that of the contemporary emotivist self is only intelligible as the end product of a long and complex set of developments.
>
> Alasdair MacIntyre (1983:31)

Authenticity, as I will argue in this chapter, is best grasped within the context of a distinct *modern culture of emotion*—principally Romantic in its origins and development—where feelings and emotions speak to us about who we are, telling us the most vital things about ourselves. Authenticity, in this sense, is a particular *language of the self*, an intensely sentimental (i.e., suffused with emotion) type of discourse; it is a way of speaking about who I am, my *identity*, which in its modern manifestation is an intense experience (and pursuit) of myself as I truly am. In what follows, as I develop these ideas about authenticity today and its continuity with its emotional and sentimental past, I examine how authenticity has been changed and intensified by contemporary media culture and how in a thoroughly media-saturated world the pursuit of authenticity—and the dramatization of the real vs. the fake, the natural vs. fabricated, the "real article" vs. the phony—has become a cultural preoccupation. Indeed, "popular culture is obsessed with authenticity and awash with artificiality," as Mukerji (2007:1) has convincingly argued and this "obsession" is played out in a number of highly visible and intensely emotional cultural practices, from the world of sports, leisure, and entertainment to those of religion and politics.

A good deal of my argument about the importance and the intensity of our pursuits of the real and the authentic concerns the special place of emotions in our contemporary culture. Emotions have become special objects of attention and elaboration for modern subjects. Most especially, emotions are integral to who and what the modern self is. Feelings and emotions are keys for unlocking who I am, my authenticity, how I perceive and how I discover my "real self." As Charles Taylor and others have shown us, this was not always the case (Taylor 1989; also see Bell 1996; Illouz 2007; Reddy 2001; Trilling 1971). Rather, the conjunction of emotion and identity is a feature of a distinct modern emotional culture, *an everyday understanding, a vernacular speech-form,* "the tendency to represent emotion as the foundation and authentication of experiences of self" (Barbalet 1998:171-72; also see Baumeister 1986, Chap.11; Lupton 1998). In Reddy's (2001:315) account of our Western "commonsense conceptions of self," emotion has become the self's "constitutive feature [...]. Like thought, memory, intention, or language, emotion is something the self has by virtue of being a self and without which it would not be a self." It is precisely this conception of emotion as something the self *has* that I wish to examine as peculiar to modern identity and its emotional culture, a dominant view of thought and feeling as "possessions of the individual" (Taylor 1989:Part II); thinking and feeling are "interiorized;" they are *mine* as is personhood itself. But by *having* emotions (and "being emotional") I also mean that "emotions" are some of the most important ways that modern persons search for and discover their authenticity: their sense of *who they really are*. Feeling deeply and intensely alive—these are moments and experiences that say to us, "This is *me*! This is who I *really* am!" (Erikson 1968:19).

A Modern Culture of Emotion

> The belief that the organic is the chief criterion of what is authentic in art and life continues ... to have great force with us ... the machine ... is felt to be inimical to the authenticity of experience and being.
>
> Lionel Trilling (1971:127)

I wish to begin with a brief recounting of authenticity's history to frame my study of today's culture of emotion.[1] Authenticity, as an idea and set of practices, is something peculiar to modern culture. Born in the late–eighteenth century, authenticity developed alongside of *individualism*, particularly the notion that the human person, as in Kant's ethical theory, is an autonomous agent directing its own actions by its own will; such agents can engage in moral self-governance. To be an authentic individual is to be a master of oneself and one's actions, a process that entails both the capability and honesty to live a life attuned to one's inner truths, to live an "authentic life." While at home in the confines of modern individualism, authenticity thrived in the waves and tremors of Romanticism, its eighteenth century progenitor. For it is to the voice within one's self and to the sentiments of one's being that the authentic person is attuned, both ideas tied to the upheaval in literature and the arts known as Romanticism. Authenticity is a self-determining freedom (cf. Rousseau), a listening to one's inner voice and urges. Each of these—the pursuit of freedom and an ear attuned to one's inner self—has its own distinct way of being in the world (cf. Herder), what it means to be me and to live according to that unique structure of mind and sentiment that is mine alone.

1 By "culture of emotion" or "emotional culture" I mean popular standards and practices about emotions, the ideas and understandings that ordinary people draw from to understand their feelings and emotions—a term identified with pioneering works in the sociology of emotions by Gordon (1981) and Stearns and Stearns (1986).

Authenticity means to *feel something* with honesty, integrity, and vitality and to express in one's life the truth of one's personal insights and discoveries.[2]

In the late–nineteenth century, portrayed as a struggle against the conventions of society, authenticity became a frequent theme of modern literature and art. Authenticity was seen as a search for personal coherence and integrity in the face of a civilization that had become an alienating force, at once mechanized and petrified through the imposition of instrumental reason in every facet of life, and a place dominated by objects and the transforming force of money, an energy that was seen to change everything into something it was not. A related theme of this period was that humankind itself had been changed, an idea clearly expressed by Marx who argued that all human relations had been changed by the material and productive forces of capitalism. In works of social philosophy of the same period (e.g. Marx, Kierkegaard, Nietzsche), humankind was believed to have lost its way, the world was found to have been emptied of meaning and human lives devoid of passion and intensity. Consequently, in works of literature of the late-nineteenth century, authenticity is represented as a heroic struggle against the (inauthentic) forces of bourgeois society. Flaubert's Emma Bovary is, perhaps, the earliest portrait of a conventional and sentimental woman who is the epitome of inauthenticity (Trilling 1971:100).

During the middle to late-twentieth century ideas of authenticity changed dramatically. It is then that we begin to see authenticity as shallow self-deception—Adorno's ([1964] 2007) "jargon of authenticity" or Lasch's (1978) "culture of narcissism"—a surrender to the dictates of popular culture, mass psychology, and their promises of pleasure and self-actualization. Authenticity-as-jargon, today's "psychobabble," is a kind of authenticity worn on one's sleeve or in one's buttonhole; it listens not to itself but to the dictates of a material civilization held in place by its therapeutic culture of self-aggrandizement (Illouz 2008; Imber 2004). But whether authenticity is viewed as an escape from the confines of a material civilization or as a kind of selling-out or material entrapment, the discourse of authenticity throughout its relatively brief history takes as its problem the pursuit of inner truth and meaningfulness in a social world of lies, deceits, and fabrications. Authenticity is always a type of self-knowledge, especially a self-knowledge that allows us to disentangle the true from the false self.

My work in emotion studies has been directed toward the most recent phase of modern emotional history, "late modernity," a time when emotions have become powerful cultural objects in their own right, parts of everyday discourse, objects of our heightened self-reflexivity, paramount features of our encounter with the world, with others, and with ourselves (McCarthy 1989, 1994, 2002, 2007). This has led me to the study of a number of "cultural practices," collective displays of emotion in different social and institutional sites. Construed as "cultural

2 On the history of modern identity and emotion, see Trilling's *Sincerity and Authenticity* (1971), Taylor's *Sources of the Self* (1989) and *The Ethics of Authenticity* (1991: 28-29), and Williams's *Culture and Society 1780-1950* [1958] (1983).

practices,"[3] culture is something—many things, really—observable and material. Culture is done, as much as it is thought and felt. But my principal interest here is in emotional cultures today and thus how these practices can be used as resources for identifying emotional cultures. In other words, authenticity will be explored within this larger "cultural package," as integral to today's culture of emotion.

To be sure "the bearers of emotion," as Barbalet writes, "are always individual persons who experience themselves as being or possessing a self ... the sense of what is meant by emotion derives from experiences of the self" (1998:187). But what emotions mean not only derives from experiences of the self, it also derives from my *identity*: who I really am (whatever that "really" refers to), *how* the self is construed, *what* it believes itself to be, *how* it is connected (or not connected) to other selves, whether or not it *believes* in its own individuality or whether it believes that its individuality is a fiction, whether it can listen to its heart, and so on. All of these aspects of identity as well as others are closely related to what I mean here by "emotional culture."

Emotional cultural practices exemplify something relatively new on the social terrain, a topic of special interest to sociologists as well as behavioral historians. Our lives today are distinguished by a distinctive and intense emotionality and a number of culturally significant "emotional pursuits" and an unprecedented demonstration of emotionality—a change in the way we readily display our pleasures and enjoyments, our frenzies of fun and feeling. For example, in leisure and sports, the rise of risk-taking activities (called "extreme games") and the pursuit of intense experiences like those described by climbers of Mount Everest like Jon Krakauer (1997) and Goren Kropp (1997); the new sites and forms of memorializing individual deaths and collective disasters, reflecting the popularity of memorializing in American culture today; the rise of media "spectacles"—extravaganzas of technology, entertainment, sports, and politics from the Superbowl and "reality" TV shows to New Year's media celebrations and TV shows like American Idol. What interests me particularly about these cultural practices are the very public displays of emotional behavior surrounding them and, in some cases, the emotional displays they evoke in their audiences; in important respects, they are emotional dramas of intense feeling, perhaps a *display* of intensity. Indeed we have come to place a special value on our feelings and on *knowing our feelings*; how the self—in its late modern manifestations—has come to be commonly understood as the *feeling* or *emotional self*; how we have become, in Irving Howe's (1967:31) memorable phrase, persons "entranced with depths," our own; how, in a relatively short span of time, a new social type was born, one who claimed to have and to live an "emotional life."

Information and entertainment media have in particular become one aspect of everyday life that is integral to many of the emotional pursuits I describe here,

---

3 The concept of *practice* is from cultural studies and is my overarching theory. For a discussion of the significance of this term in cultural studies see McCarthy (1996) and the now-classic statement on this by Stuart Hall (1980).

providing a new "torrent of images and sounds" to the world of our everyday lives, one that shares a new and distinct set of feelings and sensations, "a relentless pace, a pattern of interruption, a pressure toward unseriousness, a readiness for sensation, an anticipation of the next new thing" (Gitlin 2002:7). Contemporary everyday life is played out against this background—this flow of images and sensations—produced by television, internet, radio, but also portable electronics like car radios and CD players, iPods, and cell phones that allow for us to be plugged in almost constantly to an environment of images, messages, voices, and sounds to stimulate and entertain us.

Some of these collective practices have emerged out of new forms of media-based social identities where "participants" and "audiences" are inextricably part of the practice or event. For example, in the pursuit of "extreme games" in leisure and competitive sports websites like Everestnews.com keep audiences and journalists informed of current and ongoing events on current climbs and climbers. Leading climbers write blogs or bestselling books and become media personalities, like Jon Krakauer, the author of *Into Thin Air* (1997). Similarly, when Tori Murden, the competitive rower, crossed the Atlantic Ocean on the *American Pearl*, her website posted frequent reports while her "onlookers" sent messages of emotional support.

Or, take the collective and highly emotional responses of individuals and groups to the heroics of firefighters—such as when six firefighters in Worcester, Massachusetts gave their lives to search a burning building for homeless people. This event, discussed widely on the Internet, and the public displays that followed upon the event (US President Clinton and other dignitaries joined 30,000 firefighters from around the world in a 3-mile funeral procession) enabled firefighters worldwide to form "communities," to "gather" online, to assemble, to march and to be viewed (and to view themselves) if not in living color then in cyberspace. Information and entertainment media are vital to the formation of these cultural heroes, these "risk-takers," and the powerful collective emotions they evoke; *emotional media dramas* express and articulate the meaning of these current-day heroes to the public and to participants. There are many examples of the firefighter hero and the media dramas and iconography that surround them from the Oklahoma City Memorial to 9/11.

To construe these activities as cultural practices means, among other things, that they can be used as resources for identifying today's emotional cultures. Authenticity, then, is understood here as part of this distinctly sensate, dramatic, and media-based "cultural package," as are the emotions. And while we share a deep and lasting comradeship with our Romantic predecessors, late modern culture moves us, along with our capacity for strong feelings and emotions, out into the world, onto a stage where we have become actors "seeking identification with [our] own experiences and understandings from our audiences" (Alexander, Giesen, and Mast 2006:2). We travel to monuments and memorials to "remember" events we never witnessed (Weiseltier 2002:38); we pursue spectator sports in unprecedented numbers; we love the excitement of parades, rock concerts, and "mega-events," large-scale commercial and sports events that are dramatic and have mass appeal and international significance, like the Olympics and Expos (Roche 2000).

In some cases, these activities demand the skills of a trained actor to render an authentic performance, to be someone in touch with our deepest feelings, participants in a real life drama. The media facilitate this process, bringing us closer to something real and important "as it really happens," no matter that this sense of the real is mass produced, as is the sense of being "up close and personal" with what and whom we watch. Put differently, *playing out* our feelings and *trying on* identities (popular idioms) have taken a decidedly dramatic and performative direction. Media—especially radio, television, Internet, and movies—in both real life and fiction—"create the characters that people civil society and establish what might be called its communicative boundaries with noncivil domains" (Alexander 2006:75). They provide a distinct cognitive and emotional "media logic" (Altheide and Snow 1979) that shapes the contours of our lives. And because of this, the divide between fiction and reality has become somewhat more blurred and life has become more like a movie (Gabler 1998; Gergen 1991). Stated in decidedly academic terms, "The symbolic forms of fictional media weave the binary codes of civil society into broad narratives and popular narratives" (Alexander 2006:75). To illustrate in more depth some of these claims, I will turn briefly to the case of memorialization to explore today's changing faces of the emotional culture of authenticity.

Museums, Monuments, and Memorials

> It is now commonplace to take notice of the popularity of memorialization in American culture … With the Vietnam Veterans Memorial as a model, individuals did not hesitate to shape the meaning of a memorial through their own actions and energies.
>
> Edward T. Linenthal (2001:133-34)

One of the very first signs that "emotions" had taken on a new form—surprising, in the ways that it announced itself and by what it said about honoring the dead—were the new and very public displays of grief and mourning that began to appear on my own streets and neighborhoods in New York as well as on the nightly news. These shrines to mark the deaths of both strangers and friends, very public figures as well as those close to us began to appear across America in the late 1970s, although one of the first expressions of this kind took place in Dallas, Texas, after the assassination of John Kennedy in 1962 where in the aftermath of the assassination, mounds of flowers, candles, wreaths, and mementos were left at the site. The assassination site also became one of the first memorial museums in the US. The Sixth Floor Museum at Dealey Plaza contains a permanent historical exhibition focused on the impact of Kennedy's death on the nation and the world.

For about three decades now, there has been a surge of academic and scholarly interest in the museum, monument, and memorial as cultural phenomena, just as there has been a parallel development—popular and political—in building monuments and memorials. Today, memorializing is even described as possessing an "intensity" (Huyssen 1995:253) that points to the range of engagements with the process (scholarly, popular, journalistic, political) and to the extraordinary rise in memorials and in new forms of memorializing. Take, for example, the sheer proliferation of memorials and their popularity: Holocaust Memorials and Museums are now estimated in the thousands worldwide and visitors to these memorials are now estimated in the millions (Young 1993:x). In Washington, DC, we have witnessed the most active period of building monuments in a century: the Washington Mall alone includes the Vietnam Veterans Memorial, the Korean Memorial, the FDR Memorial, and the World War II Memorial. In fact, in 2000, US government planners unveiled 102 possible new sites for memorials and museums in Washington. Since its dedication in 1982, the Vietnam Memorial—by far, the most popular memorial in the country—has been visited by at least 50 million people and has consistently drawn visitors; despite the fact that "there is no liturgical calendar of rites there, nor is there a prescribed routine or custom that the acts of remembrance must follow; but the commemoration is regular, and everyday people go there to remember … " (Butterfield 2003:32). The Oklahoma City Memorial, dedicated in April 2000, received 340,000 visitors in its first five months (Linenthal 2001:231).

The architectural term applied to both these memorials is "minimalist," the unofficial language of modernist art since mid–twentieth century, but only recently used for monuments and memorials: Lin's Vietnam Memorial, Peter Eisenman's Holocaust Memorial in Berlin (a field of plain concrete pillars like headstones), Oklahoma City's grid of chairs. These memorials are not only important signifiers of the individual lives lost, they commemorate ordinary people, something that memorials did not do until the recent decades. In fact, as highly individualized cultural forms, they represent a type of "anti-memorial" (Kimmelman 2002), something sentimental and populist. In one critic's words, this is an art form with an "emotional intensity" and one that allows, even welcomes, the popular and emotional and individual gestures of its visitors: at the Vietnam Memorial people go to read, touch the names, leave flowers and photos—"mementos are one of the great mysteries of the Wall" (Ayres 1992).

Both the Vietnam and Oklahoma City memorials—in their minimalist muteness—allow (invite, really) for an abundance of individual and popular expressions at the sites, expressions like those at local and instant sites of loss and mourning on highways and on neighborhood streets. At the Vietnam Memorial visitors have left things—ranging from flowers, photos, letters, medals, even a Harley-Davidson motorcycle—that there is an entire warehouse to preserve them. Individual names, often traced by visitors, are also personally and emotionally significant; the names are touched lovingly, often with emotional gestures that are visible to onlookers.

For some, the emotional and personal responses of visitors—the aggrieved—are a spectacle, more moving than the wall itself. Yet the wall itself, its polished marble reflecting us back to ourselves, can also be seen as an evoker of personal sentiments (Wagner-Pacifici and Schwartz 1991:403); the names function as the objects of a highly individualized (collective) ritual. The chairs at Oklahoma City are like these names: "The bronze back and frames of the chairs themselves were dipped individually, to remind [us] that these were people. No two chairs are alike" (Rosenblatt 2000:28). Of the many emotionally wrenching objects at the Holocaust Museum in Washington, one easily recalls the signs of individuals lost: the empty shoes of the dead; the hall of photographs; the identification cards we are handed as we enter the exhibit; "this card tells the story of a real person who lived during the Holocaust," a person we carry with us through the exhibit.

Museums and memorials have been designed to be *experiential*, transformative of those who visit them. Edward Linenthal has stated that they are designed so that "the memory of the event will be as transforming as the event itself" (Rosenblatt 2000:29). They are places of "civic transformation;" one is expected to come away changed (and there are many testimonies of this occurring for those who visit these memorials); they are sites where we discover meanings as well as aspects of our identities. In Linenthal's words, "memorials are a product of who we are right now. We are a people negotiating our identities [...]. In part, we are doing this by creating and feeling the power of memorials" (Rosenblatt 2000: 30).

These new memorial sites are consequential, for they situate and frame the emotional acts described here. They are designed and arranged as settings for the masses who visit them, directing their movements—down a grassy slope to read the wall of 58,195 names, inside a steel elevator like those in the death camps, into hallways displaying life-sized photos of victims, into small movie theaters to watch films of disastrous events or to watch and listen to the stories of those who witnessed them directly. Not only do museums and memorials like these function as public stages on which to assemble, to remember, to mourn, or to undergo a cultural education about "our times," but in doing these things, they also point to something new on our social landscape: they operate as new moral spaces that borrow heavily from the familiar world of media—photos, films, TV, and recorded sound. And like this media culture we inhabit, we attend these sites as *media events*; we gather there as *spectator-participants* seeking meaningful experiences, whether memorializing the victims of the Holocaust or of the attack at New York's World Trade Center or the bombing of the federal building in Oklahoma City. It is as if these new public sites—symbols themselves—draw us to themselves to remember something we "witnessed." They also represent new "arenas of action" that combine public and private attitudes, feelings, and dispositions. These sites "beckon new types of social performances [...] new collective configurations" (Cerulo 1997:397). Public assemblies at these sites neither draw from nor strengthen common sentiments and beliefs. Yet, they are remarkably intense, enveloping spectators in experiences of something important, not in a political, but in a deeply personal sense about something that "really happened" to each of us.

Acts of Emotional Identification

Some of the emotional cultural practices described here are closely linked to processes of *identification,* a concept borrowed from both cultural studies and psychoanalysis. Identification—attachments and belongings—is constructed around *commonalities* imagined, felt, recognized, asserted, or imposed. Identification engages ideas and images about one's own or a group's solidarity and allegiance—its loss, its achievement—yet never one of these, as "identification" in modern dress is fraught with indeterminacy; identification points to a desire for, indeed, *a fantasy of incorporation* (Hall 1996:3). Identification suggests that some of these collective happenings—gatherings like demonstrations in public spaces, but also some entertainment events like rock concerts—are dramas of finding and losing, of seeking forms of self-validation and authenticity through emphatic experiences. Yet for us moderns, identification (as narrated by Freud, Marx, Durkheim) is either "too much" or "too little" (Hall 1996:2-3). For it conjures up the modern fear of being engulfed by others, while lonely in our autonomy. For we have no bonds that are unbreakable, no final attachments, we are desperate to relate, yet wary of the state of "being related," as Zygmunt Bauman writes about our "liquidity" (2005:viii).

Like all signifying practices, identifications are both "strategic" and "positional"; they entail "discursive work, the binding and making of symbolic boundaries" (Hall 1996:3). So conceived, identities today are "points of temporary attachment," ephemeral and fleeting like emotions themselves and, like some popular and local shrines assembled to commemorate a loss intensely felt, they can be quickly abandoned (cf. Holstein and Gubrium 2000).

A theory of identification can also be used to explore the new identities and attachments produced by mass media, those deeply (but fleeting) felt attachments to people we never met and whom we do not know in any immediate sense (Calhoun 1991; Meyrowitz 1985). Identification can assist us in understanding the many new forums that publics seek out to express their sympathy and grief: sites of airplane crashes, house burnings where children died (Fernandez 2007).

Another concept useful for the interpretation of these materials is that of emotives (Reddy 2001). *Emotives* are emotional expressions that describe the process by which emotions are thought about, managed, and shaped by social actors as they seek to express how and what they feel in the terms of the culture they share and produce. Emotives are instruments for directly changing, building, hiding, and intensifying emotions (Reddy 2001:105), operating on our emotions in unexpected ways. For, only as people articulate their feelings can they "know" what they feel, reflect on this knowledge, and feel yet more (Rosenwein 2002).

The idea of emotives points to a kind of freedom of persons to *navigate* the culture and styles of emotion imposed by a society and by hierarchies of class and literacy. Emotional expressions, then, do more than shape what we feel to conform to perceived norms; emotives are also *self-altering capacities*—what we can *say* about what we feel, what we *think* about our feelings—for these sayings and these thoughts enable us to navigate in the complex worlds we inhabit.

Returning to the case studies presented earlier, we are now in a better position to ask questions, and find possible answers about the significance of the public displays of emotion. One obvious interpretive avenue is that of people's *expressive capacities*, relative to the cultures they are navigating. In my studies, what people themselves make of the feelings they are having and pursuing as spectator-participants in the growing number of public stages and forums for collective action and emotion. When this is done, many of those who grieve and mourn admit an inability to understand their own feelings when public figures die, "feeling like a member of my family has passed away," one man said. A woman, speaking to a *New York Times* reporter said that "she found she was feeling sadder about the Kennedy plane crash than she did about the fatal car crash of her sister back in 1949 (Goldberg 1999:A21). Visitors to the Vietnam shrine tell us that they came *to feel something* (they needed to come here to feel their grief, to feel solace), to bring "closure" to the death of a friend or loved one. One woman reported that she found more solace after her brother's death in Iraq at *the site of a local war memorial* than she found at his funeral and burial ceremony.[4]

The idea of emotives returns us to the centerpiece of the psychoanalytic project—personal life itself—and to the idea that cultures, no matter how powerful, exist relative to something personal, inchoate, imaginary, emotional, experiential (Zaretsky 2004). In fact, Freudian analysis requires—in the face of our emotions and conflicts—that we give articulation to our inner depths; it is precisely in that articulation that we regain our freedom and our self-possession, ideas compatible with the theory of emotives.

Conclusion

There is something very important about the dramatic and public settings of the memorials I described and to the mediated quality to these and other collective actions and social performances. These settings of public actions suggest a new form of "agency"—a self-conscious, collective agency whereby social actors (when you ask them) attest to a conscious sense of the moral good of acting with others to pursue and to secure that good (victims' families seeking to authorize a public memorial, bereaved widows of fallen soldiers, mothers against drunk

4 On a related topic see Thomas J. Scheff's account of his participation in a memorial to honor the dead Americans of the Iraq War; the video, "A Wake on the Pier," and essays #46 and #59 at www.soc.ucsb.edu/faculty/scheff ; see also Scheff (2007).

driving, mourners in processions of fire fighters). When media effectively sever the connection between ourselves and physical places (Meyrowitz 1985), new social spaces, new arenas of action arise, as do "new types of social performances" (Cerulo 1997:397), and new identities and identifications. Technologies of communication provide not only a "torrent" of images and sensations, but they also provide conditions for our knowledge of distant and unknown things, previously unimagined objects and others that effectively "saturate our way of life with a promise of feeling" (Gitlin 2002:6).

Alexander and his colleagues (2006) describe such social performances as dramas of "authenticity," referring to the growing number of intense and emotional social performances today and to the fact that increasingly dramas are built into the rhythms of our everyday lives, where social actors across a range of public venues implicitly orient themselves and their actions on a public stage, "seeking identification with their experiences and understandings from their audiences" (Alexander and Mast 2006:2). Years ago, Raymond Williams alerted us to this possibility, pointing out that as a society, we have never "acted so much or watched so many others acting [...]. What we have now is drama as habitual experience" (Williams 1989:3-5). The long tradition of performance theory in the social sciences draws from this habitual experience, making mass media and the audience as the social arena where the meaning of a performance is created and where social actors "encounter their identities" (Giesen 2006; cf. Gross 1986; Schechner 2003; Turner 1988).

Charles Taylor's (2004; 2007) concept of the "social imaginary"—the deep "normative notions and images that underlie these expectations"—offers an even broader yet denser account of the cultural and personal schemes that these social dramas signify. Since the nineteenth century, he argues, a new way of construing "society" develops, a collectivity of "individuals" existing simultaneously, persons whose lives occur in (secular) time: "society" ("We the people ... ") existing horizontally, developing and changing through sequences of events. In today's "direct-access society," each of us is "immediate to the whole" (2004:158). The rise of various modern social forms and movements draws from this modern revolution in our social imaginary; today the images of "direct access" are increasingly socially diffused (2004:159-160):

> People conceive themselves as participating directly in a nationwide (sometimes even international) discussion ... We see ourselves in spaces of fashion ... taking up and handing on styles ... as part of the worldwide audience of media stars. And though these spaces are in their own sense hierarchical—they center on quasi-legendary figures—they offer all participants unmediated by any of their other allegiances or belongings.

These modes of "imagined direct access" are "egalitarian" and more of us—unlike our forebears—are free from the mediation of authorities. We imagine ourselves as part of and participants in vast communities of nation, social movement, humankind. Society itself has become construed as a "field of common agency." This modern social imaginary expands the repertory of our collective actions and creates new social spaces to act on and within *as our own*: urban centers and parks, theaters and museums, mass gatherings to hear political candidates, funerals of celebrities, but even places like television studios where fans and onlookers show up in increasing numbers. They hold out an "immense appeal" (Taylor 2004:157-61), for they are sites that contain, in some cases, the promise of shared emotion, and in others, the sense of participating in something that is happening *now*—"It's so 'now'!" The television news version is, "Breaking News."

When "real people" describe themselves in these public settings, their speech sometimes reveals that these themes are true, particularly the sense of something *real* and *emotional* and even *life-affirming* happening to them in these public places, suggesting that "authenticity" has become a vital cultural code used and pursued by social actors in an age of artifice, drama, and manipulation. So it is that visitors to memorials engage in public acts with others, becoming part of the montage they visit, participants in a "spectacle of suffering," members of an "imagined bereaved community" (Linenthal 2001:2-3). Collective acts like these operate as signs of a new phase of modern subjectivity, a new "social imaginary." This new way of construing self and society seeks to overcome—to "eclipse"—distance and separation between subject and object, to overcome the separation of the viewer and the object experienced.[5] Late modernity and its media culture disrupt the order of things, the primacy of outside reality as *there* and ourselves as distanced onlookers. It rearranges space (foreground and background) and beckons spectators to engage as participants in emotional dramas of affirmation and discovery.

Acknowledgements

Excerpt from *Unfinished Bombing* by E.T. Linenthal (2001), p. 133–4, by permission of Oxford University Press.

Trilling extract reprinted by permission of the publisher from *Sincerity and Authenticity* by Lionel Trilling, p. 127, Cambridge, Mass.: Harvard University Press.

5 "Eclipse of distance" is a theme elaborated by Daniel Bell in his *Cultural Contradictions of Capitalism* (1996). Regardless of their very different intents, it is a theme that resonates with Walter Benjamin's "The Work of Art in the Age of Mechanical Reproduction," in the collection *Illuminations* (1969: 223): "Every day the urge grows stronger to get hold of an object at very close range."

References

Adorno, Theodor. [1964] 2007. *The Jargon of Authenticity*. New York and London: Routledge.

Alexander, Jeffrey C. 2006. *The Civil Sphere*. New York: Oxford University Press.

Alexander, Jeffrey C. and Jason L. Mast. 2006. "Introduction: Symbolic Action in Theory and Practice." Pp. 1-28 in *Social Performance*, edited by J.C. Alexander, B. Giesen, and J. L. Mast. New York: Cambridge University Press.

Alexander, Jeffrey C., Bernhard Giesen, Jason L. Mast (eds.) 2006. *Social Performance*. New York: Cambridge University Press.

Altheide, David C. and Robert P. Snow. 1979. *Media Logic*. Beverly Hills and London: Sage.

Ayres, B. Drummond. 1992. "After 10 Years of Tears, Memorials Keep Healing." *The New York Times* (November 11):A14.

Barbalet, J. M. 1998. *Emotion, Social Theory, and Social Structure*. New York and Cambridge: Cambridge University Press.

Bauman, Zygmunt. 2005. *Liquid Life*. New York and London: Polity Press.

Baumeister, Roy F. 1986. *Identity*. New York: Oxford.

Bell, Daniel. 1996. *The Cultural Contradictions of Capitalism*. Second edition with a new Afterword by the author. New York: Basic Books.

Benjamin, Walter. 1969. "The Work of Art in the Age of Mechanical Reproduction." Pp. 217-252 in *Illuminations*, translation by H. Zohn, edited by H. Arendt. New York: Schocken.

Butterfield, Andrew. 2003. "Monuments and Memorials." *The New Republic*, 3:27-32.

Calhoun, Craig. 1991. "Indirect Relationships and Imagined Communities" Pp. 9-36 in *Social Theory for a Changing Society*, edited by P. Bourdieu and J. Coleman. Bolder, Colorado: Westview Press.

Cerulo, Karen. 1997. "Identity Construction. New Issues, New Directions." *Annual Review of Sociology*, 23:385-409.

Erikson, Erik H. 1968. *Identity, Youth, and Crisis*. New York: W.W. Norton.

Fernandez, Manny. 2007. "Shoulder to Shoulder, In Grief." *The New York Times* (March 13):B1, B5.

Gabler, Neal. 1998. *Life the Movie*. New York: Knopf.

Gergen, Kenneth J. 1991. *The Saturated Self*. New York: Basic Books.

Giesen, Bernhard. 2006. "Performing the Sacred." Pp. 326-367 in *Social Performance*, edited by J. Alexander, B. Giesen, and J.L. Mast New York: Cambridge.

Gitlin, Todd. 2002. *Media Unlimited*. New York: Henry Holt and Co.

Goldberg, Carey. 1999. "Feelings of Deep Grief, Even When Their Cause Surpasses Understanding." *The New York Times* (July 23): A21.

Gordon, Steven L. 1981. "The Sociology of Sentiments and Emotions." Pp. 261-78 in *Social Psychology*, edited by M. Rosenberg and R.H. Turner. New York: Basic Books.

Gross, Edward. 1986. "The Social Construction of Historical Events through Public Dramas." *Symbolic Interaction*, 9:179-200.

Hall, Stuart. 1980. *Culture, Media, Language: Working Papers in Cultural Studies 1972-1979*. London: Hutchinson.

______. 1996. "Who Needs Identity?" Pp. 1-17 in *Questions of Cultural Identity*, edited by S. Hall and Paul du Gay. London and Thousand Oaks: Sage.

Holstein, James A. and Jaber F. Gubrium. 2000. *The Self We Live By.* New York: Oxford: University Press.

Howe, Irving. 1967. *The Idea of the Modern in Literature and the Arts.* New York: Horizon Press.

Huyssen, Andreas. 1995. *Twilight Memories.* New York: Routledge.

Illouz, Eva. 2007. *Cold Intimacies.* Cambridge UK: Polity Press.

—— 2008. *Saving the Modern Soul.* Berkeley CA: University of California Press.

Imber, Jonathan B. (ed.) 2004. *Therapeutic Culture.* New Brunswick, NJ: Transaction Publishers.

Kimmelman, Michael. 2002. "Out of Minimalism, Monuments to Memory." *The NewYork Times* (January 13):Section 2:1, 37.

Krakauer, Jon. 1997. *Into Thin Air*. New York: Anchor/Doubleday.

Kropp, Goren with David Lagercrantz. 1997. *Ultimate High*. New York: Discovery Books.

Lasch, Christopher. 1978. *The Culture of Narcissism.* New York: Norton.

Linenthal, Edward. T. 2001. *The Unfinished Bombing.* New York: Oxford University Press.

Lupton, Deborah. 1998. *The Emotional Self.* London: Sage.

MacIntyre, Alasdair. 1983. *After Virtue.* Notre Dame, Indiana: University of Notre Dame Press.

McCarthy, E. Doyle. 1989. "Emotions are Social Things: An Essay in the Sociology of Emotions." Pp. 51-72 in *The Sociology of Emotions*, edited by D.D. Franks and E.D. McCarthy. Greenwich, Connecticut: JAI Press.

—— 1994. "The Social Construction of Emotions: New Directions From Culture Theory." Pp. 267-279 in *Social Perspectives on Emotion*, edited by William Wentworth and Jon Ryan. Vol. 2. Greenwich, Connecticut: JAI Press.

—— 1996. *Knowledge as Culture.* London: Routledge.

—— 2002. "The Emotions: Senses of the Modern Self," *Österreichische Zeitschrift Für Soziologie, Special Issue on the Sociology of the Senses*, 27:30-49.

—— 2007. "Public Displays of Emotion Today: Memorializing Death and Disaster." Columbia University, Seminar on Contents and Methods, February 14, 2007, unpublished.

Meyrowitz, Joshua. 1985. *No Sense of Place.* New York: Oxford University Press.

Mukerji, Chandra. 2007. "The Search for Cultural Authenticity." *Culture,* Newsletter of the Sociology of Culture Section of the American Sociological Association, 21 (3):1-2.

Reddy, William M. 2001. *The Navigation of Feeling.* New York: Cambridge University Press.

Roche, Maurice. 2000. *Mega-events and Modernity.* New York and London: Routledge.

Rosenblatt, Roger. 2000. "How We Remember." *Time*, May 29:26, 28-30.

Rosenwein, Barbara H. 2002. "Worrying about Emotions in History." *The American Historical Review* (June). Available on the Internet at: <http://historycooperative.press.uiuc.edu/journals/ahr/107.3/ah0302000821.html>.

Schechner, Richard. 2003. *Performance Theory.* London and New York: Routledge.

Scheff, Thomas. J. 2007. "Politics of Hidden Emotions: Responses to a War Memorial." *Peace and Conflict: Journal of Peace Psychology*, 13 (2):1-9.

Stearns, Carol Z. and Peter N. Stearns. 1986. *Anger, the Struggle for Emotional Control.* Chicago, Illinois: University of Chicago Press.

Taylor, Charles. 1989. *Sources of the Self.* Cambridge, MA: Harvard University Press.

—— 1991. *The Ethics of Authenticity.* Cambridge, MA: Harvard University Press.

—— 2004. *Modern Social Imaginaries.* Durham and London: Duke University Press.

—— 2007. *A Secular Age.* Cambridge, MA: The Belknap Press of Harvard University Press.

Trilling, Lionel. 1971. *Sincerity and Authenticity.* Cambridge, MA: Harvard University Press.

Turner, Victor. 1988. *The Anthropology of Performance.* New York: PAJ Publications.

Wagner-Pacifici, Robin and Barry Schwartz. 1991. "The Vietnam Veterans Memorial: Commemorating a Difficult Past." *American Journal of Sociology*, 97:376-420.

Wieseltier, Leon. 2002. "A Year Later." Washington Diarist, *The New Republic*, September 2:38.

Williams, Raymond. [1974] 1989. "Drama in a Dramatised Society." Pp. 3-5 in *Raymond Williams on Television*, edited by A. O'Connor. Toronto: Between the Lines.

—— [1958] 1983. *Culture and Society 1780-1950.* New York: Columbia University Press.

Young, James E. 1993. *The Texture of Memory.* New Haven: Yale University Press.

Zaretsky, Eli. 2004. *Secrets of the Soul.* New York: Alfred A. Knopf.

Chapter 16

Alternate Authenticities and 9/11: The Cultural Conditions Underlying Conspiracy Theories

Gary J. Krug

Where Wings Take Dream

Everything can now be known and nothing is fully believable. This is a problem. Western, Liberal democracies have traditionally organized their politics and societies around shared understandings of the world, and while differences have perhaps always existed between official means of presenting and legitimating these understandings and the local or vernacular means of legitimating them (see Coupland 2003), seldom before now has so much tension existed between these two domains. Challenges to the official versions of news, history, science, and other explanations of the world are widespread and well-organized on a range of topics. These contest the authenticity of the official stories and in so doing illuminate the often overlooked politics and practices taking place just under the surface of contemporary public discourse.

Sometimes denounced as "conspiracy theories," counter-narratives and alternative-histories of political and social events have become common place in the contemporary cultural scene in the US and in many other parts of the world. These are in no way uniform or consistent with regard to form, topic, or purpose, yet some writers have suggested some general tendencies and characteristics among them. The topics range from the alleged bio-weapon origins of AIDS, to the faking of the Apollo moon landing, to the continuing analyses of the JFK assassination. More than simple urban myths, counter-narratives (hereafter, CNs) do not address one isolated fact, but they weave together many facts, many agents, and diverse activities conducted behind the scenes to propose alternatives to the official or dominant story. Of great significance for contemporary culture among these CNs are, of course, those surrounding the events of 9/11.

On the morning of 11 September 2001, a new constellation of discourses came into being. These discourses explained the events of that day in terms of a straight, historical narrative creating a superficially coherent story of cause and effect. Nineteen Islamist hijackers commandeered four domestic jets, crashing two into the World Trade Center buildings, one into the Pentagon, and one into a field in Pennsylvania. These persons acted as agents of Osama Bin Laden and Al Qaida.

Such are the "dominant facts" and this was the narrative constructed within the news media and conveyed in other official sources such as the 9/11 Commission report. However, before the smoke had even cleared at "ground zero" and before any public, official investigation had been announced, alternative narratives and histories began to unfold that challenged the authenticity of the dominant official discourse. As subsequent historical and cultural events unfolded (such as the invasion of Iraq), these alternative interpretations gained momentum and popularity.

This chapter will not focus on the alternative histories of 9/11 *per se* but upon the profound issues for politics and for critical analysis raised through the proliferation of these CNs and their function of undermining, or at least challenging, the authenticity of dominant national narrative narratives. This is important as the CNs may rightly be called forms of cultural critique in so far as they seek first to uncover the "facts" behind shared cultural stories and beliefs, second to examine the ways in which "facts" have been constructed, and last to use these critiques to advance political agendas through their challenging of the authenticity of the official stories and facts. Sites and authors of CNs and alternative histories are in no way uniform or consistent with regard to form, topics engaged, claims made or approaches to analysis taken. Some may well be engaged in practicing the rhetorical strategy of poisoning the well, i.e. putting forward claims and arguments specifically to discredit the other sites and authors.

I'm the Decider: What Happened to Authenticity?

CNs can only exist in opposition to existing structures of knowledge and beliefs about reality, and some versions of these structures and beliefs occupy the cultural position as the official versions. This positioning as the privileged version of reality—as related in the media themselves—and of history can only exist with the support of institutions including the institutional expression of government and, of course, the institutions of the media: networks, financing, news gathering, universities, and so on. Many have demonstrated the ways in which these structures in turn shape the reality of the media (e.g. Bagdikian 2004; McChesney 2004). It is hardly novel to note that the dominant institutions in any culture utilize the media to portray reality and history in terms that provide a framework in which their actions and their existence are normalized and legitimated. A further function is to provide the symbolic material that aids in the socialization of members of that culture so that these beliefs are naturalized (Barthes 1972).

Dominant—or official or realist (Denzin 1992)—discourses create and maintain taken for granted history and narratives about what occurred. They contribute to the formation of gender, sexuality, national identity and one's fit with the social world. These constitute the background reality against which other stories and events may be compared and contrasted. Ivie (2005:89), for example, writes that

> the stories we tell about ourselves from within a culture are taken as historical fact; the stories we observe at a distance in exotic cultures and report as outsiders are understood as figurative and fictional musings about "the mysteries of life, death, divinity and existence." This latter group consists of "crucial framing stories; that *are treated* as true by the people who tell them" in order to provide justification for a social structure.

Such "crucial framing stories" have historically been a part of the seemingly uncontradictory narrative threads pulled together to provide explanation and so give meaning to the acts of terrorism of that day. Further, these explanations articulated with existing narratives of nation, narratives helping to establish the legitimacy of the government apparatus that frames them, and they once were required to provide some guarantee of continuity of cultural meaning as well as of identity (see Habermas 1973:70-72). None of these characteristics remain as unproblematic descriptions of the social world in the current day.

In the twentieth century, the mechanisms for producing and disseminating these beliefs, stories, and values—that is, the technologies of the mass media—expanded to a point where they challenged the reality of the obdurate world with their own reality. As they did so, the substance and form of the media were imbued with the language of the commercial, adjusted with persuasion technologies, and increasingly managed in always deliberate and sometimes deceptive ways (Sproule 1997). Debord (1990) referred to this mediated reality as the society of the spectacle. He observed that "the spectacle has spread itself to the point where it permeates all reality (1990:9)." Within this setting, government itself is spectacle, and the management of the media world through various persuasion technologies (propaganda, video news releases, PR, etc.) have created a "spectacular government," which Debord writes "now possess all the means necessary to falsify the whole of production and perception" and is "the absolute master of memories" (1990:10). As such, events perceived in the mass media are ahistorical and unverifiable, and equally importantly, unfalsifiable.

Some events on 9/11 did occur; this much is true, but the structure of the spectacular, mediated society guarantees that the underlying details as well as the explanation of these details are not immediately present in the moment of coverage but must be constructed afterwards; they must be legitimated and justified. Thus, the explanation and the "facts" themselves can never be validated directly but only through reference to legitimating institutions (such as the mass media, government sources) or discourses (governmental, news, etc.).

In the particular example of 9/11, nothing beyond the most basic facts can now be said without fact-checking. How did Atta's passport survive the crash in such pristine condition? Were Mossad agents arrested while videotaping the burning buildings and dancing in celebration? Who placed the "put" options on American and United Airlines, gambling on a fall in the stock price? And to what source would one turn to find "reliable" or "true" facts? Indeed, the reliance upon "facts" is one of the central problems of social discourse.

Human and Fish Can Coexist: The Loss of Social Meaning

The destabilization of "official" meanings described above takes place within the context of a general loss of cultural meaning and cohesion. As Habermas (1973) observed, "'meaning' is a scarce resource and is becoming ever scarcer. Consequently, expectations oriented to use values—that is expectations monitored by success—are rising in the civil public" (1973:73). Thus there exist social expectations for explanations of events providing quick closure of meaning as well as a clear course of administrative actions to "resolve" the problem. The continuing legitimacy of the national administration depends upon this. Further, it is entirely consistent with the philosophy of the neo-conservatives to govern in a fashion such that crises are used to construct the legitimacy of the administration.[1] Where crises do not exist, it may even be acceptable to create them as arguably occurred in the Iraq war with the systematic fabrication of evidence (e.g. see Borger 2003, Kwiatkowsky 2004). However, such manipulations of the public discourse are a shell game that, if overplayed or played too often, lead people to begin questioning the processes and to look for other examples of this "wag the dog" strategy. When legitimation is lost in one part of a government's public façade, it may precipitate crises of legitimation in other areas as well. The revelations of deception regarding the reasons for the Iraq war opened the door to questioning the official explanations of events lying at the beginning of the current crisis, events such as 9/11.

Scholars such as Lyotard (1984) and Baudrillard (1983, 1990) have explored the collapse of the realm of signification and the collapse of "grand narratives," and these are such staples of the postmodern and poststructural critical positions that they scarcely need retelling here. Nonetheless, the precise locating of the effects of the destabilization of social language within the mass media is an important first step toward understanding the social effects that follow from these changes as

1 Examples of these sorts of applications (or misapplications) of the theories of Leo Strauss abound. To take one, Ron Suskind, writing for the New York Times Magazine recounted his discussion in 2002 with a senior aide in the GW Bush White House. He wrote:

> The aide said that guys like me were "in what we call the reality-based community," which he defined as people who "believe that solutions emerge from your judicious study of discernible reality." I nodded and murmured something about enlightenment principles and empiricism. He cut me off. "That's not the way the world really works anymore," he continued. "We're an empire now, and when we act, we create our own reality. And while you're studying that reality—judiciously, as you will—we'll act again, creating other new realities, which you can study too, and that's how things will sort out. We're history's actors … and you, all of you, will be left to just study what we do."

For further discussion of the philosophies of the neoconservatives, see for examples Steinfels (1979) and Drury (1999).

these theories have generally focused on aesthetic or purely critical levels. Clearly, the spectacular society undermines many of the Enlightenment and classic Liberal assumptions about the nature of facts and knowledge, and the emergence of the spectacular is predicated on the transformation of language into a mass mediated domain with an ontology no longer dependent upon either consensus or empirical validation. The domain of mass media is completely self-contained and self-validating. Luhmann (1996:4) offers a telling analysis of the reality generated by the media, writing:

> We can speak of the reality of the mass media [...] in the sense of what *appears to them or through them to others*, to be reality. Put in Kantian terms, the mass media generate a transcendental illusion." This illusion produces a reality within the system, and as such, questions of how the media distort "the real" are specious, "for that would presuppose an ontological, available, objectively accessible reality that can be known without resort to construction, it would basically presuppose the old cosmos of essences (Luhmann 1996:7).

The necessity of having recourse to the constructionism of which Luhmann writes is key, for it establishes that nothing can be said beyond the most immediate and obdurate "facts" without employing some method of social or cultural critique. No longer confined to the domain of sociologists and cultural theorists, the utter absence of an authentic and normative shared culture makes conspiracy theorists and alternate historians of us all the very instant that we question the accepted reality of our culture. Further, this sort of challenging of the accepted cultural truths is increasingly becoming the *sine qua non* of the conscious citizen. A certain skepticism (or worse, cynicism) follows necessarily from the reality of the mass media, in part because one is positioned between that reality and the reality of the subject in his or her local lived-experience.

Let's Make Sure that There is Certainty during Uncertain Times: A Critique

Cultural criticism has become a popular leisure activity even outside of the academy. Latour (2004:228), noting this phenomenon, asks:

> What has become of critique when my neighbor in the little Bourbonnais village where I live looks down on me as someone hopelessly naïve because I believe that the United States had been attacked by terrorists? Remember the good old days when university professors could look down on unsophisticated folks because those hillbillies naïvely believed in church, motherhood, and apple pie? Things have changed a lot, at least in my village. I am now the one who naïvely believes in some facts because I am educated, while the other guys are too *unsophisticated* to be gullible.

Is not the village of which Latour writes reflective of the cynicism required to live simultaneously in the global, mediated world and the local world of lived experience? Does not Latour's example speak to the millions who no longer believe the official stories about their world; the millions who deny the moon landings, the official stories about 9/11, who have a well-established armor of skepticism toward facts in general?

This critique need not be of the naïve variety, put forward by cynics who doubt the narratives of their world. Certainly critique may be used in bad faith to undermine opposing positions. Fish (2005) makes note of this cultural and rhetorical tactic in US academic and cultural battles to destabilize meaning and so introduce doubt into the public debate in the matters of Intelligent Design and holocaust deniers. Citing phrases taken from the postmodern and multicultural domains that are used now by the right-wing of politics, such as "teach the controversy," Fish notes the people such as Phillip E. Johnson are borrowing the tactics of the postmodernists. They do not believe the ideas they are putting forward; but they find it rhetorically advantageous. "This is nothing if not clever," Fish observes. "In the work of Johnson and other Intelligent design proponents, 'teach the controversy' is the answer to no question. Instead it is a wedge for prying open the doors of a world to which they have been denied access by gatekeepers [...] who have found what they say unpersuasive" (2005: 71). Fish calls this tactic "a sleight of hand" designed "to deflect from the specific merits on one's claims by attaching them to some general truth or value that can then be piously affirmed" (2005:71).

These general truths to be piously affirmed are derived from some lines of classic liberal philosophy, notably John Stuart Mill, regarding the necessity for challenging truth, from multiculturalism's debunking of arbitrarily privileged voices in culture, and from the tendency in liberalism to prefer "tolerance over judgment" (2005:72). Fish denounces these tactics as a "shell game," writing that they say "look here, in the highest reaches of speculation about inquiry in general, and not there, in the places where the particular, nitty-gritty work of inquiry is actually done" (72). All of this sleight of hand is undertaken "in an effort to accomplish through misdirection and displacement what they cannot accomplish through evidence and argument" (72). In this manner, the ability of institutions to assert social truths is further undermined, and the possibility of "facts" is further made problematic.

A world without clearly legitimated "facts" is a world peopled with skeptics and cynics, for they are the predictable result of life in a social world that is not underpinned by a sense of authenticity. The absence cultural closure and control achieved in the mass media generate a "stereo reality" (Virilio 1994) or a "doubling" (Luhmann 2000:4) of the world for the self. On the one hand, the mediated, spectacular society is what matters and is all-present, normative, and required for one's membership in contemporary society. On the other hand, emerging generations who have never known a world that was not bifurcated constitute an increasingly media savvy audience which is dubious of the claims and authority of the media. We face the condition described by Sloterdjjk (1987:4) who writes of the modern return to the attitude of the courtly sphere and of "[a] pernicious realism through which human beings learn the crooked smile of open immorality," and in such a world "a sophisticated knowledge accumulates in informed, intelligent minds, a knowledge that moves elegantly back and forth between naked facts and conventional facades."

Such an attitude is not the cause of the disconnection between the individual person and his or her mediated culture but rather a symptom of the disjuncture. In order to participate in the culture, one cannot turn his or her back on cultural meanings and narratives, regardless of the degree to which they strain credulity. The problem for the self, for the individual person here is that "for present-day thinking, inwardness and outwardness, subjectivity and things, have been split into "alien worlds" (Sloterdjik 1987:537). To occupy one's own world *vis-à-vis* the world of mass media necessarily forces one to adopt an attitude of skepticism or cynical disregard toward either the local, the mediated or both.

This same process has been observed by others. For example, Virilio (1994 n.p.) notes that, "As I see it, new technologies are substituting a virtual reality for an actual reality." He continues: "We are entering a world here where there won't be one but two realities [...] the actual and the virtual. Thus there is no simulation, but substitution. Reality has become symmetrical." Elsewhere in the same piece he suggests that "we are in a period of 'derealization'"; the "whole of reality itself is being killed" (Virilio 1994 n.p.). In this strange new space of virtuality, one has few clear landmarks for orientation that are consistent with enlightenment practices of identity formation and truth construction.

Authenticity may be held, then, an attribute appropriate to the domain of the self. Narratives and discourses themselves may appear in conflict regarding their rightness or wrongness or regarding their veracity or mendacity, but these conflicts must necessarily circulate through the local domains of people. These people are already positioned within history and culture through their on-going implication in social activities and through webs of interlocution (Taylor 1989), and from these subjectivities they articulate a shared symbolic reality (Bormann 1972). Some component of this shared reality must draw upon narratives and discourses larger than the local, and as people are socialized through their participation in symbolic interactions with their world, there must be some sort of coherence between the internalized stories of the world and the ongoing social narratives. Otherwise, the legitimacy and authenticity of the social domain and particularly of the perceived authors of social narratives will suffer.

Subsequent to 9/11 much has been revealed regarding how the administration of George W. Bush has utilized the media for propaganda and political purposes (for examples,, Goodman and Goodman 2006; Palast 2006; Rampton and Stauber 2006; Roy 2003). Certainly previous administrations have manipulated the press, controlled reporting, and selectively provided information favorable to their plans; however, this administration raised the game to a new level. The use of video news releases, paid or otherwise corrupted reporters (e.g. Judith Miller, Armstrong Williams and others), the control of news coverage from combat areas through the use of imbedded reporters and other tactics, the creation of staged news events (the Jessica Lynch "rescue"), and other techniques, once revealed serve to undermine the credibility of the government's discourse in general. Most telling as a failed official discourse was the revelation that the justification for the Iraq war was wholly false, prompting a series of rewritings of that justification. A government may lie selectively and not lose credibility, but when so many distortions are conducted so systematically and are then exposed, there is little trust that can be expected from the demos.[2]

"Fool Me Twice, Can't Get Fooled Again"

These distortions of the media built upon and articulated with pre-existing tendencies. Described by Hofstadter (1965) as the "paranoid style of American politics," some of the cultural roots of the cynicism and critical attitude of the contemporary political sphere are long-standing and grounded in modernism itself. Some have suggested that persons confronting these splits in their own lives may develop conspiracy theories as a way of challenging the legitimacy of prevailing, dominant discourses (see Fenster 1999).

At any rate, the rise of skepticism about official stories began to accelerate as early as 2002. Distrust of the "histories" and of the administration grew in tandem. For example, a Zogby poll ("Half of New Yorkers", 2004) found that: "half (49.3 per cent) of New York City residents and 41 per cent of New York citizens overall say that some of our leaders knew in advance that attacks were planned on or around September 11, 2001, and that they consciously failed to act." While traditionally US citizens have responded to reports of attacks on their nation with sustained patriotic upwellings of nationalism and military volunteerism, the events in New York within a few years brought about a strange disbelief in the official language. It had become inauthentic. Oddly, this skepticism was not limited to the United States. The Zogby article continues, "On May 26th the Toronto Star reported a national poll showing that 63per cent of Canadians are also convinced US leaders had 'prior knowledge' of the attacks yet declined to act." This incredulity was reflected in the press as well, if not in substance at least in spirit.

Even earlier than the Zogby poll, Ann Karpf (2002 n.p.), writing for *The Guardian* observed that there had been a strange series of coincidences, fourteen by her count, regarding the "finding" of evidence about the 9/11 events and the

2 Strangely, the mediated reality of the social has become increasingly accessible through the online appearance of extensive networks of amateur historians, professional scholars, archivists of all kinds, blogs, and sites dedicated to preserving information from news services. These sites and activities serve to counteract to some extent the trend toward social amnesia and the eternal present. Thus CNs create points of relative stability in the unfolding of information that otherwise, through their constant, massive content, overwhelm social memory as well as social discourse.

subsequent linkages to al Qaida. She asks us to "think back over the past six months and it becomes ineluctable: never in the history of modern warfare has so much been found so opportunely." From the passport and suicide note of Atta to various videos and manuals seized at key moments, too many coincidences surrounded the "facts" for her to accept them at face value. In an ironic vein, she notes that:

> [y]ou could detect in them the clear hand of American propaganda. This isn't, of course, to claim a dirty tricks department somewhere in the heart of Washington. That would have you immediately accused of peddling conspiracy theories, though I'm coming to think that conspiracy theories have had a bad press. What are they, after all, but "joined-up government" by another name? (Karpf 2002 n.p.).

Karpf has hit on one of the key components of CNs and alternative histories: the curiosity of facts that do not fit, what Keely (1999) refers to a "errant data."

Keeley differentiates two classes of such errant data: unaccounted for data that "fall through the net of the received explanation" and contradictory data, "data that, if true, would contradict the received account" (1999: 118). Unaccounted for data suggest an incompleteness of the explanation, and contradictory data simply violate the logic of the explanation. Atta receiving wire transfers of large sums of money from the director of Pakistani intelligence fits Keeley's definition of unaccounted for data (reported in "General Mahmud's exit" 2001; Joshi 2001; Taranto 2001). The identification by the BBC of at least five of the alleged hijackers still alive constitutes an example of contradictory data.[3] Both of these examples have been taken up by various CNs as indicating flaws with the official accounts.

---

3 The original story, published on 23 September 2001, was titled "Hijack 'suspects' alive and well" and claimed that at least five of the named hijackers had been located by the BBC and some had been interviewed. This story may be found at http://news.bbc.co.uk/2/hi/middle_east/1559151.stm. On 27 October 2006, the BBC repudiated this story, saying that common Arabic names had caused the confusion. This story is available at http://www.bbc.co.uk/blogs/theeditors/2006/10/911_conspiracy_theory_1.html. The editors write that they sincerely regret having fueled "conspiracy theories." On this last site, one of the responses posted on the page offers the following rather thoughtful response to the BBC's:

> This column is really most unsatisfying. It seems to be political spin. Real journalism would be to further investigate the issues raised. For instance, who are the men you pictured in the article? What is their current status? Changing the photo caption at this late date seems to be inappropriate. This redaction of a historical and controversial news article smacks of Big Brother and the Ministry of Truth. If the BBC was mistaken, then the mistakes must be acknowledged and corrected in a less elliptical fashion. There must be accountability. On the other hand, if the BBC article might be correct, to the points on which this might contradict the official record in the US, the matter would then require further investigation and explication in the public interest.

There is yet a third form of errant data: *an overabundance of improbably convenient data.* The data cited by Karpf fit more into this third category, and they point toward a plausibility of CNs and alternative explanations. In addition to the data per se, there exist as well conditions under which data might be suspect. One such condition may be found in the *historical and cultural bases undermining the credibility of the current data or of the speakers and institutions that support them.* This might occur in several ways, for examples: the speaker might be positioned in context with a history of deceptive practices or, less malignly, the explanation offered for the facts is unable sufficiently to integrate complexities of history or culture.

For an example of this condition of historical and cultural bases, consider the publication of the official US government documents on the proposed Operation Northwoods written in 1962. Originally publicized by James Bamford (2001), the project was a proposed "false flag" operation[4] to justify a US military intervention in Cuba. In this plan, US operatives would conduct a series of attacks, assassinations, and bombings both in the US and in Cuba which would be constructed to appear as if Castro's agency were implicated. The plans are chillingly precise and include the simulated destruction of a civilian passenger aircraft. The existence and publication of documents such as Admiral Lemnitzer's plans for conducting fatal operations for the sole purpose of deceiving the American people as well as the entire world further undermine the credibility of mainstream narratives. If Operation Northwoods was seriously proposed (and rejected by President Kennedy), why would not a later government propose and, the reasoning runs, execute a false flag operation such as 9/11?[5]

Thus, the BBC's recanting did not bring about closure or eliminate the speculative discourses building upon their earlier reporting.

4 A false flag operation is a military or intelligence service action undertaken in such a way as to implicate a country other than the one conducting the operation.

5 Among other often-cited documents in support of the Bush administration's alleged duplicity in linking 9/11 to Saddam Hussein are the "Downing Street Memo" and the strategy paper "Rebuilding America's Defenses" by the Project for the New American Century. The Downing Street Memo was the leaked notes of a British Cabinet meeting to discuss the possible Iraq war and mentioned that the Americans would make the evidence fit the public justification for invasion. The "Rebuilding" document called for using US military might to extend influence around the world and called for a permanent base in the Middle East. Most alarmingly for some, it noted that a Pearl Harbor like event might be necessary to galvanize popular support for such undertakings. It was co-authored by (among others) Paul Wolfowitz and I. Lewis Libby, senior figures in the Bush White House, and William Kristol, a journalist and advisor to President Bush.

Not to Misremember: Historical Precedents

Tectonic strains in the US national discourse had long been noted before 2001, and the fissures between officially sanctioned stories, histories, as well as taken for granted understandings of the nation and critical alternative stories, histories, and understandings had at times become strained to breaking. The domestic unrest and urban riots in the US during the late 1960s, for example, arose in part from the disjuncture between official discourse as relayed in school books and through the mass media and the lived experience of people in the cities. The Kerner Commission report observed that "We have found a significant imbalance between what actually happened in our cities and what the newspaper, radio and television coverage of the riots told us happened" (Kerner Report 1968). After analyzing hundreds of examples of coverage and interviewing people in the urban areas, the report concluded that:

> Lacking other sources of information, we formed our original impressions and beliefs from what we saw on television, heard on the radio, and read in newspapers and magazines. We are deeply concerned that millions of other Americans, who must rely on the mass media, likewise formed incorrect impressions and judgments about what went on in many American cities last summer.

The reality of black people's experiences in apartheid America did not fit well with the dominant stories of national goodness, justice, and fair play. The failure of the national myths and the subsequent violence was cited by some of neo-conservatives and conservatives as proof of just such a breakdown.

Robert Bork, a one-time nominee to the US Supreme Court, writes of cultural collapse stemming from the loss of mythic national virtues. He asserts that:

> the manifestations of American cultural decline are even more widespread, ranging across virtually the entire society, from the violent underclass of the inner cities to our cultural and political elites, from rap music to literary studies, from pornography to law, from journalism to scholarship, from union halls to universities. Wherever one looks, the traditional virtues of this culture are being lost, its vices multiplied, its values degraded—in short, the culture itself is unraveling (Bork 1995 n.p.).

What are these writings of Bork but cultural critique, that is to say, a form of conspiracy theory, a counter-narrative? Based on interviews with several key figures in the Bush administration, Hersh (2003) writes that such counter-narrative strategies are a central tenet of the political philosophy which neoconservatives practice. For the neoconservatives, certain stories, sometimes referred to in terms of Plato's dictum of "noble lies," are necessary for the social good and for social order. There are moments in the recent history of the US where such a use of "noble lies" or deliberate manipulations of the social discourse contributed to the loss of legitimacy of the administration and, consequently, to the growth in popular appeal of CNs.

Among other historical and cultural "evidence" feeding the development of CNs was the observation that the 9/11 Commission had been formed, and then only reluctantly, not to investigate the events of 9/11 nor to assign blame but to provide the institutional support for discourses linking those events to the regime in Iraq.[6] With the appointment of Phillip Zelikow, a long-time close friend of Condaleeza Rice, as the key Commission's executive director, many people, especially the so-called Jersey Girls, widows of 9/11, questioned the intentions of the Commission. Such observations were strengthened by the conduct of the commission itself, especially its stated refusal to assign blame or identify persons responsible for failing to stop the events. For example, the first expert witness was Abraham Sofor from the conservative Hoover Institution. He had no expertise in any related field and used his time to justify the President and his war plans (see Shenon 2008:102-04). This point of the misuse of 9/11 discourse as a justification for the Iraq war was also cited in the resignation letter of a career diplomat, Jay Brady Kiesling, published in the *New York Times* on 27 February 2003. In this letter he wrote:

> The September 11 tragedy left us stronger than before, rallying around us a vast international coalition to cooperate for the first time in a systematic way against the threat of terrorism. But rather than take credit for those successes and build on them, this Administration has chosen to make terrorism a domestic political tool, enlisting a scattered and largely defeated Al Qaida as its bureaucratic ally (Kiesling 2003 n.p.).

This use of the public discourse to steer the nation's direction toward support of a war was but another in a long series of communicative acts that fragmented rather than unified the dominant narratives and that undermined the legitimacy of the institutions supporting these narratives.

Mission Accomplished

In one sense, the failed authenticity of the dominant narratives reveals a legitimation crisis within the culture. These arise when "the complementarity between the requirements of the state apparatus [...] and the interpreted needs and legitimate expectations of members of society [...] is disturbed" (Habermas 1975:48). As we have seen, there were numerous disturbances to this complementarity. To begin, the historically and culturally acceptable frameworks which historically have authenticated official language have been damaged, sometimes deliberately

6 For an inside view of the Bush administrations reluctance to investigate 9/11 and of the operation of the 9/11 Commission itself, see the interview with Senator Max Cleland in Borland (2003).

and for political advantage. This took place within a cultural moment when the critiques of modernism had challenged the use of tradition as a normative means of establishing truth. Late modernism has been reflected in a social world conveyed largely through the mass media, giving rise to a mediated world very much at odds with the public sphere envisioned in liberal philosophy. And finally, each of these factors has contributed to the spread of critique as a major mode of thought and an important rhetorical strategy in the public sphere.

Keeley writes that conspiracy theories "throw into doubt the various institutions that have been set up to generate reliable data and evidence" (1999:121). Yet, one should not be surprised at this, for the project of critique and the sociology of scientific knowledge have been engaged in precisely this project for decades. The works of Bruno Latour, Barry Barnes, Andy Pickering, Donna Haraway and others have sought to reveal the processes by which science operated, to open the largely ignored and unaccounted for social and political factors which structured these fact-producing activities and which contributed to their products. Yet Keeley is on track when he observes that conspiracy theories "reveal just how large a role trust—in both institutions and individuals—plays in the justification of our beliefs" (1999:121).

However, it is Bruno Latour (2004) who, reflecting on the current state of rampant critique and his contribution to this, writes:

> Let me be mean for a second. What's the real difference between conspiracists and a popularized, that is a teachable version of social critique inspired by a too quick reading of, let's say, a sociologist as eminent as Pierre Bordieu? In both cases, you have to learn to become suspicious of everything people say because we all know that they live in the thralls of a complete *illusio* of their real motives (2004: 228).

The majority of contemporary critique is, for Latour, engaged in a deconstructionist project, and this necessarily creates social conflict, culture wars, and the like as the various players jostle to position the other side as operating under some form of false consciousness or ideological blindness. One may reasonably propose that something like this scenario is taking place around the "facts," explanations, and theories of 9/11. The conspiracy theorists seek to reveal the hidden agency of the Bush administration, and the administration dismisses them as kooks and lunatics or as misguided and deluded.

For the language of politics, there is no longer any legitimation, either from within or without. Adorno has argued that power and governments rely upon jargon for their linguistic legitimacy. He notes that "the character of jargon would be quite formal: it sees to it that what it wants is on the whole felt and accepted through its mere delivery, without regard to the content of the words used" (Adorno 1973:8). The language of the TV commercial, of the political slogan, of the billboard and the propagandist is sufficient to convey the feeling behind the words, and the meaning has been obliterated. Anyone may speak these words so long as they do so in the using the correct forms. The person versed in the jargon "does not have to say what he thinks, does not even have to think it properly. The jargon takes over this task and devaluates thought" (Adorno 1973:9). Critique, coming from the outside, cannot speak jargon, and so cannot compete in the political arena. The state need not even acknowledge critique except to derisively dismiss it. Adorno continues that "the tone of jargon has something in it of the seriousness of the augers" (1973:9); it borrows from whatever is sacred in the culture, and in the United States, the prevailing national religion is the worship of the myth of America.

Even upon the domain of the facts of 9/11, we are still at loggerheads with no clear way to justify facts on either side. Latour continues:

> Then, after disbelief has struck and an explanation is requested for what is really going on, in both cases again it is the same appeal to powerful agents hidden in the dark acting always consistently, continuously, relentlessly. Of course, we in the academy like to use more elevated causes—society, discourse, knowledge-slash-power, fields of forces, empires, capitalism—while the conspircists like to portray a miserable bunch of greedy people with dark intents, but I find something troublingly similar in the structure of the explanation (Latour 2004: 229).

For Latour, contemporary critical culture lurches between an attitude of attacking facts and an attitude of attacking "fetishes" in the form of ideology or some other false consciousness. We are in the hands of "critical barbarity" (2004:240). He characterizes these two poles as the *fact position* and the *fairy position*, and he argues that each is inadequate both as a way of engaging the world and as a way of creating shared understandings of the world and of the creation of knowledge.

Latour suggested a new way of engaging the world that, rather than rejecting facts, fought to move closer to them, "or more exactly, to see through them the reality that requested a new respectful realist attitude" (2004:244). Latour sought to restore an interest in "matters of concern" as "matters of fact [that are] a very poor rendering of what is given in experience" (2004:244). Rather than debunk facts or challenge the beliefs of others, it is possible to explore with great care the delicate constructions of our world. In the case of 9/11, we might well being with an examination of the ranges of conditions of language, institutions, politics, rhetoric, and culture to tease out those threads necessary for our meanings to come into being, and we might well then have conversations about what these are and how we know them.

How would we undertake such conversations? Perhaps it is possible to recapture the rhetorical and political openness of multiculturalism while maintaining a sense of judgment together with an ability to discriminate between the specious and the important. Yet this, too, would require the most careful and honest of social gatherings. How else do we escape the wars for authenticity and for legitimacy? Victory, whatever that would look like, for the disingenuous, or for the dogmatic, or the politically ruthless, would further fragment the public and further undermine those institutions that help to create and maintain the legitimacy and authenticity of the social world. The only authenticity that would then exist would be that of a degraded world in which all that is knowable is already given within the jargon of power, a world of fixed objects rather than a world of evolving knowledge constructed in relationship to things.

To take an example, perhaps the most problematic event of 9/11 remains the collapse of WTC 7, a forty story structure which pancaked into its footprint at roughly 5:30 that afternoon. The official NIST (National Institute of Standards and Technology) report (NIST 2008) is unlikely to satisfy many, for it relies on contradictory data (the first ever collapse of a steel frame building from fire), and it was issued from a source that by virtue of its association with the government, is already suspect for some. Moreover, the NIST report produces a kind of closure, a final explanation that fixes the establishment explanation and ends further official investigation or examination. This is precisely the problem.

Are there no more unanswered questions, no credible dissenting voices? Has closure been achieved? Certainly a set of facts and analyses have been produced, Latour's (2004:244) "fact position" has been established. Yet, what about the "fair position?" Do the facts fit with experience, and more importantly, does the presentation of the facts invite us to examine their construction and their meaning? Do these explanations encourage more conversation, or do they devolve into the dogmatism of received knowledge? Part of the problem with authenticity is that power has too much say in what is worth knowing and how it shall be known. This is revealed in the turn to closure.

Authentic knowledge cannot exist as a political fact and is tainted by its association. Rather, the authentic must find its home in the indeterminacy of always standing on the edge of the known, always groping for another way of knowing the world, for another way of linking experience and facts in ways that are morally and ethically debatable. Let us, then, recognize the inauthentic fact as the timeless truth, the inauthentic word as that which would be the last word, the inauthentic government as the one who would stop our further discussion, and the inauthentic person as the one who acts in bad faith and secrecy to pervert our conversation. What stands in the way of our relationship with the world?

References

Adorno, Theodor. 1973. *The Jargon of Authenticity*. Trans. Knut Tarnowski and Frederic Will. Evanston, IL: Northwestern University Press.

Bamford, J. 2001. *Body of Secrets: Anatomy of the Ultra-Secret National Security Agency From the Cold War Through the Dawn of a New Century*. New York: Doubleday.

Bagdikian, Ben. 2004. *The New Media Monopoly.* Boston: Beacon Press.

Barthes, Roland. 1972. *Mythologies*. Trans. Annette Lavers. New York: Hill and Wang.

Baudrillard, Jean. 1990. *Fatal Strategies*. New York: Semiotext(e).

—— 1983. *Simulations*. New York: Semiotext(e).

Boehlert, Eric. 2003. "The President Ought to Be Ashamed." *Salon*. Accessed 2/172008 from: http://dir.salon.com/story/news/feature/2003/11/21/cleland/index.html.

Borger, Julian. 2003. "The Spies Who Pushed For War." *The Guardian*, July 17 2003. Accessed 3/21/08 from: http://www.guardian.co.uk/world/2003/jul/17/iraq.usa.

Bork, Robert. 1995. "Hard Truths About the Culture War." *First Things*, 54:18-23. Accessed 12/10/2007 from: http://www.orthodoxytoday.org/articles/BorkCultureWar.php.

Bormann, Ernest G. 1972. "Fantasy and Rhetorical Vision: The Rhetorical Criticism of Social Reality." *Quarterly Journal of Speech*, 58:396-407.

Coupland, Nikolas. 2003. "Sociolinguistic Authenticities." *Journal of Sociolinguistics*, 7:417-431.

Debord, Guy. 1990. *Comments on the Society of the Spectacle*. Trans. Malcom Imrie. New York: Verso.

Denzin, Normank. 1995. *The Cinematic Society: The Voyeur's Gaze*. London: Sage.

Drury, Shadia. 1999. *Leo Strauss and the American Right*. London: Palgrave Macmillan.

Fenster, Mark. 1999. *Conspiracy Theories: Secrecy and Power in American Culture*. Minneapolis, MN: University of Minnesota Press.

Fish, Stanley. 2005. "Academic Cross-dressing." *Harper's Magazine*, 311:70-73.

General Mahmud's Exit 2001. *Dawn* (Newspaper). Available on the Internet at http://www.dawn.com/2001/10/09/top11.htm.

Goodman, A. and D. Goodman. 2006. *Static: Government Liars, Media Cheerleaders, and the People Who Fight Back*. New York: Hyperion.

Habermas, Jurgen. 1975. *Legitimation Crisis*. Trans. Thomas McCarthy. Boston: Beacon Press.

Half of New Yorkers Believe US Leaders Had Foreknowledge of Impending 9-11 Attacks and "Consciously Failed" To Act. 2004. Available on the Internet at http://www.zogby.com/search/ReadNews.dbm?ID=855.

Hersh, Seymour. 2003. "Selective Intelligence: Donald Rumsfeld Has His Own Special Sources. Are they Reliable?" *The New Yorke*r. May 12, 2003. Accessed 3/22/08 from: http://www.newyorker.com/archive/2003/05/12/030512fa_fact?currentPage=all.

Ivie, Robert L. 2005. *Democracy and America's War On Terror*. Tuscaloosa, AL: University of Alabama Press.

Joshi, Manoj. 2001. "India Helped FBI Trace ISI-terrorist Links." *Times of India*, 9 October 2001, Accessed 2/22/08 from: http://timesofindia.indiatimes.com/articleshow/msid-1454238160,prtpage-1.cms.

Keeley, Brian L. 1999. Of Conspiracy Theories. *The Journal of Philosophy*, 96:109-26.

Kiesling, John B. 2003. "Letter of Resignation." Accessed 03/21/08 from: http://www.fas.org/irp/congress/2003_cr/h030403.html.
Kwiatkowsky, Karen. 2004. "The New Pentagon Papers." *Salon*. Accessed 9/17/2007 from: http://dir.salon.com/story/opinion/feature/2004/03/10/osp_moveon/index.html.
Latour, Bruno. 2004. "Why Has Critique Run Out Of Steam? From Matters of Fact to Matters of Concern." *Critical Inquiry*, 30:225-48.
Luhmann, Niklas. 2000. *The Reality Of The Mass Media*, Trans. Kathleen Cross. Stanford, CA: Stanford University Press.
McChesney, Robert W. 2004. *The Problem of the Media: U.S. Communication Politics in the 21st Century.* New York: Monthly Review Press.
NIST. 2008. "Reports on the Collapse of WTC 7." Accessed 8/23/08 from http://www.nist.gov/public_affairs/releases/wtc082108.html.
Palast, Greg. 2006. *Armed Madhouse*. New York: Dutton.
Project Northwoods. Original documents in pdf form available at http://www.gwu.edu/~nsarchiv/news/20010430/northwoods.pdf.
Rampton, S.J. and Stauber. 2003. *Weapons Of Mass Deception: The Uses Of Propaganda In Bush's War On Iraq.* New York: Jeremy P. Tarcher/Penguin.
—— 2006. *The Best War Ever: Lies, Damned Lies, and the Mess in Iraq*. New York: Jeremy P. Tarcher/Penguin.
Roy, Arundhati. 2003. *War Talk*. Cambridge, MA: South End Press.
Shenon, Phillip. 2008. *The Commission: The Uncensored History Of The 9/11 Investigation.* New York: Twelve.
Sloterdijk, Peter. 1987. *Critique of Cynical Reason*. Trans. Michael Eldred. Minneapolis, MN: University of Minnesota Press.
Sproule, J. Michael. 1997. *Propaganda and Democracy: The American Experience Of Media and Mass Persuasion.* Cambridge: Cambridge University Press.
Taranot, James. 2001. "Best of the Web Today." *Wall Street Journal*. October 10, 2001. Accessed from: http://www.opinionjournal.com/best/?id=95001298.
Taylor, Charles. 1989. *Sources Of the Self.* Cambridge: Harvard University Press.
Virilio, Paul. 1994. God, Cyberwar and Television. *Ctheory*. Accessed 12/10/07 from: http://www.ctheory.net/articles.aspx?id=62.

Index

For Product Safety Concerns and Information please contact our EU representative GPSR@taylorandfrancis.com
Taylor & Francis Verlag GmbH, Kaufingerstraße 24, 80331 München, Germany

www.ingramcontent.com/pod-product-compliance
Ingram Content Group UK Ltd.
Pitfield, Milton Keynes, MK11 3LW, UK
UKHW022015180926
475701UK00003B/372
* 9 7 8 0 3 6 7 6 0 3 1 8 2 *